LITERATURE AS OPERA

LITERATURE AS OPERA

Gary Schmidgall

OXFORD UNIVERSITY PRESS
Oxford New York Toronto Melbourne

Oxford University Press
Oxford London Glasgow
New York Toronto Melbourne Wellington
Nairobi Dar es Salaam Cape Town
Kuala Lumpur Singapore Jakarta Hong Kong Tokyo
Delhi Bombay Calcutta Madras Karachi

First published by Oxford University Press, New York, 1977

First issued as an Oxford University Press paperback, 1980

Library of Congress Cataloging in Publication Data
Schmidgall, Gary, 1945-
Literature as opera.

Includes index.
CONTENTS: An opening perspective.—George Frideric Handel: Orlando, Ariodante, Alcina.—Wolfgang Amadeus Mozart: Le nozze di Figaro. [etc.]
1. Opera—Dramaturgy. 2. Music and literature.
I. Title.
ML3858.S37 782.1'3 76-57264
ISBN 0-19-502213-0 ISBN 0-19-502706-X pbk.

Extracts from Benjamin Britten's *Death in Venice,* text by Myfanwy Piper based on the novella by Thomas Mann, are reprinted by permission of Faber Music Ltd.

Printed in the United States of America

for Arthur Davis Schmidgall

ACKNOWLEDGMENTS

Six of my friends and colleagues were generous enough to read the manuscript in full: William Abrahams, Elise Bickford Jorgens, Herbert Lindenberger, Paul Robinson, Marvin Tartak, and Virgil Whitaker. From their various scholarly backgrounds and personal perspectives on opera, each offered unfailingly helpful, provocative, and cautionary criticism. I am also grateful to those who read and criticized individual chapters relevant to their areas of expertise: John L'Heureux, Ann Mueller, Patrick Smith, and William Todd. Mr. and Mrs. Walton Ball, Warren Ball, Edward Bergh, Edward Colby, Clifford Cranna, Barbara Dole Kirby, James Schwabacher, and William Shank also provided their help. Sheldon Meyer, Leona Capeless, and Pat Golin at Oxford University Press made the publication of this book a distinctly pleasant experience. Every author should have one (and only one) relentlessly flattering reader. For me this person was my uncle, who it happens first excited my interest in opera. This book is dedicated to him.

CONTENTS

LITERATURE AS OPERA

one

AN OPENING PERSPECTIVE

Anything can be set to music, true,
but not everything will be effective.

Giuseppe Verdi

Literature and Opera

In the 1880s Emmanuel Chabrier addressed Shakespeare's last and perhaps greatest play with the idea of turning it into an opera. He wrote to his publisher explaining his views about its stage-worthiness:

> I now know *The Tempest* by heart; there are many good things in it, but Blau has reason to want some expanding of the love story, otherwise papa Prospero would get to be a bore. As for drama properly so called, where is it? Are they genuinely dramatic, those conspiracies of the old fogies Alonzo, Antonio, Gonzalo, Stefano? And those two debauchees Caliban and Interpocula [i.e., Trinculo]—who cares about their peregrinations around the island?
>
> So the interest will have to be spiced up elsewhere: first, in the idyll between Ferdinand and Miralda [*sic*] which is of the finest order; second, in the whole nuptial atmosphere and the spirits of air in Act IV; third, in the buffoonery with the drunkards. Is that enough to make an opera?[1]

The answer to the question appears to have been no. Chabrier never wrote his *Tempest* opera, and—to judge from his cavalier and ominously bumptious attitude—we can be thankful he did not. His letter is a reminder that when masterly literature is taken up for operatic treatment, literary values do not necessarily loom importantly in the process. In this case the composer seemed almost completely oblivious to the complicated levels of meaning in the source and has focused upon the least interesting aspects of the action: the clowning scenes and the Ferdinand-Miranda love affair, surely the most insipid in all Shakespeare. Chabrier's heart, here at least, was closer to the blithe spirit of the *boulevard* than to the grand style customary at the Paris Opéra.

Chabrier was not alone in his failure to come to grips with *The Tempest*. At least twenty-five operatic attempts have been made upon the play, more than for any other Shakespearean work. Mendelssohn consulted three librettists (a Frenchman, a German, and an Italian) about setting the play, but he produced nothing. Our greatest loss, perhaps, is the *Tempest* opera Mozart contemplated just prior to his death, though the libretto he had accepted was a peculiar one.

That no composer has succeeded in capturing the richness of Shakespeare's most musical drama seems at first glance paradoxical. One might explain this in various ways. The composer Ferruccio Busoni observed that "for the opera the only suitable subjects are such as could not exist or reach complete expression without music," and it may be that the completeness of Shakespeare's dramatic vision and the music inherent in his poetry are so self-sufficient that there is no "room" for the interlinear music an operatic treatment would provide. Or it may be that the levels on which Shakespeare is operating in *The Tempest* (autobiographical, political, magical, symbolic, philosophical) are simply too numerous; no "other" version of the play could fit them back together with the playwright's dexterity. *The Tempest* is in a sense an artistic puzzle—easy to take apart but difficult to reassemble in its original compact form. No wonder, then, that composers—adding with their music yet another important piece to the puzzle—have found it so difficult to reconstruct for their stage. In more practical terms, one might point to the uncomfortably but necessarily long expository second scene of the play, which may be virtually impossible to translate into operatic theater. Nor was Chabrier far wrong in wondering where the drama is in Shakespeare's strange late play: the dramatic conflict and development of character we have come to expect from this playwright are simply not present in *The Tempest.* Its felicities and genius are of another though scarcely less impressive order.

I have drawn attention to Chabrier's projected opera because it instances vividly how qualities of excellence in a literary work may obstruct or render impossible an operatic translation, how a work may be intrinsically ill suited to the sensibility of a composer, and how far from the true greatness of a work may be the source of its attraction for librettists or composers in a particular operatic era. Chabrier was doomed to fail if his purpose was to re-create Shakespeare's original intentions, though he might have charmed the *boulevardiers* of the mid-1880s with a comical-farcical travesty. The "real" *Tempest* was closed to him; his aesthetic and musical personality were not attuned to its subtleties.

On the other hand, a composer may approach a work with just the right key to its implicit operatic potency, and—if his musical personality blends naturally with the source—a masterpiece may result. Such was the case when Benjamin Britten chose to make a version of *A Midsummer Night's Dream.* His crucial if obvious insight was that three worlds are interwoven in the play—those of the fairy court, the noble Athenians, and the rustic laborers. Through his keen power of orchestration and an almost unique gift for setting iambic pentameter verse, Britten was able to create one of the very few truly successful musical transformations of both Shakespearean poetry and drama.

For some composers a fortuitous equivalence of literary and musical forms can make the transformation seem almost effortless; whereas, for others a disparity of artistic sensibilities causes an unbridgeable chasm. Again, Shakespeare provides an example for each case. Rossini, whose *Otello* dates from 1816, was poorly suited for Shakespeare's violent tragedy of passion. Stendhal, normally a Rossini partisan, was appalled by the opera: "It must have taken a lot of *savoir-faire* on the part of the writer of the libretto to render insipid to this degree the most impassioned of all dramas. Rossini has seconded him well." Byron added his bemused impression in a letter: "They have been crucifying *Othello* into an opera: the music good, but lugubrious; but as for the words, all the real scenes with Iago cut out, and the greatest nonsense inserted; the handkerchief turned into a *billet-doux,* and the first singer would not black his face, for some exquisite reasons." Though the opera was a success at the time of its premiere and for years thereafter, its extreme decorative bias seems to us now to sap the original play of its tragic momentum. What *Othello* required was a more vigorous, flexible compositional style capable of gathering and containing tragic forces throughout an evening. And yet it could not be divorced entirely from "number-opera" structure, for there are splendid "number" speeches imbedded in Shakespeare's dialogue. *Othello,* in short, required the style of late Verdi. The play is rich in what can only be described as operatic moments—for instance Othello's despairing renunciation:

O now, forever
Farewell the tranquil mind! farewell content!
Farewell the plumed troops and the big wars
That makes ambition virtue! O, farewell!
Farewell the neighing steed and the shrill trump,
The spirit-stirring drum, th'ear-piercing fife,
The royal banner, and all quality,
Pride, pomp, and circumstance of glorious war! [3.3.347-54]

From this to Verdi's *Ora e per sempre addio* in Act II is but a small step—the playwright even giving Verdi hints for the orchestration of his noble dirge. Introduced into the continuous texture of the opera are such standard operatic set-pieces—drinking song, love duet, vengeance duet, prayer—as Shakespeare provided musical "space" for in his play. George Bernard Shaw emphasized the fortunate parallelism between two artistic styles when he called *Othello* Shakespeare's one tragedy written in the form of an Italian opera.

This equivalence of sensibilities or form occurs in many ways. The most obvious is in the actual insertion of "musical" moments in the original—for instance Desdemona's "Willow Song" or, to take another play, the King of Thule's ballad, the Song of the Flea, and Mephistopheles' Serenade in *Faust.* Beaumarchais included nine musical events in *Le Barbier de Seville,* some of which were taken up by Paisiello (1782) and Rossini (1816) in their operatic versions of the play. Sometimes there is a particular hint that music would make a natural addition, as in Bazile's speech on the art of calumny in *Le Barbier.* Here Beaumarchais included musical metaphor in his text by using the terms *pianissimo, piano piano, rinforzando,* and *crescendo.* Both Paisiello and Rossini took full advantage of this occasion with crescendo-based arias.

In other cases an incipient operatic structure lies just below a seemingly undramatic or awkward literary format. Consider Goethe's

Sorrows of Young Werther. The collection of Werther's letters which constitute the novella might seem problematic for a librettist, but in fact the flow of correspondence is highly operatic. That is, almost all the letters represent a particular emotional climax—either of elation, depression, or a wracking mixture of both. They are the passionate highlights of Werther's year-and-three-quarters struggle with a hopeless love. They describe exalted states of consciousness, and this was exactly the potent material that Massenet turned into the highly charged lyric explosions of his *Werther.* Thus, for example, Werther's letter dated October nineteenth—its full text is simply "Oh, this void, this dreadful void in my breast! Often I think that if just once I could press her to my heart, it would be filled!"—becomes in the opera the hero's palpitating little aria in Act II, *J'aurais sur ma poitrine.* Such verbal outpouring Massenet was able to transform frequently in his score. Indeed, the title role is made up of numerous highly affective but brief lyric moments which parallel the epistolary structure of the source.

Equivalence of musical style and subject may sometimes hinge upon the language itself, as when Stravinsky found himself delighted with the Latin translation of the Greek tragedy *Oedipus Rex* for his 1927 opera-oratorio:

> What a joy it is to compose music to a language of convention, almost of ritual, the very nature of which imposes a lofty dignity! One no longer feels dominated by the phrase, the literal meaning of words . . . The text thus becomes purely phonetic material for the composer. He can dissect it at will and concentrate all his attention on its primary constituent element—that is to say the syllable.

Equations of musical and painterly styles are common: Mozart with Fragonard for their polished intimacy; Berlioz with Delacroix for their liberation of expressive coloring; Debussy with the Impressionists for their subjectivism and rejection of "line"; and Schoenberg and Berg with Klee, Munch, and Kokoschka for their Expressionist starkness and violence of utterance. Similarly, there are often remarkable equivalences in musical and literary ambience. For Diderot, this concept of equivalence was an artistic necessity: "It would be absurd to abandon the old types of music while retaining the old forms of poetry, since the poet's style must conform to that of the composer." Certain operas in the repertory encourage one to agree with Diderot: *Le Nozze di Figaro, Pelléas et Mélisande,* and *Wozzeck* to name a few. But these are a tiny minority. The exigencies of literature as opera more usually draw us into problematic areas: where the librettist (and, with increasing frequency in operatic history., the composer) finds in a source what he is looking for, but also qualities he must jettison; where he struggles gamely but in vain with an alien aesthetic in his source; where quirks of personal taste or autobiographical identification govern the process of translation. Sometimes peculiar facts surrounding the premiere—the availability of a great soprano, an excellent chorus, for example—subvert loyalty to the literary source. That Purcell was writing for Josiah Priest's Boarding School for Young Gentlewomen in Chelsea and Berlioz for the gargantuan forces at the disposal of the Paris Opéra led to extraordinarily different versions of Virgil, *Dido and Aeneas* and *Les Troyens.* Sometimes the source is simply made to fit the Procrustean bed of current operatic fashions.

The only escape from these varieties of artistic impasse is compromise. The subject of literature as opera is largely one of compromise between the excellences of the written or acted word and the unique and separate splendor of musical expression. The necessity of this spirit of compromise was finely summarized by an eighteenth-century French musical theorist:

> The theater has its own laws, statutes and conventions which, in more than one way, conflict with the methods of music. In this contest (even enmity) of two arts which are associated in order to produce one and the same effect, the task of balancing their prerogatives, regulating the sacrifices which they must make reciprocally, and pronouncing between them a pact of union from which the perfection of the performance results—this is the most difficult task we have to fulfill.[2]

Idealistic and worthy though Michel de Chabanon's sentiment is, it has little to do with the real operatic world. His equipoise of the demands of literature and music is sometimes hard to share when we encounter an opera that fails astonishingly to approach the beauties and intentions of a literary masterpiece or, on the other hand, when wretched doggerel or melodramatic plotting inspires glorious music. Which *coups de théâtre* and *coups de musique* to condemn and which to let pass (radical though the departure from the source may be) is made all the more difficult when one realizes that the sheer length of most sources makes enormous amounts of excision necessary. Composers and librettists are almost always forced to reduce a large fresco into a miniature form while somehow—through the amplifying power of music—retaining the original's expressive magnitude. Donizetti's plea to his librettist—*"la brevità, per pietà, la brevità"*—has echoed throughout operatic history.

The beauty of radical departures may often be defense enough. Ought one to chide Verdi's decision, in his first version of *Macbeth,* to give the hero a death scene on stage in accordance with eighteenth-century English theatrical and nineteenth-century operatic conventions? Ought we to condemn Berlioz in *Les Troyens* for seeking inspiration for that most wonderful of all love duets in French grand opera (*"O nuit d'ivresse"*) not in the *Aeneid* but in Shakespeare's *Merchant of Venice?* Ought we to rebuke Tchaikovsky for giving us in *Eugene Onegin* the full seriousness of deep emotions which Pushkin in fact satirized in his original poem? The answer in each case, at least for this writer, is no. But questions such as these are helpful in raising issues about the limitations upon the process of transforming literature into opera. Very often the examination of such issues illuminates the working mechanisms of opera itself, a point that will be made on numerous specific occasions in the following chapters.

What Is Operatic?

In his *Devil's Dictionary* Ambrose Bierce defined opera thus:

> A play representing life in another world, whose inhabitants have no speech but song, no motions but gestures and no postures but atti-

tudes. All acting is simulation, and the word *simulation* is taken from *simia,* an ape; but in opera the actor takes for his model *Simia audibilis* (or *Pithecanthropos stentor*)—the ape that howls.

Acerbic tone and nefarious etymology aside, Bierce does pinpoint opera's characteristic features: its divorce from artistic naturalism, its gestural mode, and its stylization. The unreality of opera is an old complaint. Finally, I am inclined to think, the ability to accept this fact of operatic art cannot be instilled by logic or persuasion. It seems the world is divided into two classes of people: those "poor, passionless, bluntminded creatures" (Stendhal's words) who dislike opera, and those to whom it comes naturally and who subject themselves as willingly to its absurdities as to its compelling expressive powers. One can speak in favor of opera, at best, on a personal and subjective level.

But what is operatic? All art is fundamentally the translation of experience into another form; what makes the operatic translation unique, if indeed it is? When we say that a work, or a scene, or a character is "operatic," do we really mean that in some sense it is poetic? concentrated? simplified? exaggerated? Can the epithet be rescued from its more common pejorative connotations? The following chapters may provide some answers to these questions, but it is worth beginning with a few tentative general comments upon the nature of opera. Laying down rules in this matter can be foolhardy.[3] One can nevertheless isolate certain qualities that many operas share. Several are mentioned here—each as a frequent hallmark rather than a *sine qua non*.

When W. H. Auden was asked why he wrote librettos, he replied that it was because opera was the last refuge of the high style. Opera has to do with heights. Exaggeration is part of its essence—whether the composer is writing for the Queen of Cathay in *Ariodante,* a seventeen-year-old maiden in *Eugene Onegin,* or a demented barber in *Wozzeck.* The world of opera is one of high relief, magnification, escalation. Metaphors of ascendancy fairly leap to mind. What results is a spectrum of increasing expressive intensity that is available to the opera composer (this holds most strongly for nineteenth-century opera):

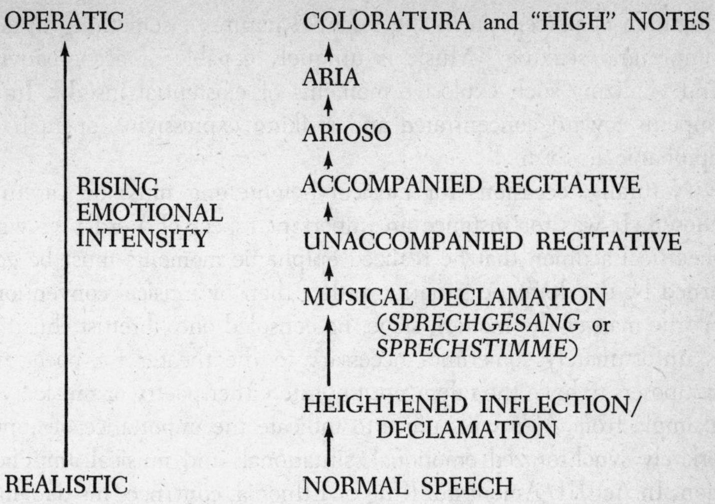

The composer's impetus is upward along this scale, and so he and his librettist must search for moments in literature—call them lyric or explosive or hyperbolic—which permit them to rise to an operatic occasion. They must, in short, think primarily as artists willing to forgo prosaic or rhetorical niceties as well as the values of realism in order to seek moments of expressive crisis—nuclear moments in which potential musical and dramatic energy is locked.

The realism of natural motion is one of the qualities we bargain away by taking opera seriously on its own heightened level of expression (though masters of stage realism like Franco Zeffirelli have in recent decades softened the bargain considerably). The power of music on the stage, if it is effective, is intensifying; just as water naturally seeks a level, music seeks emotions, characters, and situations suitable to amplification. The genre is inevitably possessed of what the Expressionists called a *Steigerungstendenz,* an inclination toward enhancement.[4] The advantage of this is an increased clarity of intention and a larger-than-life motive force in the presentation of human actions. One might compare these qualities with the effects of the epiphanies in the writing of James Joyce. The epiphany—literally a "showing forth"—is defined by Webster as "a sudden manifestation or perception of the essential nature of something usually simple and striking." Music is uniquely capable of accompanying and vitalizing such explosive moments of existential insight. In its impetus toward concentrated and striking expressivity, opera is an epiphanic art-form.

Naturally, occasions for musical heightening must be carefully chosen. It was for instance an important aspect of Verdi's growing theatrical acumen that he realized epiphanic moments must be governed by the dramatic situation rather than by musical conventions. A true man of the modern stage, he consoled one librettist thus: "It is unfortunately sometimes necessary in the theater for poets and composers to have the talent not to write either poetry or music." An example from *Aida* will suffice to indicate the importance of appropriately synchronized emotional, situational, and musical amplification. In Act III, Amonasro, King of Ethiopia, convinces his daughter Aida to betray her love for the Egyptian warrior Rhadames in order to learn the Egyptian army's battle plans. The father's persuasive tactics are urgent and brutal; it takes Aida's last particle of psychic energy to submit finally to his will. For this duet the librettist Ghislanzoni, following common practice of the time, supplied lines for a closing *cabaletta* (usually a short, brilliant aria in a pronounced rhythm and suited to coloratura variation). *Cabalettas* are excellent vehicles for expressing exhilarating emotions—most often joy, vengeance, or mastery; they are a means of moving a character's and an audience's adrenalin. For his *cabaletta* Ghislanzoni hit upon a stanza in which Aida enthusiastically agrees to deceive Rhadames.

Verdi resisted setting these lines, not only because it would have meant an implausibly sudden change in the quality of Aida's love, but also because an up-tempo expression of emotion would be psychologically ludicrous after Amonasro's torturing curses:

> I remain of the opinion that cabalettas must be used when the situation demands them . . . In the duet between father and daughter it seems especially out of place. Aida is in such a state of fear and moral depression that she cannot and must not sing a cabaletta.

Verdi realized that a moment of "moral depression" was quite unsuited to the electric effect a *cabaletta* would have at this point.

Sensing that Aida's mental prostration would permit her, at most, to utter disjointed phrases, he wrote to his colleague: "For my part, I would abandon forms of stanzas and rhythm; I would not think of having them sing and would render the situation as it is, were it even in verses of recitative." Verdi won his point. What resulted is an andante passage, dominated by a dirge-like string unison on A-flat, in which Aida must "drag herself with difficulty to her father's feet" and sing in an extremely low and veiled voice (*molto sottovoce e cupo*). The change pleased Verdi: "Now Aida, it seems to me, says what she ought to say and is truly in character [*è in situazione*]." Doubtless this duet's theatrically effective departure from convention was the reason why Verdi felt it the best of the four duets in *Aida*.

How are literary works and music connected? The answers to this question are various; we can survey but a few here. Most fundamental is the sense that the literary work must give or leave the composer something to say. This point was made very early on, in Mainwaring's eighteenth-century biography of Handel:

> If it [poetry] abounds with noble images, and high wrought descriptions, and contains little of character, sentiment, or passion, the best Composer will have no opportunity of exerting his talents. Where there is nothing capable of being expressed, all he can do is entertain his audience with mere ornamental passages of his own invention. But graces and flourishes must rise from the subject of the composition in which they are employed, just as flowers and festoons from the design of a building. It is from their relation to the whole, that these minuter parts derive their value.

Once a subject with expressive potential for music is chosen, the problem becomes one of mediating between the two art-forms. In this some composers are more receptive (Gluck, Mussorgsky, Britten) and others less receptive (Mozart, Berlioz, Strauss) to literary or linguistic "domination." Berlioz, however, best summarized the nature of the composer's difficulty: "The real problem lies in finding the means of being *expressive* and *true* without ceasing to be a musician, and to find new ways of making music dramatic." The difficulty is to avoid following the text too slavishly, on the one hand, or, on the other, ignoring it and composing thinly disguised absolute music.[5] Rossini issued a warning against the former extreme: "If the composer sets out to follow the meaning of the words with equal steps, he will write music that is not expressive by itself, but is poor, vulgar, mosaic-like, and incongruous or ridiculous." Composers who have attempted to follow Shakespeare's iambic pentameter—Britten notably excepted—have felt the force of Rossini's observation. Perhaps the most remarkable instance of an attempt to reproduce the qualities of natural speech (aside from *Pelléas*) was Mussorgsky's Gogol opera, *The Marriage*.[6] About this work the composer wrote: "My music must be an artistic reproduction of human speech, as the external manifestation of thought and feeling must, without exaggeration or violence, become true, accurate music." To the composer's friends the score was a curiosity, and he was sufficiently discouraged never to finish it. This is not surprising: Mussorgsky's experiment subverted the heightening power which is part of opera's *raison d'être*.

Not all literary styles are suitable to operatic escalation. Ferruccio Busoni declared, "What I desire from an opera text is not only that it conjures up music, but that it allows room for it to expand."* Perhaps the best way to appreciate this quality is to think of writers for whom the idea of operatic translation is virtually inconceivable—Henry Fielding, Laurence Sterne, Anthony Trollope, Jane Austen, Charles Dickens, George Bernard Shaw, and Virginia Woolf, to name a few from English literature. Pater's belief that music and prose literature are "the opposite terms of art" helps to explain why. What these authors have in common is a special dependence upon the powers of language as itself a descriptive instrument; the core of their artistry is descriptive and analytical, rather than lyrical and expressive. One might say that they are prosaic rather than poetic at heart. They may treat the strong and violent emotions that opera calls for, but these are strained through a dense conceptual or stylistic filter. Much of their drama is syntactical.

One can often say of seemingly unoperatic literary works that theirs is a theater of words, whereas opera requires a theater of action, emotion, engagement, movement, and spectacle. Consider this short

* This and other quotations in this chapter are drawn from Ulrich Weisstein's *The Essence of Opera* (1964), the best anthology on opera currently available.

passage from Sterne's *Tristram Shandy* describing that event so often celebrated in opera, falling in love:

> Not that the phrase is at all to my liking; for to say that a man is *fallen* in love,—or that he is *deeply* in love,—or up to his ears in love,—and sometimes even over head and ears in it,—carries an idiomatical kind of implication, that love is a thing *below* man:—this is recurring again to Plato's opinion, which, with all his divinityship,—I hold to be damnable and heretical; and so much for that.
>
> Let love therefore be what it will, my uncle Toby fell into it.

There is no apparent room for music here. The interest is verbal, ironic, and discursive—all qualities which, in quantity, subvert the simplifying and at the same time heightening impetus of lyric drama. Writers who hew closely to the terra firma of analytical prose neither entreat nor encourage musical enlargement. This assertion, though—like many one is tempted to make about opera—is subject to exception, as the chapter on Britten's *Death in Venice* will demonstrate.

A librettist, then, fashioning his text from a literary source, will naturally gravitate away from passages of discursive complexity and toward those that issue in psychological or physical action. A clear instance of this bias is found in Verdi's setting of *Macbeth*. Macbeth's first great monologue (1.7.1-28) is missing from the opera, and it is not difficult to see why. In this speech Macbeth weighs the implications of an assassination. It is abstracted and—to use a Shakespearean epithet—thought-sick. Nothing happens; Macbeth decides not to act. This soliloquy is consequently a dense and rhetorically involved one, as its opening lines will suggest:

> If it were done, when 'tis done, then 'twere well
> It were done quickly. If th'assassination
> Could trammel up the consequence, and catch
> With his surcease, success; that but this blow
> Might be the be-all and the end-all—here,
> But here, upon this bank and shoal of time,
> We'ld jump the life to come.

Much more attractive for operatic purposes was Macbeth's next monologue, the famous dagger speech (2.1.33-64). There is much movement here (partially, of course, only imagined by Macbeth):

the clutching after the dagger, the marshaling to action, the figure of "wither'd Murther" moving like a ghost, and Macbeth himself treading the "sure and firm-set earth." And there is also a palpable conclusion for action:

> I go, and it is done; the bell invites me.
> Hear it not, Duncan, for it is a knell,
> That summons thee to heaven or to hell. *Exit.*

This moment of resolution is one of the most famous in dramatic literature, and just such moments are a staple in opera. No wonder it inspired one of Verdi's finest accompanied recitatives (*Mi si affaccia un pugnal?*). Another line from the dagger speech—"Words to the heat of deeds too cold breath brings"—is but a variation on Verdi's own admonition to his librettists: *"poche parole, poche parole, stile conciso."* And it is to the heat of deeds and passions that operatic composers have most commonly and successfully turned, spurning as best they can the cold breath of too many and too rhetorically involved words.

Literature that is too musical may also pose difficulties. Schiller's play *The Bride of Messina* was written with operatic devices in mind, and yet it has proved one of the least attractive of his plays as operatic material. The second part of Goethe's *Faust* is extraordinarily operatic in conception.[7] And yet it is the first part which has provided the better quarry for composers. The style of Gertrude Stein presents another, admittedly special case where highly musical prose—on the contrary—encouraged the addition of a real musical dimension. Stein's prose seems almost incomplete without music; in fact, none of her plays was performed in her lifetime without it, something Stein complained about ("They could though and it would be interesting but no one has yet"). The composer Virgil Thomson, who specialized in setting Stein to music, offered the obvious explanation. He said that her writing *"likes* music. Much of it, in fact, lies closer to musical timings than to speech timings." And so it was that in composing *Four Saints in Three Acts* Thomson set exactly what Stein wrote from beginning to end. In any case, the result as lyric drama is at best curious—the music acquiescing excessively to Stein's disingenuous and yet subtle text.

One might add here that lyric dramas structured upon philosophical, aesthetic, or conceptual material rather than upon character, conflict, and dramatic situation tend to be difficult pieces for stage directors and audiences alike—though the music may prove sublime and carry all before it. Works in this category are Mozart's *Zauberflöte,* Beethoven's *Fidelio,* Wagner's *Parsifal,* Debussy's *Pelléas et Mélisande,* Schoenberg's *Moses und Aron,* Strauss's *Capriccio,* and Britten's *Death in Venice.*

In music as in nature, rhythm is life and its absence is death. Rossini turned this into an operatic theorem: "Musical expression lies in the rhythm; and in the rhythm lies all the power of music." Rhythm implies movement, and movement is a necessary quality in the opera house. Hofmannsthal described this necessity in a letter to Strauss concerning their problems with *Ariadne auf Naxos:*

> The basis of all drama is action, whether it be violent or gentle, mechanical or psychological. In opera the music comes to the support of the action—like two streams that mingle and flow on together. In this case, where there is only one real "set piece," the music does not lend assistance, does not press onward to the dramatic goal—on the contrary it has a retarding influence. Thus the thin and sluggish stream of action is constantly interrupted by passages of musical description, and the simple instinct of the public, which wants to get on with the plot, becomes restive and impatient. [letter, 8 August 1918]

Dramatists, librettists, and composers attempt to create effects of stasis or ennui at great risk. Perhaps only Beckett has truly succeeded in this on a regular basis, and then only through a paradoxically tense dialogue. *Pelléas et Mélisande,* an exception, tends to prove the rule. Lying behind Maeterlinck's play is the Symbolist desire not to name but to suggest the substance of life; the play is based upon an aesthetic of indirection and motionlessness for which Debussy's style—in its focus upon a level of almost subliminal sensation and rejection of linear progression—was perfectly suited. The opera is evocative of the mood of the original play, and for this very reason it is difficult for most operatic audiences. The average listener tends to respond to it just as G. K. Chesterton responded to the Maeterlinck play: "If we take a play like *Pelléas et Mélisande,* we shall find that unless we grasp the particular fairy thread of thought the poet rather hazily flings at us, we cannot grasp anything whatever."

Sometimes the sheer symphonic powers of a composer overwhelm the possibilities for genuine dramatic development. Jean Cocteau well observed that "certain masterpieces of the theater are not theatrical in the proper sense but scenic symphonies, which make no concession to the setting." Cocteau then cites *Boris Godunov* as a case in point, and this indeed is one possible source of that opera's problematic structure. The same balance in favor of the symphonic at the expense of the dramatic is also felt in Schumann's *Scenes from Faust* and Berlioz's *Romeo and Juliet* and *Damnation of Faust*—three examples of works that occupy a middle ground among symphony, oratorio, and opera. Even more remarkable is Beethoven's *Fidelio,* in which we are constantly reminded of the composer as symphonist: the rustic geniality of the Seventh Symphony is mirrored in Rocco; the good humor of the Eighth in the Marzelline-Jaquino affair; the monumentality of the "Eroica" in the overtures; and the ecstasy of the Ninth in the Finale of the second act. The awkward aspects of *Fidelio* are partially explained by this mixture of salient symphonic moods.

This tension between absolute musical expression and the demands of the theater is also frequently felt in Tchaikovsky's operas, and we have an admission from the composer himself that his bias was finally in favor of the music: "Uniting as it [opera] does so many elements which all serve the same end, it is perhaps the richest of musical forms. I think, however, that personally I am more inclined to symphonic music, at least I feel more free and independent when I have not to submit to the requirements and conditions of the stage." In search of an ideal in this situation we are brought back to Berlioz's desire to be expressive and true without ceasing to be a musician, or to Alban Berg's desire to "give to the theater what belongs to the theater." This requires not merely a sense of drama (what could be more dramatic than the conversation of a Haydn quartet or the intellectual self-communing of a Beethoven piano sonata?), but a sense of the theater and the requirements of the stage.[8] This necessitates a search for what Verdi called the *parola scenica*—theatrical word—that is at the same a *parola musica.* "Theater! Theater!" was

Verdi's constant plea to his librettists; that instinct is a hallmark of the greatest writers for the lyric stage.

Busoni, a too fearless lawgiver, set it down as a "fact" that opera must consist of a series of short, concise set-pieces. Whether true or not, Busoni's assertion could be supported by pointing to many works in the standard repertory. It is a matter of common sense that variety and vivid contrast are important. Verdi realized this: "To make music, one needs stanzas for cantabile sections, stanzas for ensembles, stanzas for largos, for allegros, etc., and all these in alternation so that nothing seems cold and monotonous." Berg was likewise aware of the necessity for variety when he confronted the quick succession of scenes in Büchner's play *Woyzeck*. Realizing that mere through-composition would induce boredom ("and boredom is the last thing one should experience in the theater"), Berg scrupulously differentiated each of his fifteen scenes through elaborate musical architecture. And *Wozzeck* does demonstrate the need for what Berg called, in a lecture on that work, "operatic caesurae" or stopping-points.

It may seem paradoxical to add that the variety of stage action must somehow issue in a unity and simplicity of impact. However, the effects of simplification from the original can be seen in almost every one of the operas examined in this study. Composers and librettists are not only frequently obliged to make cuts that affect the central intentions, focus, or balance of a literary work, but they must also often cut extraneous, ambiguous, or complicated material. Verdi's experience with Shakespeare exemplifies this: his art fed on focused, set-piece situations but was boggled by the overabundance of themes and complexities of double-plotting such as occur in *King Lear*. This may help to explain why, after nearly fifty years of planning for a *Re Lear*, he gave up the project. No wonder he was attracted to *Macbeth*, Shakespeare's simplest and most direct tragedy, and *Othello*, in which an entire first act and subplots could be easily ignored. At the core of Verdi's art was a desire for unified impact, and this was perhaps best expressed in a famous letter he wrote to Du Locle rejecting the idea of a new Parisian opera:

> In short, everybody would have to follow me. A single will would have to rule throughout: my own. That may seem rather tyrannical

> to you, and perhaps it is. But if the work is an organic whole, it is built on a single idea and everything must contribute to the achievement of this unity.

It is not entirely coincidental that Verdi's finest operas were written after he had gained the stature and financial security to press this "tyrannical" viewpoint in preparing his works for the stage.

One might add as a final note the most important operatic ingredient of all: eloquently passionate characters. Writing about "The Tragic Art," Schiller observed: "The state of passion in itself, independently of the good or bad influence of its objects on our morality, has something in it that charms us. We aspire to transport ourselves into that state, even if it costs us sacrifices." We seek passion in the theater especially. Hamlet even defines the theatrical experience as a "dream of passion." And passion is at the heart of opera. W. H. Auden explained its importance in one of the best essays ever written on the nature of this art-form:

> Opera in particular is an imitation of human willfulness; it is rooted in the fact that we not only have feelings but insist upon having them at whatever cost to ourselves . . . Opera, therefore, cannot present character in the novelist's sense of the word, namely, people who are potentially good *and* bad, active and passive, for music is immediate actuality *and* neither potentiality nor passivity can live in its presence . . . The quality common to all great operatic roles, e.g. Don Giovanni, Norma, Lucia, Tristan, Isolde, Brünnhilde, is that each is a passionate and willful state of being.[9]

Auden's remarks serve to conclude this brief survey, summarizing as they do some of the elements of opera we have already isolated. It remains for the reader, in the following chapters, to test these suggested connotations of the epithet *operatic* and to judge their relative importance for himself.

The Really Interesting Questions

Lytton Strachey once wrote that "the really interesting question is always the particular one, though it's always the general one that it's possible to discuss." The present format represents an attempt to cope with this paradox. Because the subject of literature as opera is full of pitfalls, unique instances, and peculiar transformational imbroglios, there is a preponderance of really interesting specific questions, and often only through them can we begin to see clearly the more general issues. I have therefor chosen particular examples from the operatic repertory for intensive analysis. My choice, however, has been made to give the reader as broad an overview of literature as opera as is possible within the purview of a mere dozen works.

First, I have considered varying "angles" on the process of translation. What happens when literary masterpieces are submitted to the vagaries and traditions of opera and to the unique technical problems of putting an opera on stage? Why are some attempts spectacularly successful, some indifferent, and some abject? Why are certain works congenial to operatic treatment and others intractable? Which operatic conventions undermine literary values, and, conversely, which amplify them? How do contemporary fashions, artistic trends, historical events, and personal aesthetics affect the translation of literature into music? Some answers to these questions will be found in the following chapters. There I have examined specific connections throughout operatic history in which the work of author, librettist, and composer coalesced in an illuminating way—sometimes with breathtaking ease, sometimes disastrously, and sometimes with a maddening mixture of fidelity and insensitivity.

Second, this study is organized according to the major periods or genres of operatic history: If operatic composers are not bound to follow aesthetic commandments chiseled in stone, they are nevertheless affected by their intellectual environment. Dryden observed that "every Age has a kind of Universal Genius, which inclines those that live in it to some particular Studies," and it follows that if we are to understand the distinctive operatic styles of succeeding epochs, we must give some attention to the "Universal Genius" of those periods. The task is one of setting composers in a larger milieu—a principle of intellectual history that goes back at least as far as Wölfflin's description of Renaissance and Baroque architectural style: "To *explain* a style then can mean nothing other than to place it in its general historical context and to verify that it speaks in harmony with the other organs of its age." In those chapters particularly concerned with stylistic parallels (Chapters Two, Three, Eight, and Nine), I have consciously attempted to make some of the extra-musical connections Wölfflin encourages. The style of a given operatic composer and librettist does not exist in a vacuum. Their creations do not spring complete from their brows, any more than Shakespeare's plays are purely Shakespearean. They are also Elizabethan, Jacobean, English, and Renaissance masterpieces.

My choice of composers and operas was thus in part governed by a desire to give a sense of the various distinctive aesthetics in operatic history. Methods and conventions that delighted one age may often prove ludicrous or impossibly constricting for another. Mozart forsook the conventions of opera seria; Wagner razed the unwieldy *scena* and *cavatina* of the bel canto period; and the musical Expressionists in turn pulverized Wagner's through-composition, "endless" melody, and elaborate leitmotiv system and also freed themselves from the restrictions of tonality. Such changes radically, if temporarily, upset the expectations raised by established fashions. They destroyed the kind of "pact" Wieland refers to: "Opera presupposes a silent agreement between the work of art and the listener." If we are to understand the nature of this silent agreement upon expectations (and how it is overturned by innovators), we should know more about opera than musicologists and biographers are able to tell us. Operas based upon important literary works, I think, provide a unique opportunity to make this more extensive exploration.

Third, my choices were also affected by the wish to survey a full range of literary genres from various national literatures. Thus, in the present study are represented an Italian Renaissance epic romance, a French domestic comedy, a German historical drama, an English romantic-historical novel, an Italian Renaissance autobiography, a Shakespearean tragedy, a long satiric Russian poem, a *fin de siècle* one-acter by an English aesthete writing in French, a short German proto-Expressionist play, and a modern German novella. Finally, I wished to represent works by composers from all the major opera-producing nations.

The underlying assumption of this study is a simple one: questions of literary history, milieu, and style ought to be of crucial concern when we approach operas based on important literary works. And my hope is to demonstrate that a comparison of a source with its operatic "edition" can illuminate the nature of opera as much as strict musical analysis or biography. It follows that the strengths and limitations of musical drama will frequently become apparent when we turn to its literary sources. Why a librettist or composer (or both) chooses a particular novel, short story, drama, or poem; what the intellectual environment of the source was; how loyal the musician was to the spirit of his source; how the ambience of source and opera compare—the consideration of such questions gives valuable insight into the composer's personality, his aesthetic, the operatic fashions he labored under, as well as into the distinctive features of literary and musical art. Surprisingly, no one has attempted a systematic study of "literary" operas with a desire to relate them to their cultural milieu—and beyond to the course of intellectual history. It is even more astonishing when one considers the large number of operas, some of them among the greatest in the repertory, that are based upon literary masterpieces.

The reason is not far to seek. There is a peculiar but common inclination not to take opera seriously and put it to the same tests of analytical rigor as, say, sculpture or poetry. There is, of course, a large and avid audience for opera, but this avidity often inspires merely an interest in trifles, personalities, high C's, and high-camp distractions. It is popular to think of opera as "bombastic and extravagantly odd" (Wagner's epithets for Meyerbeer). One is reminded of Beaumarchais's remark that one may perfectly well sing what is not worth saying, and a Beaumarchais scholar, J. B. Ratermanis, has even gone so far as to yoke opera as a "subrational entertainment" with harlequinades, spectacles, buffoonery, and low farce.

It is also hard to take opera seriously because it is so beautiful. In the sheer triumph of vocal beauty, unfortunately, we are often willing silently to sacrifice other more subtle artistic values, among them dramatic momentum, integrity of plot, intelligibility, and balance. For many who like opera, beauty is sufficient. This is partly because, as Shaw pointed out, many people "have little or no sense of drama, but a very keen sense of beauty of sound and prettiness of pattern in music."

And so opera has tended to drift out of the cultural mainstream, an art-form viewed with some bemusement or intellectual detachment—often by those who are most addicted to it. It was therefor with startled pleasure that many received Joseph Kerman's *Opera as Drama* (1956), which asserted what ought to have been obvious but was largely unrealized or at least unspoken, namely, that opera is "properly a musical form of drama, with its own individual dignity and force." I see this study as a kind of sequel and counterpart to Kerman's book: although he approached the theatrical values inherent in opera from a musicological perspective, I intend to approach the musical values of certain operas from a literary perspective. Though our vantage points differ, I conceive our final intention to be the same, that is, to bring opera back into the mainstream and reaffirm its intellectual ties with the sister arts that help constitute this most complex of all creative genres.

The book is neither definitive nor exhaustive. It could scarcely be otherwise, for this enormous topic contains so many possibilities. I have, even in this lengthy study, been able to chart only certain parts of an extraordinarily variable terrain. The result, appropriately, is an overview. One should after all have some overall sense of the landscape before rushing in with more elaborate and precise cartographer's tools.

Consequently and inevitably I was forced to ignore some famous composers and many operas that would seem to fit comfortably into a discussion of literature made into opera. An initial decision to treat no more than one work by any author or composer precluded examination of many operas that would have resulted in interesting chapters—among them *Don Carlos, Falstaff, Boris Godunov, Elektra, Peter Grimes, Billy Budd, The Turn of the Screw, A Midsummer Night's Dream.* In two cases (*Benvenuto Cellini* instead of *Les Troyens* and *Macbeth* instead of *Otello*) my priorities might seem perverse at first, but these choices are fully explained in the chapters on Berlioz and Verdi. I have also overlooked operas in which the composer and librettist have so grossly trivialized the artistic values of a source as to vitiate a "literary" approach. Bellini's *I Capuleti e i Montecchi* and Rossini's *Otello* fall into this category. So does *Faust:* the Germans emphasize Gounod's failure as a translator of Goethe by insisting on calling his opera *Marguerite.* I also hesitated to devote full chapters to works that, however important in operatic history, are not based upon literary sources that are either masterpieces in their own right or archetypes for a particular genre or period. As a result, Massenet and Puccini and Meyerbeer—who never set literature of sufficiently enduring or significant stature—are not represented at all. I made the difficult decision not to include *Carmen* or *Pelléas et Mélisande* for the same reason (in any event, much has already been written upon these operas as literary translations). Mérimée's Carmen story is certainly a minor work; the author himself referred to it as a "petite drôlerie" when it first appeared. And though Debussy wrought a unique and undeniable masterpiece from his source, Maeterlinck's play and dramaturgy have been convicted by time and can at best be seen as a tiny backwater in the mainstream of theatrical history.

For the rest, it was a question of not having world enough, time, or space. Two important topics, I finally concluded, could only be treated adequately in separate and probably lengthy studies. One was a look at operatic versions of Greek tragedy, touching for instance upon such works as Cherubini's *Medea,* Strauss's *Elektra,* Orff's *Antigone,* Milhaud's *Oresteia,* Stravinsky's *Oedipus Rex,* Honegger's *Amphion,* and Henze's *Bassarids.* The other concerned Wagner—either *Der Ring des Nibelungen* or *Tristan und Isolde.* Wagner, however, is in the matter of literary translation—as in seemingly all aspects of his art—a law unto himself. To struggle with the immense Medieval epic sources and then with the composer's involved personal and aesthetic preoccupations seemed, frankly, more than a mere chapter could possibly achieve. Finally, I have left untouched a number of peripheral or rarely performed operas that nevertheless would have offered fascinating insights into the task of making literature musical: Purcell's *Dido and Aeneas,* Busoni's *Dr. Faustus,* Janáček's *From the House of the Dead,* Prokofiev's *War and Peace,* Ezra Pound's *Le Testament de Villon,* Thomson's *Four Saints in Three Acts,* Barber's *Antony and Cleopatra,* and Carlyle Floyd's *Of Mice and Men,* just to name a few at random.

I used the term *systematic* above, and this may raise expectations that will not be fulfilled. This study is systematic only insofar as it is ordered according to the major periods of operatic history. It is not, however, an aesthetic treatise—and for good reason: elaborate theory rarely precedes the decision of a composer or librettist to set a literary work. What concerns him may instead be dramatic impact, the message or inherent music perceived in the source, the ways it will appeal to a reigning impresario—in short, any of countless contingent considerations. The decision is more often than not untutored in aesthetic niceties.

Theory comes after the fact. And I have often thought something of opera's lifeblood is lost in the more philosophical search for absolute aesthetic truths about this hybrid art-form, especially as it is pursued by writers like Kierkegaard, Schopenhauer, Wagner, and—in modern times—Theodor Adorno. Nietzsche once observed that Wagner always affected superiority toward the word *opera,* and this one feels when reading much of the literature on the aesthetics of opera. Concerted efforts to philosophize upon this genre succeed all too often in estranging it from the theatrical exigencies and realities that are to a considerable extent the concern of this study.

Herbert Graf has told of his experience directing Mozart's *Figaro* under two of the great conductors of his time, Bruno Walter and Wilhelm Furtwängler. At a climactic moment in Act II when Susanna (and not the supposed philanderer Cherubino) emerges from a closet to the amazement of both Count and Countess, there is a brief falling sequence of three-note phrases (see EX. 6, Chapter Three). Walter insisted that Graf have Susanna move at this point, since he believed Mozart was describing her "tiny steps" in his music. Graf repeated this blocking for Furtwängler, who at the same point demanded that Susanna remain motionless. His reasoning: the music represented the heartbeats of the stunned Countess. This anecdote is telling for any study of opera. Opera exists in a realm of practicalities, plural possibilities, and compromises—not material out of which fine theories may be constructed or material that encourages hasty and exclusive assumptions. Philosophers of art are valuable spokesmen, but it is doubtful that they influence the crucial decisions that are the present interest: why and how to mould a piece of literature into a form workable on an opera stage. Nor are the theoreticians the final arbiters of success, though they may be helpful in explaining it. That, after all, is for time and operatic audiences to decide. Generally speaking, operatic history has not developed according to nice aesthetic principles but through pragmatic response to particular fashions and technical innovations—simply because the complexity and expensiveness of opera have actually served to make its practitioners extremely practical-minded (Wagner being the most obvious example of this paradox). One might add, too, that composers do not always conform in practice to their own explicit theories.[10] For these reasons I have largely forsaken theory in favor of practice in what follows.

A last word should be added about the musical discussions in the following chapters. "Do not be alarmed," Shaw once wrote in a review. "I am not going to perpetrate an 'analysis.' " Of the technical analyses Shaw had in mind this study too is innocent. Though, I do attempt to comment upon the relationship of the musical language to the literary aesthetic that it seeks to vitalize. I am concerned with what the composer and librettist have to express, that is, what in the source they chose to give musical substance to and what they chose to ignore. Such discussion inevitably requires examination of the music, and the reader will find that I turn to the music primarily to illuminate the ways a composer gives life to his source, and to observe how well his musical personality agrees with the literature confronting him.

The reader will recall Michel de Chabanon's plea for equipoise. I have attempted in the following chapters to emulate his spirit and have avoided condemning what seems like radical surgery without first pursuing the symptoms of stage conventions, artistic necessity, or contradictory creative purposes that may have led to extreme measures. And I have sought to position myself between the demands of literature and the demands of music—as someone, rather like a neutral observer in a buffer zone, able to look upon both frontiers with interested detachment. It has been my experience and observation that the study of literature and music is a sadly neglected field. Professors of literature are by and large indifferent, if not hostile, to musical translations of works within their domain. Professors of music are for the better part preoccupied with performance, strict musical analysis, and musical history. This provincialism is unfortunate, since so much of the great vocal literature could be more fully appreciated, not to say more intelligently performed, if studied in an integrated way as literature *and* music. My concern is opera, but the art-song repertory also offers stupendous potential for comparative study.

Writing a general book on a topic over which specialists from both sides naturally exercise a skeptical, rigorous, and perhaps even jealous dominion represents an obvious risk. I thought the risk worth taking. Literature as opera is too large and intriguing a subject to be left entirely to either literary or musical faculties. The intention of the present study, then, is to encourage a better rapport between the two disciplines and a willingness to make those reciprocal sacrifices Chabanon speaks of. Readers unable to take the words of Shakespeare's Coriolanus to heart may find this a maddening book: "On both sides more respect."

two

ORLANDO
ARIODANTE ALCINA

He sent his faculties out upon discovery,
into worlds where only imagination can travel.

Samuel Johnson, *Life of Milton*

Claude Debussy, thinking mainly of Handel and Scarlatti, wrote once that "the dead are really sometimes too diffident and are willing to wait too long for the sad meed of posthumous fame." Debussy's observation applies less to Handel's oratorios than to his operas. The former gave the composer an undisputed place on the musical Parnassus while he lived, and—thanks to strong choral traditions in England and Germany—Handelian oratorios have been performed consistently in succeeding centuries.[1] On the other hand, Handel's Italian operas, of which thirty-nine survive, have been obliged to wait more patiently for revival. Italian opera enjoyed a great vogue in the first quarter of the eighteenth century among London's upper class. In 1722 Gay could write to Swift, "There's nobody allow'd to say I sing but an Eunuch [castrato] or an Italian Woman. Every body is grown now as great a judge of Musick as they were in your time of Poetry. And folks that could not distinguish one tune from another now daily dispute about the different Styles of Hendel, Bononcini, and Attillio." In the 1730s, however, this vogue began to wane. Indeed, the decline of Italian opera was breathtaking. By 1760 Goldsmith could observe of Handel that "though his English oratorios are accounted inimitable, yet his Italian operas are fallen into oblivion."

The disenchantment with Italian opera in England derived from many influences: the rise of a more vigorous, English-language ballad entertainment inaugurated by *The Beggar's Opera* in 1728, the success of Handel's first oratorios *Athalia* and *Deborah* in 1733, the decline in quality of imported Italian divas and divos, the ruinous competition between the two London opera companies, and a simple tiring of the public with a genre that never seemed to change its basic format.[2] But Handel persevered in the composition of Italian operas in spite of their increasingly chilly and financially risky prospects. A more shrewd judge of his public and its changing taste—

Handel let six years slip by after *Athalia* and *Deborah* were written before returning to the oratorio with *Saul*—would have changed his colors sooner.

That Handel did not do so is fortunate for the history of opera and for the purposes of the present study: three of his late operas written in spite of changing fashions are among the greatest that composer or indeed any Baroque composer ever wrote. They are based upon one of the finest and most popular literary sources for Baroque composers, Ludovico Ariosto's *Orlando Furioso*.* Handel's *Orlando* (1733), *Ariodante* (1735), and *Alcina* (1735) are also perfectly placed near the stylistic watershed separating Baroque and Classical operatic conventions. They contain not only the typical vistas of Baroque opera but also brilliant moments in which Handel breaks away from the conventions of his time to look ahead to Mozart, Verdi, and beyond. These operas also provide occasion to explore the qualities of Ariosto's epic poem that proved so appealing to the particular musical aesthetic that flourished in England and on the Continent in the early eighteenth century.

Handelian opera was and is an easily despised genre. Sir Isaac Newton's response to Handel's *Radamisto* in 1720—"The first Act he heard with pleasure, the 2d stretch'd his patience, at the 3d he ran away."—is not an unusual one even today. In its heyday Italian opera was much maligned by Londoners as an exotic, if not downright foolish piece of work. Many of the most learned and prominent ears of the time were made of tin—Swift, Pope, Steele, Addison, and Johnson, just to name a few. The various wits and sages complained then with the same haughty condescension toward opera one often experiences today. Addison could scarcely begin deprecating opera because its "absurdity . . . shows itself at the first sight," and he added the corollary among composers of Italian opera, "That nothing is capable of being well set to music, that is not nonsense." Samuel Johnson was satisfied to call opera "an exotic and irrational entertainment," and Swift's manly intellect gave the newly immigrated art-form short shrift, speaking of "that unnatural Taste for Italian

* Ariosto's work (1st ed., 1516) will henceforth be referred to by its full title, Handel's opera as *Orlando*. Ariostan quotations are from the William Rose translation (1823-1831), ed. Stewart Baker (1968).

Musick among us, which is wholly unsuitable to our Northern Climate, and the Genius of the People, whereby we are overrun with Italian Effeminacy and Italian Nonsense." James Miller spoke for all of the detractors when he complained in 1731 of singers who

> In unknown Tongues mysterious Dullness chant,
> Make Love in Tune, or thro' the Gamut rant.

What annoyed Handel's contemporaries is precisely what tends to infuriate the modern listener. We nervously abide (in the form of countertenors) what one writer called "the shrill Whine/ Of gentle Eunuchs" for whom Handel wrote many heroic roles. We bridle along with Charles Avison (*An Essay on Musical Expression,* 1753) at "that egregious Absurdity of repeating and finishing many Songs with the first Part" which is demanded by the da capo convention. Like James Beattie (*Essays on Poetry and Music,* 1776) we tire of the "long divisions (or successions of notes warbled to one syllable)" which "set us staring at the flexibility of the performer's voice." And there are preposterous, facile, and labyrinthine plots—incredible even by normal operatic standards.

But for two important reasons, we might therefor leave Debussy's "veil of death" covering Handel's three *Furioso* operas. The first is that—renowned though the detractors of opera were—there was also in the eighteenth century a vociferous chorus of admiration for Handel's musical powers. The age took great delight in Handel, especially after he burst upon a larger, more democratically constituted audience with his oratorios. When James Harris came to praise men who exploited "the genuine Charm of Music, and the Wonders which it works," he added in a footnote: "Such, above all, is George Frederick Handel; whose Genius, having been cultivated by continued Exercise, and being itself far the sublimest and most universal now known, has justly placed him without an Equal or a Second" (*Three Treatises,* 1744). Toward the end of Handel's career William Hughes could observe—taking his cue from Shakespeare's *Julius Caesar*—that the composer "does bestride the Musick World/ Like a Colossus" (*Remarks Upon Musick,* 1758). And if we look at the list of his operatic rivals, which includes Porpora, Hasse, Veracini, and Bononcini, we can only agree that history has vindicated Hughes's early assessment. Handel was admired as Milton was, for striking out into worlds where only imaginative genius could travel. He died supreme among the "great Professors" of music and was buried with pomp in Westminster Abbey.

Of course, Handel acquired his large, admiring audience primarily after he turned to vocal music composed for English texts.[3] The following for his Italian operas was limited to an elite that could appreciate their more refined, essentially Continental beauties and afford the expensive price of admission. Goldsmith well noted that the middle and lower classes of London "have neither taste nor fortune to relish such an entertainment; they would find more satisfaction in the 'Roast Beef of Old England,' than in the finest closes [cadenzas] of an eunuch, they sleep amidst all the agony of recitative." The pleasures of Italian opera were strictly for sophisticated society. Jonathan Richardson made just this point in 1719 in *A Discourse on the Dignity, Certainty, Pleasure and Advantage of the Science of the Connoisseur:* "The Noblest Works of *Rafaelle,* the most Ravishing Musick of *Hendell,* the most Masterly Strokes of *Milton,* touch not People without Discernment" (p. 203).

All this is by way of warning that, though Handel's reputation changed radically with the advent of the oratorios, his fundamental vocal-dramatic art did not. This brings me to the second reason for interest in the *Furioso* operas, which is simply that the experience of them (I am speaking, unfortunately, of recent recordings, not the optimal experience of live performances) is attractive, engaging, often dramatically compelling, and beautiful. The impression is strong that, as with so many masterly operas, close study will be repaid. After sensitive cutting, what remains is unmistakably stageworthy, sometimes startlingly powerful; characterization proves far from primitive; the richness and special effects of orchestration become manifest; and modifications of Baroque conventions begin to emerge.

We should not be surprised to find the brilliant qualities of the oratorios prefigured in Handel's Italian operas. It might seem plausible to think of the operas as merely so many grinding wheels upon which Handel sharpened the genius displayed in his climactic masterpieces, but *Orlando, Ariodante,* and *Alcina* ruin this assumption.

They are splendid works in their own right. Each displays too many marks of genius to support the harsh division of Handel's *oeuvre* into forgotten operas and remembered oratorios. What follows is an attempt to draw the former somewhat into the favoring light that the latter have never lacked, as well as to examine why the Handelian aesthetic combined so naturally with Ariosto's romance to produce three operas exemplary of eighteenth-century operatic tastes.

Handel, the Passions, and Eighteenth-Century Aesthetics

At Handel's death "An Attempt towards an Epitaph" appeared in the *Universal Chronicle* of 21 April 1759:

Beneath this Place
Are reposited the Remains of
GEORGE FREDERICK HANDEL.
The most excellent Musician
Any Age ever produced:
Whose Compositions were a
Sentimental Language
Rather than mere Sounds;
And surpassed the Power of Words
In expressing the various Passions
Of the Human Heart.

The anonymous writer of this epitaph (which was not used) pierced to the essence of Handel's vocal writing—the various passions of the human heart. Handel's operas, it soon becomes obvious, amount to a series of passionate or affective vignettes, while the plot itself moves largely during the interstitial recitatives. This followed the Neapolitan operatic tradition of which Handel is something of a culmination. One might assume that this piecemeal way of portraying human actions was due to the formulaic nature of Baroque music, with its "terraced" structure, rhythmic rigidity, and limited modes of expression. There is, however, much more behind the "sentimental language" of passions as we find it in Handel than musical history alone can reveal. Handel was a man of his age not only as a composer, but also as a thinker, psychologist, and musical dramatist. To understand his operas and judge them fairly, we must place Handel's passion-based aesthetic, not against our more supple and complicated modern psychology, but against the philosophy of human motivation prevalent in Handel's own time. In his operas lie many crucial philosophical and aesthetic assumptions of the period.

To our modern age, so well versed in Freud and Jung and aware of the labyrinthine tangle of psychic impulses which issue in human action, the passions as they are represented in Handelian opera must seem terribly generalized and few in number. Even in his own time Handel's talent could be roughly summarized under three headings—"Airs expressive of the Rage of Tyrants, the Passions of Heroes, and the Distresses of Lovers" (James Ralph, "The Touch-Stone" 1728). This, of course, grossly underestimates Handel's powers of discrimination, for within these categories exist a variety and power of nuance that only a familiarity with the operas can possibly reveal. Still, insofar as the typical Handel aria is an idealization of one of the passions of the human heart, it manifests the eighteenth century's bias in favor of the generalizing intellect. "Great thoughts," wrote Samuel Johnson, "are always general." Beattie applied this idea in his *Essays on Poetry and Music:* "The ideas of Poetry are rather general than singular; rather collected from the examination of a species or a class of things, than copied from an individual."[4] Handel's age avoided the eccentric, idiosyncratic, and curious, and so in large part did Handel's librettists in their choice of emotions for musical setting. Handel's strength lay in the main line of human experience—filial devotion, jealousy, melancholy enervation, dalliance, connubial bliss, and courage, for example.

A second general point that must be made about Handel's passions is that they are *human* passions. J. S. Bach did not heed (nor would have conceived it desirable to heed) Pope's famous admonition,

> Know then thyself, presume not God to scan;
> The proper study of mankind is man.

But Handel most certainly did. No matter how high-born the Handelian character or how exotic his surroundings, he or she always expresses human emotions. The special gift of Handel's era was the expression in a generalized way of the various common emotional events of human life. It is no wonder that his music struck such a responsive chord, for this was precisely the combination of generalized yet sympathetic art that neo-Classical connoisseurs desired. James Harris might have been thinking of Handel when he specified "Men and Human Actions" as the proper subject of art—and its proper intention as being "to lay open the internal Constitution of Man, and give us an Insight into Characters, Manners, Passions, and Sentiments." The sympathetic urge was strong among these men, as Beattie's remark upon poetry might suggest: "Mere descriptions, however beautiful, and moral reflections, however just, become tiresome, where our passions are not occasionally awakened by some event that concerns our fellow-men" (p. 34).

Handel's essentially cheerful and optimistic age—it has been called the Age of Exuberance—turned eagerly away from the dreary, chaotic, and rather chilling world view of Locke to embrace the more enthusiastic, convivial ideas of a man like Shaftesbury. Shaftesbury's ideas were suited to the temperament of Handel's time: they possessed vigor, an overmastering right-mindedness, and an earthy solidity. And the Shaftesbury philosophy was heartily social: "The highest Principle, which is the Love of God, is best attained not by dark Speculations and Monkish Philosophy, but by moral Practice, and Love of Mankind, and a Study of their Interests."[5] Johnson's famous reaction to *Paradise Lost* evinces the same bias in favor of art that attempts to mediate between man and mankind on the common subjects of human existence, and against art preoccupied with abstruse philosophy. Though Johnson asserted that "before the greatness displayed in Milton's poem all other greatness shrinks away," yet he was ill at ease in its presence:

> The want of human interest is always felt. *Paradise Lost* is one of the books which the reader admires and lays down, and forgets to take up again . . . Its perusal is a duty rather than a pleasure. We read Milton for instruction, retire harassed and overburdened, and look elsewhere for recreation; we desert our master, and seek for companions.

I often leave Bach, who like Milton was not intent upon recreation, and go to Handel for the same reasons. I leave the theological master of the *Passions* and the *B-Minor Mass* and seek human companions in Handel. The inspired moments in his operas and allegedly sacred oratorios are nearly always focused upon that "human interest" Johnson found lacking in Milton. Handel's sympathy with the character in his or her moment of emotional need often blossoms into extraordinarily poignant music. This was due to that "friendship with mankind" (to use a phrase from Shaftesbury) which Handel possessed and which was so prized by his admirers.

The eighteenth century's interest in human passions, their nature and sources, was a product not only of a sympathetic "friendship with mankind" but also of a general relaxation of inhibitions against emotional catharsis. These men were not afraid of emotional excess, and this is perhaps why they tended to think Stoic repression a grievous perversion. Robert South could thus defend the expression of human emotions from his pulpit:

> The soul during its abode in the body does all things by the mediation of passions and inferior affections. And here the opinion of the Stoics was famous and singular, who looked upon all these as sinful defects or irregularities, as so many deviations from right reason, making *passion* to be only another word for *perturbation* . . . To us, let this be sufficient, that our Saviour, Christ, who took upon him all our natural infirmities, but none of our sinful, has been seen to *weep,* to *be sorrowful,* to *pity,* and to *be angry.*[6]

To the eighteenth century, expression (and delight) in strong passions was part of the human condition—and it became in due course an important part of artistic expression.

John Dryden observed in his preface to *Troilus and Cressida* (1679) that "To describe them [passions] naturally, and to move them artfully, is one of the greatest commendations that can be given to a poet." He was expressing a rationalistic theory of passions which was to become dominant in the next century. This theory was based upon the Cartesian assumption that passions or emotions are definite in character, concrete in form, and separable in the mind. However crude this concept of passions as somehow palpable entities, it did lead to some important insights into what is now called human psychology. Shaftesbury, for instance, was one of the first to assert human affections or passions rather than reason to be the "springs of action." Given a certain objective life of their own, passions could then be categorized. Shaftesbury sifted them into three species: (1) the "natural" or "social" affections which are directed toward the general welfare; (2) the "self" or "private" affections which are directed toward an individual's own good; and (3) the "unnatural" affections which are directed toward neither. Like most simplifications, this concretizing of emotions made initial analysis easier but also was carried to absurd extremes. Nevertheless, such categorizing eventually influenced musical theory. Charles Avison in his *Essay on Musical Expression* (1752), for instance, postulated three main compositional styles and their respective subheadings: the Grand (the Sublime, Joyous, Learned), the Beautiful (the Cheerful, Serene, Pastoral), and the Pathetic (the Devout, Plaintive, Sorrowful). Many Handel arias fit comfortably into one of these categories.

The implications of such a theory of the passions for the arts were overwhelming. "Passions are Nature's never-failing Rhetorick," we learn in *The English Theophrastus* (1702), "and the only Orators that can master our Affections." The "rhetoric" of much of the art of this time is concerned with "raising" appropriate emotions in the spectator or listener.[7] This was true in music, particularly in Germany where the theory of the passions was systematized into the *Affektenlehre* (doctrine of the passions). The *Affektenlehre* prescribed how sentiments could be portrayed in music, and thus the idea that dramatic music must deal in various specific human emotions and evoke a pathetic response became a central element of late Baroque opera.

Opera suggested itself as the most challenging vehicle for the display of a composer's talent. Johann Mattheson, Germany's most prodigious writer on music in the eighteenth century and an acquaintance of Handel's, praised opera quite baldly as offering means for displaying skill in the management of passions:

> One can find [in operas] so to speak a conflux of all of music's beauties. For in them a composer has excellent opportunity to give free reign to his powers of invention. In them he can imitate very naturally, with grace, and with thousands of variations, Love, Jealousy, Hatred, Gentleness, Impatience, Desire, Lethargy, Fear, Revenge, Valor, Timidity, Magnanimity, Terror, Dignity, Baseness,

Pomp, Poverty, Pride, Meekness, Happiness, Laughter, Crying, Pleasure, Pain, Bliss, Despair, Storm, Calm—yes, even Heaven, Earth, Sea, Hell and all of the human activities associated with these passions (especially if our eyes are willing to give just a little aid to our ears).[8]

English musical theorists were of the same party. Beattie observed: "Music, therefore, is pleasing, not because it is imitative, but because certain melodies and harmonies have *an aptitude* to raise certain passions, affections, and sentiments in the soul." Charles Avison summarized the power of music to "raise a Variety of Passions in the human Breast":

> By the Musician's Art, we are often carried into the Fury of a Battle, or a Tempest, we are by turns elated with Joy, or sunk in pleasing Sorrow, roused to Courage, or quelled by grateful Terrors, melted into Pity, Tenderness, and Love, or transported to the Regions of Bliss, in an Extacy of divine Praise. [p. 4]

Handel's ability to do all these things is epitomized in his 1736 setting of Dryden's heroic ode, "Alexander's Feast, or The Power of Music" (1697). This noble narrative poem, dramatic enough to be staged as an opera in its Handelian form, symbolizes the foundation of opera of the time upon the theory of discrete passions. The plot tells of a performance by the musician Timotheus at the nuptial festivities for Alexander and Thais. Timotheus' power to evoke different moods is the theme of the work. In its original poetic form it was seen as a vehicle for the artful moving of passions—as Pope's handy synopsis in *An Essay on Criticism* makes clear:

> Hear how Timotheus' vary'd Lays surprize,
> And bid Alternate Passions fall and rise!
> While, at each Change, the Son [Alexander] of Lybian Jove
> Now burns with Glory, and then melts with Love;
> Now his fierce Eyes with sparkling Fury glow;
> Now Sighs steal out, and Tears begin to flow:
> Persians and Greeks like Turns of Nature found,
> And the World's Victor stood subdu'd by Sound!
> The Pow'r of Musick all our Hearts allow;
> And what Timotheus was, is Dryden now. [374-82]

That Handel should have eventually set the ode seems in retrospect inevitable. Much of the praise Handel received in his career marked him as the obvious eighteenth-century Timotheus. In "The Touch-Stone" (1728) James Ralph approvingly noted that "*H*[ande]*l* would warm us in Frost or Snow, by rousing every Passion with Notes proper to the Subject." And one of Handel's many eulogists asked rhetorically,

> Who cou'd like *Handel* with such art controul
> The various passions of the warring soul?
> With sounds each intellectual storm assuage,
> Fire us with holy rapture, or with rage?

Handel was the last great professor of this affective tradition in opera.

Not surprisingly, the librettist for *Alexander's Feast,* Newburgh Hamilton, felt Handel was the only composer capable of doing justice to Dryden's poetry. And the expectations of so perfect a combination as Dryden's "energy of words, vivacity of description, and apposite variety of numbers" (Beattie) with Handel's "wonderful talents in the sublime and pathetic" (Avison) were not disappointed. This is articulated in the occasional poem "To Mr. HANDEL, On his setting to Musick of Mr. Dryden's 'Feast of Alexander' " written by Hamilton:

> That Artist's [Timotheus'] Hand, (whose Skill alone cou'd move
> To Glory, Grief, or Joy, the Son of *Jove;*)
> Not greater Raptures to the *Grecian* gave,
> Than *British* Theatres from you receive;
> That Ignorance and Envy vanquish'd see,
> Heav'n made you rule the World by *Harmony.*

Handel is shadowed forth in his musical Timotheus, just as there is much of Shakespeare the playwright in his Prospero. It is worth noting, too, that *Alexander's Feast* was written at the final stage of Handel's operatic period: the art displayed in this work he learned while writing for the operatic stage. The power of music celebrated in *Alexander's Feast* is essentially the power of Handelian opera seria—of which the three *Furioso* operas are the last great examples.

R. A. Streatfeild, an important Handel defender of this century, wrote of the Dryden setting:

> *Alexander's Feast* is a wonderful series of pictures, each one dashed off in broad splashes of colour by the hand of a master. When Handel is in this vein his simple directness of method is overpowering. He seems to hurl his effects straight in your face. It was of such music as this that Mozart was thinking when he said, "When he chooses, he strikes like a thunderbolt."[9]

Streatfeild's gallery metaphor helps us to focus on the structural implications of the theory of passions. The creative artist, quarrying among the full range of emotions, must finally arrange them in some kind of order—make each emotional crux picturesque. The result was operas comprised of passionate set-pieces arranged in a linear fashion—musical picture galleries. Baroque librettists were primarily interested in giving life to the crucial emotive moments in the action of their story. They fixed upon the most affecting "frames" in the moving plot, froze them momentarily in place, and composers then filled them with a self-contained musical life and color. These composers were looking for the painterly moment in which to display appropriate musical and thespian gestures. Naturally the methods of the painter and composer were frequently analogized in this regard.

"Of necessity," wrote James Harris, "every Picture is a *Punctum Temporis* or Instant." Great Baroque paintings are frequently depictions of massive, complex motion frozen at just the most acute and compelling point in time. Nothing in the painting of the Baroque so closely resembles a Handel opera as Rubens's pomp-and-circumstance series depicting the life of Marie de Medici. These stupendous paintings capture the salient moments in the life of the Queen, highlighting the continuous action of her reign much as Handel arias highlight an operatic story line. Many of Rubens's paintings in this series contain musical instruments, especially "The Debarkation at Marseilles" and "The Felicity of the Regency." One can almost hear Handelian strains as one studies them. The effect of Rubens and Handel, continuing the painterly analogy, is to give a rich perspective and resonance to climactic dramatic situations.

In his *Essay on the Theory of Painting* (1715) Jonathan Richardson observed that "Every Historical Picture is a Representation of one single point of Time; This then must be chosen; and That in the Story which is most Advantageous must be It." Throughout the arts, this search for the most advantageous moment was crucial. Lord Clarendon was praised as a prose-portraitist ("never was there a better Painter in that kind") for his ability to catch his subjects in characteristic moments. It was high commendation for Milton that Richardson saw his *Paradise Lost* in painterly terms:

> In reading the *Iliad* or *Aeneid* we Treasure up a Collection of Fine Imaginative Pictures as when we read *Paradise Lost;* Only that from Thence we have (to speak like a Connoisseur) More Rafaelles, Correggios, Guidos, & C. Milton's Pictures are more Sublimely Great, Divine and Lovely than Homer's, or Virgil's, or those of Any Other Poet. [p. clx]

It took but a short step for William Hayes in his *Remarks on Mr. Avison's Essay on Musical Expression* (1753) to extend such praise of Milton to Handel:

> For there is not a Scene which Milton describes, were Claude Lorrain or Poussin to paint, could possibly appear in more lively Colours, or give a truer Idea of it, than our Great Musician has by his *pictoresque* Arrangement of musical Sounds; with this Advantage, that his Pictures *speak.* [p. 67]

It may help us to appreciate the disjunctive structure of Handelian opera to remember that it was born of an aesthetic whose kernel was a belief in the reality of individual passions and the artistic efficacy of framing them and rendering them picturesque. The best of Handel's arias are indeed speaking pictures.[10]

This painterly analogy requires a caveat in defense of Handel. It would play too easily into the hands of anti-Handelians to say that his finest arias represent "stop" motion, or that his operas betray that staid inertness of a picture gallery. Handel's pictures are emphatically speaking *and* moving ones. When the plot becomes stationary in a Handel opera, the characters begin to move or be moved in their own emotional spheres. It is excessively literal-minded to consider Handel's arias—where everything but the plot moves—merely as static episodes.

Before leaving the subject of the picturesque, I want to mention the eighteenth-century "English" garden. The position of the English garden in the history of landscaping bears some interesting parallels to the place Handel occupies along the continuum between the older Italian Baroque opera and the Classical opera of Mozart. Eighteenth-century theorists of landscaping turned their backs on the magnificence of Italian and French formal gardens. They decried the elaborate, artificial, and studiously symmetrical terraces so popular at the height of the architectural Baroque. "Is there anything more shocking," asked Batty Langley in *New Principles of Gardening* (1728), "than a stiff regular garden?" Men like Langley despised that great Baroque feature, the sculptural fountain; they wished instead to banish the "professed art" of man from their vistas. In so doing they tried to "improve" and "heighten" the natural qualities of the terrain rather than bulldoze it into grandiose visual set-pieces created with line and compass. "The living landscape was chastened or polished, not transformed," said Walpole.[11]

The new emphasis in landscaping was upon the picturesque. Walpole praised the invention of the ha-ha (a sunken, concealed fence) for making the walk through a fine garden like the experience of "a succession of pictures." He concluded of England's innovations in natural landscaping: "Enough has been done to establish such a school of landscape as cannot be found on the rest of the globe. If we have the seeds of a Claude [Lorrain] or a Gaspar [DuGhet] amongst us let him come forth." Walpole praised a particular avenue at Stanstead by saying that it "recalls such exact pictures of Claude Lorrain that it is difficult to conceive that he did not paint them from this very spot." For Handel's century all gardening, as Pope allegedly observed, was landscape painting.

What were the artistic methods behind this change in the concept of gardening? Pope, who doted upon his garden at Twickenham, gives us the specifics: "All the rules of gardening are reducible to three heads: the contrasts, the management of surprises, and the concealment of bounds." Mozart, as we shall see, was able to apply exactly these techniques to the large-scale musical forms and conventions of the Baroque in order to create a more flexible expressive style. The relaxation of physical boundaries in landscaping—and of the bonds of traditional forms in music—led finally to a new freedom of expression. Walpole's analysis of the effect of the ha-ha on gardening is worth quoting in full, for it symbolizes the kind of innovative daring that Handel displays in his three *Furioso* operas:

> The contiguous ground of the park without the sunk fence was to be harmonised with the lawn within; and the garden in its turn was to be set free from its prim regularity, that it might affort with the wilder country without. The sunk fence ascertained [i.e. delimited] the specific garden; but that it might not draw too obvious a line of distinction between the neat and the rude, the contiguous outlying parts came to be included in a kind of general design: and when nature was taken into the plan, under improvements, every step that was made, pointed out new beauties and inspired new ideas.

The "sunk fence" brought the art of man and the art of nature closer together, made the distinguishing line more subtle. Artists, as Walpole observed, "leaped the fence, and saw that all nature was a garden." In opera, Handel was having the same effect. In his operas we see the struggle between traditional formulas and the urgency of natural, truly dramatic expression—in other words, the struggle between artificial "neatness" and incisive, direct "rudeness." We see the relinquishment of the da capo aria where it would be painfully redundant, the development of differing emotions in duets and trios, a new simplicity of utterance (which looked forward to the artistic Rococo), and we see more refinement of the flexible arioso and even more flexible accompanied recitative. We frequently see Handel abandon what Walpole called the "prim regularity" of tradition.

Walpole thought William Kent the primary inventor of the "new style" of landscaping and praised him thus: he "disdained to make every division tally with its opposite; and though he still adhered much to straight walks with high clipped hedges, they were only his great lines; the rest he diversified by wilderness, and with loose groves of oak." Kent's breakthroughs made possible the masterpieces of his great successor Capability Brown. Handel, for opera, stands in a similar position. He was among those who made use of new methods that later composers like Mozart and Gluck were to perfect—the brilliant *scenas*, the spectacular accompanied recitatives, the preparation for and creation of musical-dramatic surprises, and the increasing concealment of musical formulas within theatrical contexts. The progress in landscape was from formal to pictorial effects; the progress in music was from ritual and formal to dramatic effects. Kent and Handel were, in their respective arts, both partially responsible for this progress. Handel stands out as one of the great figures mediating between the Baroque age of monumentality and pomp and the Classical age of human dimension and drama.

Ariosto, Handel, and Baroque Opera

One of Don Quixote's inspirations in Cervantes's masterpiece is Ariosto's *Orlando Furioso,* and if it is madness to be swept by the power of the imagination into the magical, exhilarating world of romance, then the knight of la Mancha was certainly lunatic. We are constantly made to feel that Quixote's madness is a glorious one. There is scarcely a sadder moment in literature than the one when he renounces the books of knight-errantry and—having thus extinguished the vital flame of imagination—dies.

The so-called Age of Reason—profoundly empiricist by nature—was not so susceptible to Quixote's madness and was consequently not attracted to the pleasures of the imagination the great Renaissance romances evoked. Indeed, the dominant attitude in the eighteenth century toward romance is well represented by Cervantes's eminently moralistic, down-to-earth Canon:

> Who could really believe in . . . all those palfreys, all those wandering damsels, all those serpents, all those dragons, all those giants, all those battles, all those desperate encounters, all that fine raiment, all those love-lorn princesses, all those squires who become counts, all those facetious dwarfs, all those love letters, all that wooing, all those courageous ladies and, in fact, all those monstrous absurdities contained in books of chivalry? For myself, I can say that they give me a certain pleasure when I read them—so long as I do not deliberately reflect that they are all triviality and lies. But when I consider what they are I throw the very best of them against the wall. [Pt. I, Ch. 49]

Samuel Johnson sounds like the Canon when he addresses himself to the Italian epic poets: "Ariosto's [de]pravity is generally known;

and, though [Tasso's] *Deliverance of Jerusalem* may be considered as a sacred subject, the poet has been very sparing of moral instruction." Addison, along with his French neo-Classical counterpart Boileau, felt that "one verse of Virgil is worth all the clinquant or tinsel of Tasso"; he doubtless cared even less for the more earthy and carefree Ariosto. Addison's and Johnson's age expressed itself best in prose (and, at that, in the brief essay form) and naturally looked with a chilly glare upon the rambling, irregular, fanciful romance genre. What Dryden called "the fairy way of writing" was not to its taste.[12]

What displeased men of reason, however, perfectly suited the operatic stage. Since the very inception of the operatic art-form in the elaborate courtly entertainments of the sixteenth and seventeenth centuries, romances had been quarried for plots. These romances also gave rich inspiration for the fabulous scenic effects made possible by important Baroque advances in stage technology, especially in lighting, movable scenery, articulation of perspective, and spectacular special effects. *Orlando Furioso,* with its forty thousand lines of intertwining and yet easily separable plot lines and wealth of exotic events, proved to be one of the most common sources for the court masque—the most important of all proto-operatic courtly entertainments. The masque depended for its attraction upon lavish costumes, breathtaking special effects (such as sudden transformations and cloud cars), and elaborate ballets. When Dryden defined "opera" in 1685 as "a poetical tale, or fiction, represented by vocal and instrumental music, adorned with scenes, machines, and dancing," he was thinking primarily of the court masque. When he further observed that the subject of a typical opera, "being extended beyond the limits of human nature, admits of that sort of marvelous and surprising conduct which is rejected in other plays," he draws our attention to the primary reason for the appeal of *Orlando Furioso,* namely, its fictional world of wonder and marvels. Francesco Algarotti (*Essay on Opera*) observed as late as 1754 that "well-suited [operatic] subjects could be drawn from Ariosto and Tasso, especially since here, in addition to the familiar stories and strong passions, the charms of magic are apparent."

Those who defended the romances in the eighteenth century argued strongly in favor of the pleasures of illusion and the attractiveness of an escape from the real world. One of the most eloquent apologies for romance literature and Ariosto's "golden dreams" is Richard Hurd's *Letters on Chivalry and Romance* (1762). He observed that romances address themselves to "the Imagination, a young and credulous faculty, which loves to admire and to be deceived" (p. 95). Such was the operatic audience for which Handel wrote: it loved to admire and be deceived by clever stage effects of the sort that occur in the *Furioso* operas. The worlds of Ariosto and of opera seria were dazzlingly illusionistic, so it is no wonder that, for instance, the Ginevra-Ariodante episode was set to music no fewer than twelve times between 1708 and 1753. Nor is it surprising that Hurd's defense of Ariosto can serve as a defense not only of Handelian opera, but of opera as an art-form:

> Critics may talk what they will of Truth and Nature, and abuse the Italian poets, as they will, for transgressing both in their incredible fictions. But believe it, my friend, these fictions with which they have studied to delude the world, are of that kind of creditable deceits, of which a wise antient pronounces with assurance, "That they, who deceive, are honester than they who do not deceive; and they, who are deceived, wiser than they who are not deceived." [p. 103]

Handel's operas were amusements for a monied, leisured audience—escapist at heart. *Orlando Furioso* was an obvious choice, then, for librettists intent upon creating worlds into which such an audience could be enticed. That is how John Hughes, an early editor of Spenser's *Faerie Queene,* explains the attraction of romances: "For as Mankind is departed from the Simplicity, as well as the Innocence, of a State of Nature, and is immers'd in Cares and Pursuits of a very different kind; it is a wonderful Amusement to the Imagination to be sometimes transported, as it were, out of modern Life, and to wander in these pleasant Scenes." Ariosto's poem must still hold this escapist attraction. In 1970 an Italian company visited New York with a theatrical adaptation of the epic. Of this the critic John Lahr wrote: "Theater must usher us into the unknown, offering us an extraordinary and unique world as an alternative to our daily lives. *Orlando Furioso* does this."[13]

As the descriptions of the scenes and transformations in *Ariodante, Alcina,* and *Orlando* suggest, the possibilities in Ariosto's poem for creating special effects are enormous. That Handel wrote three operas based upon it (and three other "magical" romance operas: *Rinaldo, Teseo,* and *Amadigi*) is indication enough of the importance of spectacle in opera of the time. This recommended Ariosto to countless composers of Handel's time and later; the central Orlando story alone was treated, for example, by Peri (1619), Lully (1685), Steffani (1691), Haydn (1782), and Thomas (1843), just to mention better-known composers.

Even more interesting are the qualities of *Orlando Furioso* that bear particularly upon Handel's operatic artistry. The *Furioso* operas are all dramatically cogent settings of important Ariostan episodes.[14] And—as we shall frequently find in the course of this study—this is largely due to special affinities of personality and artistic sensibility shared by author and composer. Some of these we can look at briefly here.

The most important shared quality is simply their human dimensions. For all the formulaic poetic and musical machinery and spectacular events, the characters inhabiting the poem and the operas are real people feeling themselves in situations not fetched far from everyday experience. Speaking of *Orlando Furioso,* C. S. Lewis wrote, "What lies immediately below the surface of the Italian epic is simply the actual—daily life of travel, war, or gallantry."[15] And C. P. Brand, in one of the few English studies of Ariosto, carefully notes how the poet constantly brings his characters down to human proportions—how, amid all the panoply, we are suddenly startled to find ourselves reading about average men and women in common amorous imbroglios. These frequent flashes of common humanity in *Orlando Furioso* were one major reason for its appeal to Baroque librettists. No matter how exotic the decor and plot, they had to set the emotions of the human heart. Ariosto supplied these emotions.

Orlando Furioso's accessibility for opera becomes especially clear if one compares it with that vast allegorical epic it helped to spawn, Spenser's *Faerie Queene.* "In Ariosto, we walk upon the ground, in a company gay, fantastic and adventurous enough. In Spenser, we wander in another world, among ideal beings."[16] It is no wonder that

Spenser's disembodied allegorical characters have never thrived on the operatic stage, where Ariosto's characters feel so much at home.

Handel was primarily a feeling rather than a thinking artist, and Ariosto provided him with numerous moments of inspiring human drama. One might point, for instance, to the King's expression of paternal love in *Ariodante* (*Al sen ti stringo e parto,* S6), the racking fury and depression of Orlando's mad scene (*Ah! Stigie larve,* S4), or the pins-and-needles agony of the spurned queen in *Alcina* (*Ah! mio cor!,* S4).* The most brilliant moments in Handel's operas are invariably those where interesting characters enter into interesting situations, and there are many such in *Orlando Furioso.*

Edward FitzGerald's famous assessment of Handel's aesthetic brings us to another characteristic shared with Ariosto:

> [Handel] was a good old Pagan at heart, and (till he had to yield to the fashionable Piety of England) stuck to Opera, and Cantatas, such as *Acis and Galatea,* Milton's *Penseroso, Alexander's Feast,* etc., where he could revel and plunge and frolic without being tied down to Orthodoxy. And these are (to my mind) his really great works.[17]

Ariosto, too, was a good old pagan at heart. It was only posthumously that moralizing allegorists like his first English translator John Harington subjected *Orlando Furioso* to Christian and Humanist dogma. If there is any "moral" in the poem, it is to be found not in the life hereafter, but in the silly, devious lives mortals—especially mortals tangled in love affairs—lead on earth. It ultimately concludes that our life is, as Ariosto called the whole epic, a "dance of folly." His Montaignesque assessment of man's so-called rational intentions is precisely the same we should derive from Mozart's *Così fan tutte:*

> O feeble and unstable minds of men!
> How quickly our intentions fluctuate!
> All thoughts we lightly change, but mostly when
> These from lover's quarrels take their date.
>
> [Canto XXIX.1]

It is a mark of Handel's closeness to some of the main philosophical currents of his time that he was comfortable with the human dimen-

* Since only one recording is available for each opera, I will indicate the side where each aria appears: S4 = side four.

sions of *Orlando Furioso.* Handel was not at ease with "men of cold dispositions and philosophical fancies" (Hurd's phrase) such as those who attacked romances. We can see from his operas and the thinly disguised operas which travel under the alias of oratorio that he preferred real emotions to moralizing cant.

In this, Shaftesbury can speak for Handel. (If there is an unmistakable Handelian ring in any of the philosophy of the time, it is in Shaftesbury's "Apostrophe to Nature" of 1711.) For Shaftesbury, the task of art was to give a sympathetic, imaginative representation of human experience—to judge characters from life, not solely by moral convention. He praised writings that "pointed out real *Characters* and *Manners* . . . exhibited 'em *alive,* and set the Countenances and Complexions of Men plainly in view. And by this means they taught us not only to know *Others;* but, what was principal and of highest virtue in 'em, they taught us to know *Our-selves.*" Shaftesbury sees the best poet as one who describes "no qualities or Virtues; censures no Mannners; makes no Encomium, nor gives Characters himself; but brings his actors still in view. 'Tis they who shew themselves." These are just the virtues displayed in Handel's operatic characters—and, indeed, in the characters of almost all great operatic composers.

Handel was, like Shaftesbury, interested in arousing response, not in giving moral instruction. In the oratorios this bias is often obvious—even in such a piece as *Theodora* where the text was very much against him. A passage from that work—

> Ought we not to leave
> The free-born mind of man still ever free?
> Since vain is the attempt to force belief.

—is probably not far from Handel's (and Shaftesbury's) own philosophical latitudinarianism. It was enough for Ariosto and Handel to set their characters "plainly in view." They did not feel obliged to follow them with the obsessive moralism of a Spenser, Milton, Johnson, or an Addison. Animated characters inspired these two men, and if it is pagan to be attracted to such characters who act foolishly, selfishly, or irrationally, then these two men were good old pagans indeed.

It follows as a corollary that neither Ariosto nor Handel was an intellectual artist. Ariosto seems to have had no strong beliefs. Benedetto Croce called him "the opposite of a philosopher." Though many scholars have attempted to find an encompassing intellectual pattern in *Orlando Furioso,* none has succeeded. John Hughes realized that Ariosto did not compose his work with Aristotelian niceties in mind:

> In the *Orlando Furioso,* we every where meet with an exuberant Invention, join'd with great Liveliness and Facility of Description, yet debas'd by frequent Mixtures of the comick Genius, as well as many shocking Indecorums. Besides, in the Huddle and Distraction of the Adventures, we are for the most part only amus'd with extravagant Stories, without being instructed in any Moral.

Orlando Furioso is a monument to Ariosto's vitality, not his powers of architecture. Its great moments are tiny vignettes that come briefly but vividly to life. Sometimes they last a stanza or two; sometimes they flourish and vanish in a few lines. As for the long view or overriding "themes," there are scarcely any. The art of Ariosto is ultimately a simple, humane, and sympathetic art.

Handel, likewise, was not a deep thinker, never lost himself in philosophical introspection. He left the realm of mystical religious experience to Bach. Indeed, Eduard Hanslick's praise of Bach shows just how utterly that composer differed from Handel: "That Bach was able, without undue effort, to exclude all worldly and fleshly elements and still absorb the listener in an area of human sensation so rigorously circumscribed is the supreme testimony of the strength of his genius." Handel's music, on the other hand, is almost entirely made up of those "worldly and fleshly elements" so rarely met in Bach. One might call Bach's emotions theological; Handel's are more quotidian. But then, Bach composed for the next world; Handel composed for this one.

That Handel was no theoretician is clear from his few extant letters. In 1719 the German musical factotum Mattheson sent his book on the Greek modes to Handel for comment. His reply reveals an ingenuous pragmatism that is the mark of history's operatic geniuses:

> I do not see why one should not choose the route that leads *most* easily and in the shortest time to the desired end. As to the Greek Modes, I find, Sir, that you have said all that there is to say. Knowledge of them is no doubt necessary to those who would practise and execute ancient music that has been composed according to these modes; but since we have freed ourselves from the narrow bounds of ancient music, I do not see of what use the Greek Modes can be for modern music.

The masterpieces of Spenser, Milton, and Bach—all profoundly cerebral men—have given rise to large, toilsome scholarly followings. This is because their sublime beauties lie to a great degree below the surface and require careful excavation. What can be said of Milton's epic applies as well to much of Bach and certainly to *The Faerie Queene*:

> A Reader . . . must be Always upon Duty; he is Surrounded with Sense, it rises in every Line, every Word is to the Purpose; There are no Lazy Intervals, All has been Consider'd, and Demands, and Merits Observation. Even in the Best Writers you Somtimes find Words and Sentences which hang on so Loosely you may Blow 'em off; Milton's are all Substance and Weight.[18]

Ariosto's epic and Handel's *Furioso* operas make no such burdensome demands. They have lazy intervals; all is not the fruit of meticulous calculation. They are more congenial to the relaxed and pleasure-seeking mind. They do not induce meditation or introspection, but rather introduce us to a world of vivid experiences. There is no overbearing intellectual system—but much life—in Ariosto and Handel.

Certain specific aspects of *Orlando Furioso* are relevant to the *Furioso* operas. The first is the subject of the poem, which Ariosto announces in his famous opening lines:

> Of Loves and Ladies, Knights and Arms, I sing,
> Of Courtesies, and many a Daring Feat.

The poet's promise is most auspicious for a composer whose acknowledged gift was for "Airs expressive of the Rage of Tyrants, the Passions of Heroes, and the Distresses of Lovers." However, it is possible to narrow further the focus of the poem (or at least the three episodes Handel used) to the subject of love. The brief explanation of the plot of Handel's *Orlando* that appeared in the libretto for its premiere serves easily for all three operas:

> [The story] tends to demonstrate the imperious Manner in which Love insinuates its Impressions into the Hearts of Persons of all Ranks, and likewise how a wise Man should be ever ready with his best Endeavours to reconduct into the Right Way, those who have been misguided from it by the Illusion of their Passions.

In *Orlando Furioso* love is a forest

> where parforce
> Who enter its recesses go astray;
> And here and there pursue their devious course.
> [Canto XXIV.2]

The devious course of lovers is the direct cause of the complicated plots in all the *Furioso* operas. Take for example *Alcina,* whose plot may be summarized in this way: A (Morgana) loves B ("Ricciardo," who is really Bradamante in disguise), B loves C (Ruggiero), C loves D (Alcina), and E (Oronte) loves A; the plot is set in motion when E attempts to make C jealous of B by implicating B in an affair with D. This convoluted plotting was typical of epic romances and opera seria. Yet, these complex plots had a simple outcome: they gave Handel his opportunity to create a panorama of the various human passions evoked by love. With Ariosto as his basis, he could describe the "manifold and dread" penalties suffered by those characters bound in "the chains of love" (XXXI.1). Handel's gifts were apt for such a task. The Handelian aria is perfectly suited to the access of emotion, and nothing incites such an event better than love or its complications. Thus, in Act I of *Ariodante* alone we find successive arias expressing the rejection of love (*Orrida agli occhi miei*), the impotent longing for love (*Apri le luci e mira*), the fury of rejected love (*Coperta la frode*), a celebration (*Volate, amori*) and a proclamation (*Voli colla sua tromba*) of love, a feigned love (*Spero per voi*), the longing for love (*Del mio sol vezzosi rai*), and a love-plighting duet (*Se rinasce nel mio cor*).

Mario Praz observed in *The Flaming Heart* that the "time-hallowed Mediterranean sex-centered point of view" triumphs in *Orlando Furioso,* and one must agree that the cynosure of interest in the epic—and in the three operas—is sex and the love-games men and women play with each other. If one can look beyond the romance machinery of the poem and the structural formality of the operas, the observation of human beings in love reveals a high degree of psychological acumen. Alcina's "fatal island" is not merely an exotic sensual paradise. It is the sexual arena. Orlando is not an aimless lunatic but rather a study in uncontrollable jealousy that is not too distantly related to Othello's. The plot of *Ariodante,* too, has much in common with *Othello* as a study of great love subverted by a kind of motiveless, diabolical malignity (Polinesso = Iago).

Something must also be said here about the theory of passions and Ariosto's poem. Great operatic characters have in common a certain immensity of passion and self-will. And whatever greatness the characters in *Ariodante, Orlando,* and *Alcina* possess is due to Handel's ability to evoke such willful, overmastering states of being. Handel was given ample opportunity for this by Ariosto, for the poet was quite as intrigued with the emotional state of his characters as he was with the kaleidoscopic rush of events. C. S. Lewis feels that Ariosto's characters "are drawn from the outside and drawn by one who is more interested in the general nature of 'passions' (it is the Latin way) than by idiosyncrasies." So it was that Handel's aesthetic, based upon the eighteenth century's generalized human passions, applied with consummate ease to Ariosto. Ariosto was clearly delighted by the little *scenas* his figures create under love's duress, and *Orlando Furioso* is consequently rich in vignettes where the passions of love come to poetic life (see, for example, V.40-41; VII.17; VIII.73-74; XXIII.112-13). Such passages translated effortlessly into the stanzas necessary for a da capo aria.

Finally, we should pause to appreciate that quality which, if any single one does, marks *Orlando Furioso* and the *Furioso* operas: the command of pathos. Through their magical worlds walk characters who, if not realistic in the sense of extended development, nevertheless do experience highly realistic moments. Suddenly in the stylized poetic and musical setting we are startled by the genius of profoundly empathic artists. Ariosto's Alcina may be a formidable enchantress and Ruggiero a famous knight, but their mutual infatuation (VII.17-30) is described in terms of any consumingly blissful human coupling. No epic poet could thus observe his hero waiting for his beloved and be accused of lacking a realist's eye and human sympathy:

> At every movement heard on distant floor,
> Hoping 'twas her, Rogero raised his head:
> He thinks he hears; but it is heard no more,
> Then sighs at his mistake: ofttimes from bed
> He issued, and undid his chamber door,
> And peeped abroad, but still no better sped;
> And cursed a thousand times the hour that she
> So long retarded his felicity. [VII.24]

Equally affecting are Ariosto's descriptions of Orlando's painful discovery of Angelica's love for Medoro and his torturing madness of jealousy and envy (XXIII.101-21) and of Ariodante's agony upon seeing his supposed Ginevra in the arms of Polinesso (V.51ff). Today one reads *Orlando Furioso* largely, I believe, for such passages of acute psychological observation.

The overwhelming sense with Ariosto is of a moral latitudinarian (one could hardly imagine a less judgmental bent), a lover of action rather than contemplation, and an artist of great sympathetic range. And behind all this is a kind of force or *virtù*. One review of the recent theatrical version of Ariosto's poem helps to pinpoint this force:

> *Orlando Furioso* is essentially street theater; and this is a viable format—with its bravado and parody—for the operatic [!] exaggeration of its actors. Gestures must be broad in order to be seen; emotions must be grandiose in a play imitating heroic legend. Performing is outrageous; what is real is not the outer façade of action, but the inner emotion driving the body to such extremes . . . The performing in *Orlando* is explosive, not contained.[19]

Unwittingly, this reviewer describes precisely those qualities that made the romance so agreeable a source for opera composers. The "façade of action" (that is, the plot) is not as important as the moments of "inner emotion" that drive the characters—and the characters' voices—to extremes. In Handel's case, the vocal extreme was the full-fledged aria. The *Furioso* operas, too, amount to series of musical explosions into heightened emotion and gesture.

When he was inspired, Handel could invest these passionate explosions with powerful musical impact—an impact that was for George Bernard Shaw the essence of his greatness.[20] The finest moments in Handelian opera result from a combination of expressive force and command of pathos. Handel was, with the exception of Monteverdi, the first composer to reveal consistently this combination of artistic powers indispensable for great opera. And this is why one might say of Handel's operatic achievements (paraphrasing C. S. Lewis on the *Orlando Furioso*): when you are tired of Handel, you must be tired of the world.

Handel's Wig and the Furioso *Operas*

FitzGerald once wrote that "Handel never gets out of his wig—that is, out of his age."[21] This view, held even by some Handelians, is one of the myths that have led to an underestimation of his operas. If nothing else, this view has plausibility to recommend it. After all, he kept rather conventional company: in his own time Avison regarded Lully in France, Scarlatti in Italy, and Handel in Britain as the three composers who "enjoyed the highest local Reputation, having been the reigning Favourites among the People, in the several Countries where they resided." And, too, it was Handel's livelihood to satisfy the tastes of his audience; this sometimes led him to join his rivals in sacrificing his art "to the gross Judgment of an indelicate Audience" (Avison). These tastes were certainly not of the sort to inspire radical experimentation. Even the supreme man of reason, Voltaire, made modest demands of opera: "Such is the entire interest I have in an opera. A lovely spectacle well-varied, containing brilliant festivities, plenty of arias, little recitative, brief acts—that is what pleases me." To complacent tastes like this Handel and his librettists catered, and his operas in fact generally follow Voltaire's specifications (except the last!).

Many conventional aspects of Handel opera are disagreeable to modern sensibilities. They are as unblinkable as a powdered wig. Before considering the intriguing moments when Handel doffed that wig and struck out on innovative paths, we should confront the Handel of the portraits and engravings: fully wigged. Without trying to excuse the traditions of the Baroque completely, we can at least attempt to see them in the perspective of eighteenth-century tastes.[22]

The Italian castrato Nicolini arrived in London in 1708 and established one of the greatest vocal careers of the time. Colley Cibber intended the highest praise for him when he wrote in *An Apology for the Life of Colley Cibber* (1740): "There is scarce a beautiful Posture, in an old Statue, which he does not plant himself in, as the different Circumstances of the Story give occasion for it." Such was the kind of representation encouraged by da capo opera, which required the singer to "raise" himself to the three dimensions of a statue rather than those of a "real" character by modern naturalistic standards. That Handel's characters are statuesque idealizations is due to the period's belief that representations, such as those in opera seria, had to be artfully generalized or exaggerated. According to the standards by which Handel was judged, mere realism would simply not suffice. Richardson's *Essay on the Theory of Painting* (1725) forcefully expresses the aesthetic of the grand style as we experience it in Handel's operas: "A Painter must raise his Ideas beyond what he sees . . . He must as it were raise the whole Species, and give them all imaginable Beauty, and Grace, Dignity, and Perfection; Every several Character, whether it be Good, or Bad, Amiable, or Detestable, must be Stronger, and more Perfect." This is the aesthetic behind Handel's operatic characters.

Nature, according to Richardson, must be the source of inspiration, but this must be artistically amplified: "Provided Natural Truth is at the bottom, Nature must be Heighten'd, and Improv'd, and the Imagination fill'd with Finer Images than the Eye Commonly sees, or in some cases Ever can, whereby the Passions are more Strongly touch'd" (*A Discourse,* 1719). Richardson's aesthetic applies almost without qualification to Handel's operas: our passions are most strongly engaged in those arias where the kernel of psychological truth is magnified and raised to the sublime by music. As especially fine examples of this technique, consider Orlando's *Già lo stringo* (S5), Alcina's *Mi restano le lagrime* (S6), and Ariodante's *Scherza infida* (S4). "Greatness is Essential," concluded Richardson, "and

Truth is not." If this central dictum of the grand style—which crushes our puling modern desire for "real" characters—holds for any opera, it holds certainly for Handelian opera.

The da capo aria is today probably the single most indigestible ingredient of Baroque opera. Unfortunately, it is the core of Handel's operas: in the *Furioso* operas there are altogether seventy arias; only three lack a da capo. The da capo aria (consisting of an A section, a B section in a different key and sometimes a new tempo, and then a repetition of A, da capo—"from the beginning") had its critics in Handel's day. Avison, as we have seen, complained of the "egregious Absurdity of repeating and finishing many Songs with the first Part." Given the aesthetic of opera seria, based upon virtuosic execution, the da capo aria does not deserve utter condemnation. Pier Francesco Tosi gives us the pro and con:

> If whoever introduced the Custom of repeating the first Part of the *Air* (which is called *Da Capo*) did it out of a Motive to show the Capacity of the Singer, in varying the Repetition, the Invention cannot be blam'd by Lovers of Musick; though in respect of the Words it is sometimes an Impropriety.[23]

The period of pre-eminence for the da capo aria was the first period in the bel canto age, and the essence of the da capo aria lay in extemporaneous embellishment of the repeated section. Da capo arias would be much less tedious if singers were today encouraged to make the most of the repetition for purposes of variation. In this respect, the recording of *Alcina* is the most satisfying; the *Orlando* and *Ariodante* recordings are disappointingly timid.[24]

The obvious alternative, admittedly a "modernization" of Handel, is excision of B sections and the repetition in some arias. Most Handel operas are, in any case, too long for modern audiences, and the da capos should be the first place to look with scissors in hand. This act of mercy is performed twelve times in the *Alcina* recording (the conductor Richard Bonynge observes in the liner notes that this accords with Handel's own practice in subsequent performances of *Alcina*). The other two recordings, however, favor excision of entire arias and retention of the da capo.

A large number of the da capo arias in the *Furioso* operas, on the other hand, have excellent dramatic rationale behind them. Ruggiero's magnificent *Sta nell'Ircana pietrosa tana* (S6) from *Alcina* is a case in point: here Ruggiero describes the tigress desiring to meet the hunter in A, then its maternal desire to stay and protect its young in B. The return of A nicely sets in balance the conflicting feelings being expressed. Elsewhere in *Alcina* conflicting yet tensely counterpoised emotions are effectively captured through the da capo formula: Bradamante's pyrotechnic *È gelosia* (S1), Alcina's jealous hysteria in *Tornami a vagheggiar* (S2), and her heart-rending *Ah! mio cor!* (S4).[25]

Handel's habit of borrowing musical material from himself and others was a common practice in his time.[26] However, since *derivative* and *plagiarized* are harsh epithets to modern ears, it is perhaps worth observing that here also Handel was working well within the bounds of eighteenth-century convention. Innovation was in Handel's time not greatly valued in itself. Nothing else could explain the incredible frequency of plot devices like the prison scene or the poisoned cup or the threatened suicide, the endless stream of easily categorized arias (*aria infuriata, aria di bravura, aria cantabile,* etc.), and the countless, interchangeable heroic personages of Baroque opera. Handel's age was no age for the principle of copyright. No doubt he would have defended his borrowings (if, of course, some one had thought to accuse him) just as Walpole defended the practice in landscaping—

> Ought one man's garden to be deprived of a happy object, because that object has been employed by another? The more we exact novelty, the sooner our taste will be vitiated. Situations are every where so various, that there never can be a sameness, while the disposition of the ground is studied and followed, and every incident of view turned to advantage.

—or as Richardson defended the practice for painting:

> Nor need any Man be asham'd to be sometimes a Plagiary, 'tis what the greatest Painters, and Poets have allowed themselves . . . indeed 'tis hard that a Man having had a good Thought should have a Patent for it for Ever. The Painter that can take a Hint, or insert a Figure, or Groupes of Figures from another Man, and mix these

> with his Own, so as to make a good Composition, will thereby establish such a Reputation to himself, as to be above fearing to suffer.

Handel was certainly thought by his contemporaries to be above fearing on this point.

Modern audiences also find the predominance of female voices in Handel's operas disconcerting. For one must accustom oneself to the roles of heroes like Ariodante, Orlando, and Ruggiero sung by mezzo-sopranos and villains like Polinesso sung by contraltos. Those who cannot may wish to take their Handelian pleasure in those late almost-operas *Solomon, Samson, Semele,* and *Hercules* that contain no roles written for Italian castrati. In these later works (there being, of course, no English-speaking castrati) the highest male roles were written for a genuine tenor. Modern producers of these works are thus spared the necessity of casting lower female voices in order to approximate the castrato's vocal timbre.[27]

There is no getting round the modern distaste for the vocal qualities of the male alto, male contralto, or countertenor. Handel composed his operas at a time when the audience doted upon the castrato voice and could hardly have cared less about tenors. His audience, one suspects, would find today's ear-shattering tenor high C from the chest a rather vulgar, scarifying vocal feat. This clash of modern and Baroque fashions, more than any other, requires the broad-mindedness of a Streatfeild: "The conventions of one age always appear foolish to another, but we must not let them blind us to the value of the work with which they are associated."

But what of Handel without his wig? For all the conventionality of the *Furioso* operas, they look forward in history too. In each of these works glimpses of Mozart and the later Italian bel canto composers are sprinkled. Handel was adept at compromising between tradition and dramatic exigency; it was part of his nature to compromise (he took to spelling his middle name Frideric—midway between the English Frederick and the German Friedrich). In the *Furioso* operas he frequently evaded the dead hand of tradition, and some of their modern aspects are worth noting before turning to his successor, Mozart, in Chapter Three.

First, one can see in Handel's contrast of mood in successive arias the embryonic beginnings of the great *scenas* of the next century. The very first numbers in *Ariodante,* for instance, in which Ginevra expresses her love for Ariodante, converses with her maid, and then rejects Polinesso, are structured almost exactly as a Verdian *scena,* Violetta's in Act I of *La Traviata,* for example:

ARIODANTE	LA TRAVIATA
Vezzi, lusinghe e brio (andante, arioso)	*Ah, fors' è lui* (andantino, *cavatina*)
Ami dunque, o signora? (recitative)	*Follie! Follie!* (accompanied recitative)
Orrida agli occhi miei (allegro, aria)	*Sempre libera* (allegro brillante, aria)

A similar flexibility of organization resulting in an extended scenic event is the climactic moment when the mad hero is overcome by Zoroastro's powers in Act III of *Orlando.* Here Handel relies upon a sequence of accompanied recitative, arioso, dry or unaccompanied recitative, and then accompanied recitative, with a closing *sinfonia.* Handel avoids use of the aria completely and the passage is all the more impelling therefor.

Handel's sophistication of the accompanied recitative is noteworthy, especially in *Orlando.* Orlando's mad scene in Act II (based on XXIII.128ff) is a musico-dramatic display that concedes nothing to the more flexible means at the disposal of Mozart and Verdi. Here Handel takes his hero through a careening series of rapidly contrasting emotions: furious rage over Angelica's treachery (4/4 time with a salient rising motif); utter prostration (andante, flat melodic line); terror as he imagines himself crossing the Styx (5/8 time used for the first time in opera, andante); terror as he sees Cerberus (6/8 andante, grim unison strings); a reflux of vengeful rage at Medoro (4/4); breathless suspension as Orlando's love gets the better of him (adagio); and a mellower, pastoral interlude as Orlando exhausts his fury (4/4, tempo di gavotta, then 3/4 larghetto). This scene is a fine depiction of the manic-depressive lover; its criss-crossing of light and dark orchestration is worthy of Mozart. Also striking and dramatically effective are three other accompanied recitatives in *Orlando:* Zoroastro's introductory *Gieroglifici eterni!* (S1), Dorinda's exquisitely rustic *Quanto diletto* (S2), and Zoroastro's invocation *Tu, che del gran Tonante* (S6).

Nor was Handel chained to the solo aria. The concerted numbers in the *Furioso* operas are, in their dramatic discrimination of competing vocal lines and the naturalness of juxtaposition, oriented toward the operatic future. The Ginevra-Ariodante duet in Act I (*Prendi da questa mano,* S1) performs exactly the function of the love duet in Act I of Verdi's *Otello* and is, though much shorter, quite as affecting. Handel has the delighted father interrupt the duet at its climax—a happy dramatic stroke. Only one of *Ariodante*'s four duets, incidentally, has the usual da capo. The duet between the mad Orlando and Angelica (*Unisca amor,* S5) is finely observed by Handel, who emphasizes through separate tempos (largo 3/4 for Orlando, andante 4/4 for Angelica) their inability to communicate. A similar method vitalizes the later Act III duet for the same characters (*Finchè prendi ancor,* S6).

The *Furioso* operas also offer two excellent trios. In Act I of *Orlando,* Medoro and Angelica console the shepherdess Dorinda for her unluckiness in love. This trio (which Dean calls "highly irregular, if not unique") is nearly the last word in Handelian pastoral elegance, and its essentially da capo structure fits well with Dorinda's unwillingness to be consoled. In the last act of *Alcina,* Ruggiero and Bradamante join forces to resist Alcina's last desperate pleas. The result is a fine example of Handel in his "salient" posture.

One may not normally think of Handel as a tone-painter, but passages in the three operas argue otherwise. The *sinfonia* that opens Act II of *Ariodante* (a moonlit night near the royal garden) is a beautiful example of Handel's Shaftesbury-esque sympathy with nature, though underneath the pacific violins Handel places an ominous descending figure portending the success of Polinesso's plot. Dorinda's arioso (*Quando spieghi i tuoi tormenti,* S3) opening Act II of *Orlando* is typical of the vernal Handel. It is a whispered hint of the Nightingale Chorus from *Solomon* and the rustic glories of *L'Al-*

legro. One could also refer to the perfect epitome of pastoral melancholy in Dorinda's following aria *Se mi rivolgo al prato* (S3). Angelica's sublime *Verdi piante, erbette liete* (S4), with its wafting semiquavers and soprano recorders, examples Handel's ability to depict nature almost weeping for the sad human in its midst. Also in this genre is the pleasure-sated languor of Alcina's palace depicted in her aria *Di', cor mio* (S1) and Ruggiero's farewell to the delights of Alcina's island, *Verdi prati* (S4)—an aria such as one would want to hear upon leaving Paradise.

Though Goldsmith observed that Handel required "the full band," he was by modern standards limited by the constitution of a Baroque orchestra. Nevertheless, he could create fine effects through the sparing use of certain instruments at dramatically auspicious moments. Two such instances come near the opening of *Orlando.* Zoroastro attempts to convince the love-stricken Orlando to return to the field of honor, glory, and battle. His aria *Lascia Amor, e segui Marte,* S1) is typical of the call-to-arms Handel. Just where we expect to hear trumpets or horns, however, he specifies flutes, the instrument of amorous dalliance: Zoroastro is perhaps scaling his pleas to the situation. Orlando's reply (*Non fu già men forte Alcide,* S1) is equally ironic, for here Handel has the hero reject the warrior's life to the accompaniment of the usually military horns. Handel thoroughly domesticates them, even to the extent of requiring effeminate, flute-like trills. Other special effects of orchestration can only be mentioned in passing: the unexpected entry of recorders in *Verdi piante* (S4) in *Orlando;* the withholding of the trumpets until the last scene of *Ariodante,* where a stage orchestra plays antiphonally with the main orchestra; the prominent horns in the heroic aria for Ruggiero in Act III of *Alcina;* the plaintive solo violin in Morgana's *Ama, sospira* (S5) from the same opera; and the bassoon, expressing the void left in Ariodante's heart by Ginevra's supposed betrayal, that dominates his splendid *Scherza infida* (S4).

Finally, there are the moments when Handel rises to a simplicity of utterance worlds apart from the long-winded arias frequently associated with Baroque opera (a typical "bad" example, incidentally, is Lurcanio's *Il tuo sangue* (S4) in *Ariodante*). In the last act of *Ariodante* alone are three excellent examples of Handelian concision.

The first is Ginevra's sorrowful farewell to her father (*Io ti bacio,* S5). Handel achieves a profoundly plaintive quality with a largo assai and a vocal line paralleled by four violins; he actually raises a lump in the throat in the fourth bar. This aria is twelve bars long (seven for A, five for B); that the last section and da capo are cut in the recording is a shame. A little later Ginevra is given another wisely calculated and compact aria (*Si, morrò,* S6). After a relaxing five bars, largo e piano, she bursts suddenly into an allegro explosion of righteous indignation worthy of a Lucrece. This aria is just thirty-nine bars long, and Handel—a Baroque composer but no fool—required no da capo here. Finally, with Ginevra in prison, Handel permits himself just five bars of arioso (lesser hands would have set a grand aria here) before the *Fidelio*-like trumpets of a *sinfonia* announce her rescue.

This overview of some modern features of the *Furioso* operas can merely hint that Handel was, if not the only, certainly the most successful of Baroque innovators. To paraphrase his nineteenth-century biographer, Chrysander, Handel walked in the steps of earlier Baroque composers, but his feet were larger. Those who become familiar with the *Furioso* operas—and I do not pretend to have discussed them more than cursorily in this chapter—will perhaps find *their* Handel best represented visually by Roubiliac's sculpture of the composer in Westminster Abbey. For there Handel is to be seen without his wig.

three

LE NOZZE DI FIGARO

I'll laugh and cry at the same time.

Figaro, *Le Mariage de Figaro*

Mozart was one of the least biased artistic geniuses who have ever lived, and his operas display a consequent willingness to observe without brow-beating interventions the subtle antagonisms and ambivalences of human nature. He rarely passes harsh judgments in his music, rarely declares his allegiance. Mozart was willing to give the mortal fools he created the benefit of the doubt, leeway to act either wisely or foolishly but always to act as human beings. Even his comic butts behave with a distinctly human credibility. This is why *human* is an epithet so often used to describe the essence of this composer's appeal.

This artistry of multiple focus and equipoise is uniquely capable of displaying the underlying contradictions of human actions. In Mozart's most popular operas these contradictions are constantly in animation and conflict. Stage directors and commentators who impose their own approach frequently do Mozart serious injustice, for it is in their interest to obscure or eliminate the rich potentialities in the musical character that the composer left open. Mozart challenges us to envision his characters—who may appear simple at first glance but nearly always become more complex, more human as we get to know them—with the same expansive and yet finely reticent powers of observation he has focused upon them. This task requires the shrewdness and gravity of a philosopher and the gaiety of a child. In other words, Mozart's seriousness is gracious and ebullient.

Mozart could communicate much while leaving final conclusions unspoken. This characteristic has naturally encouraged myriad analyses of his operas and extraordinary contention about their essential nature. *Don Giovanni* has perhaps been buffeted in the polemical storm more than any other. *Die Zauberflöte* has suffered rather less, if only because its arcane symbolic foundations permit interpreters more freedom of action. And until quite recently *Così fan tutte* has elicited surprisingly harsh judgments. As late as the 1950s Joseph

Kerman called it "Mozart's most problematic" work and "immoral and frivolous." Since then, however, increasing familiarity and the recent sexual Enlightenment have helped to establish *Così* as one of Mozart's four supreme operas.[1] Still, those who love Mozart will probably always be most attracted to *Le Nozze di Figaro*. This opera elicits, and can bear up under, the subtlest distinctions. It draws us in many directions—not necessarily but plausibly. On the other hand, with *Figaro* we are in constant danger of reaching a hasty conclusion or sounding a premature cadence. It carries us away now and again, as it did Brigid Brophy (who called it "the most purely erotic opera ever composed") or W. J. Turner (describing *Non so più* as "one of the loveliest things the genius of an artist has ever created in the history of the world"). We want to praise *Le Nozze* extravagantly, yet its wonders escape superlatives.

Perhaps most maddening is an inability to answer the simplest, most fundamental questions about our experience of the opera. What is the most fulfilling moment? One will say (and Mozart would agree) the Act III sextet; another responds with the Act II Finale; yet another will say the Count's final plea for pardon. Dramatically or musically, who is the central character—the Count, the Countess, Figaro, or Susanna? A case can be made for each of them. Ought *Le Nozze* to make us laugh or cry, or—as the epigraph suggests—are we to do both simultaneously? We rightly feel that such queries ought to be easily answered, yet they are not. The reason for this is a Mozartean equipoise of spirit and art—what Romain Rolland called his "heroic dualism." This quality can be but poorly felt without placing the opera not only in the immediate literary context of its source, the Beaumarchais play *Le Mariage de Figaro,* but also in its more general cultural context. While much has been written of Mozart's (and Haydn's) miraculous emergence from the relatively colorless decades of rococo that ensued after Bach's death in 1750, little has been said of Mozart's literary milieu. This milieu illumines his achievement in *Le Nozze di Figaro*—his first great opera, as well as the first opera never to require a revival. What follows is an attempt to examine it in a broader perspective—to lift our eyes from Mozart's magical score to the surrounding stage he entered upon.

Mozart and Beaumarchais: The Classical Style

Consider the first eighteen bars of the *Sinfonia* that opens *Le Nozze di Figaro* (EX. 1). Thus begins—how can one resist saying so?—the

Example 1

most splendid of comic overtures. With breathless and breathtaking concision, we are introduced to the two primary comic modes of the opera. In bars one through six the strings and bassoon capture the droll, sinuous machinations that keep the plot in perpetual motion. The very arch of this first theme reflects the many comic complications that materialize, heighten in intensity, wane, and evanesce as the action unwinds. The tiny imbroglio solved by the return to D in bar seven leaves in its wake the increased energy (in the form of an octave D in the cellos and a dynamic increase from pianissimo to piano) to reach in bars eight to eighteen an expression of the contrasting comic mode of quasi-military assertiveness. This more aggressive, masculine fanfare is appropriately sounded by the winds. As in so many instances of comic self-assertion throughout the opera, the "rise" and "fall" is carefully graded: horns and oboes take bar eight, flutes and clarinets play bar nine, then both groups join in bars ten and eleven, and the full orchestra sounds a momentary climax in bar twelve. Of course, such "superiority" never lasts long, and in the minuscule coda of bars fifteen through seventeen Mozart exhausts this comic moment of what Hobbes, in his definition of laughter, called "sudden glory." At bar eighteen another revolution of the comic wheel begins.

This careening fifteen-second passage, though sounding reckless and overflowing in its energy, is a carefully ordered and balanced entity. Indeed, its balance bears some resemblance to a typical couplet from Pope (this one, incidentally, describing the comic crux of both play and opera):

> Oh thoughtless Mortals! ever blind to Fate,
> Too soon dejected, and too soon elate!
> "The Rape of the Lock"

The passage from the *Sinfonia* has this same nice balance and closure. The abundance of these qualities in *Le Nozze* is no doubt what led Richard Wagner to observe: "With what aplomb he treated *Le Nozze di Figaro:* on the set foundation of Italian opera buffa he reared a building of such perfect symmetry."[2]

One lingers over the first bars of the opera not only because their ingenuity is a recurrent feature of the score (the first twelve bars of *Non più andrai* or the first eighteen of *Dove sono* would have served as well) but, more crucially, to suggest that the structural equipoise of the Mozartean style is in this opera invariably apt to the drama of the moment. As Charles Rosen has observed, Mozart's genius was to see the potential for dramatic application in the musical conventions and forms he worked with.* In his operas, life does not seem to conform arbitrarily to the exigencies of musical formulas but rather is invigorated by them.[3] Mozart applied the rules of the classical era imaginatively, broke them when necessary. Though no composer respected or thought more in terms of these rules, they seem to be utterly at his mercy. Mozart was, in short—paradoxes surround the man—a rebellious conservative.

The idea that Mozart was bound by rules and forms will probably never be eradicated. One can only reply that classicism is not neces-

* Charles Rosen, *The Classical Style: Haydn, Mozart, Beethoven* (1971). Quotations from Rosen will appear in the text. It is hoped that the present discussion will complement Rosen's extended musical analysis of Mozart's classical style.

sarily a matter of deadening rules applied to living ideas, but a more vital combination of traditional forms and innovative intellect. Delacroix described the "classic" in a general way that most of us feel is near its essence: "I call classic all works in which regularity predominates, those which satisfy the mind not alone by painting sentiments and things in an exact or grandiose or piquant manner, but also by unity and logical order." But even the arch-Romantic Delacroix went on to observe that in true classicism rules may predominate but are not frigidly unbending ("Many people do not separate the idea of coldness from that of the Classical"). In *The Life of Forms of Art* Henri Focillon also defends classicism from the usual detractions of coldness and inert severity:

> Classicism consists of the greatest propriety of the parts one to the other. It is stability, security, following upon experimental unrest. It confers, so to speak, a solidity on the unstable aspects of experimentation . . . Classicism: a brief, perfectly balanced instant of complete possession of forms; not a slow and monotonous application of "rules," but a pure, quick delight. [pp. 11-12]

This summation could well refer to Mozart, for *Le Nozze* displays precisely that "possession of forms" Focillon speaks of. The overture may indeed be, as musicologists will say, in sonata form but lacking a development section. But it is more; Mozart has repossessed the form and made it an exhilarating preparation for the following comedy. It captures the entire opera's alternation between experimental (i.e., comic) unrest and the security of the return to an anticipated tonic or final cadence (i.e., a happy end). *Le Nozze* is the epitome of classicism's "pure, quick delight" in experimental risk-taking with musical forms. What Figaro says in Beaumarchais—"There's nothing in taking risks, but to take risks and at the same time turn them to your advantage—that's something!"—goes far to explain the genius of Mozart's score.

It is something of a myth that the Age of Reason (*Aufklärung, siècle des lumières,* or Enlightenment as it is variously called) was a rule-bound age. Many men of the time were indeed aware that the life of the mind, particularly if it was the mind of a genius, is not to be guided solely by custom or even so apparently honorable a counselor as reason. Alexander Pope—who felt the bonds of rhyme and meter most and yet was freest in them—expresses memorably the ideal combination of formal restriction and pragmatic license that distinguishes Mozart. Significantly, the musical art helps him make his point:

> Some Beauties yet, no Precepts can declare,
> For there's a Happiness as well as Care.
> Musick resembles Poetry, in each
> Are nameless Graces which no Methods teach,
> And which a Master-Hand alone can reach.
> If, where the Rules not far enough extend,
> (Since Rules were made but to promote their End)
> Some Lucky Licence answers to the full
> Th'Intent propos'd, that Licence is a Rule.
> Thus Pegasus, a nearer way to take,
> May boldly deviate from the common Track.
> Great Wits sometimes may gloriously offend,
> And rise to Faults true Criticks dare not mend;
> From vulgar Bounds with brave Disorder part,
> And snatch a Grace beyond the Reach of Art.
>
> *Essay on Criticism* [I. 141-55]

Such is Mozart's art in *Le Nozze*. As Pope praised the "lucky license" that ignores decorum, so was Mozart guided by a sense of theatricality and dramatic appropriateness. For Mozart as for Pope, freedom was a rule with special priority. In a letter to his father in October 1781 Mozart complained bitterly about the pedantic librettists he had to deal with: "Poets almost remind me of trumpeters with their professional tricks! If we composers were always true to our rules (which were very good at a time when no one knew better), we should be concocting music as unpalatable as their libretti." Mozart's respect for rules was, like Pope's, neither truculent nor submissive but simply reasoned and pragmatic. He could have boasted as Beaumarchais did of his own career: "I have remained free in the midst of fetters."[4]

As we shall see elsewhere in this study, the greatest operatic translations of literature usually are the result of fortunate coincidences—be they aesthetic, biographical, or historical. The coincidence perhaps most responsible for the brilliant lyric transformation of *Le Mariage* was one of essential artistic sensibilities: the play's world view and dramatic style drew perfectly upon Mozart's equilibrating art.* Indeed, of the three Beaumarchais comedies, one feels only *Le Mariage* could have tapped this art fully. In a preface to the last of the Figaro plays, *La Mère coupable,* the playwright distinguished their differing tones:

> After having laughed heartily, on the first day, in *Le Barbier de Seville,* at the turbulent youth of Count Almaviva, which is practically that of all men; after having, on the second day, gaily considered, in *Le Mariage de Figaro* the faults of his maturity, which are too often our own; come and be convinced by the picture of his old age in *La Mère coupable,* where we see that every man who is not congenitally knavish always ends up a good sort when he leaves the age of passions behind and, above all, when he has tasted the sweet pleasure of being a father.†

How fortunate we are that Rossini, whose gift was to elicit the hearty laugh, was destined to set the first play to music. And how fortunate that Mozart was drawn to the play most delicately criss-crossed with gaiety and the "faults" of maturity, rather than to the turgidly moralistic last part of the trilogy (which Milhaud did set to music in 1966).

Not only is the tone of *Le Mariage* a volatile mixture of seriousness and levity, but the very form of the play is also strangely mixed. The influence of various genres can be felt: Italian comedy, sentimental melodrama (*comédie larmoyante* in France), opera with spoken dialogue (*opéra comique* or *comédie mêlée d'ariettes*), the rococo drawing-room comedy typified by Marivaux, not to mention the philosophical style of Voltaire and Diderot. As many have noted, the constituent parts of the play—its situations, characters, and dialogue—are almost all derivative, as are Da Ponte's Mozart libretti. Beaumarchais's skill, however, was in amalgamating everything and giving it

* Henceforth, the French title and French spelling of the dramatis personae will refer to the Beaumarchais play. Quotations from *Le Mariage* are cited in the text by reference to page number in the Penguin paperback translation by John Wood (1964).

† *Œuvres Complètes* (1828), Vol. II, pp. 237-38. Subsequent citations from Beaumarchais's works are included in the text.

breathtaking pace and verve. He disposed and integrated the familiar building-blocks of various traditions into a unified whole, and Mozart was uniquely able to reconcile Beaumarchais's amalgam of theatrical styles with the wide range of musical styles at his disposal. He rose to the challenge of the effects we find in *Le Mariage*—"the skilful moves and countermoves of the chief protagonists; the minor variations in a fast general tempo; the pleasures of complications and perplexities; and the ingenious unwinding of plot."[5] The newly won flexibility of the classical musical style permitted Mozart to match the wit, drollery, and expressiveness of the play's dialogue in his music. His expertise in the "drama" of tonal adventure, experimentation and final resolution fit as a glove the requirements of the play's numerous imbroglios. The supple tempos of the new classical style allowed Mozart to follow Beaumarchais's comic pace with epoch-making sensitivity.

Perplexity over the true nature of the classical style perhaps is explained by its sense of balance. For it is in the fine balancing of opposing forces—strength and gentleness, sadness and joy, hope and despair, tears of happiness and pain—that the finest moments of Mozart's operas are found. Beaumarchais sent the King of Sweden a note accompanying a finely bound copy of *Le Mariage:* "Sorrow issues from joy, and gaiety itself produces grief." He was alluding to the play's mingled sense of life's levity and sadness. The same oscillation Mozart infused in his opera. Indeed, any opera that can comfortably encompass the lambent sentiment of *Dove sono,* the malevolence of *Vedrò mentr'io sospiro,* the innocence of *Non so più,* the theatrical cynicism of Basilio's *In quegli anni,* the parodic recognition scene, and the noble *Contessa perdono*—such an opera must, like its source, be considered a miracle of balance. Stendhal was right: "Mozart's opera [*Le Nozze*] is a sublime mixture of wit and melancholy which has no equal."[6]

A more general coincidence—and perhaps the most telling—is worth a fleeting mention. This concerns the peculiarly hermaphroditic genius of Beaumarchais and Mozart, that spiritual balance which colors the essential qualities of their art. Beaumarchais recognized this quality in himself; of *La Mère coupable* he wrote: "I have composed it and with a purpose both direct and pure; with a man's cool head and a woman's heart, as has been said of Rousseau. I have noticed that this combination, this moral hermaphroditism is less rare than has been believed." In his attempt to explain the "infinitely ambiguous" nature of Mozart's music, W. J. Turner referred to the same concept, declaring that "*intellectually* all men of genius are hermaphroditic."[7] Whether Turner's generalization is sound, its force for Mozart is strong. The idea of the hermaphrodite suggests the same tense equilibrium Focillon found in the classical style and which we find in Mozart. The concept may help to explain the interlacing qualities of passion and wit that tie *Le Mariage* and *Le Nozze* so closely together.

Augustan Mozart: A Literary Context for His Style

Boileau wrote in a letter to Racine that Baroque music would never produce good opera because it did not "know how" to narrate action. He even added that Baroque music could not express itself in dialogue ("La musique ne sait pas dialoguer"). But the advent of the classical style changed this. Mozart, with his Augustan genius, helped effect this change.[8] With Haydn and Mozart it becomes possible to speak of musical language and of musical grammar or rhetoric. Classical methods not only made dialogue possible—it *was* dialogue in essence. No musical period has come closer to portraying the pleasures and give-and-take of conversation. It is not entirely coincidental that music became, in the words of Rolland, "eminently sociable" toward the end of the Augustan age—the first age to take its "literary" pleasures in the social atmosphere of the coffeehouse or salon and in the art of conversation. Rolland also observed that with Mozart "free speech" was united with "free music." *Le Nozze* is the first great manifestation in opera of this revolutionary collaboration.

Classical music, perhaps more than any other in history, is syntactical. The methods of syntax (from the Greek = to arrange together) apply to the poet, the prose stylist, and to the classical composer alike. This is why Rosen's syntactic analysis of the classical style is so illuminating. What he calls the "syntactic art of dramatic movement" was becoming possible in the time of Haydn and Mozart. Together, these men explored and perfected the widest possible range and flexibility of musical elocution. In a way, they expanded their art-form just as John Dryden broadened the horizons of the English language:

> Perhaps no nation ever produced a writer that enriched his language with such variety of models. To him we owe the improvement, perhaps the completion, of our meter, the refinement of our language, and much of the correctness of our sentiments. By him we were taught *sapere et fari,* to think naturally and express forcibly . . . What was said of Rome, adorned by Augustus, may be applied by an easy metaphor to English poetry embellished by Dryden, *lateritiam invenit, marmoream reliquit,* he found it brick, and he left it marble.[9]

Samuel Johnson's "easy metaphor" can also be extended to describe Mozart's impact upon the language of operatic music. Johnson, of course, was not ignoring the brilliance of England's great Baroque poet Milton—just as we cannot ignore the contributions of Mozart's predecessors Bach and Handel. That Mozart's or Dryden's art is more flexible and in a sense more humane—that is, closer to the natural dimensions of human experience—may be the very reason they seldom rise to the austere majesty or metaphysical profundity of Bach and Milton. Neither inferiority nor superiority is implied; the accomplishments are merely in different styles.

To appreciate how Mozart differs from Bach or Handel and why this difference made the former peculiarly able to translate *Le Mariage,* we may usefully put the composer in the larger context of Baroque and neo-Classical rhetorical traditions, in the context of the rhetorical polarity between the grand style (*genus grande*) and the plain style (*genus humile*) whose history stretches back to ancient Greece. Dryden, Pope, and Johnson succeeded upon a century in English literature when the grand style held sway, just as in music Mozart and Beaumarchais succeeded upon a century dominated by the grand style of the *tragédie héroïque* and opera seria. To understand the nature of the Augustan and Mozartean departure from the Baroque, let us look briefly at the earlier style.

As early as Longinus's treatise *On the Sublime* (1st century of the Christian era) the existence of two great polar styles—one concise and the other expansive—was already established:

> Demosthenes' greatness is usually more abrupt; he is always forceful, rapid, powerful, and intense; he may be compared to the lightning or the thunderbolt which burns and ravages. Cicero, to me, is like an enveloping conflagration which spreads all around and crowds upon us, a vast steady fire which flares up in this direction or that and is fed intermittently . . . the tense greatness of Demosthenes is more suited to moments of intense and violent passion when the audience must be altogether swept off its feet. The right time for the Ciceronian copiousness is when the audience must be overwhelmed by a flood of words. [Grube tr.]

It is clear from this passage, I think, that opera as we now know it was not to flourish until a musical equivalent of Demosthenes' style appeared, for this genre is very much tied to "moments of intense and violent passion."

Cicero fathered the grandiose syntax. The Ciceronian sentence is an immense juggernaut, full (as is much Baroque music) of long rolling cadences, symphonic and carefully graded movement, and a sense of monumentality. Its effect is one of slowly accumulating energy and a suspense that builds until the end of the period (a period in punctuation signifying a full stop). The Ciceronian style is exampled in English prose by Hooker's famous sentence from *The Laws of Ecclesiastical Polity* (1593) in which he imagines a world without divine order. It cannot be quoted partially. It must be savored whole or not at all, so compelling is its momentum:

> Now if nature should intermit her course, and leave altogether though it were but for a while the observation of her own laws; if those principal and mother elements of the world, whereof all things in this lower world are made, should lose the qualities which now they have; if the frame of that heavenly arch erected over our heads should loosen and dissolve itself; if celestial spheres should forget their wonted motions, and by irregular volubility turn themselves any way as it might happen; if the prince of the lights of heaven, which now as a giant doth run his unwearied course, should as it were through a languishing faintness begin to stand and to rest himself; if the moon should wander from her beaten way, the times and seasons of the year blend themselves by disordered and confused mixture, the winds breathe out their last gasp, the clouds yield no rain,

> the earth pine away as children at the withered breasts of their mother no longer able to yield them relief: what would become of man himself, whom these things now do all serve?

Such prose is glorious for the same reasons Bach and Handel are glorious, containing as it does expressive majesty, immensity of scope, and a closely knit but prodigiously extensive design. With what relief and sense of consummation we reach the thundered rhetorical question of its climax. Hooker's unified rhythmic texture (the *if*'s keep the momentum flowing), the vast wave of eloquence, and the seemingly perpetual motion—the sentence could end anywhere, one feels, or continue indefinitely—are qualities traditionally identified with Baroque music. It is possible, for instance, to work in the opposite direction and apply Rosen's description of Baroque music to Hooker's sentence: "Given the fluid, continuous, and self-generating rhythm of Baroque music the only way to stop a piece was a forceful tonic cadence" (p. 49). This is exactly how Hooker concludes his sentence, the strong accents of the last seven words even requiring the rallentando or slowing of tempo that accompanies the final cadence of a Baroque musical movement.

The poetic equivalent for Hooker is Milton. The first ten lines of *Paradise Lost* or its most wonderful and characteristically Miltonic period—

> Him [Satan] the Almighty Power
> Hurl'd headlong flaming from th'Ethereal Sky
> With hideous ruin and combustion down
> To bottomless perdition, there to dwell
> In Adamantine Chains and penal Fire,
> Who durst defy th'Omnipotent to Arms. [I. 44-49]

—exemplify the muscularity and epical breadth associated with this poet. In their density, uniformity of heightened diction, and cumulative power, these passages bring us very close to the Baroque aesthetic. When a scholar says of Milton that he must be quoted at length or not at all, we might add the same of Bach or Handel. When Addison describes Milton's "Pomp of Sound" we are put in mind of a Bach cantata or a Handel oratorio. And Johnson describes

Milton's style in a way we might easily apply to the composer of the Matthew and John *Passions:* "The characteristick quality . . . is sublimity. He sometimes descends to the elegant, but his element is the great. He can occasionally invest himself with grace; but his natural port is gigantick loftiness. He can please when pleasure is required; but it is his peculiar power to astonish." In a moment of weakness, we might even agree with Johnson that the Baroque masters can overstay their welcome: what he felt of *Paradise Lost* ("None ever wished it longer than it is") one sometimes feels about the *B-Minor Mass* or the *Messiah*.

Mozart's age (like the Augustan age) vainly aspired to the "gigantick loftiness" of former generations. When it essayed Milton's terrific didacticism it produced only prescriptive bombast such as Addison's *Cato,* Diderot's *Père de famille,* and even Beaumarchais's *Eugénie*. Aiming at the sublime, it brought forth pomposity. Its productions in the genres normally associated with the grand style—tragedy, opera seria, epic, for example—are now almost completely forgotten. Rather, men like Mozart and Pope leaned in the direction, as Longinus phrased it, of "abrupt greatness." Augustans succeeded in the smaller forms—the epigram, heroic couplet, essay, and coffeehouse anecdote. Pope was praised for his "minute attention" to the world around him, and this phrase is a hallmark for the period—which exercised its keen empiricism and gift for precise articulation upon man as he actually is. For Augustans the proper study of mankind was man, not the mythological deities and exotic emperors who populated Baroque opera.

Beaumarchais, too, was at heart an Augustan—even if his was the very last breath of Augustanism in France. Much as Johnson had criticized *Paradise Lost* because it concerned neither "human actions nor human manners," so did Beaumarchais attack the *tragédie héroïque* with its grandiose personages and bloated diction:

> The subjects [in heroic tragedy] being so distant from our own manners and the characters so alien to our social station, our interest in it is less pressing than in the action of realistic drama; its morality is less direct, more arid, often worthless and quite lost on us, at least so much as does not serve to console us in our more humble situations. [I. p. 12]

Beaumarchais wrote one opera libretto, *Tarare* (1787), which was set to music by Mozart's Viennese rival Salieri. In his preface to *Tarare,* "To Opera Subscribers Who Wish to Love Opera," Beaumarchais put himself on record as a critic of the opera seria with all its fantastic luxury and exotic plotting.

Samuel Johnson believed that the writer's primary task was to convey "accurate observation of the living world," and the creator of *Le Mariage* shared this bias in favor of realism. This realistic bent gave Beaumarchais's plays their great initial popularity and was finally responsible for their revolutionary undertones. As the Baroness d'Oberkirch trenchantly observed at the time, the realism and natural vigor of *Le Mariage* were so captivatingly novel that its first aristocratic audiences failed to see the play's social implications.[10]

Precise syntax, elegant diction, curt phrasing, and a pervasive feeling of down-to-earth common sense made Augustan prose especially apt as a tool for analysis and balancing. Its clarifying powers were extraordinary, as Johnson's comparison of Dryden with Pope may serve to suggest: "If the flights of Dryden are higher, Pope continues longer on the wing. If of Dryden's fire the blaze is brighter, of Pope's the heat is more regular and constant. Dryden often surpasses expectation, and Pope never falls below it. Dryden is read with frequent astonishment, and Pope with perpetual delight." This same pristine balancing of phrase and sentiment is manifest throughout *Le Mariage*. Even the tipsy gardener Antonio has the knack for balanced epigram: "That's all that distinguishes us from the beasts, Madam—drinking when we aren't thirsty and making love whenever we feel like it" (150). We will shortly see how Mozart realized musically the Augustan qualities of the play's dialogue.

The child of equipoise is irony: masters of balance are by definition distanced from the extremes of behavior they observe. Ironists are masters of context. Their realistic, skeptical, and detached sensibilities give them the power to see isolated actions, temporary crises in a larger perspective. The Augustan age was the great age of satirical irony, as *The Tale of a Tub,* "The Rape of the Lock," *Gulliver's Travels,* the *Tatler* and *Spectator* essays, and "A Modest Proposal" suffice to indicate. In "Verses on the Death of Dr. Swift," Swift even claimed with tongue in cheek the discovery of irony as a literary mode:

> Arbuthnot is no more my Friend,
> Who dares to Irony pretend;
> Which I was born to introduce,
> Refin'd it first, and shew'd its Use.

Beaumarchais and Mozart were successors to the ironic tradition in their own time. The ironist will always vanish behind the façade of his work, and this was Beaumarchais's stated intention, explained in an anecdote from the preface to *Le Mariage:*

> A very witty gentleman who perhaps is a bit too stingy of his cleverness, said to me one evening at the theater: "Tell me then, I beg of you, why one finds in your play so many negligent phrases which are not in your usual style?" "In my style, sir! If I am unlucky enough to have but one, I should endeavor to forget that fact when I write a comedy. I know of nothing so insipid in the theater as those stale pieces of dullness where everything is blue, where all is pink, where everything is the author, no matter what." [II. p. 34]

When Beaumarchais comes to explain how he creates his characters, he reveals with droll self-mockery the stance of a true ironist: "When my subject seizes me, I conjure up my characters and place them in situations . . . What they will say I haven't a clue; it is what they will do that occupies me. Then, if they are in good fettle, I write from their rapid dictations, certain that they will not betray me . . . each speaks his own language; may the god of what is natural preserve them from speaking otherwise!"

Mozart's opera gives us the same sense of a creator who vanishes behind the various local effects he is creating with his wildly disparate musical characterizations. Each figure speaks his or her own musical language, Mozart giving full emotional play to the sincerity of the moment (in comedy sincerity rarely lasts longer). How else can one explain Figaro's acerbic *Aprite un po' quegl'occhi* in his otherwise comic role, the stately sentiment of *Porgi amor* and *Dove sono* for a Countess who is also a comic intriguer, and the haunting beauty of Barbarina's bathetic Act IV aria? These discontinuities do not jar because Mozart and Da Ponte were able to place them in the plot's overall comic context. The comic perspective may not always be apparent to us in the midst of an aria or ensemble, but as soon as it is over this perspective tends to reassert itself. That we are dizzied by alternating invitations to believe and then to disbelieve the emotions expressed in *Le Nozze* is due to the ironist's master hand.

Mozart was, of course, more than an Augustan. His "literary" milieu extends beyond the chiseled, rather aloof clarity of Pope to the Richardsonian penchant for the affective sentimental scene; one who has read *Clarissa* or *Pamela* will know the Countess better than most.[11] And there is something of Mozart in the clever machinations and irony of Fielding's *Tom Jones*. Still, if terms from literary history can be applied to Mozart at all, Augustan is the most obvious one. The Augustan style wins us over by trenchancy, not inundation. Such is Mozart's style, with its clever articulation of dramatic moments. The Augustan style is organized in smaller modules; its momentum is less than the Baroque; still, its movement is more consistently interesting in its eventfulness. The same is true of Mozart's music: "The clearest [element] in the formation of the classical style . . . is the short, periodic, articulated phrase. When it first appears, it is a disruptive element in the Baroque style, which relied generally on an encompassing and sweeping continuity" (Rosen, p. 57). The Augustan sensibility was ultimately comic, and so is the Mozartean style. No period has produced finer comedy—in absolute music or operatic music—than did the classical period.

Once the juggernaut of what one might call the Ciceronian conventions of the Baroque was overturned, the potential for more local and aurally discernible dramatic effects in music was realized. Imaginative arrangement of sequential events became possible in music, and with this proliferated the comic possibilities that follow from the syntactical power to disrupt meaning and expectation suddenly. One writer finds in *Le Mariage* that "the plot unfolds as an endless series of surprises, adventures, novelties, and incredible happenings, worlds apart from the centered harmony one experiences in a play by Molière."[12] The increasing atomization of the "centered harmony" of Bach and the Baroque—which had been taking place for nearly half a century—culminated with Mozart. He was uniquely able to do what had not been possible on such a large scale hitherto: render into music the surprises, tiny crises, and incredible happenings that are the staple of comic theater.

If a counterpart for Mozart's style and spirit is to be found in English literature, we should look to that poet of stable poise, perfect ease, and sureness of transition, Alexander Pope. We are not now in the habit of analyzing genius as painstakingly as the Augustans (the nature of genius peculiarly intrigued them). Nevertheless, there is in Johnson's description of Pope's genius an apt summary—in a prose style itself characteristic of the Augustan age—of the genius Mozart displayed in music:

> Pope had, in proportions very nicely adjusted to each other, all the qualities that constitute genius. He had Invention, by which new trains of events are formed and new scenes of imagery displayed and by which extrinsick and adventitious embellishments and illustrations are connected with a known subject . . . he had Imagination, which strongly impresses on the writer's mind and enables him to convey to the reader the various forms of nature, incidents of life, and energies of passions . . . he had Judgement, which selects from life or nature what the present purpose requires, and, by separating the essence of things from its concomitants, often makes the representation more powerful than the reality; and he had colours of language always before him ready to decorate his matter with every grace of elegant expression.

Play and Opera: Milieu

There has been much discussion of the revolutionary content of *Le Mariage* and, to a lesser extent, *Le Nozze*. The revolution clarioned by these works, however, was not only political but artistic. They represent a revolution of theatrical sensibilities. In their respective genres Beaumarchais and Mozart turned the tide, if not initially at least significantly, against the reigning taste for heroic tragedy. They established (in the playwright's case re-established) the *vis comica* on the dramatic and operatic stage.

Beaumarchais's achievement must be savored against the background of eighteenth-century European stage history, which was largely a story of declining vigor and stagnation. The audience was inclined less and less to laugh. By 1746 the Duc d'Aumont could observe that the plays of Molière were "entirely abandoned by the public." This eclipse of Molière's ribald, forceful, prosaic comedy is accountable for two main reasons. First was the increasing prestige of heroic tragedy. After some decades Voltaire could well observe: "Everything is permitted in this tedious genre."

Second, and more subversive because more directly competitive with Molière's laughing comedy, was the growing popularity of two comic subgenres: the highly polished salon comedy exemplified by Marivaux (1688-1763) and the sentimental comedy inaugurated by La Chaussée (1692-1754) that flourished at mid-century. These dramatists provided a more mundane, decorous, cosmetic, and less searching theatrical experience; violent emotions lay concealed behind a refined gallantry. No wonder, as Bachaumont indicates in his *Mémoires* (1764), that the pointed satire and earthy vigor of earlier French comedy was not attractive at this time: "Our scrupulous exactitude in matters of decorum forbids us to laugh as much at this piece [*Le Malade imaginaire*] as one did in Molière's time." The plays of Marivaux—who has been called the psychologist of femininity and the philosopher of feminism—were, though limited in their comic scope and depth, at least valuable in the development of an agile theatrical language. The assertion that Marivaux was the "master of the most flexible language which had ever been written to be spoken" is indication enough of the influence he must have had on Beaumarchais.[13] More subversive still was the influence of the sentimental comedies that proliferated in the second third of the eighteenth century (the same time, it might be noted, that the tearful novels of Richardson took France by storm). With these "weeping" comedies sentimentality triumphed over satire; laughter was drowned in moralizing cant.

Upon such a scene, where laughter had been banished for decades, Beaumarchais arrived. The circumstances he faced were the same circumstances Oliver Goldsmith brought to the attention of the London public in his "Essay on the Theatre: A Comparison between Laughing and Sentimental Comedy" (1773). Though this brief piece, which argues for the former mode, appeared a decade or so before the premiere of *Le Mariage,* it offers many parallels with the theatrical history surrounding Beaumarchais's stage works. In fact, a few years earlier, in a preface to *The Good-Natured Man* (1768), Goldsmith had looked disparagingly across the Channel: "French comedy is now become so very elevated and sentimental, that it has not only banished humor and Molière from the stage, but it has banished all spectators too." In the "Essay" Goldsmith laments the lost taste for the rollicking comedy of Congreve, Wycherly, and Vanbrugh, much as Bachaumont felt the lost taste for Molière. He fears the new sentimental comedy may eventually cause the "art of laughing" to vanish. His rueful description of the recipe for a sentimental play is worth quoting in full:

> It is only sufficient to raise the Characters a little, to deck out the Hero with a Ribband, or give the Heroine a Title; then to put an Insipid Dialogue, without Character or Humour, into their mouths, give them mighty good hearts, very fine clothes, furnish a new sett of Scenes, make a Pathetic Scene or two, with a sprinkling of tender melancholy Conversation through the whole, and there is no doubt but all the Ladies will cry, and all the Gentlemen applaud.

The response in England to Goldsmith's challenge was his own *She Stoops to Conquer* (1773) and Sheridan's *The School for Scandal* (1777). In France Beaumarchais did his part with *Le Barbier de Seville* (1775) and *Le Mariage de Figaro* (1784).

Though Beaumarchais was not able fully to escape the influence of weeping comedies, he was the first to make a conscious effort to avoid their hackneyed features. Taking his cue from Diderot, who favored the exclusion of burlesque at the comic extreme, and the marvelous and magical at the tragic extreme, Beaumarchais evolved the concept of the *drame sérieuse,* which he elaborated on in his preface to *Eugénie.* This essay encompasses the central theorems of the new, more natural dramaturgy. It urges the redirection of attention from gods and kings to more humane situations: "The genuine interest of the heart, its true expression, is of course always that of a man to a man, and not between a man and a king." Inspired by the Encyclopedists, the playwright sought a dramatic style that would "show men absolutely such as they are." This encouraged a more economical style and led Beaumarchais to reject the heaving bombast of tragedy and the effete badinage of salon comedy. Only after the artificial clutter was swept away, he felt, could the "genuine interests of the heart" emerge in a believable context:

> Serious theater admits only a simple style, without flowers or garlands; it ought to derive all of its beauty from the depth, texture, interest and course of action . . . Its true eloquence is that of situations; and it must be colored in language that is vital, urgent, concise, tumultuous, and true in its passions—far from the influence of the poet's caesura and the affectations of rhyme. [I. p. 22]

Beaumarchais helped drama return to the prose and speech men actually use. And he revitalized the "art of laughing" on the French stage. This very intention he expressed in a letter to Baron de Breteuil concerning *Le Barbier,* saying he hoped to "return to the stage the genuine gaiety we once knew, combining it with the subtle, delicate, airy tone of the humor of our own day." French audiences, and soon audiences elsewhere (twelve German translations of *Le Mariage* were circulating within a year), responded enthusiastically. *Le Mariage* enjoyed the greatest success of any French play of the century, running for sixty-eight successive performances and grossing a third of a million livres.

The aesthetic revolution that Beaumarchais achieved on the legitimate stage Mozart was destined to participate in for opera. By a significant coincidence, Mozart did this by turning away from the "pompous trains, the swelling phrase, and the unnatural rant" (to use Goldsmith's description of heroic tragedy) of opera seria. After having seen his seria *Idomeneo* through a difficult gestation, he wrote to his father on 7 May 1783 of a new direction he wanted to pursue: "The most essential thing is that on the whole the story should be really *comic:* and, if possible, he [the librettist Varesco] ought to introduce two equally good female parts, one of these to be *seria,* the other *mezzo carattere,* but both parts quite equal *in importance and excellence.* The third female character, however, may be entirely buffa, and so may all the male ones." Mozart appears not to have completed an opera with Varesco according to this plan. What we do know is that less than a year later, on 27 April 1784, *Le Nozze di*

Figaro received its premiere, sweeping Europe thereafter. We might well see in Mozart's specifications just quoted the dim outlines of what was to be his next opera: the seria figure is the Countess, Susanna is *mezzo carattere* (and both roles are equally important), and buffo does impinge upon all the male roles. Mozart eventually wrote the opera he had felt within him in May 1783.

The first intimation of opera seria's mortality was Pergolesi's *Serva Padrona* (1733). This comic one-acter for three singers was eventually to ignite at mid-century in France the War of the Buffoons between partisans of seria and the new Italian comedy. With *Le Nozze*, however, the fate of opera seria was sealed—just as surely as the storming of the Bastille sealed the fate of Louis XVI. If, as Danton is said to have remarked, Beaumarchais's Figaro killed the nobility, Mozart's Figaro certainly had a hand in the demise of opera seria. This genre, like the great Baroque gardens with their expansive promenades, grandiose sight lines, and ordered monumentality, was subjected to a comic revolution similar to that represented by the Augustan taste for the "natural" garden—carefully landscaped, more human in proportions, less static and regular. Seria opera is, in a sense, a bravura sequence of ornate, greatly enlarged "frames" selected judiciously from the plot; we see only selected moments and are made to pause over them for three, five, eight minutes. Seria librettists like Metastasio were primarily interested in reaching moments of stasis where emotions could be expanded upon and elaborate similes disgorged. Movement of plot or development of character was not a pressing concern.

Beaumarchais, however, pressured Mozart to fit his music to a play that is constantly in motion. The dramatist saw the "true eloquence" of his art in situations and thrust his characters into them, not with a poet's ear for fine sounds and diction, but to see what they would do. This put Mozart on a treadmill demanding consistent musical movement. (It is worth noting that the most seria-like numbers in the opera, *Dove sono* and *Deh vieni, non tardar*, are just the ones that have no basis in the lines of the play.) *Le Mariage*, with its supple and sinuous action and sudden inflations and deflations, required from Mozart not merely movement but a distinctive sense of comic pacing. As Rosen so well describes, it was Mozart's good fortune that the conventions of the classical style, together with his own genius, made him capable of responding to this challenge. And so was produced the first great comic antidote to the Metastasian opera seria.

That Mozart was able in *Le Nozze* to expose the comic potential of the classical style is due in part to the innovative qualities of the Beaumarchais play. The playwright was his own fondest admirer, and his description of *Le Mariage* convinces us just how successfully Mozart translated its felicities:

> [In *Le Mariage*] I have attempted what no man of letters has heretofore dared: a play that combines moralities of general effect and of detail spread on a sea of inalterable gaiety, a rather vivacious dialogue whose facility hides its workmanship, an effortlessly spun out intrigue where art conceals art and which knots and unravels itself ceaselessly through a crowd of comic situations, and piquant, varied tableaux which sustain without tiring the audience throughout the three-and-a-half-hour-long performance. [II. p. 38]

Mozart, too, was forced to write an unprecedentedly long opera for his time: it runs about the same time as the play. Its first performance in Italy was even split into two evenings. But Mozart must have discerned in the flurry of situations that knot and unwind the potential applications of his own style. With *Le Mariage*—that something "really comic" he had been searching for—he and Da Ponte set to work.

Le Mariage *and* Le Nozze: *What Da Ponte and Mozart Did*

STRUCTURE

What must startle the reader of *Le Mariage* who is already familiar with Mozart's opera is the latter's faithfulness to the structure of the original. Interestingly, what was long felt to be *Le Nozze*'s weakest act, the third, is problematic for reasons related to the only major change Mozart and Da Ponte made in the play. The situation is complicated but worth setting out briefly, since it shows how the minor practical headaches of producing opera can have major and lasting implications.

The problem arose when Da Ponte cut the long courtroom scene in Act III of the play in which the case of Marceline *v.* Figaro is heard. This was wise, for it is a highly digressive scene, born no doubt of Beaumarchais's long personal history of litigation. Cutting it was really the only hope for keeping the opera within the bounds of reasonable length. The excision caused a new difficulty: how to give a sense of elapsed time between the Count's announcement that he will hold a judicial session and the rendering of a decision. This matter has worried many since then, for in the score and all printed versions of *Le Nozze* the courtroom battle must take place during the Count's recitative and aria *Vedrò mentr'io sospiro* (about six minutes).

Recently Robert Moberly and Christopher Raeburn have cast light on Mozart's resolution of the problem—and how he was foiled at the last minute.[14] Moberly and Raeburn suggest that Mozart intended to cover the passage of time for the courtroom battle by inserting a scene with no literal basis in the play—the Countess's recitative and aria *Dove sono*. This original order can be shown thus:

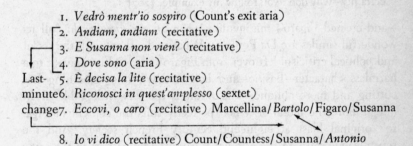

1. *Vedrò mentr'io sospiro* (Count's exit aria)
2. *Andiam, andiam* (recitative)
3. *E Susanna non vien?* (recitative)
4. *Dove sono* (aria)

Last- 5. *È decisa la lite* (recitative)
minute 6. *Riconosci in quest'amplesso* (sextet)
change 7. *Eccovi, o caro* (recitative) Marcellina/*Bartolo*/Figaro/Susanna

8. *Io vi dico* (recitative) Count/Countess/Susanna/*Antonio*

Why do we find numbers two through four nestled between seven and eight? Moberly and Raeburn convincingly demonstrate that this is because the same singer doubled in the parts of Bartolo and Antonio in the first performance. At the last minute, presumably, it was discovered that the singer had no time to change from the doctor's to the gardener's costume. Realizing that nothing else in the preceding action was expendable except the interpolated aria *Dove sono,* Mozart probably decided to make the obvious change—though he must have sensed the awkwardness this would create. The immediate problems of performance won out over an otherwise nice solution to a typical problem of the operatic translator: how to make a large cut as delicately as possible. Of course, the original order is preferable when there are two singers for the roles of Bartolo and Antonio.

Aside from the one large change, Da Ponte altered little of importance. Of course, it was necessary to tone down for the Austrian Emperor passages which might have offended an aristocracy that had been warned of Beaumarchais's political barbs. Da Ponte wrote to Joseph II assuring him that he had "left out and shortened whatever might offend the refinement and decorum of an entertainment at which Your Majesty presides." Figaro's famous tirade in Act V was the first to go, but even here it is fascinating to see how Da Ponte and Mozart retained something of its essence. The tirade begins and ends upon the domestic note of Suzanne's infidelity. Da Ponte took the cue from this, in combination with a subsequent speech—

> You foolish husbands who rely on hired investigators and spend months struggling with your suspicions and never arriving at any certainty—why don't you follow my example? [207]

—and created Figaro's misogynist *Aprite un po' quegl'occhi* (all its wonderful similes are Da Ponte's). What to do, then, with the social and political criticism left over from Figaro's tirade? First, give it to a harmless character—Basilio—and boil it down into something less cutting and more oblique. The result is the wry little fable of *In quegli anni,* the moral of which perfectly suits the content of Figaro's original blast at eighteenth-century French society. And the seven-league satire of the original is captured by Mozart in the aria's marvelous musical theatrics. It is a shame that *In quegli anni* is nearly always cut in performance.

Something, too, must be said of the ways Mozart and Da Ponte accommodated set-piece conventions to the play's incessant pace. In some cases the dramatic action and an appropriate number parallel each other perfectly. The action of the "slanging-match between two angry women" (114) blends quite naturally into the Act I Marcellina-Susanna duet. Mozart's perpetual-motion *Aprite, presto aprite* is a perfect accompaniment to the tense moment when Cherubino leaps from the balcony. Even the astonishing Act II Finale, which grows steadily in distinct modules from duet to trio to quartet to quintet to the final septet, accomplishes all of Beaumarchais's comic crises in about twenty minutes, the same running time as the play.

Because set-piece opera must develop in a modular fashion, it is of necessity unable to match the continuity of normal dramatic dialogue. The miracle of *Le Nozze* is that the constraints of set-pieces are so little apparent or, rather, do not seem to hinder the course of action. One reason is that Mozart and Da Ponte were able to localize multiple events or gradually developed themes in single arias. What may seem an action-stopper is, if we know the original play, often an action summarizer. One example is the Count's violent explosion of frustration in Act III, *Vedrò mentr'io sospiro*. Throughout the action the Comte is embarrassed by, as he says, "some evil genius" who keeps thwarting his plans. (We know the genius is a comic one.) His aria, then, comes as a credible explosion as the frustrations of the day wear him down.

We also find the gathering of plot threads in the Countess's two arias. The first, *Porgi amor,* results from Suzanne's mere hint that her mistress is a neglected wife, and it is—Mozart's concession to the pace of the play—left without the rapid second section that normally follows a larghetto aria. The sorrow of the Comtesse, Mozart and Da Ponte must have realized, is the foundation of the play's impact. Against her sad situation all the comedy of *Le Mariage* is balanced. In the play the Comte explains to his wife (disguised as Suzanne): "Our wives think they do all that is necessary in loving us. Once it's settled that they love us—they go on doing so. *How* they go on! (Assuming they do love us!) They are so compliant, so acquiescent" (206). Though it has no literal basis in the play, *Dove sono* is still necessary. For it shows the Countess making the alleged "mistake" the Comte here complains of. *Dove sono* displays her anguish and thereby amplifies the disturbing undertones Beaumarchais sprinkled throughout his play. Mozart could well have found his inspiration for the Countess's bittersweet role in Beaumarchais's own explanatory note on her character: "Torn between two conflicting emotions she should display only a restrained tenderness and very moderate degree of resentment, above all nothing which might impair her amiable and virtuous character in the eyes of the audience."

Marcellina's Act IV aria, *Il capro e la capretta,* is a third example of Da Ponte's ability to summarize character change in one stroke. Marceline's role in the play is problematic (as the very first actors realized), changing from a comic butt in Act I to a sympathetic, truth-speaking figure after she recognizes Figaro as a long-lost son. If the change seems "operatic" in its abruptness, the playwright is to blame. Marcellina's aria has a provenance similar to Basilio's *In quegli anni.* Marceline is given her own brief day in court on behalf of the feminine sex (comparable in some ways to Figaro's tirade), and what she says must have struck a 1784 audience as daring: "Even in the more exalted walks of life you [men] accord us women no more than a derisory consideration. In a state of servitude behind the alluring pretences of respect, treated as children where our possessions are concerned we are punished as responsible adults where our faults are in question!" (176). These sentiments—worthy of a Women's Liberationist—Da Ponte set in another of his fabular condensations in *Il capro.* Still, it is faithful to Marceline's rhetorical flourish and the point Beaumarchais makes through her, namely, that men are a cruel and arrogant race.

Another group of arias is structurally unexceptionable simply because Beaumarchais's own speeches or his own *moments musicales* inspired them. This is true of *Non più andrai*—

> Good-bye, my dear Chérubin. You are going to a very different life. By Jove, yes! No more running round all day with the girls, no more cream buns and custard tarts; no more 'tig' and blind-man's-bluff. Soldiers of the Queen, by Gad! Just think of 'em, weather-beaten and ragged-arsed, weighed down with their muskets, right turn, left wheel, forward march! On to the field of glory and no flinching on the way—unless a round of shot . . . [126]

—and Cherubino's breathless *Non so più:*

> I don't know what's coming over me. For some time I have had such a strange feeling within me. My pulse quickens at the very sight of a woman. The word love makes my heart go pit-a-pat. In fact, I feel such a need to say "I love you" to someone that I catch myself saying it to myself walking in the park, to your Mistress, to you, to the trees, to the clouds, to the wind which wafts them away with my fleeting words. [117]

Beaumarchais's first theatrical success, *Le Barbier,* was originally intended as an opera libretto, so it is hardly surprising that he should have been eager to intersperse musical events in *Le Mariage.* This desire was of course conditioned by the popular tradition in France of the *comédie mêlée d'ariettes*—comedy with arias interspersed—where most of the text was spoken. Chérubin's song amounts to eight quatrains set to a French folk tune. This is pronounced by the Comtesse "naïve and sentimental"—just the qualities Mozart invests in *Voi che sapete.* The bridal festivities of Act IV in the play were also meant to be a musical event, specifically requiring the bland peasant tunes and fandango Mozart gives us in the opera.

This leaves, then, a few numbers that are without basis in the play—though one need not seek far to justify their presence in the opera. In the opening pages of *Le Mariage* poor Bartholo can scarcely get a word in edgewise, so skillful is the repartee of Figaro and Marceline. But scattered phrases ("incorrigible babbler," "worthless scoundrel") clearly suggest he is anxious to get even with Figaro. Given the chance, he would surely burst into the harmless bombast of the vengeance aria Mozart gives him. The drollery of *La vendetta* —its effect is of a gasbag noisily exhausting itself—is all the more delicious when juxtaposed with the genuinely malevolent feelings of vengeance expressed in *Se vuol ballare,* which just precedes it.

Some puzzlement surrounds Barbarina's *L'ho perduta* in Act IV. True, Fanchette (Beaumarchais's original name) does open the play's final act, but her concern to get food to Chérubin is far from her operatic counterpart's worry about the lost pin. Even more odd is the self-consciously affective tone of the music—the only number in the opera that remains entirely in the minor mode. Is it merely padding—an *aria di sorbette* during which the audience can relax its attention? This raises a problem of authorial intention of the sort which has puzzled readers of the play. For instance, was the recognition scene (*Riconosci in quest'amplesso* in the opera) meant to be taken seriously or as a parody of the ubiquitous recognition scenes in sentimental comedies? Perhaps we should take our answer from the music Mozart provided for the scene, which is very tongue in cheek.[15] Might not the same be true of Barbarina's aria? Surely the bathos expended over a lost pin, in an opera where much more serious things are in danger of being lost, is meant as parody. Surely this little affectedly purple patch must remind one of the mock-epic irony of "The Rape of the Lock."

Paradoxically, the most obviously interpolated aria in the entire opera, Susanna's *Deh vieni, non tardar,* is musically and dramatically the most indispensable. Da Ponte and Mozart took their cue from this brief exchange:

> *Suzanne:* Your Ladyship is trembling. Are you cold?
> *Comtesse:* The evening is damp. I'm going to go inside.
> *Suzanne:* If Your Ladyship doesn't need me I'll take the air a little under the trees. [203]

Musically, the aria provides a moment of repose before the complex denouement that follows. It functions as would the slow movement of a Mozartean concerto, which is usually succeeded by an eventful, propulsive finale. It also provides a necessarily soothing moment that looks backward to ease the harshness of Figaro's vicious *Aprite un po' quegl'occhi* and forward to prefigure the nobility of the Countess's pardon. And, of course, it sets a glorious nocturnal mood (which a stage designer must always try to match visually).[16] Lastly, the sheer eloquence of the aria convinces us that the follies of this day are to be ruled finally by the *deus amor,* not by an evil genius but by a comic one who not only brings the characters to see themselves as they really are, but also brings them together in a quadruple marriage celebration.

Both in small and in large, *Le Nozze* is loyal to its source. One scarcely need add that the play is full of small comic gestures. Its métier is verbal wit and its most piercing effects are often the result of fleeting innuendo, squelch, or riposte. It would be a tedious catalogue that attempted to point out the many instances where Mozart translated into music what one nineteenth-century critic of *Le Mariage* called the "quaint snip-snap" of its dialogue.[17] Suffice it to say many of the tinier verbal felicities of the play find expression in Mozart's music. At best one can point to a few instances where musical humor works hand in glove with Beaumarchais.

Foremost is Mozart's ability to capture a comic stance with the utmost economy. The opening of the Act I trio provides three ex-

Example 2

amples of this: the Count's salient yet nearly speechless fury is caught in the rising but not really potent music accompanying his first words (EX. 2); Basilio's toadying politeness gets a musical setting that fairly trumpets his hypocrisy (EX. 3); and Susanna's vocal line flutters anxiously in search of a way out of her dilemma at the line *"Che ruina! me meschina!."* Mozart's ability to capture the comic rage so often operating behind sham formality in *Le Mariage* is an important aspect of the opera's pleasures. How he controls comic fury and allows it to escape is exemplified in the initial Marcellina-Susanna battle of words and in *Se vuol ballare*.

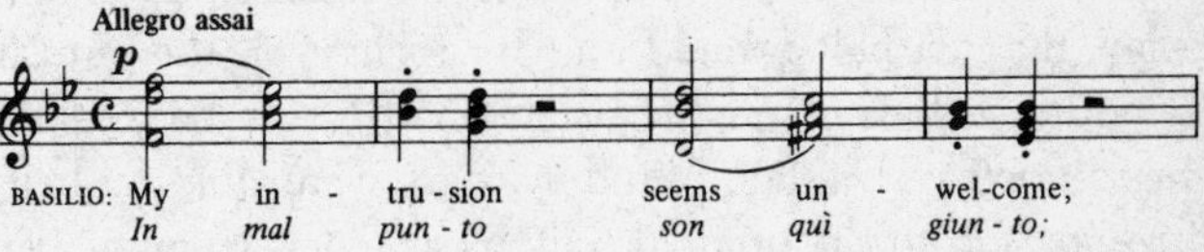

Example 3

Arch musical inflections also help Mozart achieve his witticisms. Much of the comedy is sparked by the imperious gesture, and Mozart captures such gestures often—sometimes with vocal leaps such as when the Count warns of his coming revenge (EX. 4). Often

Example 4

Mozart must take the edge off the possible seriousness of a comic situation, and this he frequently does with staccato markings and trilled notes, for instance, in the second Figaro-Susanna duet in Act I, in the middle section of *Se vuol ballare,* in the Count's interrogation in Act II (*Conoscete, signor Figaro*), and in *Aprite un po' quegl'occhi.*

Finally, Mozart's orchestration provides delicious moments. Aside from the well-known horns that announce the cuckhold at the end of Figaro's Act IV aria, there is the ominous staccato horn motif hovering in the subtly revolutionary *Se vuol ballare,* the giddy string motif of Bartolo's windy revenge aria, and the airy play of the strings in *Non più andrai* reflecting the carefree life Cherubino must leave. But Mozart's surest sign of innuendo is the bassoon, which comments upon the stage action at so many of the unforgettable comic moments —in Susanna's aria coaching Cherubino in his female disguise, at her exit from the closet, when the Count begs pardon in Act II, and in the archly mechanical duet in Act III in which the Count makes his assignation with Susanna.

The overall contours of play and opera are essentially the same. As in the play, the first half (Acts I and II) focuses on the punishment of the Count's jealousy, and the second half (Acts III and IV) exposes his infidelity. Da Ponte and Mozart were able to heighten, emphasize, or add to the original only what seems from our vantage point of hindsight necessary for the full experience of Beaumarchais's intentions. That they were able to achieve this within the context of operatic conventions makes their success all the more remarkable.

BEAUMARCHAIS'S CHARACTERS AND MOZARTEAN EQUIPOISE

We have already had occasion to observe Mozart's gift for sustaining an equipoise in his musical effects, and that the variety of moods and oscillating emotions in *Le Mariage* forced him to exploit this gift. When the Comte ponders the strange effects of irresolution in Act III, he becomes lost in the same quandary we in the audience must feel about much of the play: "I don't get the thread of it all . . . there's something not clear somewhere . . . How do I come to be involved in this preposterous entanglement . . . It just shows where not knowing one's own mind leads one" (158). Brid-oison (distilled by Mozart and Da Ponte into the role of Don Curzio) echoes this bafflement at play's end when he is asked for his opinion of the events: "All I can say is—I don't know what to think!"

The crux of the play—and most comedy—is the bafflement of plans and intentions, as Figaro announces at the opening of Act IV: "That's the way things are: one works, one schemes, one arranges things in one way: fortune determines them otherwise" (181). The characters in the play are comic, and so many of its crises arise, because there is intrinsic ambiguity in their actions. Dual interpretations shadow virtually everything in the play. Marriage—the play's institutional focus—is a puzzlement, as Bazile suggests: "Of all seriious things marriage [is] the most farcical." Marceline says of women, "our sex is ardent but timid" and finds men equally anomalous, "proud and terrible simpletons." The play even leaves us with mixed feelings about its class structure: it remains strong and in the end unimpaired, but we cannot help feeling that *something* in Sevillian society is falling apart. *Le Mariage* is, in short, a play where the comic villains and butts sometimes merit less than our scorn and where the comic heroes merit less than our complete admiration. Our allegiances are constantly subverted by the unexpected.

An intentional ambivalence in characterization is also important in play and opera. It hangs about Suzanne, as the Comte explains why he is attracted to her: "More variety perhaps, more liveliness of manner, some indefinable quality that constitutes charm: an occasional rebuff perhaps? How do I know?" And in his note on Chérubin, Beaumarchais requires a similar ambiguity: "The basis of his character is an undefined and restless desire." Even more crucial is the ambivalence built into the roles of the Comte, Comtesse, and Figaro. These are worth examining in detail.

A production of *Le Nozze* succeeds or fails insofar as the role of the Count is explored in the fullness of its ambiguity. We must leave a performance of the opera feeling, as does Marceline, that "one doesn't know just how to describe the Comte." For he is neither a complete villain nor a bungler for whom—like Don Giovanni—nothing on this particular day seems to go right. He is not a tragic character lost in the comedy of *Le Nozze,* nor is he purely a comic butt.

He is cruel, but we cannot really feel his cruelty is entirely willful. He is arrogant, but tradition has helped him to be so. He sins but never enjoys the fruits of sin. He retains some of the levity of Almaviva in *Le Barbier,* and yet there is more than a little of Giovanni's evil hubris in him.[18] Beaumarchais knew the Comte presented a crucial problem for his impersonator, and he knew how important the role was in achieving the right tone for the play as a whole. His note on the role applies equally well to the operatic Count:

> Comte Almaviva should be played with great dignity yet with grace and affability. The corruption of his heart should in no way detract from the elegance of his manners. It was customary *in those days* for great noblemen to treat any design upon the fair sex in a spirit of levity. The part is all the more difficult to play well in that it is always the unsympathetic role. [II. p. 44]

The baritone who approaches the role in this way will have solved many of this role's traps of interpretation. He will also be sensitive to the ambiguities Mozart invests in his music. The Count's role is a mixture of evil moments and droll ones—malevolent power succeeded by comic impotence. If the operatic Count takes his evil bluster too seriously and allows the posturing of a Scarpia or Pizarro to overwhelm his performance, the audience will exult rather than laugh over his downfall. If, on the other hand, he plays the role in a buffoonish, Falstaffian manner, the comic letdowns will strike us as trivial. The challenge is to keep the balance between these extremes.

If the comic moments depend first of all upon the Count, the serious moments are related most strongly to the Countess. Beaumarchais himself thought this the play's most difficult role. She is the gravest, most ruminative character; every now and again the action catches her deep in thought, abstracted from the goings-on around her. No wonder a respected tragedienne was chosen for the premiere. Before we even meet the Comtesse we have been told that she is a neglected wife (by Suzanne), that she is "listless, languishing, pining away" (by Marceline), and that she is "noble, beautiful, but how unapproachable" (by Chérubin). She is clearly the same Rosine who asked Comte Almaviva in *Le Barbier,* "Isn't that the most dreadful fate imaginable—to hate when one knows that love is what one is made for?" That she is still "made for loving" Mozart makes very clear. What makes the role challenging, then, is that the plot requires this dignified personage to become an intriguer—something not only below her station but also a painful admission of her sad plight. Beaumarchais sensed the only way out of the dilemma was in acting the part with a "restrained tenderness" and "moderate resentment"—the two adjectives of equipoise must be close to the heart of any successful interpretation of the role. To assess the Countess fully we must consider the two arias central, of course, but we must keep in mind her vigorous theatricality in the Act II Finale, the composure she retains in the painful disguised tryst with her husband, as well as her surprisingly businesslike pardon at the end of the opera. We must be able to see in Mozart's Countess a woman who can give in to her emotion or keep it in firm control as occasion demands. Of all the opera's characters she is closest to mastering her situation and to seeing it in context. She is consequently the least comic character on stage.

It is a commonplace that Figaro was an autobiographical shadow of Beaumarchais himself. A recent biography is even entitled *The Real Figaro*. La Harpe's contemporary description of Beaumarchais approximates what we expect in a good stage Figaro: "His face and voice were equally lively, lit up by eyes full of fire, with as much expression in accent and look as of delicacy in the smile. Above all, he had a sort of assurance inspired by the consciousness of his own powers, and which he knew how to communicate to others." But there is more to Figaro than the mere self-confidence and verve Rossini's Figaro in *Il Barbiere di Siviglia* might lead us to expect. As Robert Niklaus summarizes, Figaro represented a crucial moment in theatrical history when one tradition was dying and another gestating. The equipoise of his character derives from this:

> Figaro is the last of the valets, the inheritor of countless generations of clowns, but the first incarnation of the man of the Revolution, the individual bent on self-betterment and without prejudice or scruple, the challenger of the establishment, and the shining apostle of the free man who makes his own destiny as best he can. A man of infinite resource, he appears to be dangerous, yet is deeply human and ultimately attractive.[19]

If *Le Nozze* fails anywhere as a translation, it is in not fully capturing this brilliant ambivalence of the original Figaro. Da Ponte was obliged, perhaps, to forsake too many of Figaro's devastating retorts, not to mention much of his social criticism. In the opera we must look rather too carefully for signs of the temperament of the revolutionary individualist. Fortunately, Mozart—who once wrote to his father, "I may not always say what I like, I may at any rate think it"—was able now and then to express Figaro's menacing turn of mind through music. One thinks of the ominous, conspiratorial strings that accompany the recitative preceding *Se vuol ballare*. The aria itself is a marvelous account of furious energy held just barely within the decorum of the minuet. Figaro's veneer soon wears thin and brute power exerts itself through the piano attempts at reserve. Disconcerting, too, is the haunting horn phrase that adds much nervous energy to the aria. This sense of loose energy is heightened by the trills in its presto section, which climaxes in the powerful moment when Figaro suddenly reverts to the stilted formality of the minuet. Aside from his Act IV outburst, an entirely domestic matter, Figaro's purpose in the opera is largely that of master intriguer. This makes it difficult to retain Beaumarchais's original balance between Figaro's philosophical bitterness and acerbic wit on one hand and his levity of spirit on the other. The playwright was concerned that the interpreter not favor the latter over the former—

> I warn the interpreter of Figaro . . . not to play the role with too great a frivolity. For that could make a farce of the work. Figaro is a bad character, though in his expressions delicate, cunning, well-educated—but never a jokester.

—but the emphasis of the Da Ponte libretto makes this difficult. We have in *Le Nozze* a more lightweight and less charismatic title figure, perhaps because in the opera Figaro is far too preoccupied with Susanna and his imminent marriage to indulge in the philosophical asides, critical digressions, and sheer love of witty exchange in the play.

COMIC RHYTHM: THE FINALE TO ACT II

The follies of the day on which *Le Mariage* takes place are numerous, and each folly is prepared by a brief span of action in which combustible comic ingredients (such as the Count's suspicious nature, the machinations of a servant smarter than his master, and the sudden intrusion of an outsider) are packed together and exploded at just the right moment.

To see how Mozart translated this procedure of serial complication and denouement into music, we can turn to the Finale of Act II. It is not merely the dramatic heart of the opera but also one of the most beautifully realized comic scenes in all opera. As well, the Finale is a supreme instance of almost literal translation from its source and exemplifies how comic energies are gathered up and released through musical means. A schematic rendering of the Finale will clarify the following analysis:

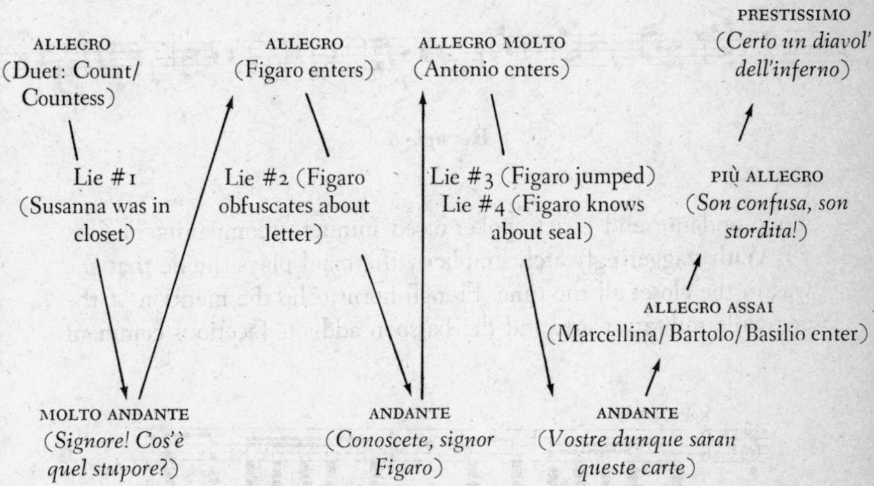

The Finale opens in allegro dudgeon, with the Count threatening, crowbar in hand, to break down the door hiding Cherubino. An insistent rising phrase, made even more bristling by forte-piano and staccato markings, accompanies his menacing gestures. The Countess tries to calm him, but the quick tempo gives the lie to her soothing legato line. In desperation she turns to the truth, but in comedy the truth often gets one nowhere. The duet develops erratically, the Count's blind jealousy and his wife's fear epitomized in a giddy roller-coaster woodwind phrase (EX. 5). Nothing stops a comic plot so

Example 5

quickly as a Big Lie, and this happens as the Count and Countess reach a climactic impasse. In a few bars Mozart contrives for all the furious energy to vanish into thin air as Susanna issues from the closet (EX. 6). Mozart reflects this sudden deflation in a relaxation to

Example 6

molto andante and a new poker-faced minuet accompaniment (EX. 7). With staggeringly arch simplicity the maid plays the lie that she was in the closet all the time. French horns echo the mention of the erstwhile military page, and the bassoon adds its facetious comment

Example 7

on the Count's mystification. Before long, however, the Count recovers his balance. As his skepticism mounts the tempo escalates to allegro, and a restless phrase establishes a new sense of nervously mounting comic energy (EX. 8). The following passage shows a more controlled elegance as the Countess warms to the task of taking advantage of her husband's sudden deflation (EX. 9). The trio ex-

Example 8

Example 9

pands on this wafting theme until a climactic unison passage (*"Da questo momento"*) where the verbal fencing reaches a standoff.

The next section of the Finale opens with Figaro's announcement of preparations for his wedding. The Count quickly imposes upon Figaro's allegro verve, for his doubts have still not been put to rest. The situation becomes tentative again for all concerned, and Mozart translates this into the andante interrogation about the letter that had sent the Count to his wife's chambers in the first place. The Count's vocal line reeks with false formality. The mechanical nonchalance of the underlying semiquavers and the trills and staccati of this passage belie the ulterior motives of his line of questioning.

Figaro and the Count face each other off (while Susanna and the Countess add their own nervous observations) until another unison impasse is reached, this exploding into a furious allegro molto at the entrance of the irate gardener. As the truth begins to impinge upon the tissue of falsehoods, the pace quickens. When Antonio explains his trampled plants, the Count's brutal force and the nervous tension caused by the new disclosures alternate in the orchestra (EX. 10). The following rush of triplets ends only with the third Big Lie

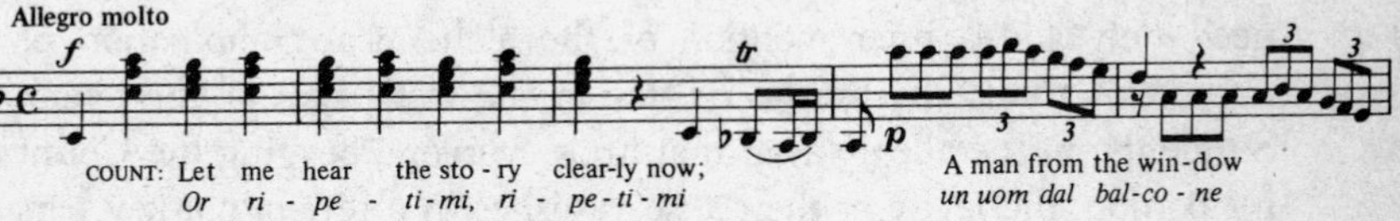

Example 10

of the Finale, Figaro's assertion that he had leapt from the balcony. Just as with Susanna's exit from the closet, the comic rhythm collapses into an andante "holding pattern"; the music nearly stops as the characters all cope with Figaro's daring falsehood. A fourth lie is necessitated when Antonio produces some papers dropped in the leap from the balcony. The ensuing interrogation is laid over an impassive staccato phrase that seems to tick off the time Figaro needs to answer for the contents of the papers (EX. 11). Each of the characters now on stage is avoiding giving his or her true feelings away, and Mozart's wry music captures just how tentatively and close to the vest each is behaving.

Example 11

Figaro's deceit keeps the events in control (that is, at a deliberate tempo) until the last section of the Finale brings another mini-catastrophe—the entrance of Marcellina, Basilio, and Bartolo demanding satisfaction of Figaro's nuptial contract with Marcellina. As the stage becomes crowded and the situation more knotted, the musical pace likewise increases, at first from the piquant andante to a propulsive allegro assai. When the Count finally announces a session in court, the tempo rises to più allegro as plotters become victims and vice versa. The Finale plays itself out in typical buffo fashion from this point, registering one manic prestissimo burst of energy in its last moments.

The pages of this Finale are among the greatest in comic opera. To give a sense of Mozart's overall achievement in *Le Nozze,* one need only add a brief mention of the alchemical combination of tragic and comic rhythm he creates in the last pages of the opera. Suddenly, in the allegro assai that finds everyone begging the Count for pardon, the levity of the music vanishes in a few minor-key bars at the Countess's words *Almeno per loro.* This deliquesces into the

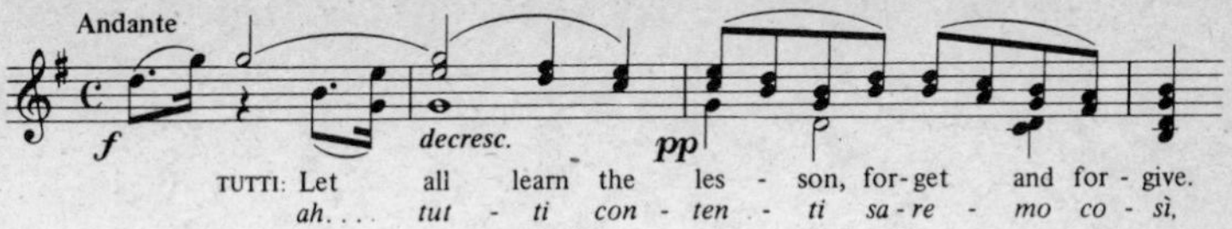

Example 12

noble andante of *Contessa perdono*. In the gorgeous reclining phrases of the following benedictory passage (EX 12), with its plangent harmonies and hushed seriousness (it is to be sung in a whisper), is the denouement of the tragic side of the plot. Then, in the opera's most magical moment, the solemnity transforms delicately into a final joyous allegro assai (EX. 13). As in each of the tiny episodes in *Le Nozze,* the comic genius is reaffirmed and ascendant at the final curtain.

Example 13

From a musician's standpoint, Rosen found the essence of the classical style in "the symmetrical resolution of opposing forces." In dramatic terms, too, *Le Nozze* represents the symmetrical resolution of the comic and the tragic forces that have been at work throughout the action. The last minutes of the opera are a supreme example of this equipoise. We leave the opera having wept—if we weep at all—tears of joy and sadness.

four

MARIA STUARDA & LUCIA DI LAMMERMOOR

Hail to thee, blithe Spirit!
Bird thou never wert,
That from Heaven, or near it,
Pourest thy full heart
In profuse strains of unpremeditated art.

Higher still and higher
From the earth thou springest
Like a cloud of fire;
The blue deep thou wingest,
And singing still dost soar, and soaring ever singest.

Shelley, "*To a Skylark*"

Schiller, Scott, and the Blithe Spirit of Bel Canto

If Romanticism meant anything (and it meant many things, depending upon which scholars one consults), it meant escape from the bonds of neo-Classicism on one hand or realism on the other, as well as escape from the customary restraints of society. It meant the ascendancy of subjective emotional experience over rational experience and a keener development of and relish in the artist's own individuality. Romanticism was a flight into the unique and individual soul. To express the agony and ecstasy of this escape Romantic poets, traveling as Keats put it on "the viewless wings of Poesy," frequently relied on the imagery of birds and their soaring escape into the empyrean. Keats found an image for his spiritual emancipation in the "full-throated ease" of the nightingale. Shelley compared himself as a poet to the skylark,

Singing hymns unbidden,
Till the world is wrought
To sympathy with hopes and fears it heedeth not.

Talk now of bel canto, however, and the average person will almost surely conjure a mindlessly warbling songbird whose art is all too premeditated. This ungainly aviary image is our inheritance from generations of detractors and satirists of opera. It is an unfortunate one because it makes us forget the positive side of the image Romantic poets so famously celebrated. Bel canto opera can also be inhabited by the sleek, soaring, and affectingly beautiful creatures evoked in Shelley's "To a Skylark" or Keats's quintessential Romantic poem, "Ode to a Nightingale." One may condescendingly imagine that Jenny Lind, the Swedish Nightingale, and her bel canto colleagues were admired as so many songbirds. But it would not be amiss, as a way of counterbalancing this popular myth, to read Keats's Ode as a plausible encomium for bel canto vocalism. This poem, at the very least, goes far to explain what enthusiasts find so attractive in operas of the bel canto genre.

One may in short approach bel canto in two ways. The first is with reserve, clinically—perhaps with the pathetic image of a caged bird in mind. The result is bound to be a somewhat unpleasant satiety such as Delacroix experienced at a performance of *Lucia di Lammermoor:* "Ornament takes up all the room there is in this music; you get nothing but festoons and astragals: I call it sensual music and only that; it is designed just to tickle the ear for a moment." Many cannot abide bel canto opera for the same sober reason. Such people will always feel a little guilty in the presence of what one writer has called "naked, ear-delighting, absolute, melodic melody—a delicious meaningless sound."[1]

For those attracted to bel canto, on the other hand, its pleasures are not so shallow or ephemeral. What one might call the Shelleyan or Keatsian approach to the genre is to give oneself over to the music of the skylark, nightingale, or coloratura singer—to resign oneself to the pleasures of elaborate, sensual, even sometimes meaningless beauty. The true bel canto devotee feels himself at one with Keats in his exclamation: "O for a life of Sensations rather than of thoughts!" This bias requires a certain will to self-indulgence, which is after all a crucial aspect of the Romantic aesthetic generally and that of bel canto especially. It requires an ability merely to revel—just as Shelley revels in the skylark's "rain of melody," "harmonious madness," and "triumphant chaunt." An enthusiastic response to bel canto vocalism is expressed in Balzac's story "Massimilla Doni," where a performance of Rossini's *Mosé in Egitto* is elaborately described. What the figure Capraja says of the coloratura cadenza provides an idea of bel canto's escapist and exhilarating attractions:

> The clear cadenza is the acme of art; an arabesque adorning the chief room of the house; too little, it becomes nothing; a shade too much, it becomes confusion. The cadenza is set to arouse the soul to a thousand sleeping ideas—it ascends, takes its flight through space, scatters seed upon the air to be received in our ears to bloom in the heart . . . To [the tenor] Genovese it is due that I was enabled to escape from my old husk for a few minutes; short minutes, perhaps, by actual count of time, but long when measured by sensation.

For no period in the history of opera is the phrase "on wings of song" more apt. The image both warns and promises. It warns that if we wish to soar with bel canto singers we shall have to do so unhindered by ponderous ideas or complex human themes; it promises a kind of untrammeled exhilaration or, as Shelley put it, "unbodied joy" in the simple ecstasy of sound. No one has captured in words this delectation of the human voice better than Joyce:

> It soared, a bird, it held its flight, a swift pure cry, soar silver orb it leaped serene, speeding, sustained, to come, don't spin it out too long breath he breath long life, soaring high, high resplendent, aflame, crowned, high in the effulgence symbolistic, high, of the ethereal bosom, high, of the high vast irradiation everywhere all soaring all around about the all, the endlessnessnessness . . .[2]

The heart of bel canto opera lies in this almost orgasmic pleasure—and Joyce brilliantly expands it—in the powerful airborne melody climaxing somewhere above the staff.

In the following pages we will see how one composer, with his librettists, drew from important works by Romantic authors to create masterpieces in this genre of catapulting vocalism. *Maria Stuarda* and *Lucia di Lammermoor* are not merely brilliant examples of the melodic richness and vertiginous aerial delights of bel canto. They also interest us because they are based with considerable faith upon sources that permit one to make some strategic generalizations about the relationship between bel canto opera and early Romantic literary values.

Among authors important in the dawning age of Romanticism stand Friedrich Schiller (1759-1805) and Walter Scott (1771-1832). Together with Byron and the revived Shakespeare, these two men heralded Romanticism on the Continent. In his famous essay "The Romantic School" (1833) Heine wrote of Schiller:

> The spirit of the age took strong hold of him, Friedrich Schiller, he wrestled with it, was conquered by it, followed it to battle . . . Schiller wrote for the great ideas of the Revolution; he destroyed the Bastilles of the intellectual and spiritual world; he helped to build the temple of liberty, that very great temple which is to embrace all nations.[3]

Schiller's greatest theatrical contribution to European Romanticism was his passionate and salient heroes and heroines—characters of extraordinary self-consciousness and eloquence. His popularity as a literary figure was considerable. He was a friend and near equal to Goethe, and, what is more, Schiller's reputation—particularly as an aesthetician—has maintained itself into the twentieth century.

Scott's contributions to the Romantic movement were widespread and influential. Though, because of the genre he chose to work in, they were of a mundane nature. Robert Louis Stevenson probably put the novelist's case most positively when he wrote that "with Scott the Romantic movement, the movement of an extended curiosity and an enfranchised imagination began." But there was, really, little Blakean profundity, Byronic vitality, or Shelleyan grace in Scott's Romanticism. Scott himself defined the Romantic novel simply as one whose interest "turns upon marvelous and uncommon incidents." The modern Marxist critic George Lukács has stated Scott's achievement quite differently in *The Historical Novel* (p. 35): Scott's "greatness lies in his capacity to give living human embodiment to historical-social types. The typically human terms in which great historical trends become tangible had never before been portrayed so superbly, straightforwardly and pregnantly." What Scott most importantly achieved—and this is crucial when one comes to explain his popularity with opera librettists—was a re-creation of the "life" of past history. Scott's Waverley novels are the scenic and historical wonders of the Romantic era; for its spiritual wonders we must turn to Wordsworth, Byron, Shelley, and Keats. The richness of Scott's novels is brilliant but limited, as Heine was to point out in a remark on one of Scott's Continental imitators: "Like the works of Walter Scott, so also do Fouqué's romances of chivalry remind us of the fantastic tapestries known as Gobelins, whose rich texture and brilliant colours are more pleasing to our eyes than edifying to our souls."

What cannot be gainsaid, however, was Scott's popularity throughout Europe. Byron wrote to him: "Of whom could you be jealous?—of none of the living certainly—and of which of the dead?" William Hazlitt could state flatly in 1825 that "Sir Walter Scott is undoubtedly the most popular writer of the age." Goethe, Balzac, Hugo, and Dumas all admired the Waverley novels. Thomas Carlyle wrote in the *London and Westminister Review* (January 1838) that the "Waverley series, swift following one on the other apparently without end, was the universal reading; looked for like an annual harvest, by all ranks, in all European countries." Scott's reputation in the 1820s and 1830s was supreme.[4]

Both Schiller and Scott, too, are important figures in the history of opera, for their works possess distinctly operatic characteristics and as a consequence were popular sources for librettos. Every one of Schiller's plays was set to music at least once. Most notable among the Schiller operas are Verdi's *Giovanna d'Arco, I Masnadieri, Luisa Miller,* and *Don Carlos,* Rossini's *Guillaume Tell,* Tchaikovsky's *Maid of Orleans,* and Donizetti's *Maria Stuarda.* Even his unfinished *Demetrius* was made into an opera, and his adaptation of Gozzi's *Turandot* was eventually to inspire Puccini.

Schiller himself was no stranger to opera. His first extant work is a libretto for an opera seria based on the Semele myth. He also entertained the idea of a libretto based on Wieland's *Oberon.* This he finally abandoned for the excellent reason, explained in a letter to Goethe, that "if you do not have a very skillful and popular composer I fear that you are putting yourself in danger of having an ungrateful audience, for in the performance itself no libretto will redeem an opera if the music is not successful." In 1796, a few years before writing *Mary Stuart,* Schiller directed a revival of Gluck's *Iphigénie en Tauride* and was thrilled by the experience. That he was attuned to techniques from the lyric theater is obvious from the various "operatic" aspects so often remarked upon by commentators on his plays, especially in *The Maid of Orleans, The Bride of Messina,* and *Mary Stuart.*

Scott's novels were quarried even more eagerly by nineteenth-century librettists, though unfortunately Scott attracted primarily second-rank composers. Auber and Scribe attempted a version of *The Bride of Lammermoor* in 1829, six years before Donizetti. Scribe and Boieldieu had a few years earlier brought out *La Dame Blanche* (based on *The Monastery* and *Guy Mannering*), which had a staggering vogue over the next fifty years. Carafa set *The Heart of Mid-Lothian;* Nicolai attempted an *Ivanhoe* opera (as did Arthur Sullivan much later). Flotow wrote a *Rob Roy,* Adolph Adam a *Talisman,* and Bizet a *Fair Maid of Perth.* This leaves unmentioned many others set by forgotten composers. Of all the attempts to transform the sprawling, invertebrate, fancy-dress Waverley novels, Donizetti's *Lucia* is the finest and certainly the most popular.

Scott's influence, for better or worse, stretched beyond his own works—since he was among the most lavishly and often artlessly imitated authors of the century. Some excellent authors, too, felt Scott's presence. Hugo adapted *Kenilworth* for the stage as *Amy Robsart,* and this play is important for understanding Hugo's radical departures in *Cromwell, Hernani* (entertained as a subject by Bellini and finally set by Verdi), and *Lucrezia Borgia* (set by Donizetti). The first clear manifestation of Scott's influence in Italy—Grossi's *I Lombardi alla Prima Crociata* (1826)—was to become an opera by Verdi. Bulwer-Lytton followed in the Scott tradition, and his *Rienzi, Last of the Roman Tribunes* (1835) became Wagner's old-fashioned juggernaut *Rienzi.*

Two works could hardly be farther apart, not merely in genre but also in their underlying artistic qualities, than Schiller's play *Mary Stuart* and Scott's novel *The Bride of Lammermoor.* When transformed into opera by Donizetti, however, they become in many respects reverse sides of the bel canto coin. The two great dramatic themes of bel canto opera are the conflict of strong personalities and the thwarted love-plight. Schiller's play gave Donizetti the opportunity to create the ultimate example of immense conflict in the battle of wits and voices between Queen Mary and Queen Elizabeth, just as *Lucia* is an archetypal example in the bel canto repertory of ill-fated love. Both end in death, a sign of the bel canto rebellion against the "happy ending" of the earlier opera seria. Both *Maria Stuarda* and *Lucia* show, each in its own way, what composers looked for in order to display the series of arias and ensembles that constitutes the typical bel canto opera. Each of the two, again in its own manner, provides a basis for general comments upon Italian opera in the 1820s and 1830s. But most importantly, each is a masterpiece of the genre. If not the summit of achievement for bel canto (Bellini's *Norma* or *I Puritani,* to my mind, deserves that place), both are nearby.

Whereas Mozart crystallizes human passions and Verdi tears them to tatters, Donizetti's habit is to translate salient characters, strong passions, or dramatic crises into ear-filling vocal events—some extravagantly arabesqued, others startlingly simple. Though his set-pieces may seem formulaic, they are often towering, heroic expressions of human nature. Bel canto opera is extraordinarily humane—no seria gods or goddesses here, few aberrant or heterodox emotions either—but its humanity is both simpler and larger than life. Donizetti's music frequently has an immensity of impact that may seem to modern ears self-indulgent. But Romantic composers were nothing if not self-indulgent of their melodic invention, their singers' voices, and their characters' passions.

The crux of bel canto, then, is to transform mere self-indulgence through commitment and virtuosity into something which transcends. Shelley expressed the Romantic ideal in "Adonais":

> A godlike mind soars forth, in its delight
> Making earth bare and veiling heaven . . .

Bel canto audiences learned to expect god-like voices soaring forth and making earth seem a little bare. Such vocalism must at its best be levitating, and one would be hard-pressed to find two operas from the period that provide this effect more frequently than *Maria Stuarda* and *Lucia*—while remaining faithful to important literary sources.

Bel Canto and Early Romantic Drama

There is considerable feeling that *Mary Stuart* (1800) is Schiller's finest play.* One writer could even assert in 1934 that it is "probably up to now the most rigorously crafted tragedy in German literature."[5] And, doubtless because of its emphasis on the nobility of the martyred Catholic queen, the play became the favorite of Schiller's works south of the Alps.[6] A first Italian translation appeared in 1821, and operatic versions were produced by Casella (1813), Mercadante (1821), and Coccia (1827) before Donizetti ended the competition in 1835.

Mary Stuart is an enormous affair—a hundred lines longer than Shakespeare's longest play, *Hamlet*. It was the unenviable task of Donizetti and his librettist Giuseppe Bardari to translate it into the approximately fifteen to twenty arias, ensembles, and choruses that make up the typical bel canto opera. How the essential structure of the play helped them, what scenes were raised to special importance, what characters, themes, and plot lines were excised—all these questions give us insight into the literary attractions of bel canto composers and their audience. It would be fruitless, however, to plunge into such specifics without commenting upon *Mary Stuart's* general subject and tone, since they so strongly appealed to Donizetti's special gifts. One of the best brief summaries of Schiller's intentions is found in Thomas Carlyle's *Life of Schiller* (1825):

> To exhibit the repentance of a lovely but erring woman, to show us how her soul may be restored to its primitive nobleness, by sufferings, devotion, and death, is the object of *Mary Stuart*. It is a tragedy of sombre and mournful feelings; with an air of melancholy and obstruction pervading it; a looking backward on objects of remorse, around on imprisonment, and forward on the grave. Its object is undoubtedly attained. We are forced to pardon and to love the heroine: she is beautiful, and miserable, and lofty-minded; and her crimes, however dark, have been expiated by long years of weeping and woe . . . they seem less hateful than the cold, premeditated villainy of which she is the victim. Elizabeth is selfish, heartless, envious; she

* In order to avoid confusion with the opera, I shall refer to Schiller's play in English and the opera in Italian.

violates no law, but she has no virtue, and she lives triumphant: her arid, artificial character serves by contrast to heighten our sympathy with her warm-hearted, forlorn, ill-fated rival.

Virtually everything Carlyle specifies about the play recommends it for bel canto transformation. Bel canto thrived upon sensational incidents and violent appeals to emotion, in short upon melodrama; *Mary Stuart* is the work of a melodramatist of genius. The transparently stagey quality of the play, as we will see, metamorphosed effortlessly into the set-pieces of the opera. Mary's situation, too, as Carlyle describes it, is perfect for bel canto purposes: it rests on a firm basis of the imprisoned Queen's gloom and noble equipoise (full of inspiration for Donizetti's characteristic melodic vein of suave melancholy) and a contrasting loftiness and pride of spirit (perfect for Maria's more pyrotechnic effusions). In the age of bel canto a "beautiful, and miserable, and lofty-minded" heroine was as much as one could wish for in a title role. Nor are violent appeals to emotion limited to Mary's character: the glint of the headsman's axe supercharges the entire atmosphere.

The larger-than-life contrast between Mary and Elizabeth that Carlyle describes is worth noting. Here was perfect grist for the bel canto mill. In matters of good and evil, bel canto opera was not scrupulous; blacks and whites were sufficient to its purposes, and particular niceties of shading are infrequently met. Thus, Donizetti's Elisabetta is colored in far darker shades than the more complex Elizabeth in Schiller would justify. Because bel canto existed for the display and conflict of stupendous voices, the main concern was to put on the stage conflicting characters of appropriately large magnitude. For this purpose *Mary Stuart* was most apt.

Perhaps most importantly, Schiller's play is one of striking contrasts—in political themes, characterization, overall structure, and even in diction. This fondness for sharp juxtapositions is epitomized in the great confrontation scene—which never, in fact, occurred historically. The bel canto aesthetic was likewise profoundly dependent upon striking contrasts in differing vocal registers, in the variation of set-pieces such as *cavatinas*, duets, and choruses, and also within set-pieces, where acceleration from larghetto to allegro to vivace is a commonplace. It is a measure of the operatic quality of the Schiller source that the extreme compressions and elaborate contrasts of Donizetti's *Maria* do it very little essential damage.

The ways Donizetti and Bardari pared the original into an opera-length scenario explain something about bel canto priorities. The elaborate symmetry of Schiller's play, for one thing, proved helpful: there the scenes are equally divided between Mary's prison and Elizabeth's court; Acts I and V are focused on Mary, II and IV upon Elizabeth, and III on the confrontation. A different but equally effective balance was achieved in the opera by giving Act I to Elisabetta, the first part of Act II to Maria and the rest to the confrontation, and then Act III first to Elisabetta and last to Maria. Schiller's symmetrical organization also facilitated the judicious parceling of vocal assignments to singers who were always jealous of the relative importance of their roles. Thus, the three principals (Leicester completes the triangle) are each given an introductory aria with *cabaletta,* and the three important duets are divided equally among them. All the cast take part in the sextet, which is placed at the middle of the opera. Only in the closing prayer and scaffold aria does the balance finally and necessarily tip in favor of Maria.

Other exigencies of the bel canto stage required some radical changes. The dramatis personae were reduced with relative ease from seventeen to the more or less typical half-dozen vocal assignments. In the play Leicester, a would-be supporter of Mary's cause (but very complexly drawn by Schiller), is balanced by Mortimer, a hot-blooded young intriguer also in her party. Bel canto, however, did not, on the whole, favor quadrangles in conflict (moreover, four principals may not have been available or financially possible for the La Scala premiere). So Mortimer was excised and some of his duties in the plot taken over by Leicester. A more significant change relative to Leicester is that in the opera the triangle of Maria, Elisabetta, and himself is far more clearly a love triangle than a political triangle. In the opera Elisabetta is more a woman jealous of Maria as a rival in love than, as in Schiller, a queen fearful and awestruck by the personal charisma of a potential contender for her throne. Leicester, in short, becomes a pawn in the Queens' competition for his loyalty and affection. Inevitably, he is not a particularly remarkable Donizetti hero—certainly not on a par with Edgardo di Ravenswood. History dooms Leicester's plans as a peacemaker and lover to end in failure. *Maria Stuarda* presents a woman's world—no place for male heroism but rather for discretion, both in deeds and vocalism.

Further compressions of the cast were made possible by having Cecil alone represent the party favoring execution of Mary and having Talbot become the only spokesman for mercy. Talbot also becomes Maria's confessor in Act III (Melvil performs this ritual in the play).

All these maneuvers still left an exceedingly long play. More radical cutting was necessary: Act I of the play was the first to go. It is worth looking at this act for a moment to see what in it was so undesirable from the bel canto point of view. First of all, there is much filling in of past events in bland narrative fashion. Only a few situations rise to an emotional pitch that would be suitable for music—for instance, a brilliant exit speech for Mary:

> Let her not clothe in holy garb the bloody
> Audacity of naked violence.
> Deceit like this must not deceive the world!
> She can assassinate me, but not judge me!
> Let her give up combining fruits of crime
> With the external holy look of virtue,
> And let her seem to be just what she *is!* [966]

With those incendiary exclamation points, this should have made a fine *aria di sortita* or exit aria, but it happened to be embedded in highly rhetorical speeches about the drumhead trial set up to convict Mary. The speech could not be plausibly salvaged.

Other material in Schiller's Act I must have seemed needlessly complicating to Bardari—for instance the discussion of Mary's complicity in the murder of her Scottish husband Lord Darnley (an issue still unsettled by historians). Though Mary's past crimes are alluded to in the opera, emphasis upon them would clearly have undermined the essential nobility of the heroine Donizetti was intent on creating. There are also attempts by Schiller in his Act I to emphasize through second-hand conversations Mary's personal charisma. Knowing rightly that this is best done directly, Donizetti waited to establish this momentous quality, with Maria on stage, in her first scene in Act II of the opera. Finally, Schiller attempts in Act I to establish indirectly Elizabeth's vacillation in the face of a difficult dilemma. Bel canto was never very successful at expressing dubiety or indecisiveness of character. Its greatest moments are either those of prostration and stasis (and its related states of ennui, misery, and despair) or those of oath-making, love-plighting, and malediction. So it is no surprise that the ambivalent agony of Schiller's English Queen is not strongly developed in the opera. Rather, what has attracted Donizetti's interest is a queen bent on vengeance, a queen with an exhilarating streak of vindictiveness about her.

Schiller's first act, then, is largely a forensic display, heavy with rhetorical flourishes, given to forensic rather than lyric eloquence. This was not the stuff of bel canto opera, and so it was wholly abandoned. Fortunately, the loss is small for listeners aware of the familiar historical events. The kinds of cuts made on a more piecemeal basis throughout the play are typified by what happened to Schiller's first act. Mortimer has occasion to exclaim to Leicester: "What little steps / So great a Lord must measure in this court!" Donizetti was decidedly uninterested in the "little steps" of courtly intrigue and debate between royal counselors. For his vocal style to take flight, big steps were necessary: Leicester's decision to liberate Maria (introducing his *cabaletta, Se fida tanto,* S2), Elisabetta's decision to executive Maria (*È morta ogni pietà* in the Act III trio, S4), or Maria's awesome determination to bear herself nobly in the last two scenes.*

Mary Stuart *and the Donizetti Style*

Having put to one side the aspects of Schiller's play that were musically inert, Donizetti and Bardari could begin to focus on the moments which seemed to plea for lyric explosion into aria or ensemble. The focus of bel canto opera is situational. That is, a character is put into a trying or ambivalent situation and must "sing" himself or herself out of it by making a decision. The omnipresent *scena* or *cava-*

* References to passages in *Maria Stuarda* are keyed to the Audio Treasury recording of the opera featuring Beverly Sills (S2 = side two). London has also released a version of the opera with Joan Sutherland.

tina was quite simply the chief "decision-making" formula of bel canto theater; it usually consisted of a slow aria, a gear-changing section usually in dialogue with another character or a chorus, then a fast aria with an even faster, absolutely determining *stretta*. Schiller offered Donizetti a perfect *cavatina* situation when Mortimer (Talbot in the opera) approaches Leicester with Mary's secret letter and portrait:

> *Mortimer:* The Queen of Scotland sends you this.
> *Leicester:* (*startled, reaches for it hastily*): Speak softly, Sir—What is this I see! Her picture! Ah! (*He kisses it and gazes at it with rapture*) [1726]

Donizetti accepts this invitation to an aria expressive of the tenor's devotion (*Ah! rimiro il bel sembiante,* S2). What then follows in the play is comparable to an operatic bridge passage; here Leicester is won to Mary's side. Donizetti sets this in twenty-three bars, moving quickly to the announcement of Leicester's decision to protect Maria in the demanding aria *Se fida tanto*. This same process can be discerned in the Act I duet in which Elisabetta interviews Leicester. Having become convinced of his love for Maria in the larghetto, *Era d'amor l'immagina* (S2), she promises decisive and fatal consequences in the closing vivace ensemble, *Sul crin la rivale*.

The third act of *Mary Stuart* is the finest and, by a fortunate coincidence, the most operatic in texture. As the act opens we find Mary enjoying momentary freedom in the park of Fotheringay Castle. Schiller rises here to the challenge of making this scene an overpowering lyric contrast to the rhetoric of his preceding action. Donizetti and Bardari arrange this scene as our introduction to Maria: the result is an archetypal bel canto scene and also one of the happiest instances of the parallel between literary and musical forms. As such it is worth looking at carefully.

The operatic aspects of Schiller's *Mary Stuart* have often been noticed, and it is not surprising to find one writer describing the action in terms also available to musicians: "Parallelisms, triads, repetitions, and augmentations follow one another as the verse sails on from one splendid climax to the next."[7] The same writer refers to the "allegro furioso" of the confrontation, and he is not far wrong: the allegro tempo is more predominant in Donizetti's confrontation scene than in its two framing acts.

The dramatist's "operatic" heightening intentions, however, are made even clearer in the scene just preceding the collision of the Queens. Here four eight-line stanzas are inserted amid the unrhymed blank verse dialogue between Mary and her nurse. These four lyric flights that Schiller gives to Mary are among his most famous lines. Donizetti sets two of them memorably in the following manner: after a brief orchestral introduction and a short recitative interchange, he sets a portion of the first stanza and part of Mary's next speech—

> Let me delight in freedom new-found
> And be as a child,—O be one too!
> And on the meadows' greensward round
> Let my winged foot now dance on the dew. [2074]

—to nine gentle andante bars. As Schiller then reverts to blank verse in Mary's next speech, so, too, does the score revert to recitative for the equivalent of these lines from the play:

> I want to dream myself to happy ease . . .
> I rest upon the broad lap of the sky,
> Unfettered now and free, my eye
> Roves through its vast immensities.
> And yonder where the grey mist-mountains rise
> The borders of my realm advance,
> And yonder cloud that toward the south-land flies
> Is searching for the distant shores of France. [2089]

The moment calls now for an even greater burst of lyricism, and Schiller provides this in the next stanza:

> Hastening cloud, you sailer in air!
> Happy are they who with you may fare!
> Greet for me the land of my youth.
> I am a captive, in bondage I lie,
> No other messenger have I,
> Free in air is your highway,
> You are not under this Queen's sway. [2098]

These lines become the text for Maria's aria *Oh nube! che lieve per l'aria* (S3). This is quintessential Donizetti, representing all those arias that equate the escape of the soul from misery or oppression with the escape of the singing voice above the staff. It makes the greatest virtue of airily light orchestration, the plainest strophic organization, and that utterly simple, arching melodic line that is a bel canto trademark (EX. 1).

Example 1

Taken by Schiller's sudden and brilliant lyricism, Bardari at this point attempted to set the last of Schiller's four stanzas. Donizetti, however, must have sensed that this would be dramatic and musical overkill. He also realized that operatic convention required very shortly a *cabaletta* display number at an increased tempo, this to be connected by a transition passage justifying a faster tempo. Schiller's next page gave him just what he wanted, namely, the sound of the horns of the Queen's hunting party—and the attendant confusion in Mary's mind about the imminent meeting. This becomes fifty-six bars of allegro, ending with the nurse's announcement, "The tyrant passes through the park."

We have now reached a crucial moment. The character (and the performer) must take a stand. Vigor, determination, ascendancy—these are the dramatic and musical values the bel canto audience would expect at this point. Nor did Donizetti have to ignore Schiller to achieve these effects. For in the play Mary suddenly turns under the stress to show another side of her personality:

How I was going to move her, touch her pity.
Now everything is suddenly forgotten,
Nothing lives within me at this moment
Except the burning sense of sufferings.
My heart within me turns against her in
Fierce hatred, all my good thoughts flee away,
And with their heads of serpent-locks all shaking,
The evil spirits up from hell surround me. [2180]

These lines were apparently too strong for Bardari, but he was nevertheless able to convey the same pride of spirit in Maria's *cabaletta, Nella pace, del mesto riposo* (S3). Donizetti's music for this is vintage bel canto in its "salient" mode, with its compelling rhythm, stately tempo (*moderato e fiero*), and upwardly lunging melodic line (EX. 2). Hatred and its allied emotions of vengeance and repulsion were a bel canto staple, and this situation led to a typically exultant piece of musical abomination.

Example 2

Following Maria's introductory scene is another example of the Schillerian and Donizettian delight in the succession of strongly contrasted scenes. Maria having just given vent to her anger, Leicester enters to persuade her to assume a deferential attitude toward Elisabetta. In *Da tutti abbandonata* (S3) Maria shows a third side of her character, this expressing the ennui of oppression. Leicester counters with the utmost sympathy. This inspired one of Donizetti's loveliest duets, a sweet, limpid masterpiece tinged with his characteristic melancholy. The duet passes through a bridge section in which Leicester expresses the common bel canto will to vengeance on Maria's behalf; Maria in turn tells of her fear for his safety. This leads to yet another heavily accented duet in the "aggressive" mode with an impelling dotted rhythm (*Ah! se il mio cor tremò giammai,* S3) which—though not based on Schiller—admirably prepares for the increased level of excitement in the following confrontation. (It is all the more effective in the recording where, with her last, unwritten high D-flat of defiance still ringing in our ears, Maria must soon abase herself before Elisabetta.)

We come now to the climactic scene of both play and opera, the collision of immovable object and irresistible force. Some critics have complained of the stagey, rhetorical nature of the scene in the play. But these melodramatic and artificial qualities were congenial for translation into opera. All the preceding action Schiller focused on this scene, and there is nothing subtle in his announcement that the moment of catastrophe has arrived. As soon as the eyes of the two Queens meet, Schiller specifies a "general silence." Bel canto thrilled in such climactic, dumb-striking moments. In the form of large ensembles it could expand such moments outside the "running time" of the action itself. (Rossini anticipated this practice with the *a capella* ensembles that begin some of his finales.) So, after requiring his own *breve silenzio,* Donizetti filled this stop-action with a sextet. With this peculiarly operatic device he was able to express the varying inner thoughts of the characters at exactly the instant of greatest impact: Elisabetta's vindictiveness, Maria's trepidation, Talbot's (baseless) relief, Anna's foreboding, Leicester's sympathy, and Cecil's politic bloodthirst. It is a masterpiece of simplicity and understatement, with its ominous, *sempre piano,* slowly dying close. Compared with the sextet in *Lucia,* which is almost twice as long and reaches a more brilliant climax, this sextet may seem disappointing. The difference, however, is dramatically founded. The very arrival of Edgardo at the wedding festivities *is* in a sense the catastrophe of the story; in the sextet there is an expression of an accomplished crisis. In *Maria,* however, the catastrophe (Maria's caustic speech to Elisabetta) is yet to occur. The sextet is only anticipatory, and so brevity would here seem in Donizetti's favor.

Donizetti's actual confrontation is an unwontedly scintillating bel canto interchange, and this may be attributed to his decision to treat it as a duet very freely intermixed with accompanied recitative and interjections from the Queens' attendants. Tension is expressed by means of a pulsing allegro of broken chords, but Donizetti superimposes on this a skittish yet gracefully spun out melody of the kind for which he is noted (EX. 3). This is the basis of the exchange between

Example 3

the Queens. But for the climactic moment when, harried beyond endurance, Maria finally returns viciously in kind, Donizetti relaxes into the most commonplace yet effective rustle-and-thunder accompanied recitative:

> Wanton daughter of Anne Boleyn
> Is it you speaking of dishonor?
> Obscene, unworthy prostitute.
> I blush for you.
> The English throne is sullied,
> vile bastard, by your foot! [Bardari libretto][8]

As the disaster of these words sinks in, the orchestra begins a tremulous rise to full power. On Maria's last phrase, *dal tuo piè,* there is a dizzying release of energy at an increased tempo. Elisabetta calls for guards and departs. In just nineteen bars of rising musical excitement the stupefaction of everyone present is registered.

At this point comes another of those bel canto silences that announce a stop-action and an imminent explosion into musical time and space. Such is the Finale (*Va, preparati furente,* S4) that follows at a torrid allegro vivace, gathering strength as vocal mass and orchestration broaden. This Finale acts in a sense as a resolution for the sextet that introduced the confrontation, each character expressing the fulfillment or destruction of hopes evinced earlier. This Finale closes Act II, one of the supremely successful translations of literature for the bel canto stage.

Something should be said about the strengths, limitations, and means of characterization in *Maria Stuarda*. Opera, especially bel canto opera, requires in some degree a stylization of literary sources, and one reason Donizetti's version of the play works is that Schiller himself intended his play to have a stylized quality. Dramaturgically, *Mary Stuart* represented for Schiller a gradual though distinct swing away from realism toward both a lyric and rhetorical enrichment of his language. (As we have observed, Donizetti responded primarily to the former.) This intention is made clear in a letter Schiller wrote in 1801 expressing his dissatisfaction with an actress who played the role of Mary in Weimar:

> Unzelmann plays this role with delicacy and great understanding; her declamation is beautiful and sensible, but one would wish in her rather more force [*Schwung*] and a more tragic style. The prejudice in favor of our beloved naturalism still rules her too strongly, and everything becomes to me too realistic in her mouth.

Donizetti, and in succeeding decades Verdi and Wagner in particular, thrived upon characters who exhibited the *force,* the motive power that Schiller sought to instill in his characters. If there is a key to the essence of *Maria Stuarda*'s bel canto nature it is in Schiller's observation that Mary "feels or excites no tenderness; her destiny is only to experience herself and inflame others with vehement passion." Donizetti's heroine accomplishes this with the aid of music. All her emotions—vindictive jealousy, sympathetic devotion, noble sufferance—are the staple of bel canto, and Donizetti set them to music with an easy mastery. Maria is a focus of emotional energies and, therefor, a perfect bel canto heroine.

The character of Elizabeth presented a challenge that neither the bel canto aesthetic nor Donizetti was fully able to meet. Bel canto composers were never to succeed completely in capturing the charisma of genuine villainy (the villains must sing so beautifully). To express Elisabetta's wickedness Donizetti relied upon the tried-and-true means of simple vocal browbeating. This is not to say he was not frequently effective—the sputtering octave commands in the confrontation scene are spine-tingling. But Elisabetta's wickedness is finally not so much moral or political as simply vocal.

With other aspects of Elisabetta's character Donizetti was more successful. In the introductory aria, *Ah! quando all'ara scorgemi* (S1), Donizetti deploys the voice in this apparent expression of love for Leicester in a distinctly threatening, perversely whimsical manner. The love of this woman is clearly dangerous. In the following, supposedly positive-minded *cabaletta* (*Ah! dal ciel discenda un raggio*) Donizetti allows the subject of mercy only seven bars before the horns announce Elisabetta's more typical preoccupation, vengeance. Elisabetta is a monster of cruelty; her motivations are strong, and here, with vivace rhythmic drive and a rising, heavily accented, propulsive, dotted-rhythm melodic line (EX. 4), the composer succeeded in creating a fine evil foil for Maria.

Example 4

We have spoken sufficiently of the different aspects of Maria's character displayed in her first three numbers of Act II. It remains to consider the special ways the Donizetti style assured a successful narration of Maria's last moments. The tone of the last scene—suavely measured grandeur—is set by one of those long, seemingly effortless Donizetti melodies in the clarinets: Maria's struggle is clearly over, all is peace. This melody, like so many in bel canto operas, is sounded once and thrown away. The brief recitative that follows is derived from these lines of Schiller, in which Mary reassures her faithful retainers:

You should be glad with me because my goal
Of grief is reached at last, my fetters fall,
My prison opens, and my joyous soul
On angel wings soars up to everlasting
Liberty. [3481]

The familiar image of flight poises us once again for vocal uplift, this time in the form of Maria's prayer. This prayer is not in the play, though Mary is overheard praying at one point by Leicester. At any rate, prayers were, like mad scenes and vengeance duets, stock events in bel canto operas. Here Donizetti achieves the most powerful effect with the simplest means. The tempo is andante commodo, the orchestral support is the mere arpeggiated chord, and the theme is simplicity itself (EX. 5). The structure of this ensemble is

Example 5

one of repetition (the theme recurs seven times) and augmentation of orchestral mass and choral accompaniment. By the fourth repetition Maria's voice and soul are airborne in a stunning pianissimo G held a full eight bars and rising to B-flat. The prayer continues to intensify, ending as do so many bel canto ensembles of this kind, with the soprano soaring far above an increasingly thunderous coda.

In bel canto musical accompaniment, less is often more, and this certainly holds for Maria's scaffold aria. The opening larghetto (*D'un cor che muore,* S6) is the plainest amalgam of descending phrases and Beethoven's "Eroica" motif. Yet it is still deeply affecting. After the pulse of the aria rises slightly, it evanesces in a few bars of coloratura flourish. Donizetti, in the following bridge section, brings everyone's blood to a boil as a second cannon shot announces the procession to the execution. This ends with a *lungo silenzio* that, we have seen, usually ushers in an increased tempo and level of tension. What Donizetti in fact provides is surprisingly understated but perfectly apt to the dramatic situation: another stately aria, naturally marked maestoso, with yet another of his absolutely simple and symmetrical melodies (EX. 6).[9] The repetition of this melody is taken at the same noble pace, releasing into a splendidly succinct closing finale at the third cannon shot. In every respect Donizetti provided a fittingly poised and affecting end for Schiller's Queen. The playwright's heroine expresses herself nobly and forcefully, and Donizetti made her operatic in the same terms.

Maestoso
p
MARIA: Ah! se un gior - no da que - ste ri - tor - te il tuo braccio in - vo-lar - mi do - ve - a,

Example 6

One last observation might be made upon the strong bonds between Schiller's proto-Romanticism and Donizetti's bel canto style. With the exception perhaps of the *Wallenstein* trilogy, Schiller's œuvre is one of immense idealism and little sustained psychological subtlety or detailed insight. Georg Büchner, whose *Woyzeck* is the subject of a later chapter, despised Schiller on this count. One writer has commented upon this important limitation: "With Schiller the nerves remain out of the action. He left utterly closed the Pandora's box of unconscious sexual forces opened by the Romantics."[10] The bel canto aesthetic was similarly constrained in its powers of expression, and this constraint was due largely to its ultimately melodic orientation. Bel canto paid a price for its fertile melodism. Stendhal well observed that "melody can do nothing with emotional half-tones and suggestions; these qualities are found only in the under-currents of orchestral harmony." With Berlioz, then Wagner, and finally Strauss and Berg, purely orchestral modes of expression developed sufficiently to deal with emotional half-tones, psychological complexities, nameless desires and fears. Nevertheless, one must marvel at the dramatic strength Donizetti achieved with *Maria Stuarda* in spite of these limitations of Romantic heroic drama and bel canto opera.

Bel Canto and the Sir Walter Disease

The metamorphosis of Walter Scott's *Bride of Lammermoor* (1819) into *Lucia di Lammermoor* (1835) represents one of the happiest lyric translations in the history of opera, especially because its story focuses upon the "other" great bel canto theme, passionate love plighted and thwarted, but also because Donizetti's best-known opera (and he wrote seventy) happens to be based upon one of the most highly regarded of the thirty-two epoch-making and epoch-delighting Waverley novels. The year it appeared the reviewer for *Blackwood's Magazine* described *The Bride* as "a pure and magnificent tragical romance." J. G. Lockhart, Scott's son-in-law and first great biographer, called it "the most pure and powerful of all the tragedies that Scott ever penned."[11] De Quincey found it to be Scott's closest approach to Shakespeare, and the Shakespearean undertones in the novel—largely from *Romeo and Juliet* and *Macbeth*—must have added measurably to its popularity in the midst of the Romantic revival of the playwright's works.

Other aspects of the remarkable coincidence that resulted in *Lucia* are worth noting. First, it was composed not only at the chronological midpoint of Donizetti's career but also near its apex: *Lucia,* unlike *Maria Stuarda,* was an immediate success and established the composer as the pre-eminent writer for the European operatic stage. His only rival, Bellini, died in 1835, just when *Lucia* was in rehearsal for its Neapolitan premiere, and Verdi's first success, *Nabucco,* was still seven years in the future. Second, *Lucia* happened to be Donizetti's first collaboration with one of the period's most successful librettists, Salvatore Cammarano.

It is symbolically fitting that one of the first Scott-based operas (Rossini's *Donna del Lago,* 1819) and the greatest one were written, respectively, by the first and the last major purveyors of the pure late Italian bel canto style. For what Mark Twain called the "Sir Walter disease" was most widely epidemic during the period—1815 to approximately 1840—when bel canto reached its culmination. (Donizetti's *Don Pasquale* (1843) might well be recognized as one of the last pure blossoms of bel canto.) Perhaps because the aesthetics of Scott and Donizetti were geared for the main chance and for immediate fashionable success, their decline occurred with equally breathtaking rapidity: the more extreme the faddishness of success, the less likely its durability. The posthumous reputations of both novelist and composer tend to bear out this generalization. Bagehot could in 1858 call Scott's art "old-fashioned"; in 1864 Henry James could condescend to state that "old-fashioned, ponderous Sir Walter holds his own."[12] Rather the same thing happened to Donizetti. He and much of bel canto were swept away, partially at first by French grand opera, at which Donizetti tried his hand late in life, then more devastatingly by the Wagnerian revolution. The popularity of neither survived intact beyond mid-century.

Nevertheless, when Donizetti and Scott flourished they did so together, and there is more than a little coincidence in the simultaneous taste for their works. Both sought and found success in an age, as Carlyle put it, "altogether languid, without either skepticism or faith." The audiences for which they wrote wished to be entertained, not exercised by radical ideas or incendiary political themes.[13] One highly incensed contemporary reviewer excoriated Scott for the pleasant but ephemeral preoccupations of his novels:

> The other class of writers, who find their resources in every thing that can create an interest, however transitory and vulgar, who describe scenes merely for the purpose of describing them, and heap together circumstances that shall have a value in themselves, quite independently of the characters of those whom they act upon;—it is the doom of such men to compound melo-drames, and the prize of their high calling to produce excitement without thought . . . on the whole [Scott] has ministered immensely to the diseased craving for mere amusement.[14]

Bel canto comes under the same fire here leveled at Scott—*melodramma* is, after all, another term for the bel canto operatic genre. It was a confectionary aesthetic of heroic deeds and passions designed to amuse rather than challenge. Bel canto was, we must admit, more often than not intended to produce excitement without thought. As in the novels of Scott, political creeds and religious faiths were merely data and not of intrinsic interest; they were pretexts for extraordinary clashes and personal bravery. In short, bel canto heroes and heroines are the progeny of melodrama. It is the cross they bear.[15]

Bel canto, again like Scott's novels, is almost completely innocent of ideas—moral, political, philosophical, or otherwise—and that is why (since tragedy must finally deal in ideas or, rather, idealized constructs of human experience) there is little genuine tragedy in operas of this genre. Hazlitt put the matter harshly but accurately when he said of Scott that "his speculative understanding is empty, flaccid, poor, and dead." But this lacking made Scott a perfect soul-mate for his bel canto contemporaries, in whose hands ideas withered while passions flourished. Carlyle called Scott's style in the Waverley novels one of "intellectual shampooing," and the enemies of bel canto could scarcely find a better phrase for their pejorative arsenal.

To this serious charge there is one crushing retort, and Bagehot made it long ago in Scott's defense: "The labours of the searching and introspective intellect, however needful, absorbing, and in some degree delicious, to the seeker himself, are not in general very delightful to those who are not seeking." Donizetti's audience was not seeking in the fashion Bagehot describes. He realized this and wrote accordingly. Only the engulfing charisma of a Wagner succeeded in channeling opera in the direction of speculation: his Tristan, Hans Sachs, Wotan, and Amfortas possess Bagehot's "searching and abstract intellect." But it is risky to denigrate bel canto for not producing such profound figures. When condescension is easy, one can quickly assume an ungallant pose. Bel canto should be approached on its own terms, without judgmental hauteur, as Henry James was able to do with Scott:

> We are arrested by the sudden conviction that it is useless to dogmatize upon Scott; that it is almost ungrateful to criticize him. He, least of all, would have invited or sanctioned any curious investigation of his works. They were written without pretence: all that has been claimed for them has been claimed by others than their author. They are emphatically works of entertainment. As such let us cherish and preserve them.

Scott also mirrored the bel canto aesthetic in his conservatism or, even more to the point, his essentially apolitical sensibility. He may have written illuminatingly about how politicians, sectarians, and rulers make history, but he was no real partisan himself. Flourishing in the decades before the revolution of 1848, Scott was firmly preoccupied with the past. The man who wrote *The Antiquary* was himself one. Such was the burden of an unsigned obituary in the *Monthly Repository* of November 1832:

> He was eminently the man of the past. In a literary sense, he thought little of the world to come; his heart was in the bygone world. Reform was a trouble to his mind; he dwelt in the fading shadows of feudality, and was appalled at the growing glare of democracy.

Scott was a stranger to the struggles of his time, and so, too, was the world of bel canto. This was due in no small way to powerful censors, but admittedly we must look carefully to find any evidence of political consciousness (so superabundant in Verdi and Wagner) in the works or correspondence of Rossini, Bellini, and Donizetti.[16] Whatever damage to this generalization Rossini caused by writing *Guillaume Tell* (it was, at any rate, his librettist's idea) was more than balanced by the idle epicureanism of his long Parisian retirement. The bel canto artistic establishment had no call to investigate theories of society or of the psyche and would not have tolerated anyone who, like Wagner, was so inclined. In this Scott was bel canto's man; both were guiltless of dogmatism.

Another trait shared by Scott and Donizetti—a more personal one—was an extraordinary facility. And they both suffered a common fate of prolific artists: their genius did not always keep pace with the creative pressures to which they subjected themselves. Scott's later Waverley novels suffered particularly when, in order to extricate himself from an enormous debt, he resorted to dictation in an effort to increase his productivity. Sheridan once quipped that easy writing sometimes makes damnably hard reading, and most modern readers would happily sink many Scott novels with that charge. The untidiness of much that he wrote is captured with fair cynicism by one review in 1832: "He plays with them [his characters], and 'exquisite fooling' it is, till the required quantity of letter-press is completed, and then he huddles up the catastrophe, and sends them about their business in a hurry." *The Bride* leaves a reader feeling very much this way: Edgar's climactic entrance (the midpoint of the opera) takes place on page 419 of the 454-page novel!

Similar disparagement can be made of Donizetti's spree of seventy operas, many of them perfunctory works of nondescript aspect. As with Shakespeare's remains—cursed be he who moves their bones. But it must be said in Donizetti's defense that the constant pressure for new works was something an operatic composer in Italy at this time was obliged to face if he wished to make a name and a living for himself. Donizetti was neither as shrewd nor as lucky in avoiding numerous and harsh deadlines as his rival Bellini, whose production line ran much more slowly. He left ten operas at his death at the age of thirty-five, while Donizetti had over four times as many to his credit when he reached that age. By the time Donizetti was wealthy enough to relax his pace, he was no longer constitutionally willing or able to slow down. The progress of syphilis eventually forced him to do so. Donizetti was in short victimized by the omnivorous opera houses of Italy and Paris, the latter demanding fewer but longer works: of his *Les Martyrs* he exclaimed, *"Oh, cosa eterna!"* In another operatic age Donizetti might have written fewer and better works.

Historical Romance as Opera

The story of *The Bride of Lammermoor* is far more compelling as an opera than in its original narrative form. It is better because Cammarano ruthlessly cut reams of the extraneous material that clogs the pages of Scott's novels. One example must suffice. At the stupefying moment when Edgar flings open the door on the signing of the nuptial contract between Lucy and Arthur Bucklaw—the moment for Donizetti's sextet—Scott gives us this paragraph:

> He planted himself full in the middle of the apartment, opposite to the table at which Lucy was seated, on whom, as if she had been alone in the chamber, he bent his eyes with a mingled expression of deep grief and deliberate indignation. His dark-coloured riding cloak,

> displaced from one shoulder, hung around one side of his person in the ample folds of the Spanish mantle. The rest of his rich dress was travel-soil'd, and deranged by hard riding. He had a sword by his side, and pistols in his belt. His slouched hat, which he had not removed at entrance, gave an additional gloom to his dark features [et cetera].*

Here, painfully exposed, is the primary deficiency of Scott's novels, the tendency to become swamped in external details at the vital and dramatic moments when the reader is really interested in how characters think and feel. Here is the baneful side of the rage for the picturesque, the visual at the expense of the inner human emotions. Stendhal said all there is to say about this penchant: "The doublet and leather collar of a medieval serf are easier to describe than the movements of the human heart." Passages like the above, which hobble the pace of the novel, become just so much information for the costume and set designers for *Lucia di Lammermoor*.

Such passages, when multiplied many times over, have the inevitable effect (common to Balzac and Hugo too) of obscuring the central action of the plot, that is, when Scott is able to provide one at all. The author had little gift for plotting and knew it. In his journal for 18 October 1826 he wrote: "But woe's me! that [making a well-contrived story] requires thought, consideration—the writing out a regular plán or plot—above all the adhering to [one]—which I never can do." The besetting weakness of Scott's novels, then, is a casualness resulting from overripe descriptions, pointless divagations, and huge casts of characters. In his most exasperating novels it is difficult sometimes to discern what indeed is central and what is peripheral. *The Bride of Lammermoor,* however, presents no such problem: one senses immediately where to begin jettisoning Scott's excess narrative baggage. First to go is the elaborate explanation of the "ambidexter ingenuity of the bar" at the root of the Ashton-Ravenswood feud; Scott was himself a lawyer and this material came all too easily for him. Gone are all but six of the novel's thirty characters—an unusually small number for a Scott novel! Lucy's father (the crafty lawyer: "he had good intelligence and sound views, and

* Quotations are taken from the *Border Edition of the Waverley Novels,* ed. Andrew Lang (1897), Vols. 14 and 15.

sold out in time"), his satanic wife (a shade of Lady Macbeth), her older brother, Sholto, and her younger one, Henry (a harmless juvenile)—all these are boiled down into Donizetti's blood-and-thunder protector of the family name, Enrico. Especially happy is the disappearance of Edgar's insanely faithful old retainer, Caleb Balderstone—an outrageously crude comic figure who is cordially hated by all critics for spoiling *The Bride*. Bel canto scenarists, incidentally, had little use for low-born characters—the creation of which is now recognized as one of Scott's most important novelistic innovations.

Vanished from the opera is virtually everything of unimportance. One seeks vainly for an event or a character whose absence is sorely felt—though the "detestable and diabolical" Lady Ashton might have inspired a more intriguing villain than we have in Enrico. We are left with the minimal necessities for narrative sense, the remarkable events of the central story, and what scraps and hints of characterization Scott meted out to his two lovers. We are left, in short, with the romantic snatch of actual history upon which Scott based his novel and to which he alludes in its closing pages:

> By many readers this may be deemed overstrained, romantic, and composed by the wild imagination of an author, desirous of gratifying the popular appetite for the horrible; but those who are read in the private family history of Scotland during the period in which the scene is laid, will readily discover, through the disguise of borrowed names and added incidents, the leading particulars of AN OWER [i.e., absolutely] TRUE TALE.

In an 1830 edition of the novel, Scott himself wrote an introduction explaining the real-life events that inspired him. His synopsis strikes one as very much like that of Donizetti's opera.

This residue from *The Bride,* small though it may seem, still contained more than enough to satisfy the bel canto aesthetic.[17] One may remark first upon the setting of the novel, which must have had an attraction similar to the one expressed by Schiller:

> Who does not prefer to feast his eyes upon the wild streams and waterfalls of Scotland, upon its misty mountains, upon that romantic nature from which Ossian drew his inspiration—rather than to grow enthusiastic in this stiff Holland?

Donizetti was never particularly successful in capturing geographical flavor on a sustained basis, but *Lucia*—though one can hardly call it "Scottish"—is one of his more atmospheric operas. The "fountain" scene in Act I glistens with aethereal brilliance; the storm which introduces the Wolf Crag castle is quite equal to Scott: "A wilder, or more disconsolate dwelling, it was perhaps difficult to conceive . . . a symbol of unvaried and monotonous melancholy, not unmingled with horror." And Donizetti's details of orchestration are unusually effective—in the use of the harp, in frequent haunting flute and woodwind tones, most obviously in the specification of the eerie glass harmonica in the mad scene.

There is also a distinct and pervading exaggeration of character and event throughout *The Bride* that, as we have seen with *Mary Stuart,* must have recommended it for operatic treatment. Scott favored the bold and animated in everything he wrote. It was what he knew best, and what bel canto thrived on. The operatic quality of Scott's writing is hinted in a generous comment he made about his only serious rival, Jane Austen (than whom there could hardly be a less "operatic" writer):

> That young lady had a talent for describing the involvements and feelings and characters of ordinary life which is to me the most wonderful I ever met with. The big bow-wow strain I can do myself, like any now going; but the exquisite touch which renders ordinary commonplace things and characters interesting from the truth of the description and the sentiment, is denied to me.

The big bow-wow strain—that was the strain for bel canto composers. They could not have had less desire to make "commonplace things and characters" interesting. The exquisite touch was not their strong point. Needless to add, none of them was ever attracted to *Emma* or *Sense and Sensibility*.

Something should here be said about Scott's heroes and heroines, since Italian bel canto depended so heavily on them.[18] They are by all accounts among the least captivating in all literature. There is not an Hernani, William Tell, or Mary Stuart among them. Of Scott's leading men one writer said:

> They have little personality. They are all of the same type; excellent young men—rather strong—able to ride and climb and jump. They are always said to be sensible, and bear out the character by being unwilling sometimes to talk platitudes. But we know nothing of their inner life.[19]

The writer then adds, fortunately for us, that "if there is an exception, it is Edgar Ravenswood"—a view that is corroborated by other judges in the matter. Of Scott's heroines generally one can put the best face on it by describing them as well-bred, unaffected young women who are highly principled, spirited, and capable of warm attachments. Farther than that it is risky to venture.

The miracle of Donizetti's opera is that he is actually able to bring Scott's Edgar and Lucy to passionate life with only the most meager hints to guide him. If we judge by the result, however, they were the perfect hints. One wonders if the reference to "the silver tones of Lucy Ashton's voice" was noticed by Cammarano and Donizetti, for there is in the role of Lucia a silvery pallor and delicacy—most obviously in *Regnava nel silenzio* and the mad scene. We learn also that "Lucy Ashton's exquisitely beautiful, yet somewhat girlish features were informed to express peace of mind, serenity, and indifference to the tinsel of worldly pleasure." Donizetti masterfully deploys the powers of coloratura to give Lucia the detached and strangely airy cast of mind that Scott seems to imply. Vocal dexterity also helps him to color the character of this young girl who is wont to erect "aerial palaces" in her daydreams, "of strange adventures and supernatural horrors." Lucy, for all her passivity of character, does swear eternal devotion to Edgar, and within the bounds of familial piety she suffers greatly by maintaining her vow. This passionate devotion —of which there are breaths and hints in the novel—Donizetti fully captures, especially in *Quando, rapito in estasi.*

Scott gave Donizetti little to go on in creating Edgardo. We are told that "his soul was of an higher, prouder character" than most, that he is "a devilish deal prettier" than his rival Bucklaw, and that no one in Lucy's experience displayed "a mien and features so romantic and so striking as young Ravenswood." This, though, was apparently enough for the composer; his Edgardo is a romantic hero of far more potency than the Edgar of the novel. Edgardo is indeed the hero Scott ought to have given us in the first place. In one trait Edgar was especially amenable to the bel canto style: "His was a mind unwillingly roused from contemplative inactivity, but which, when once put in motion, acquired a spirit of forcible and violent expression." Could there be a hero more agreeable to the slow aria/fast aria *cavatina* formula so beloved by Donizetti? Consider Edgardo's *Sulla tomba* in Act I and his interview with Enrico in Act III.

Finally, however, it is the way Scott organized his melodrama in terms of situations that was most helpful to Cammarano and Donizetti. As Hazlitt well observed, "Sir Walter places his *dramatis personae* in romantic situations, and subjects them to extraordinary occurrences, and narrates the result." His novels develop with a firm sense for strong contrasts and for the possibilities of instantaneous impact or ignition (though, alas, he rarely fans the fire once it is started). Scott saw this flaw in his own novels: "The insipidity of this author's heroes may be also in part referred to the readiness with which he twists and turns his story to produce some immediate and perhaps temporary effect." Much opera generally, and bel canto opera in particular, is structured in this way to create salient situations, provide emotional tinder, then place the character in the midst and let the music ignite everything.

The particular situations the librettist and composer singled out from *The Bride* are exemplary of the sorts of events bel canto librettists favored. Oaths, for instance, are a staple, and the rivalry between the Ashtons and Ravenswoods makes them important in Scott's story. The entire first act, with the exception of Lucia's *cavatina,* is given over to oaths. Both ends of Enrico's introductory *cavatina* (*Cruda, funesta smania* and *La pietade in suo favore*) amount to oaths of vengeance. Edgardo is soon swearing his own oath upon the tomb of his father (*Sulla tomba*). And the act closes as Lucia and Edgardo swear their eternal devotion (*Verranno a te sull'aure*). Outrageously, Scott accomplishes the crucial love-plight without a single word of dialogue: "The whole passed so suddenly, and arose so much out of the immediate impulse of the moment, that ere the master of Ravenswood could reflect upon the consequences of the step which he had taken, their lips, as well as their hands, had pledged the sincerity of their affection." Happily ignoring Scott's craven expedience, Donizetti gave his lovers the dreamily arching love-duet theme, which breathes as much as anything in Donizetti the essence of bel canto romantic love.

Of dramatic confrontations enough has been said. One need only point with admiration to the Act III vocal collision of tenor and baritone in the Wolf Crag castle. It is bel canto pure and simple, based upon the meeting in the last pages of the novel between Colonel Douglas Ashton and Edgar.

The advantage Donizetti enjoyed as an operatic composer over Scott is nowhere more evident than at the climactic moment when Edgar suddenly appears at Ravenswood castle. Scott builds the moment for all it is worth in this paragraph:

> Lockhard and another domestic, who had in vain attempted to oppose his passage through the gallery or antechamber, were seen standing on the threshold transfixed with surprise, which was instantly communicated to the whole party in the state-room. That of Colonel Douglas Ashton was mingled with resentment; that of Bucklaw, with haughty and affected indifference; the rest, even Lady Ashton herself, showed signs of fear, and Lucy seemed stiffened to stone by this unexpected apparition. Apparition it might well be termed, for Ravenswood had more the appearance of one returned from the dead, than a living visitor.

Scott succeeds in falling flat on his face in the next paragraph (quoted on page 137). Not Donizetti. He saw the invitation for an ensemble and delivered the famous sextet, *Chi mi frena in tal momento?* If ever an author gave a composer an operatic moment, it is this. It is rendered even more spectacular by the following finale (which must have helped Verdi in the end of the gambling scene of *La Traviata*).

A word or two about the mad scene, another common bel canto event. Donizetti's setting is, obviously enough, splendid. More than that, though, it rises to the challenge of the one "theme" it may be said that Scott actually develops in the characterization of his heroine. Scott gives us a fragile young sensibility with a penchant for "weaving her enchanted web of fairy tissue, as beautiful and transient as the film of gossamer, when it is pearled with the morning dew, and glimmering in the sun." Scott very nearly does his job of showing us a delicately minded heroine who is passive almost to the point of feebleness but who still possesses a perversely strong sense of emotional commitment. Under the pressure of events, it is all too natural for her to collapse mentally between these two very different characteristics of recessiveness and determination. Donizetti's rendering of Lucia's madness accords exactly with the description of her symptoms in the novel:

> Lucy was transported to her own chamber, where she remained for some time in a state of absolute stupor. Yet afterwards, in the course of the ensuing day, she seemed to have recovered, not merely her spirits and resolution, but a sort of flighty levity, that was foreign to her character and situation, and which was at times chequered by fits of deep silence and melancholy, and of capricious pettishness.

These qualities were particularly amenable to coloratura expression. The description just quoted occurs before the attack on Bucklaw (in the novel, incidentally, he survives), but it does capture the essence of Lucia's actions in the operatic mad scene, which is, in fact, derived from this passage:

> The next evening, the physicians said, would be the crisis of her malady. It proved so; for although she awoke from her trance with some appearance of calmness, and suffered her nightclothes to be changed, or put in order, yet so soon as she put her hand to her neck, as if to search for the fatal blue ribbon, a tide of recollections seemed to rush upon her, which her mind and body were alike incapable of bearing.

The last scene of *Lucia* does not strictly concern us, since it has no basis in Scott's novel. Still, Cammarano's means of conclusion are not farfetched. Scott makes it quite clear that Edgar's world-weariness is complete, and his actual death—met while recklessly crossing a stretch of quicksand on his way to duel with Colonel Ashton—is really a kind of self-destruction. This last scene, however, does provide the occasion to make an observation without which a chapter on bel canto would be incomplete—namely, that Donizetti wrote his operas with specific singers in mind. He structured his operas and designed the tessitura and breadth of each role with particular voices as a guide. His correspondence makes very clear that his prime concern for the premiere of a new opera was an able cast. The selection of singers was the most he could do to protect himself. Thus he wrote to the famous French tenor Gilbert-Louis Duprez concerning the cast for his first Paris opera: "I need to know the singers from up close, this because I don't want to risk ruining it or ruining me." Once a good cast was agreed upon, Donizetti was willing to leave the rest "in the hands of destiny." The contract he signed for *Maria Stuarda* has the agreed-upon cast added at the bottom.

This attention to singers probably lies behind the rather unusual closing scene for tenor, since Donizetti had at his disposal for the Neapolitan premiere Duprez himself.[20] With such an important personage in the hero's role (and with a soprano, Persiani, singing Lucia rather early in her career), Donizetti was able to make a departure from the customary opera-ending bravura piece for the prima donna. And he wrote for Duprez two of his most meltingly beautiful and sombre arias (*Fra poco a me ricovero* and *Tu che a Dio spiegasti l'ali*). The scene is one of the happiest results of the quirks of bel canto casting.

A chapter on bel canto opera cannot close without a few further comments about *Lucia* and the genre in general. The first concerns the libretto, which, though written by one of the most respected librettists of the time, is not a very estimable piece of work. The generally poor quality of bel canto librettos can be attributed to at least two related facts. First, as Patrick Smith makes clear in his chapter on Italian *melodramma* in *The Tenth Muse,* in the artistic consortium that produced opera in the 1830s the librettist "brought up the rear." He had to serve obediently and self-effacingly the whims of impresarios, headstrong singers, and—if they were stubborn enough to have their way too—composers. Italian opera of this period was highly conventionalized, and librettists were obliged to tailor their creations to its rigid demands. Second, audiences were not particularly disposed to pay attention to *what* was being sung. In his travels Hector Berlioz found himself in Milan for a performance of Donizetti's *L'elisir d'amore* (this was three years before *Maria Stuarda* opened there):

> The noise of the audience was such that no sound penetrated except the bass drum. People were gambling, eating supper in their boxes, etcetera, etcetera. Consequently, perceiving it was useless to expect to hear anything of the score, which was then new to me, I left. It appears that the Italians do sometimes listen. I have been assured by several people that it is so. The fact remains that music to the Milanese, as to the Neapolitans [who heard the *Lucia* premiere], the Romans, the Florentines and the Genoese, means arias, duets, trios, well sung; anything beyond that provokes only aversion or indifference.[21]

Hardly the atmosphere in which self-respecting poet-librettists could practice their trade with dignity.

"Really, when I think of those people [singers]," Rossini reminisced, "they were wild animals." "Singers! What a race!" Berlioz exclaimed. The operatic genre of which *Lucia* and *Maria* are prime examples was designed to serve and display such a headstrong and voice-strong race. *Lucia* is not mounted except where an impresario feels he has a heroine who can carry the action on the strength of her coloratura artistry. *Lucia* without such a heroine would be as plausible as *Hamlet* without a charismatic Prince. As a result, in many modern bel canto performances the "presence" of a prominent exponent in the prima donna role tends to disbalance the entire proceeding. This emphasis on the personality of the executant is, now as always, an unavoidable part of the bel canto ethos. During the period of Donizetti's popularity, as sometimes today, this "personality" was stretched into a truly demonic egoism. Berlioz captures this vulnerable part of the bel canto aesthetic in his description of the psychology of one self-willed diva of the time:

> She would consider herself to have failed if she did not monopolize the attention of the house, rightly or wrongly and by whatever piece of stage business, in every scene she appears in. Her whole manner suggests that she sees herself as the focus of the drama, the only character with whom the audience need concern itself. "What? Listening to that fellow? Admiring the composer? Interested in that chorus? How can you be so misguided? Look over here, this is what you should be attending to. I am the libretto, I am the poetry, I am

> the music. The one object of interest this evening is me. The sole reason for your coming to the theatre is me!"[22]

Wilhelmine Schröder-Devrient was not the only singer guilty of this arrogance. Not far below the surface of most bel canto heroines like Maria and Lucia lies this psychology of artistic virtuosity and self-indulgence.

In his *Life of Rossini* Stendhal had the occasion to observe that "Walter Scott found the courage to be *simple.*" This was a courage that the creators of bel canto opera could well appreciate, for simplicity—whether of dramatic structure, of melodic development, of harmonic and orchestrative technique, of diction, of character development, or of human emotions—is a hallmark of this operatic epoch. With this courage to be simple, bel canto composers and librettists created what many feel to be the most quintessentially "operatic" operas in the repertory.

five

BENVENUTO CELLINI

In literature mere egotism is delightful. It is what fascinates us in the letters of personalities so different as Cicero and Balzac, Flaubert and Berlioz, Byron and Madame de Sévigné . . . Humanity will always love Rousseau for having confessed his sins, not to a priest, but to the world, and [Cellini's works of art] have not given it more pleasure than has that autobiography in which the supreme scoundrel of the Renaissance relates the story of his splendour and his shame.

Oscar Wilde, *"The Critic as Artist"*

Toward the end of his life, which became increasingly clouded by misanthropy, Hector Berlioz made two judgments about his career as a composer. One concerned his future popularity: "If I could only live to be a hundred and forty, my musical life would end by becoming quite fascinating" (*M*, 496).* This mordant prophecy proved approximately accurate: the great Berlioz revival seems to have spanned roughly the sesquicentennial of his birth and the centennial of his death in 1869. Now the music of Berlioz generally enjoys the respect and sensitive performances that this tragically proud composer sought vainly in his lifetime. One might add, as a gesture symbolic of the tardy appreciation the French often accord their own artistic geniuses, that only in 1974 did the Bank of France issue a ten-franc note bearing the picture of Berlioz conducting an orchestra. The reverse side shows him with a guitar in front of the Villa Medici in Rome, where he resided as a holder of the Prix de Rome. And one should note also that Berlioz is finally receiving a full scholarly review in the form of the New Berlioz Edition.

The other prediction referred to his operatic output: "I would consider myself extremely fortunate if I were able to produce two good ones in my life" (*M*, 445). Berlioz never did write more than two operas. *Béatrice et Bénédict* scarcely falls in the same class as

* For purposes of citation in the text, *M* will refer to the *Memoirs of Hector Berlioz,* tr. David Cairns (Norton paperback, 1969); *E* refers to Berlioz's *Evenings with the Orchestra,* tr. Jacques Barzun (Phoenix paperback, 1973); *A* refers to Benvenuto Cellini's *Autobiography,* tr. George Bull (Penguin paperback, 1956).

Benvenuto Cellini or *Les Troyens,* and Berlioz himself rightly called *La Damnation de Faust* a "descriptive symphony" rather than an opera. The two operas are beginning to attract attention through the recordings of Colin Davis, and the inundating beauty of *Les Troyens* in particular has brought that work to many of the world's major opera houses.

The "other" opera is emerging only slowly from oblivion. This situation must eventually be righted, for *Benvenuto Cellini* is among the finest neglected masterpieces of the lyric stage. It has the consistent human and musical interest of a *Carmen* or *Rigoletto. Die Meistersinger* and *Boris Godunov* are hardly more immense in orchestral panorama. Though its plot does not unwind as smoothly and credibly as *Le Nozze di Figaro* or *Il Barbiere di Siviglia, Cellini*'s charm, verve, and wit are on nearly the same level. Berlioz's immense opera of his youth (as *Les Troyens* is of his somber twilight) is more: an archetypal Romantic opera and, along with Rossini's *Guillaume Tell,* a unique blend of Italian bel canto vocal style with the scenic traditions of French grand opera. *Cellini* is one of the first operatic expressions of the rights of the individual as against those of society and contemporary morality. Its hero is the antithesis of Mozart's Don, who is finally condemned according to Sevillian social mores. Cellini ("To hell with my statue, and the Pope, and the law!") is triumphant. *Cellini* is also one of the first operas to touch on the question of artistic freedom.

The opera is by no means a perfect specimen. Delacroix described Berlioz's music as "un héroïque gâchis" (a heroic mess), and there are some who would find the phrase well suited to *Benvenuto Cellini.*[1] Its gestation was complicated by the necessity of transforming it—as happened with *Carmen*—from a spoken-dialogue Opéra Comique to a through-composed Opéra version because the former theater rejected the libretto. Its stage history, one of massive cuts and transpositions, has left the score in confusion, which the New Berlioz editors have yet to resolve. Nor can one ignore the strange mixture of the most venerable stock events (among them the *Figaro* "closet" trick in the first scene, Fieramosca's harmless buffo bombast, and Teresa's "prayer" scene) with a truly revolutionary level of sheer expressive energy and ingenuity of orchestration. The plot—on paper an Opéra Comique confection—is stagey in its facility. And to this one must add that there are some weak musical moments, the most serious being the final scene, though imaginative and spectacular staging can overcome its defects.

In spite of these admissions, *Benvenuto Cellini* deserves our attention for a number of reasons. Most important is the sense that, notwithstanding its flaws, it is an impressive work. If it is dangerous to praise it uncritically—as has been my inclination—it is a danger many have courted. Gautier called it a "bold, original, thoroughly novel work." Liszt wrote to Berlioz after its performance in Weimar (21 March 1852): "Without puffery, I am able to tell London and Paris of its success. I thank Berlioz deeply for the noble pleasure which study of *Benvenuto Cellini* has given me. It is one of the most powerful works I know of. It is at once both the glorious sculptor himself and the vital, original statue." In 1883 the pianist-composer Marie Jaëll wrote that when it is revived "how many other glories will fade! For it will live as long as French music itself; no one will write another *Cellini:* it is more Gallic than anything Gallic that has been written. There is in it Rabelais and Voltaire . . . this dazzling effervescence of mind and wit no one has captured like Berlioz, and it will be his undying glory."[2]

The opera is also important among Berlioz's early works as a full-fledged example of the orchestrative revolution he was to effect. It is worth recalling that the composer was virtually *born* a rebel; there was no slow innovative progression like Verdi's or Wagner's. The epoch-shattering "Symphonie Fantastique" was a mere Opus 14 and premiered when Berlioz was twenty-six. *Cellini,* too, belongs to that seminal period when—to borrow from the metal-casting jargon—the art of Berlioz was congealing in its characteristic mould. The composer's fertility of melodic invention, massiveness of sonic scope, reckless demands upon his orchestra (and, incidentally, his chorus), and the rich colorism and finesse of his orchestral palette are all present in the opera.

A third reason for turning to *Cellini* is related to the purposes of the present study. Often a literary work is chosen for operatic treatment for reasons tied to events in a composer's life or to his personal world view. Autobiographical elements influenced the choice of at least three of the operas discussed in succeeding chapters (*Eugene Onegin, Wozzeck, Death in Venice*), but in the Berlioz work we have perhaps the most obvious and affecting autobiographical nexus between literary source and a composer's life in the entire repertory. Autobiography was an important aspect of the ethos of Romantic egotism, and Berlioz, like so many Romantics, wore his heart if not on his sleeve at least very close to the surface of his art. His subtitle for the "Symphonie Fantastique" is "Episode in the Life of an Artist." The artist was, of course, Berlioz, and the program he wrote for the piece was born of his love affair with the English actress Harriet Smithson. "Harold in Italy" was also planned on the foundations of the composer's own experiences:

> My idea was to write a series of orchestral scenes in which the solo viola would be involved, to a greater or lesser extent, like an actual person, retaining the same character throughout. I decided to give it as a setting the poetic impressions recollected from my wanderings in the Abruzzi, and to make it a kind of melancholy dreamer in the style of Byron's Childe Harold. [*M*, 225]

Cellini can be seen as the last and most elaborate part of Berlioz's "autobiographical" trilogy. It is no less than a thinly disguised, at times painfully touching, operatic memoir, a self-portrait of musical Romanticism at its most luminous. It tells us—as *Les Troyens* cannot—of the essential Berlioz of the early years when he wrote most of his enduring masterpieces and when he was at his most vibrantly optimistic.

Finally, the opera is one excellent key to the French Romantic movement. A lyrical setting of not only one of literature's finest autobiographies but also of one of our most illuminating re-creations of Italian Renaissance humanism, the Berlioz opera is partially a product of the artistic renaissance which had been taking place in France during the 1820s and 1830s. True to its source, *Cellini* brims with fire, youth, enthusiasm, and aesthetic adventure—just the qualities that describe the first wave of the somewhat belated Romantic movement in France. Berlioz's gregarious hero is a reflection of the immense reserve of self-confidence the new aesthetic demanded of its first proponents. "Timidity," wrote Théophile Gautier, "was not the weak point of that time."* In the thrilling sense of individualism and sheer psychic freedom emanating from the pages of the *Autobiography,* Berlioz must have sensed Cellini's affinity with those first years of liberation from the bonds of French neo-Classicism and from the polite, restrained Age of Reason. "What a wonderful time it was!" wrote Gautier. "It was all so youthful, so new, so richly coloured, and of so strange and intoxicating savour, that it turned our heads and we seemed to be entering into unknown worlds."

One recourse for those who detested the sterile beauties of neo-Classicism was the art and literature of the Renaissance, whose healthy externality and rugged, direct, colorful expressiveness were all the more exciting by comparison. Cellini's *Autobiography* (written between 1558 and 1566, unknown outside Italy until the nineteenth century) benefitted from this new Romantic taste. Goethe himself translated it into German, and by 1822 it appeared in France. (Berlioz and his librettists appear to have used the Farjasse translation of 1833.) In the primal vigor and élan with which Cellini confronted great or trivial artistic annoyances, the spiteful enmity of his old-fashioned colleagues, the unpredictability, indifference, and ignorance of his patrons—in these the harassed Romantics surely found someone to identify with and, since misery loves company, to console them. As we shall see, this was true for Berlioz. His first opera thus tells us as much of French Romanticism as it does of the man and the artist who created it.

Autobiographical Truth

We are concerned here not only with Cellini's memoirs, but also with the composer's personal identification with his source. So we should pause to consider a pervasive difficulty of the memoir as a literary form, namely, the fact that truth and autobiography are almost by nature mutually exclusive. Alexander Pushkin put the problem succinctly in a letter describing his own attempted self-description (which he later burned):

* *The Complete Works,* tr. F. C. de Sumichrast (1909), Vol. VIII, p. 139. All quotations from Gautier in this chapter are from this volume, which contains *A History of Romanticism* and *Romanticist Studies* (including an essay on Berlioz).

> It is both tempting and pleasant to write one's mémoires. There is nobody one loves as much, or knows as well, as oneself. It is an inexhaustible subject. But it presents difficulties. It is possible not to lie; but to be sincere is a physical impossibility. The pen will sometimes stop, as a runner draws up at an abyss, before something an outsider would read with indifference.[3]

Pushkin provides a good caveat for a reader venturing upon Cellini's *Autobiography,* which distinctly lacks an air of veracity and scrupulously avoids even the pretense of introspection or self-doubt. The events of Cellini's life are told by an author with a weakness for self-serving stage management; the characters of his friends and enemies, one instinctively feels, have passed through a roseate, self-gratifying filter. It is hard to be stern with Cellini in his fancifications, however, for he is disingenuous, even honest, about his intentions as a memoirist. The very first lines hint at the bigger-than-life artist in store for us: "No matter what sort he is, everyone who has to his credit what are or really seem great achievements, if he cares for truth and goodness, ought to write the story of his own life in his own hand . . . I intend to tell the story of my life with a certain amount of pride" (*A,* 15). No autobiography supports Pushkin's idea that one can love nobody so much as oneself better than Cellini's. It is at once an apologia and a swaggering spree of doting self-enjoyment.

Berlioz also wrote his memoir, though, unlike Cellini, he knew it would be published. It has much in common with the *Autobiography.* As with Cellini, there is nothing sanctimonious or weak-kneed about it. Berlioz warned in his preface, "I do not have the least pretension to 'appear before God, book in hand', declaring myself 'the best of men', nor to write 'Confessions' " (*M,* 29). Rather, Berlioz's *Memoirs* is the apologia of a battle-scarred artistic gladiator, a relation of his "agitated and laborious career." Both memoirists are combative, uninhibited in praise and condemnation; their enemies are painted with the full palette of sarcasm, irony, ridicule, and jest. The niceties of correct chronology they leave to our more scholarly century. They are not purveyors of historial truth, either; to an event narrated in the *Memoirs* Berlioz adds his own arch footnote: "This is quite untrue, and an eample of the proneness of artists to write for effect"

(*M*, 180). Cellini's work is full of delightful "effects" (some turned to happy purpose in the opera), and so is the *Memoirs*, whose author had such a stunning gift for satiric fictionalizing in his treatment of the musical idiocies of his time. In their writing both men manifest a gift for posing. They reach, as prideful artists often will, after something other than strict truth. Often they seek simply for approval—in what Berlioz himself admitted to be "a desperate craving for limitless love" (*M*, 501). Cellini characteristically notes the effect of his works upon the faces of his patrons: "He uttered an expression of astonishment like you do when you see a miracle." Cellini loved to see the delight and amazement his creations produced, and something of this pride runs through the *Memoirs* of Berlioz.[4]

Cellini's *Autobiography* was among the first Renaissance expressions of the integrity of the individual, of fierce and proud self-esteem. One of Romanticism's central philosophers, Friedrich Schlegel, wrote that "he who has his center of gravity within himself is an artist." In musical history Berlioz, possessing this internal center of gravity, stands alongside Beethoven as one of the first musicians to assert independence from aesthetic dictates and dictators. Largely for this reason they both stood alone, belonged to their own schools. Clearly it was not Cellini's art but rather his artistic *stance* that fired the imagination of Romantics like Berlioz. It was not so much the contours of the Perseus (a flawed *chef d'œuvre*, most art historians agree) as the statue's symbolism of the artist's conquest over a grudging intellectual environment that Berlioz felt:

> Music is the most poetic, the most powerful, the most living of all arts. She ought to be the freest, but she is not yet . . . Modern music is like the classic Andromeda, naked and divinely beautiful. She is chained to a rock on the shores of a vast sea and awaits the victorious Perseus who shall loose her bonds and break in pieces the chimera called Routine.[5]

Berlioz, in a way, believed himself a modern musical Perseus and throughout his life composed works he hoped would have the effect of Cellini's masterpiece: that of breaking the serenely dull musical peace.

If, as Pushkin suggests, veracity in matters autobiographical is not possible, perhaps the very humanity of Cellini's lack of candor is the essence of his appeal. The Cellini who never lived except in the selective and falsifying light of memory is more important to us now. Jacob Burckhardt suggested as much:

> It does him [Cellini] no harm when the reader often detects him bragging or lying; the stamp of a mighty, energetic, and thoroughly developed nature remains . . . He is a man who can do all and dares do all, and who carries his measure in himself. Whether we like him or not, he lives, such as he was, as a wholly recognizable prototype of modern man.[6]

There is considerable truth in the *Autobiography,* but it is humane rather than historical truth. The same must also be said of the Berlioz *Memoirs.* The composer developed his own persona when he took to his writing desk, and his imagination typically took hold on the slightest details. He let down his guard now and then—especially in his last years; then, in bitter asides, we sometimes glimpse what Gautier called the "Promethean melancholy" of the man. But whether we have in the *Memoirs* the true, essential Berlioz remains an unanswered question. Saint-Saëns, to name one, thought they did not offer the full picture.

But the *Memoirs* does tell us the nature of Berlioz's aesthetic, the frequent agonies and infrequent ecstacies of his musical life in Paris, and the home truths of his art. And this brings us to the "truth" of *Benvenuto Cellini*—or rather, its truths. For Berlioz not only succeeded in capturing those qualities of the Florentine goldsmith and sculptor which are most endearing, he also divined in Cellini's efforts as an artist his own status. Berlioz saw, as did Burckhardt, that this artist's importance was not the tangible measure of his works but the intangible measure of his own personal vitality. In addition, Berlioz realized in himself a Cellini-esque independence of intellect, and this identification must lie behind the character of the operatic Cellini. By a marvelous coincidence of events and personalities, Berlioz was able to be true to the tenor of his literary source, to himself, and to his aesthetic. This perfect coincidence, as the present study must hint, is rare in operatic annals and must help to explain the vitality and appeal of *Cellini.*

The Premiere and Anti-Romanticism

To appreciate the autobiographical implications in *Cellini* we must examine the reasons for the failure of the opera at its premiere on 10 September 1838. The sad tale is typical not only for Berlioz but for many Romantic artists. The opera was doomed first of all by the extraordinarily inclement conditions of the first production. These are pathetically recounted in the *Memoirs:*

> I shall never forget the horror of those three months. The indifference, the distaste manifested by most of the singers (who were already convinced that it would be a flop); [the conductor] Habeneck's ill humour, and the vague rumours that were constantly going round the theatre; the crass objections raised by that whole crowd of illiterates by certain turns of phrase in a libretto so different in style from the empty, mechanical rhyming prose of the Scribe school—all this was eloquent of an atmosphere of general hostility against which I was powerless, but which I had to pretend not to notice. [*M*, 243]

Burdened with an orchestra by no means unanimous on the composer's behalf, a conductor who transformed incompetence to deal with the intricate score into outrage at Berlioz, a production full of half-measures, and a tenor in the title role uncomfortable with its demands and cynically resolved to perform it diffidently—the opera was bound for defeat.[7] Of the first night audience Berlioz reports, "The overture received exaggerated applause, and the rest was hissed with admirable energy and unanimity." Fourteen years later Berlioz was at last able to see the opera revived *"avec un succès pyramidal"* at Weimar under Liszt's baton. Of this he wrote sadly to Auguste Barbier, one of the librettists: "To tell you that I have experienced a melancholy joy in making a comparison between this well-intentioned production and the miserable cabal to which we were subjected at the *Opéra* would be difficult. It makes me sick at heart." With the first Teresa contracted to leave Paris after two weeks and the tenor eager to throw over his role, *Cellini* was withdrawn after three performances. Receipts were well below Meyerbeerian levels, so the money-hungry management nailed shut its coffin all the more eagerly. As many must have joked, *Benvenuto* was in fact *malvenuto.*

Other reasons for the failure of the opera can be attributed simply to the anti-Romantic bias, and these are worth glancing at. To show in a brief space how the opera's hero, its libretto, its musical personality, and even Berlioz himself excited animosity, we may conveniently turn to two contemporary articles from the prestigious *Journal des Débats* and the *Revue des Deux Mondes*. The first is a review by the literary lion of the day, Jules Janin, and the second is a long, condescending tirade by Henri Blaze.[8]

The emphases of Janin's feuilleton are illuminating. Most intriguing is its reaction to the hero: "But what a hero! What a subject! A bully, a bandit, a hare-brained sort only the slightest bit poetic, always in the pay of someone or other, always suspected of thievery or murder, stretching out an open palm to all the princes of the world and all their mistresses, upset with his fate, a kind of adventurer and great artist by the luck of the draw." Janin succeeds in putting Cellini in the worst light, complaining that he is not a Michelangelo, even suggesting that a wiser composer would have set *that* more socially acceptable artist's life to music:

> Now Michelangelo, that poetic figure! A political man, as well as a soldier, a serious artist, a devout Christian artist, a zealous republican, a man important for his virtue as for his genius, the imperishable honor of Italy—one who would look with the same unspeakable horror upon a Cellini, a goldsmith, taking his place as upon an Ariosto, a buffoon, taking the place of Dante.

Janin's idea of an artistic hero would have accorded well with the pious rationality and refined, high-flown diction of a by then superannuated neo-Classicism. I pause over his wishful thinking because, in its discomfort with Ariosto (a genuine Cellini of Renaissance poets in his colloquial vigor) and with Cellini, it expresses a hidebound stuffiness that Berlioz seemed always to be struggling against. The spirit if not the genius of the *siècle des lumières* was still nurtured among the Janins of the time, and these men still demanded sophistication, learning, periphrasis, and self-conscious art. No wonder Janin found Cellini a "vulgar and trivial hero" and merely a "glorious vagabond."

Romantics like Hugo, Delacroix, and Berlioz burst upon an era in

French cultural history that could hardly be called exciting. Gautier observed of the period, "It is impossible to realize the depth of insignificance and colourlessness literature had fallen into; and the case of painting was no better." And one might add that in music the first two decades of the nineteenth century were among the dullest in French history. But with the advent of Shakespeare, Beethoven, and Goethe in the 1820s in Paris, the scene changed radically. The pressure upon timeworn conventions increased; an eagerness to explore new forms of expression grew inevitably. The desire for direct, powerful, vivid expression increased, just as did the disposition to ignore the rules and proprieties of the former age. To satisfy the thirst for new experiences, Romantics looked to faraway places, to eccentrics, to social outcasts, to grotesques. But above all, they looked to times that were at least artistically more free—for instance to the humanist Renaissance, that vital intellectual interregnum between the age of faith and the age of reason that was dominated by neither the ancients nor the moderns. The Romantics looked for an era as lively and promising as their own, and they naturally sensed that the times of Cellini, Rabelais, and Shakespeare suited their needs. Gautier felt the parallel even in 1830: "A movement analogous to that of the Renaissance was taking place. A sap of new life was running hotly; everything was germinating, budding, blooming at one and the same time; intoxicating scents filled the air."

The popularity of Cellini among the new generation was to be expected, for here was a man with an encompassing egotism that drove all before it, a tenacity of feeling, and a down-to-earth quality—just what Romantics found in themselves and wanted in their art. They wanted, in short, a hero who would admit (as Cellini did in his *Treatise on Goldsmithing*), "I can't do your fine elegant manner of writing." They did not care that he lacked an inspirational artistic gravity, or even that he was a bit vulgar and trivial. They liked the turmoil and invigorating pace of Cellini's world. They were instinctively drawn to this *bandit de génie*—a man who shocked the 1830s just as he shocked the 1530s.

Giorgio Vasari, a contemporary of Cellini, described him as "in all his doings of high spirit, proud, lively, very quick to act, and formidably vehement." These qualities stand out in the pages of the

Autobiography and in the score of *Cellini.* It was not in Janin's power to conceive the colorful kind of heroism that Berlioz was to invest in his score, a heroism based upon an inner *virtù* that clears its own path and pays out grudgingly the allegiance demanded by society. The Cellini of Berlioz is an archetypal Romantic hero on a par with Hugo's Hernani. No wonder he grated the sensibilities of Janin's pre-Revolutionary aesthetic.

The second major offense for which Janin indicts *Cellini* is its libretto. He could scarcely ignore the horrors committed upon the language: "However, if you have the power to push the unfortunate and maladroit text to one side, if you close your ears to the silly words and the wretched rhymes, what a talented score this is!" It is now hard to imagine what exactly offended Janin. Specifics are few, but the tone is breathtakingly arch:

> The language in which the libretto is written I need scarcely bother with. It is ludicrous. There must be underneath such a style some poetic theory that is easily disguised and which I could not discover. For it is most certain that verse of this sort could only have been written on purpose. Here are the last two lines of the piece, judge the rest by them:
>
> Il réussit, j'en étais sûr!
> Ma fille, embrasse ton futur!
>
> [He has won! I was sure of it!
> My daughter, embrace your future husband!]

Janin is apparently objecting to the simple-mindedness of Balducci's last words to his daughter. One might excuse them by observing that Balducci is given, throughout the opera, the buffo character of a man with a stunningly simple turn of mind.

Berlioz, who we know was trying to improve upon the boring rhymes of the Scribe style, found this violent reaction to his more vigorous and earthy libretto quite incomprehensible:

> Auguste Barbier, here and there in the recitatives, may have let slip a word or phrase unashamedly deriving from the vocabulary of the people and therefore unacceptable to the niceness of modern taste; but it is hardly credible that the following lines, which occur in a

duet written by Léon de Wailly, should have struck most of the singers as ridiculous:

> When I came to my senses,
> The rooftops were shining in the first light of dawn,
> the cocks were crowing, etcetera, etcetera.
>
> "Ah, the cocks!" they said, "ha! ha! ha! The cocks! It'll be the hens next!" and so on in the same vein. What could one say to such idiots? [*M*, 243]

The tradition that the opera failed because of an indifferent libretto was taken up in due course by many subsequent commentators. However, anyone who peruses it will find a libretto of verve and imagination, if also some occasionally heavy-handed rhyming. It is hard to fathom why it was rejected while the dull prosody of Scribe was praised and patronized.[9]

This strange state of affairs becomes less surprising, however, given the surrounding literary terrain. The rejection of this libretto reflects yet again the classicist bias in favor of modesty and finesse and against the prosaic or colloquial. If we turn to the notorious evening when Hugo's play *Hernani* received its premiere (25 February 1830), we find the same violent skirmishing over the most mundane lines. Gautier sarcastically examined the silly clash between Romantics and Classicists:

> How can one explain, for instance, that this line—
>
> Est-il minuit? Minuit bientôt.
> [Is it midnight? It is about to strike.]
>
> —should have raised a storm and that the battle raged for three days around that hemistich? It was adjudged to be trivial, familiar, improper. Behold a king asking what time it is in the language of a commoner, and answered as though he were a clodhopper! Serves him right! If he had used a fine periphrasis, he would have been replied to politely, somewhat in this fashion—
>
> . . . l'heure
> Atteindra bientôt sa dernière demeure.
> [The time / Will soon have reached its latest hour.]

The same silly scruples helped to cause the furor over the *Cellini* libretto. Trivial, familiar, improper—the same epithets that were hurled at Hugo were hurled at Barbier and de Wailly. If their text failed to meet the expectations of an audience addicted to the pallid beauties of Scribe, then it was an *insuccès d'estime.*[10]

In spite of his reservations about the subject and libretto, Janin was sympathetic to its music. He admired the first aria for Teresa, found the love-tryst trio "charming," the end of the first scene full of color, enjoyed the buffo aria for Fieramosca, and noted among the "beautiful things" of Act II Cellini's narration, the grand duet, Ascanio's aria, and Cellini's romance. Janin tried as best he could to extricate Berlioz from the supposed debacle: "For those who know how to listen and understand, M. Berlioz has survived this trial as a great artist, a profound musician." (Janin and Berlioz were, incidentally, colleagues on the *Journal des Débats.*)

To find criticism of Berlioz's music that does throw in relief the Classic-Romantic antagonism, we are obliged to turn to the article by Henri Blaze, a musician and critic perhaps best known for the massacre he committed upon Weber's *Der Freischütz* for performance in Paris.[11] The Blaze article (on Berlioz's music generally) manages to allege most of the failures and flaws commonly associated with this composer. They are the flaws of Romanticism as seen through the eyes of a deep-dyed reactionary. Blaze fears Berlioz as an unpredictable, arrogantly self-willed barbarian,

> a character who is energetic and uncivilized, though loyal, open, and generous . . . whatever the disorderly caprices to which he abandons himself, one must attribute these to the impetuosity, the eccentric flair of his revolutionary temperament.

The composer is pictured as a bull in the china shop of musical tradition: "I defy anyone to cite one glorious tradition in music which M. Berlioz has respected. Melody, rhythm, the human voice"[12] His response is expressive of a common reactionary failure of the imagination ("Berlioz persists in searching for effects that it is not possible for music to express"). He finds nothing in Berlioz but a "genius for destruction," yokes him damningly with Hugo, and even criticizes him for trying to write a musical equivalent of Hugo's notorious preface to the play *Cromwell* (which attacked the dramatic unities).

For Berlioz the response was simple: declare war on musical conventions. "If it suited me," his friend Hiller reported Berlioz as saying, "I would marry the natural daughter of a hangman and a negress." There was some truth in the Blaze description of Berlioz—"an impetuous sort, resolute, proud, proclaiming only the genius blessed by his own hands"—as a man who would naturally grate upon his colleagues and rivals and enemies. He had a refractory streak, a sharpness of intellect, a cynicism about human motives and debilities that—human nature being what it is—begged for retribution. No doubt many in Paris looked sanguinely upon his premieres with revenge in mind—much as the Pope looks upon Cellini in the Finale of the opera's third tableau:

> Now he will feel less proud
> Of his mad effrontery.
> His insolence was too great;
> I have to punish him.
> There will be no saint or guardian angel
> To aid his efforts.
> He defied my authority.
> It has gone too far; my indulgence is exhausted.

And it is equally certain that Berlioz, at least in his early years, looked upon his enemies with the same defiance Cellini expresses at the same time in the Finale:

> My spirit is too full of power
> For failure to be possible.
> I defy their vengeance.
> God favours the bold
> And grants them success.
> Their crude vengeance
> Will not prevail.

Beriloz paid the price for his personality. Many of those who hissed the first performance of *Benvenuto Cellini* thought they were dropping an insolent musical troublemaker a few notches.

An Operatic Cellini: 1838

With a sense of this hostile environment into which Berlioz thrust his first opera, we can begin to see what appealed to him in Cellini's autobiography. That there was an identification is clear from the first story in the composer's witty collection of tales about musical life in Paris, *Evenings with the Orchestra* (*E*, 9-26). While dull, banal operas are being performed on stage, members of the orchestra exchange anecdotes, critiques, and parables (only the trombones and bass drum need attend to the music). This story is called "The First Opera, A Tale of the Past," and it is cast in the form of an exchange of letters between Benvenuto Cellini and a distraught opera composer, Alfonso della Viola—Berlioz himself. Viola writes to tell Cellini of the "bittter pangs of the artist who has been outraged in his art and in his person." In his attempt to get the first opera performed, Viola appears to suffer the same indignities meted out to Berlioz. At the last minute the Grand Duke of Florence has a change of mind: "The Duke, whose golden words had filled an artist's heart and kindled an artist's imagination, now made sport of it all, ordering that imagination to cool off, that heart to be still or to break—it didn't matter which to him! In short, he halts the production." (The events Viola describes are most pertinent to the imbroglio surrounding the commissioning postponement, and eventual performance of the *Requiem*. See the *Memoirs,* Chapter 46.)

Viola writes to Cellini for comfort and advice about a method of revenge. Cellini replies with the tale of his own trials and adds this advice: "I know you, you will persevere. You will reach your goal in spite of everything. You are a man of iron mold, and the stones thrown in your face by the low and envious who lie in ambush along your path, far from breaking your head, will strike fire from it." In his letter Cellini even alludes to his difficulties with the statue of Perseus: "These, my dear Alfonso, are dire sufferings and persecutions hard to bear . . . I suppose you haven't forgotten the mocking nicknames hurled at me, the insulting sonnets placarded nightly on my door, the secret intrigues by which Cosimo was persuaded that my new casting process would not work and that it was folly to entrust me with the metal." Cellini concludes with an exordium that

Berlioz himself was forced to believe in throughout his troubled Parisian career:

> Yes, I tell you, I have endured every sort of buffet that fate can inflict upon an artist. And yet I live. And my living fame is a torment to my enemies. I knew it was to be, so now I am able to bury them in my contempt. This kind of revenge comes slowly, it is true, but for an inspired man who is sure of himself, who is strong and patient, it is a certainty.[13]

If Berlioz survived a half-century of Parisian battle with his sanity and musical beliefs intact, it is because he believed in these words he puts in Cellini's mouth. The two artists were soul mates at core. This characteristic self-reliance is mirrored in the crucial lines from Cellini's prayer in the last minutes of the opera:

> Lord, use Thy power!
> Thou holdest the only remedy.
> If Thou dost not wish me to give way
> To despair,
> Then help me, since I help myself.

Cellini's motto in the last line was the motto for the composer too.

For the denouement of the little parable Berlioz has Cellini arrange to meet Viola in Florence. On his way to meet him at the Baptistery, Cellini stops to gaze at his statue of Perseus. "The artist contemplated his immortal work, wondering whether an obscure life and an ordinary mind were not to be preferred to glory and genius." These musings express the heartsickening desire to free oneself from the struggle, to abandon one's art for peace of mind:

> "Why am I not a drover from Nettuno or Porto d'Anzio?" he mused. "Like the cattle in my care, I should lead a rough, monotonous life, but it would at least be free from the turmoil which since childhood has bedeviled my existence. Treacherous and jealous rivals—unjust or ungrateful princes—relentless critics—brainless flatterers—continual alternations of success and adversity, of splendor and of poverty—overwork without end—never any respite, any comfort, any leisure—wearing out my body like a mercenary and feeling my soul forever chilled or aflame—can that be called living?"

These thoughts nearly paraphrase the text for Cellini's air in Act II, just before the casting of the statue (*Sur les monts les plus sauvages*):

On the wildest mountains
Why am I not a simple shepherd
Leading from pasture to pasture,
Day by day, my wandering flock!
At large, solitary, untroubled,
Free from exhausting toil,
Roaming far from the din of cities,
I would sing like a lark;
And then at night in my hut
Alone, my bed the earth,
I'd sleep as peacefully
As in my mother's arms.

It has been felt that the sentiment of this air is "surprising," but not if one sees it as the poignant autobiographical statement it is. At the end of the aria Cellini responds to the call of his art and supervises the miraculous casting of the Perseus. He tears himself away from the pleasant dream of tranquillity. Like his hero, Berlioz also resisted until the very last years the temptation to retire from the fight for his musical beliefs. Berlioz, too, was chained by the bonds of pride to his art.[14] When the orchestra members celebrate their last "Evening" each player makes a toast. The one made by the Conductor is pure Berlioz: "I drink to those artists whom nothing can debase or dishearten, the true, the valiant, and the strong!" (*E*, 300).[15]

Why was this courage necessary? We have in his writings frequent and often witty descriptions of the "Lilliputian inanities" that threatened Berlioz from every side. Perhaps most fundamentally, Berlioz found himself in the ignorant and whimsical hands of the powerful—men "who have never done anything, do not know anything, do not believe in anything, do not care about anything, neither want nor are capable of anything, and in addition to the indispensable attributes of ignorance, apathy and incompetence, are gifted with a kind of primordial inertia only just removed from imbecility" (*M*, 398-99). In France at the time the bourgeois class was finally asserting a prerogative answering to its economic power. Opera became a genuinely public domain and, as a consequence, an adjunct of the commercial system. Beginning with Véron and Duponchel, directors of the Opéra were businessmen first and artists second, if at all. To Berlioz the business ethic ruined the institution: "These unsavory, if short-lived, alliances [between art and commerce] are always brought about by money—the greed for rapid gain that can corrupt the most high-minded people" (*M*, 342).

The consequence for Berlioz was an Opéra almost by definition closed to him—perhaps the single most crippling and humiliating fact of his entire musical career. His attitude toward that institution became merciless:

> The Opéra is madly in love with mediocrity. In order to possess mediocrity, do honor to it, give it a home, pet it and cherish it and glorify it, it will stop at nothing, shrink from no sacrifice, and accept any hard labor with enthusiasm. With the best of intentions, the utmost goodwill, it works itself up to ecstasy over platitude, shows a raging appetite for the insipid, and burns with the fever of love for what is lukewarm. It would turn poet in order to sing the praises of prose. [*E*, 106-7]

For the Parisian audience to which the Opéra management catered, Berlioz saved some of his most contemptuous utterances. Naturally, managers catering to a public which "as a whole is not very bright, but frivolous rather, unjust, indifferent, changeable" (*E*, 307) would scarcely have time to pay heed to aesthetic niceties, or to what Berlioz believed was the essentially aristocratic nature of music.[16] Visual panoply overwhelmed dramatic truth and artistic economy on the stage Berlioz had attempted to storm with *Benvenuto Cellini*. There was no public for mere simple, unpretentious beauty, and this is cleverly suggested by an episode in the opera. This is the lampoon of the musical tastes of a figure dressed up to look like Teresa's father Balducci. This takes place at the Roman Carnival in Act I. In the mimed contest to determine the finest tenor, Harlequin performs a tender ariette (its theme is familiar from the Roman Carnival overture) that possesses the indubitable stamp of Berlioz:

During this the feigned Balducci falls asleep. When the second contestant, Pasquarello, offers a mindless *cavatina* to this accompaniment—

—the impersonated Balducci is delighted, even beats the drum (so despised by Berlioz for overuse) against the rhythm. This scene is a droll comment upon the plebeian tastes that pervaded the Opéra stage, and to which Berlioz so often alludes in *Evenings with the Orchestra*.

Money was always a problem for Berlioz, except in his later years when he had little strength to enjoy it. He must have identified with the anxiety of the last pages of *Cellini* (in which the need for "more metal" threatens destruction of the Perseus project at the last minute) because he often suffered torture over the financing of the concerts of his music he himself organized. The necessity for money was a lesson Berlioz carried away from the ordeal of his first opera: "The composition of *Cellini* occupied a good deal of time. But for a friend who came to my rescue, I would not have been able to finish it by the appointed date. One must be free of all other work when writing an opera; that is, one's livelihood must be assured for a certain period" (*M*, 246). The composer, however, was never so lucky. He had to depend upon wages received for the articles he so hated writing, from the benevolence of friends like Legouvé and Paganini, and from the receipts of his successful German and Russian excursions. Like Cellini, Berlioz's financial existence was tenuous and unpredictable. The cry "more metal!" echoed frequently.

Enough has already been observed of the difficulties Berlioz faced in preparing his works for performance. His writings are littered with passages describing emotions of disgust, amusement, outrage, and depression arising from many causes: the pomposity of singers, the incompetence of conductors, the bumble-brained behavior of inept or ungenerous musicians, the insolence of impresarios, the unethical and ignoble intrigues of rivals, and the whimsy of governmental agencies. Like many artistic geniuses, Berlioz felt himself profoundly out of joint with the times—and with his countrymen:

> What the devil was the good Lord thinking of when he had me born in this pleasant land of France? Yet I love our absurd country, whenever I can forget art and the impossibly unstable politics. What gaiety there is, how amusing things are, between whiles! What a hotbed of ideas it is (verbally, at least)! How they tear the universe to pieces with their fine white teeth and scratch its Creator with their exquisite nails! How they dance on the pin-point of a good phrase! How royally they play the fool—and republicanly! [*M*, 124]

Only this typically cynical buoyancy kept Berlioz's tribulations from becoming a genuinely funereal catalogue aria. The treatment he received at the hands of his countrymen reminds one of Tchaikovsky's *bon mot* about Parisians: "Curious people! It is necessary to die in order to attract their attention." The composer was a victim of his own genius. As Byron observed, talent can be forgiven, but genius never—and Berlioz was only posthumously forgiven by his fellow Parisians for the excesses to which genius led him. There is a handsome, newly installed monument at the composer's grave in the Montmartre cemetery to prove it. How Berlioz would have mocked the gesture!

Benvenuto Cellini *and Cellini's Autobiography*

As I have already suggested, the interest of *Cellini* is due in no small measure to the biographical and cultural-historical parallels between

Cellini's and Berlioz's worlds. The appeal of the *Autobiography* for the composer was based, in addition, upon a strong artistic affinity with the outstanding qualities of Cellini's writing. No composer in history has been so completely bound up with great literature as Berlioz; almost all of his important works are inspired by or based upon masterpieces of men eminent in Western literature.[17] No composer despised with more venomous hatred the musical enervation of great literature. (His reaction to Bellini's *Romeo and Juliet* opera is typical: "Disgusting, ridiculous, impotent. That little fool has apparently not been afraid that Shakespeare's shade might come and haunt him in his sleep.") And no one sought more fervently and fruitfully to preserve the qualities of literary splendor in his musical transformations.

The *Autobiography* was a perfect vehicle for what Berlioz knew he could portray best. Intense passion, animation, and unpredictability are the dominant qualities of Cellini's personality and his prose style, and Berlioz described the "modern tonality"—of which he and Beethoven were the progenitors—as essentially dramatic, passionate, and expressive (*E*, 191). Precisely these qualities assured the *Autobiography* a place in world literature. Cellini naturally dramatized the events of his life, and the composer also possessed a sophisticated dramatic sense. Paul Dukas wrote that "With Berlioz everything—symphony, oratorio, sacred music—becomes drama."[18] Cellini wrote with a virile colloquialism and a minimum of "artistic" overlay. The same qualities are the essence of Berlioz's credo as an artist, expressed so well in the *Evenings:*

> We must ever show the warmest regard for theatrical compositions in which music is respected and passion nobly expressed, and in which are displayed common sense, naturalness, plain truth, grandeur without bombast, and strength without brutality . . . A work in good taste, truly musical and coming from the heart—why, in our time of exaggeration, vociferation, dislocation, mechanism, and manikinism, we must adore it. [*E*, 306]

J. A. Symonds, the most famous Cellini translator, described the statue of Perseus as having "something of fascination, a bravura brilliancy, a sharpness of technical precision, a singular and striking picturesqueness." This applies verbatim to the *Cellini* score. The finest scenes in the opera are true to the *joie de vivre* of the *Autobiography*. In its restless, careening, alternately stentorian and languorous character, the Overture prepares us for the entire opera. All of the characteristics of the "Symphonie Fantastique" are present here and in the opera generally: fiery orchestration, rhythmic inventiveness, melodic riches, and the uncanny sense for the modulation of emotion and control of suspense. Words one might use to describe Cellini himself—energetic, sinewy, daring, ingenious, naïve, salient—apply with ease to the Overture. Its melodies were even delineated in terms of Cellini's art by Weingartner: "each plastic, sharply characterized, wonderfully chiselled, varied, developed, climaxed and concluded."[19]

Upset by an apparent insult, Cellini admits in his *Autobiography*, "I was utterly determined to make mischief, and anyway I am rather hot-blooded by nature" (*A*, 37). Real blood—often hot—never ceases to flow in the veins of the Berlioz hero, and as in the original he always subjugates the stage when he is present. Cellini's bent was not for the long, hard pull. Rather, he operated upon the sudden jet of emotion, depending upon the agility and quickness of his wits, not upon a gravity of design. Cellini readily admits that he was often passion's slave, and Berlioz is careful to make sure his own Cellini remains precisely that—even devoting Cellini's Act I romance (*La gloire était ma seule idole,* S2) to an expression of the pull between duty and passion. Rolland called Berlioz an "untrammeled spirit" and perhaps it takes one to know one, for the orchestral fire never dies out under the role of Cellini. Nothing better captures his catapulting Romantic individualism than the duet *Quand des sommets de la montagne* (S5) for Cellini and Teresa in Act II. Marked allegro fuoco ma non troppo, this restless, fervent duet truly takes flight. One is reminded of Hernani's horn summoning the mountain hawks, with which Hugo shattered the repose of the neo-Classical old guard.

It would be mistaken to conclude that *Cellini* is a completely innovative work. Though in subject and execution something new on the horizon, it is nevertheless based upon old operatic traditions. Old-fashioned plot threads are woven with the new. Teresa's first scene is based upon the *cavatina*/recitative/*cabaletta* organization so well developed by Rossini and carried on by Verdi. The feckless suitor to Teresa, Fieramosca, is given a buffo aria (*Ah! qui pourrait me résister?*, S3) worthy of comparison with Basilio's "calumny" aria in *Il Barbiere*. There is a charming coloratura dexterity in the pants-role scene for Ascanio (*Mais qu'ai-je donc?*, S7) that comes suspiciously close to the character of Isolier in Rossini's *Le Comte Ory*. And the added by-plot of Teresa, her self-important father Balducci, and the tenor lover remarkably parallels the story of *Il Barbiere di Siviglia*—which Berlioz called a "dazzling masterpiece" in spite of his low opinion of Rossini's effect on operatic tastes. (Teresa's first big scene performs exactly the function of Rosina's *Una voce poco fa.*) What sets these "highlights" above the average is their psychological truth, the personality Berlioz infuses in these traditional forms and themes. Ascanio's aria is a case in point. Here is a brilliant sketch-in-an-aria that somehow captures the eagerness, juvenile flightiness, and charm of all the helpers Cellini mentions in his memoirs.

Within these traditional contexts Berlioz created many scenes whose dramatic effectiveness derived from the source. One of Cellini's penchants was for making his enemies look foolish—a gift we know from the *Evenings* was shared by Berlioz. Lattanzio Gorini, who harassed Cellini during the casting of the Perseus, is described as "a lean harsh man . . . this little pipsqueak, with his spidery hands and tiny gnat's voice" (*A*, 315). When Cellini and the "filthy, ruffianly blockhead" Bandinello confront each other in the presence of Duke Cosimo, there is little doubt who triumphs: "The Duke stood there, listening with great enjoyment, and while I was talking Bandinello kept twisting and turning and making the most unimaginably ugly faces—and his face was ugly enough already" (*A*, 336). Cellini seems always to come out on top, battered but unbowed, and Berlioz faithfully keeps his hero buoyed above the pettiness and self-indulgence of Balducci (a composite of all the courtier villians in the *Autobiography*) and Fieramosca (a composite of all Cellini's vicious and inept professional rivals).

The introduction of Balducci in the first scene is a perfect example of Cellini-esque caricature transformed into music. From the stalking little fugato—Berlioz was a very circumspect friend of the fugue—

which accompanies his entrance, the nervous tick in the strings, and the crazy, swaggering trills, we know we are in the presence of a comic butt. None of Cellini's rivals in art, except Michelangelo, survives the author's dashing wit, and Berlioz likewise puts all his energies of deprecation and lampoon into the characterization of the papal sculptor Fieramosca. As a parody of the artist without artistry, a grotesque suitor, and a jelly of false courage, Fieramosca is a precursor of Wagner's Beckmesser; and Beckmessers hounded Berlioz all his life. Especially amusing and reminiscent of Beckmesser's rule-mongering is Berlioz's description of the procedures established by the Academy of Fine Arts for awarding the Prix de Rome (*M*, 107-18). Like Wagner's self-indulgent pedant, Fieramosca is also crushed by the plot. He is a delectable comic butt and, along with Balducci, a perfect foil for the free-spirited, passionate Cellini.

Berlioz and his librettists were not afraid to make extreme alterations of the plot for their opera. Pope Clement, for instance, replaces Duke Cosimo de' Medici as the patron of the statue. And Pompeo's murder in Act I is handled differently from the source. The change, however, is in specifics rather than in the essence of the dramatic event. Cellini's Pompeo is not a swordsman but a jeweler and, for reasons not entirely clear, a personal enemy. His demise is sparked by a public confrontation of the kind common in Mediterranean societies: "After Pompeo had been standing there for the length of time it takes to say two Hail Marys he laughed scornfully in my direction, and then, all laughing together, he and his companions made off, snapping their fingers at me and provoking me with their insolent gestures" (*A*, 134). Intent on revenge, Cellini manages shortly to meet Pompeo. The deed is described with chilling nonchalance:

> I grasped my little sharp-edged dagger, forced my way through his guards, and put my hands on his chest so coolly and swiftly that none of them could stop me. I aimed to let him have it in the face, but he was so terrified that he turned his head and my dagger struck him just under the ear. I followed this up with only two stabs more, for at the second he fell dead; not that that had been my intention, but, as they say, there are no rules in war. Then I retrieved the dagger with my left hand, while with my right I drew my sword to defend my life.

In the operatic version the essential aspects are the same: Pompeo is still an unpleasant, swaggering sort whose demise is no great sadness, the murder is committed in the heat of the moment (because of spoiled elopement rather than a personal affront), and it is done in the midst of a crowd. To be sure, the eerie detachment of Cellini's version is undercut somewhat by having Cellini and Pompeo fairly dueling each other.[20]

The murder of Pompeo and Cellini's flight are turned to effect in Act II, in which the hero is given the opportunity to relate his escape from the Piazza Colonna. This breathless recitative passage (*Ma dague en main*, S5) perhaps captures more vividly the literary quality of the *Autobiography* than any other in the opera. For it puts the operatic Cellini in the position of the memoirist, attempting to re-create the drama of a past event by charging it with an emotional energy. Here is our one direct glimpse of Cellini the writer in the opera.

The casting of the Perseus is the climax of Cellini's memoirs, as it is of the opera. The librettists had very little to do in this last scene but follow the source. All things needful for an exciting denouement are in the *Autobiography:* the tearful desperation, the melodrama of the uncertain forge and the last-minute lack of metal, the eagerness for failure on the part of Cellini's enemies, the wavering courage of the forgehands, the sudden but effective piety of Cellini's prayer, and above all the sense of Cellini himself omnipresent, roaring his orders, and straightening out the "terrible confusion." It is unfortunate that at this point Berlioz could not rise fully to the challenge of transforming the tension, momentum, and suspense into music.

The present approach to *Cellini* has not offered sufficient opportunity to observe some of the score's musical felicities, something that can only be briefly done here. One would point to the passionate trio in the first scene between Cellini, Teresa, and the concealed Fieramosca—especially the breathtaking allegro in which the lover's rendezvous is planned. Underlying it is an orchestral fine-point and delicacy of humor comparable to the Queen Mab Scherzo in *Romeo and Juliet*. The choruses of *Cellini* are among the most invigorating and richly characterized in the literature, and there are no less than five important choral events in the opera. The "Song of the Metalworkers" is brilliant and carries with it a beautiful text in praise of the goldsmith's art. The gathering of the populace for the *commedia dell'arte* in the Piazza Colonna is full of humor and is rather more successfully observed than its scenic counterpart in *Pagliacci*.

The power of the ensemble passages, especially the conclusions of Acts I and II, cannot be overemphasized. They lead one to remark that almost every scene ends with a tremendous orchestral upswing. If ever there was an operatic "upper," *Cellini* is it. The stupendous climax of the "Symphonie Fantastique" occurs, if this can be imagined, seven or eight times in the score. If one may call *Don Giovanni* an "attacca opera" in which the pace never slackens, never touches ground for a moment, then I think *Cellini* might be called an attacca/allegro opera. That marking—allegro con fuoco, allegro vivace, allegro animato, allegro deciso con impeto, allegro con fuoco assai—dominates the score and gives it its extraordinary momentum.

After the casting is performed, Cellini adds in typical fashion, "I was a little boastful and inclined to show off about it, so I preened myself a little." He even relates that his enemies suspected him of being "some powerful fiend, since I had done the impossible, and some things which even a devil would have found baffling." The devilish Cellini of the *Autobiography* lives in the opera because, as Berlioz himself observed in a letter, "There is a diabolical fire in that score."[21] With considerable right, Berlioz, too, could look back upon his handiwork and boast: "I have just examined it seriously, after having forgotten it for thirteen years, and I swear that I shall never more recapture that animation and Cellinian impetuosity, nor such a variety of ideas."[22] All of these powers helped Berlioz to capture in his opera the fascinating mixture of piety and roguery, honesty and self-indulgent special pleading, tenderness and brutality, shrewdness and naïveté that makes Cellini such a unique literary and historical figure.

six

MACBETH

To copy reality is a good thing, but to
invent reality *is better, much better.*
A contradiction may seem to exist in
these three words to invent reality,
but just ask Papa Shakespeare.

Giuseppe Verdi

Samuel Johnson opened his defense of the witches' scenes in Shakespeare's "Macbeth" with this admonition: "In order to make a true estimate of the abilities and merit of a writer, it is always necessary to examine the genius of his age, and the opinions of his contemporaries." This sentiment is particularly relevant to Giuseppe Verdi's first attempt to bring a Shakespearean play to the operatic stage. For *Macbeth,* the tenth of his twenty-seven operas, has been obliged to rest in the shadow of the composer's two culminating works, which also happen to be based upon Shakespearean plays.* *Macbeth* is a work of the composer's relative youth (he was thirty-three when he wrote it), and we rightly sense that it is still tangled in the traditional influences of old conventions prevailing in Italy in the 1840s. Nestled among *Alzira, Attila, I Masnadieri,* and *Jérusalem* in the Verdi canon, *Macbeth* has suffered much from the condescension, not to say worse, regularly heaped upon the bulk of the "early" and "middle" operas. This is to a degree natural: the attractions of budding genius will pall once we have experienced its final luxuriant bloom.

But *Macbeth* is a trap for those who are too hasty in their condescension—and there have been many such. Even a writer as perceptive as Joseph Kerman has fallen into the trap, writing that "the relationship between opera and play is insignificant in the early works up to and including *Macbeth.*"[1] This peremptory judgment is unfair to *Macbeth,* partly because Kerman has failed to take Dr. Johnson's

* In this essay plays are set in quotation marks, operas in italic type. Musical quotations are from the Schirmer score, except for those made from the Paris version. Shakespearean quotations are taken from the Riverside Shakespeare edition (1973).

advice and examine the opera against a background of Verdi's operatic epoch and against the play itself. Far from insignificant, the relationship between play and music is remarkable, even historic. We must look at the opera, in a sense, through the eyes of contemporaries if we are to understand its stunning effectiveness and its significance in the development of musical drama. We may then begin to understand why the first Lady Macbeth, Barbieri-Nini, described it as "something unheard-of, something quite new, something unimagined." We will also find that the opera's finest passages bring Shakespeare's memorable moments strikingly to life and, conversely, that some of the opera's vulgarities, melodrama, and hasty character development are to be blamed—if blame must be dispensed at all—not upon the composer but upon Shakespeare himself. The opera is a far more faithful setting than has been realized heretofore, and we owe Verdi the belated justice of considering play and opera in close juxtaposition.

Verdi and Shakespeare

In his last months Verdi was asked to set a prayer written by the widow of the recently assassinated King Umberto. He declined, explaining that his doctors forbade the strain composition would entail, but did remark: "I should add that I would not have set a rhymed version of this prayer to music. In the original prose of the Queen there is more sincerity, more abandon, and a primal coloring which is naturally lacking in the verse" (*C*, 723).* This brief comment expresses the single most deeply felt and historically significant of Ver-

* Quotations from Verdi's correspondence come from various sources. Those designated by (*W*) are from *Verdi: The Man in His Letters,* eds. Franz Werfel and Paul Stefan, tr. Edward Downes (1942). For some letters my own translation seemed preferable, in which case I consulted *I Copialettere di Giuseppe Verdi,* eds. Gaetano and Alessandro Luzio (1913). These are denoted by (*C*). A new translation of selected letters by Charles Osborne (1971) is, however, now the most accessible.

I am indebted in this chapter to Julian Budden's *The Operas of Verdi* (1973), Vol. 1. When the second volume appears, this will be the most complete treatment of Verdi's works in English. The *Macbeth* chapter is most illuminating. I have sought to avoid repetition of Budden's observations and hope that what has resulted will serve as a companion essay to his.

di's creative principles: that the direct, primal expression of human feeling must be the supreme artistic goal. In fact, as Verdi's credo, the words of his idol Shakespeare could scarcely be bettered:

> Suit the action to the word, the word to the action, with this special observation, that you o'erstep not the modesty of nature: for any thing so o'erdone is from the purpose of playing, whose end, both at the first and now, was and is, to hold as 'twere the mirror up to nature.

Hamlet's speech to the players may seem most relevant to the period of *Otello* and *Falstaff* when Verdi had abandoned the set-piece structure we associate with Rossini, Bellini, and Donizetti. But we have not realized just how early in his career Verdi personalized Hamlet's principles, or how courageous and persistent an artist had to be in the 1840s if he did not care to overstep the modesty of nature. His modern ideas about realism in the lyric theater were already forming in these years, and *Macbeth* is his first clear example of this new sensitivity to literary and dramatic values.

Verdi's letters from this period in his life suggest that he was making operatic history. It might not be utterly fanciful to assert that the age of bel canto ended and the age of verismo began on the day—28 November 1848 to be precise—when Verdi objected to a soprano under consideration for the role of Lady Macbeth at the Neapolitan premiere: "Tadolini has a beautiful, lovely figure, and I would like Lady Macbeth brutish and ugly. Tadolini sings to perfection, and I would like a Lady Macbeth who doesn't really sing. Tadolini has an astonishing, clear, limpid, potent voice, and I would like in Lady a harsh, suffocated, veiled voice. Tadolini's voice is angelic; I would like Lady's voice to seem diabolical" (*C*, 61). The era of the singing actor was finally dawning.

All four Shakespearean settings Verdi produced or contemplated forced the composer to break new ground,[2] but perhaps the most important in terms of his overall artistic growth was *Macbeth*. This early opera forced him to become a verismo composer, "untimely ripped" from the highly ornamental aesthetic prevailing at the time. Where Rossini's, Bellini's, and Donizetti's preoccupation was to give the singer room to sing, Verdi was becoming anxious to give room—

as he wrote much later concerning *Aida*—for the actor to act (*campo ad azione per l'attore*). In order to create this "space" for acting, Verdi was willing to forgo any artistic custom or nicety, something his librettists were often reluctant to do.

Verdi was above all a man of the theater. By the time he came to write *Aida* in 1870 he could be brutally candid with his librettists about his dramatic priorities: "It seems to me that the right theatrical phrase is missing, or if it's there it is buried under rhyme or the verse, and doesn't leap out nicely and clearly as it should" (*C*, 639). Whenever he was presented with a dramatically moribund text that lacked the "theatrical word," back it went for the kiss of life. "Theater! Theater!" was his constant cry, and in pursuit of this he harassed his librettists above all for passion and energy.

Small surprise that Verdi found these qualities in Shakespeare. Italy, like all Europe, had just discovered the vitality of that playwright's art, and through the efforts of Italian Romantics his vogue culminated in the early 1830s. Two prose "Macbeths" and one in verse appeared in Italy in 1830. Verdi was the poet's most successful Italian exploiter mainly because he was ultimately interested in recreating the sublime sentiments, stupendous situations, and surpassing grandeur so abundant in Shakespeare. In an operatic environment of intoxicating roulades and trills, elephantine set-pieces, and stupefyingly complex and inert plots, Verdi fought for an aesthetic of simplicity and vigor. "An art without naturalness and simplicity," he wrote, "is not art." This was his lifelong belief and it fit well the contours of Shakespearean dramaturgy.

Verdi looked around him and found the high style suffocating the operatic stage: "To me, our opera nowadays sins in the direction of too great monotony . . . They have but one burden to their song; elevated, if you like, but always the same" (*W*, 175). Shakespeare's plays offered Verdi a way out of this syndrome. The poet may have written untidily—Ben Jonson wished he had "blotted" a thousand lines; his talent may have been melodramatic in essence; and he could stoop to vulgarity at times. But intense energy and passion were all-sufficient to Verdi. "Just put plenty of passion into it," he asked of his librettist for *Alzira* in 1844 (a few years before embarking on *Macbeth*), "and you will see that I compose quite passably." Like

Shakespeare, Verdi was always looking for the impact of a situation. For both men the scenic segments almost always add up to something greater than the plot as a whole. Their power develops in consecutive bursts, not cumulatively as in a Greek drama. Perhaps for this reason the Shakespearean play submitted more readily and satisfactorily to an essentially set-piece construction than to the sophisticated architecture of Wagnerian *Gesamtkunst* theory.

Indeed, we might press further this aesthetic dichotomy, particularly as it relates to Shakespeare. As Verdi had his Wagner, so Shakespeare had his Jonson (and Ariosto his Tasso, one might add). That is, on one side were men essentially of feeling and visceral response—of directness, enthusiasm, and vigor; on the other side were men of theory, elevation, allegorical heightening, and extreme artistic polish. Attempting to make his own position clear, Verdi admitted, "Tasso's work may be better, but I prefer Ariosto a thousand times. For the same reason I prefer Shakespeare to all other dramatists, including the Greeks" (*W*, 175). What Verdi undoubtedly found in Ariosto—variety, humor, humanity, a coarse naturalness, rich if a bit untidy poetic invention—he found likewise in Shakespeare. What infuriated him in Tasso must have been that poet's rhetorical flourishes, the staggering learning crammed in every nook, the immensity of his art that seems to outstrip human proportions. The point made implicitly by Verdi in preferring Ariosto is spelled out in no uncertain terms in a letter to Camille du Locle. Verdi is rejecting the idea of writing an opera according to the Parisian style:

> I believe in *inspiration;* you people believe in construction. I don't object to your *criterion,* for the sake of argument, but I desire the *enthusiasm* that you lack, in feeling and in judgment. I strive for *art,* in whatever form it may appear, but never for the *amusement, artifice,* or *system* which you prefer. [*W*, 269-70]

Verdi aligned himself on the side of Shakespeare's passionate if unrefined art—and this is not in greater evidence than in "Macbeth." This second shortest of the thirty-eight plays is a masterpiece of concision and passion. The great Shakespearean A. C. Bradley wrote: "Macbeth" is "distinguished by its simplicity—by grandeur in simplicity, no doubt, but still by simplicity."[3] And Verdi was compelled by the nature of the play to simplify and trim the ornament and complexity operatic traditions would have forced upon him. The sleek, focused contours of the play, Verdi fully realized, could easily be ruined by the addition of extraneous effects. When *Macbeth* was being readied for its Paris premiere, Carvalho, director of the Thèâtre Lyrique, wished to strengthen the role of Macduff by giving him part of Lady Macbeth's drinking song in the banquet scene. This was doubtless, as one Paris critic noted, to assuage the *amour-propre* of the tenor Montjauze. As so often in Verdi's career, he was obliged to reject the idea out of hand for reasons of simplicity and dramatic impact:

> We ought not to try for effects with a high C from the chest, or a fresh voice, or a secondary role. But we should try to produce a solid, lasting impression with whatever good there may really be in "Macbeth." Be guided by this: there are three roles in this opera and three roles only: *Lady Macbeth, Macbeth,* and the *Chorus of the Witches.* [*W*, 237]

In the end Carvalho and Montjauze did as they pleased, and poor Verdi was taken to task by the *Journal des Débats* for "risking the compromise of an opera's success" by catering to the whims of singers!

Verdi was, of course, right to sense the tripartite focus in "Macbeth," for Shakespeare himself had ruthlessly concentrated his dramatic interest upon the two central figures, and he based the structure of the play upon the prophecies of the witches. Bradley, wondering at the relative spareness of the play and the lack of differentiation in its dramatis personae, came to this conclusion:

> All this makes for simplicity of effect. And, this being so, is it not possible that Shakespeare instinctively felt, or consciously feared, that to give much individuality or attraction to the subordinate figures would diminish their effect, and so, like a good artist, sacrificed a part to the whole? And was he wrong? He certainly avoided the overloading which distresses us in "King Lear", and has produced a tragedy utterly unlike it, not much less great as a dramatic poem, and as a drama superior.

Had Verdi needed one, this is the best defense for the focus of his opera. Bradley also provides the best hint why Verdi was never able to cope to his own satisfaction with the plot of "King Lear." Verdi's art fed upon concentrated, set-piece situations like those in "Macbeth"; but his art was boggled by overabundance, dramaturgical ambiguities, and complexities of double plotting such as occur in "Lear."

Before looking to the opera itself, we can note one further parallel between Shakespeare and Verdi—concerning the matter of realism. This is necessary largely because so many of Verdi's operas are criticized for lack of psychological finesse and sheer credibility. There is, of course, a basis for these complaints. But Verdi knew well the limitations of realism in art, and these he learned at least partially from Shakespeare. In 1876 he wrote to Clarina Maffei what is quoted in the epigraph, and he added, "Copying reality is a nice business, but it is photography not painting" (C, 624). This lesson, so peculiarly hard for opera despisers—and many critics—to grasp, Verdi learned early in his career, very possibly as he struggled with the composition and production of *Macbeth*. The mirror held up to nature is not the inert, dutiful, exactly reproducing mirror of photography or literal sense; it is a poetic mirror that may distort reality in order to illuminate essential qualities of the human condition. Copying reality can, if pressed to extremes (as the Renaissance Dutch school of painting did), lead to triviality or aesthetic inertia. There is something slavish and unedifying in the process, as Verdi meant to suggest in his reference to photography. Hence he was in his art forced to go beyond mere daguerreotype reality to something more awesome as a means of expressing human feelings.

In this sense Verdi was a true Shakespearean, and the defense mounted for the play's lack of psychological consistency or realism also exonerates the composer: "Shakespeare was not so much concerned with the creation of real human beings, but with theatrical or poetical effect. He was fascinated by the very difficulty of making the psychologically improbable, by sheer virtuosity, appear possible."[4] The man who created such operatic roles as the Macbeths, Abigaille, Rigoletto, Azucena, Iago, and Falstaff was driven by the same fascination with larger-than-life characters—and was also an ardent explorer in the realms of psychological improbability. Verdi's pleasure in the choice of adventurous subjects is captured in a letter concerning his plans in 1853 for *La Traviata*:

> I want plots that are great, beautiful, varied, daring . . . daring to an extreme, new in form and at the same time adapted to composing . . . Another person would perhaps not have composed it because of the costumes, because of the period, because of a thousand other foolish objections.
>
> I did it with particular pleasure. Everybody cried out when I proposed to put a hunchback on the stage. Well, I was overjoyed to compose *Rigoletto,* and it was just the same with *Macbeth,* and so on. [*W,* 172]

Verdi's interest in setting the play "Macbeth" must have been great, for it contains all the qualities that most excited the composer's artistic impulses. The central figures are not nicely but awesomely characterized. There are ample tour de force possibilities in the play which beg for musical amplification—the murderous invocations and their conscience-stricken aftermath, the banquet scene, and the sleepwalking scene, to name a few. And there is the darksome, vertiginous tone of the play as a whole that first attracted Verdi. Indeed, the basic tone of the opera was formulated before the libretto was written. To Francesco Maria Piave, the librettist, he wrote, "Once it [the introduction] is done I'll leave you all the time you want, because I've got the general character and the color of the opera into my head just as if the libretto were already written."

The result was something new, as Verdi warned Piave at the outset: "The sketch is clear . . . unconventional . . . and short." It is no wonder that in 1848, with thirteen operas already to his credit, Verdi found himself more attached to *Macbeth* than any of the others. His first service to "Signor Guglielmo" (thus Verdi referred to him) was an inevitable and congenial conflation of two theatrical sensibilities alike in many important ways. That it is—given the operatic conventions of its day—a largely faithful transformation of the source is no small reason to respect it. In *Macbeth* we find Verdi following, as will all innovative geniuses, his own lights and not those of his time.

Macbeth *and Italian Opera in the 1840s*

"But sure he's proud—and yet his pride becomes him." This line from "As You Like It" might apply to Verdi in his lifelong struggle to write operas on his own terms rather than those of venal impresarios, headstrong or indifferent singers, and outraged critics. Verdi was a man of fierce pride and self-confidence, particularly when his artistic principles were jeopardized. Though it annoyed him to be called petty, he did not object to his reputation as the lion of Busseto. To the director of the Teatro San Carlo he confided, "I am sorry it appears to you that I am assuming touchy or precious airs, when I am extremely frank, decisive, occasionally irascible, even savage if you like—but never touchy or precious" (*C*, 57). Verdi's independence of mind is expressed in an 1852 letter to Antonio Barezzi, the guardian angel of the composer's youth. Barezzi had criticized Verdi for living out of wedlock with the singer Giuseppina Strepponi (he finally married her in 1859), and Verdi responded indignantly: "With this long chatter I have meant only to say that I demand my freedom of action, because all people have a right to it and because my whole being rebels against conforming to other people" (*W*, 170). A man of such strong character—and great artistic innovators in their own time must possess one—was bound to have an effect on the opera of his time. It is not fashionable or common to think of Verdi as a great operatic innovator on a par, say, with Mozart or Wagner, but the fact is Verdi performed the necessary operations which made growth out of the Rossinian bel canto aesthetic possible. *Macbeth's* novelties especially show the nature of the traditions Verdi struggled to reform in his early years, and certain traditions (Budden discusses others) are worth pausing over before examining the process of transformation itself.

The essence of Verdi's innovations lies in his belief that what might be called free-floating vocalism does *not* come first in importance in the opera house. The composer's priorities are illuminated in a letter he wrote expressing doubts about the success of a performance of *La Forza del Destino* in 1869:

> A curious thing—and discouraging at the same time! While everyone cries out about *Reform* and *Progress*, the audience sits on its hands and the singers can only manage arias, romances, canzonettas effectively. I know that dramatic scenes [*scene di azione*] are popular now too, but indirectly, as a frame for the rest. The order is reversed. The frame has turned into the picture!!! [C, 619]

Verdi then goes on to make a distinction new in the operatic world, a crucial distinction that a Rossini or Donizetti would never have thought to make: "I believe and am convinced that, while the solo and ensemble numbers may have been marvelously done, the opera, mark well, the *opera* or the lyric drama [*dramma scenico-musicale*] was imperfectly executed." This Verdian allegiance to the drama of an opera rather than its vocalism marked an advance beyond the confines of the decorative aesthetic of bel canto, where towering passions are expressed through immense arabesques of coloratura, stunning high notes, and grandiose ensembles—all vulnerable to vocal excesses. Verdi was not interested in opera as display for the participants but as *dramma scenico-musicale*. Texts with no dramatic "space" for his melodic imagination to breathe, without the igniting *parola scenica,* lacking scenes that proffered opportunity for singers to sing *and* act—these left him cold.

This crux of the mature Verdi's aesthetic—that if the drama is vital then the musical values will follow naturally and be fulfilled—stands out for the first time in his letters and instructions concerning *Macbeth*. Particularly in the extant letters he wrote to Felice Varesi, the first Macbeth, we have many indications of Verdi's preoccupation with dramatic effects. "I will not cease to recommend that you study the dramatic situations and the words: the music will follow on its own. To sum up, I shall be more pleased if you serve the *poet* rather than the composer."[5] Verdi is the picture of tact, telling the fine baritone where he may shine vocally but reserving his greatest emphasis for the verbal and theatrical highlights of the score ("this is the most beautiful point—dramatic and poetic," "the following poetic ideas, which are extremely fine"). The entire Act I duet, he warns, should be "spoken in a whisper, in a voice both darksome and transfixed with terror." Verdi emphasizes yet again that in this scene "the orchestra will play extremely softly and you must really sing with your mutes on [*con le sordine*]." In another letter Verdi assures the baritone that he will succeed in the death scene if "you will unite your singing with the carefully reasoned action." How many times Verdi must have given his singers that advice.

Verdi knew that his age was addicted to the beauties of the human voice and, as a consequence, was populated largely by self-infatuated and willful singers. He also knew that *Macbeth* could not achieve its proper effect if singers were allowed to "beautify" it. Hence his objection to the soprano Tadolini. Verdi realized it would take time to inculcate the "ugly" qualities of dramatic and vocal character that are crucial to the roles of Macbeth and, more importantly, his wife. He warned the impresario of the Teatro Pergola in Florence that his new opera would require "many orchestral and stage rehearsals," and in the end he even made the unheard-of demand for a full-dress final rehearsal. The first Lady Macbeth described in her memoirs the incredible rehearsal period of three months. More than one hundred piano and orchestral rehearsals took place, and Barbieri-Nini added that she and Varesi were forced to sing the Act I duet one hundred and fifty times. "Verdi," she wrote, "was determined that in our mouths the music should seem rather spoken than sung." And throughout the opera Verdi does, by means of directions like *cupo, voce muta, con voce fioca, soffocato,* and *sottovoce,* take extreme pains to rein in his singers at points where crude baritonal or soprano power might subvert a dramatic point. Knowing the penchant of most singers, Verdi warned Cammarano, who was rehearsing the Neapolitan premiere of *Macbeth* in 1848:

> Tell them that the most important numbers of the opera are the duet between Lady Macbeth and her husband and the sleepwalking scene. These two numbers absolutely must not be sung:
> They must be acted, and declaimed in a dark, veiled voice:
> without which they can have no effect. [C, 62]

The spectacle of singers being asked not to sing was not the only novelty in Verdi's opera.[6] Of the *cabaletta, Vada in fiamme* which originally ended Act III, Verdi wrote to Varesi: "It is not after the common pattern, because following all the preceding action a *cabaletta* in the usual form and with the usual refrains would result in a trivial effect." The composer may also have adumbrated the usual *cabaletta* sequence in Macduff's one aria for the same reason. Verdi also warned that Macbeth's death scene would be something new in its simplicity. It would be "a very brief death scene, not one of those usual, mawkish deaths," and he broached the matter again in another letter to Varesi. "You will understand very well that Macbeth must not die as does Edgardo [in *Lucia di Lammermoor*] or Gennaro [in *Lucrezia Borgia*]; therefore it is necessary to carry it off in a new manner. It must be pathetic, but more than that, it must be terrible." As well, Verdi was willing to lengthen his accompanied recitatives where the action required it—as in the "dagger speech" soliloquy in the first act. Budden justly calls this recitative the best Verdi wrote prior to *Pari siamo* in *Rigoletto*. But it was above all on the matter of acting that Verdi was most adamant. The bass who was to sing Banquo at the premiere refused to appear as the ghost of Banquo in the banquet scene, and Verdi responded angrily to the impresario:

> I am annoyed that the singer who is to do Banquo doesn't want to do the ghost. Why so? Singers must be engaged to sing and to act, and furthermore it is high time to do away with such leniencies. It would be monstrous for someone else to play the ghost, for Banquo must preserve exactly the same appearance when he is a ghost. [*W*, 121]

It is a mark of the theatrical obtuseness of the time that Verdi was obliged to argue this point, or that he had to drill into the heads of his artists—what should have been patently clear—that the duets between the Macbeths are the heart of the opera. But such were the battles Verdi found himself fighting throughout his career. Many years later, when he was preparing *Macbeth* for the Paris stage, Verdi could write with a touch of sadness about the tribulations of his profession: "I know the world in general but the theater in particular, so I am not surprised at any perfidies, great or small, which may be committed there" (*W*, 242).

Verdi and Shakespeare's "Macbeth"

Of Shakespeare's mature tragedies "Macbeth" must have struck Verdi as the most amenable to operatic transformation. "Julius Caesar" and "Hamlet" are sprawling stories of political machinations and inner psychic struggle; unsurprisingly, Verdi never seriously considered setting either of them to music. Nor did he ever take up the possibility of "Antony and Cleopatra"—perhaps because the great poetry of the two lovers is set within a most complex scenic structure. This leaves the two tragedies Verdi did set, "Othello" and "Macbeth." The former is the supreme play of passion, a fiery tragedy that finds the playwright at the crest of his powers. Likewise, Verdi's *Otello* is representative of the composer's peaking genius. But "Othello" is a very long (3700 lines, compared to 2500 in "Macbeth") and far more complex play. No wonder that Verdi delayed his attempt upon the noble Moor until he had the money, leisure, and masterly librettist to deal with it on his own terms.

We can, then, see why "Macbeth" appealed to a harried young composer accustomed to writing one or two operas a year. Here was a short play with no mincing of words or effects. The qualities of compression, pregnancy, energy, and violence of emotion Verdi favored were all abundant. Bradley has described the play as "the most vehement, the most concentrated, perhaps we may say the most tremendous, of the tragedies," and it is clear from Verdi's letters that these characteristics sparked his imagination.

Verdi's demands for compression might well be reflected in Lady Macbeth's line, "Words to the heat of deeds too cold breath brings" (2.1.61). In no Shakespearean tragedy does the poetry cling so tightly to the action. There is surprisingly little rhetoric, little verbal byplay to dampen the heat of passionate and ambitious acts. The result is a sense of motion and inevitability. This gathering momentum is a crucial part of the opera's architecture and underscores the extreme clarity of the play's focus, namely, the hastening doom of the Macbeths' traitorous ascent to power. For Verdi and Piave there was very little to change, excise, or puzzle over in the play. It had the great virtues of extreme dramatic impact and strongly delineated characters—and little of the Shakespearean vices of diffuseness, punnish wordplay, or ambiguity of intention.[7]

What is more, Verdi's reading of the play shows a perceptiveness that would do honor to any Shakespearean. As we have seen, he held doggedly to the view that there are only three focuses of dramatic interest in "Macbeth": Macbeth, his wife, and the witches. As in Shakespeare, the faceless surrounding cast is never allowed to draw our attention from the dilemma of the Macbeths. Edward Dowden has called the play a "tragedy of the twilight and the setting-in of thick darkness upon a human soul,"[8] and Bradley has noted that the memorable scenes all take place under the "blanket of the dark." While emphasizing that the mise en scene for his opera must be very dark ("*La scena estremamente scura*"), Verdi filled his score with dark orchestration, the deadening pall of frequent modulation to the minor tonality, and themes based on the falling half-tone. These same techniques Verdi was to invest, with more refinement, in his two later "dark" operas *Simon Boccanegra* and *Don Carlos*.

Critics have called *Macbeth* Verdi's opera *senza amore,* and this too is in keeping with the original—where the oases of humor, beauty, and love are painfully brief. The world of the play and the opera is coarse, brutal, essentially masculine, and martial. Verdi has also remained faithful (with a few exceptions to be noted below) to the basic dichotomy of the play: the first half finds Lady Macbeth in control, while in the second Macbeth—increasingly courageous in his desperation—takes command of the action. Verdi's reading of "Macbeth" uncannily focuses upon the lines prominent in most basic studies of the play, and this unerring sense of precisely where theatrical interest resides is perhaps the best indication of Verdi's excellence as a musical dramatist.

Finally and most importantly, Verdi was able to capture in his score the tragic tension without which "Macbeth" is nothing. This tension is instilled in the opera primarily through his always important rhythmic underpinnings and the frequent use of what might be called motives of incessancy or repetition. These help to describe the gnawing effects of evil intentions and stricken conscience. Indeed, it is almost enough to follow the development of the plot by reference to the rhythms which underlie the crucial points in the opera. At the outset is the most basic divided-string accompaniment to Macbeth's first reaction to the prophecies, the duet *Due vaticini* (EX. 1). Though a rhythmic cliché, in its measured flatness it is able to support both the evil and the noble responses warring in Macbeth's mind, as well as the first hint of the different personalities of Banquo and the eventual regicide. This slow staccato rhythm (Verdi uses the staccato marking effectively throughout the opera) is—like the witches' predictions—inscrutable in its simplicity, soothing yet tentative. The evil awakened now in Macbeth is hinted at in other ways: the hollow mating of woodwinds at the first access of bloody thoughts (*Ma*

Example 1

perchè sento rizzarsi il crine?), the vacillating opened and closed phrasing in Macbeth's vocal line, and the unsettling passage through contrasting keys.

In his early works Verdi was most effective in expressing overmastering willpower through rhythm, and a typical instance of this Verdian hallmark is Lady Macbeth's first *cavatina* (*Vieni! t'affretta!*). Based upon the lines "Hie thee hither, / That I may pour my spirits in thine ear, / And chastise with the valour of my tongue" (1.5.25-27), this number harnesses the catapulting energy of evil that ignites the action in Lady Macbeth's first aria (EX. 2). Under the blandish-

Example 2

ment and "valour" of a tortured vocal line we find a simple, driving rhythm that sets the climb to power in motion. It is typical of that family of "salient" rhythms Verdi often used to express the will to love, pleasure, power, or victory. A new rhythm with more tortuous qualities appears in Lady Macbeth's next eruption of evil psychic energy, *La luce langue* (EX. 3). Here the accompaniment wanders in a

Example 3

narrow melodic span with more evenness. The aptly brutalized vocal line rests upon this sinuous motive—reflecting the idea of evil that is even more dangerous when cloaked in restraint and indirection.

Verdi's rhythms also serve to distinguish the characters of Macbeth and his wife in the duet following just after the murder of Duncan. In the play Lady Macbeth is clearly the more intelligent, calculating, and complex of the two characters; Macbeth is slim of intellect, more straightforward, and given all too easily to the powers of suggestion. In keeping with this disparity, Verdi's music for his heroine is the more complex rhythmically. The contrast of complex and simple rhythm is particularly telling as Lady Macbeth nervously tries to control Macbeth, whose fear, so to speak, petrifies him into the lyric passage, *Com'angeli d'ira* (EX. 4).

There are two vital rhythmic events in the banquet scene, the first accompanying Macbeth's reaction to Banquo's ghost:

Example 4

> Avaunt, and quit my sight! let the earth hide thee!
> Thy bones are marrowless, thy blood is cold;
> Thou hast no speculation in those eyes
> Which thou dost glare with! [3.4.92-95]

This is a crucial point in Macbeth's tragedy, for at this moment he is steeled in sin. This is his worst horror, and if he can survive it (as he barely does) nothing will make him flinch. Verdi's music puts him to a severe test. In the 1847 version the giddy rolling motion of the strings proved almost enough to suggest how close Macbeth is to fainting (EX. 5A). But when Verdi came back to this moment in revising for Paris he added to Macbeth's vertigo the skipped heartbeats of an erratically accented bass line (EX. 5B). After a few agonizing moments he is released from this torture through the musical balm of a modulation to the major at the words *La vita riprendo!* ("I am a man again," 3.4.107).

What next takes place is a stroke of genius as well as an indication of Verdi's awareness of Shakespeare's intentions. The composer in-

Example 5

serts (as the first part of the Act II finale) an anti-climactic largo for the line, "It will have blood, they say; blood will have blood" (3.4.121). The rhythm of this section is relentless and utterly even, yet it absorbs terrifying connotations from the dramatic context. For this is the moment when Macbeth begins to realize in his heart that he is treading a path to dusty death. Through the second half of the play Macbeth becomes less and less the honored general and more an animal tracked down by an unalterable fate. Such imagery even occurs to him in his final moments: "They have tied me to a stake: I cannot fly, / But bear-like I must fight the course" (5.7.1-2). The stalking of the beast effectively begins in the banquet scene, and in this extremely brief respite of the largo—mixed so well by Verdi with gathering strength, fatalism, and determination—the nature of Macbeth's fall is first hinted. The Macbeth of the last half of the play is a stupendous mixture of doom and desperation, nihilism and fearlessness. Starting with this passage (*Sangue a me quell'ombra*), in which Macbeth succeeds heroically to a kind of self-possession, we find Verdi exploring this explosive amalgam of opposites with simple yet effective rhythmic means.

Characterization through rhythm in the sleepwalking scene is scarcely excelled in any Verdi opera, and certainly, for psychological acumen, in any of the countless "mad scenes" of the period. The point here is that there is no rest for the weary sinner, no escape from the bite of conscience. Bradley has written of this scene in the play: "The effect is extraordinarily impressive. The soaring pride and power of Lady Macbeth's first speeches return in our memory, and the change is felt with breathless awe." This is just the effect Verdi achieves in his music: the scene is crowded with dislocated shards of Lady Macbeth's once-great will (and vocal power). Even in the introduction we sense a mind that reaches a conclusion (or a cadence) only with painful effort (EX. 6). The atmosphere is an eerie mixture of starkness and blandness. Rhythmic relics of the past now seem to have an odd insistency as well as a pointless, inconclusive quality. And what is worse, they all hammer mercilessly in Lady Macbeth's mind, as in the andante (EX. 7). The octave dirge on D-flat, the painful repeated alto oboe sigh on A-natural/A-flat, the

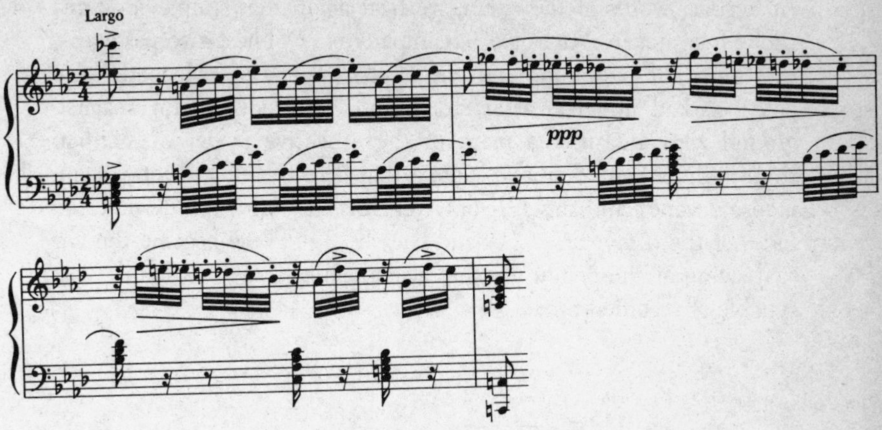

Example 6

Example 7

incessant string thirds—all suggest that psychic forces have driven the heroine insane.

Throughout the scene there is an oppressive sense of a winding down to extinction. Lady Macbeth's tired mind assumes a mechanical quality; all vitality is lost. Her repetitious last speech marks a profound spiritual enervation; she has not even the "poetic" power to speak in iambic pentameter:

> To bed, to bed; there's knocking at the gate. Come, come, come, come, give me your hand. What's done cannot be undone. To bed, to bed, to bed. [5.1.66-68]

At her last words in the opera, we hear again that simple rhythmic cliché first met in Act I (EX. 8; compare EX. 1. These two passages—in a sense the beginning and end of the tragedy of "Macbeth"—are both marked andante assai sostenuto). We have again reached ground zero, but it is a mark of the evocative power of Verdian rhythm in a strong dramatic context that here the effect is one of immense vacancy and stasis. It only remains for Verdi to alternate the tones of the octave dirge (second bar, EX. 8). These become the virtual swing of the pendulum that accompanies Lady Macbeth's "last syllable of recorded time."

Example 8

Macbeth's final aria, too, reflects this terrifying inertia, but in a more lyrical vein. *Pietà, rispetto, amore* is based upon Macbeth's speech in Act V:

> I have liv'd long enough: my way of life
> Is fall'n into the sear, the yellow leaf,
> And that which should accompany old age,
> As honor, love, obedience, troops of friends,
> I must not look to have; but in their stead,
> Curses, not loud but deep, mouth-honor, breath,
> Which the poor heart would fain deny, and dare not. [5.3.22-28]

The text of this beautiful aria—Macbeth's one lyric display—is based only on the third through sixth lines of the speech, that is, upon the lines where Macbeth *imagines* the good which he has lost and the evil he is heir to. But by now Macbeth's imagination is fitful. It sometimes reveals the harsh face of truth, which would make other men wince:

> I have supp'd full with horrors:
> Direness, familiar to my slaughterous thoughts,
> Cannot once start me. [5.5.13-15]

Opposed to Macbeth's waning powers of imagination is the growing sense of the flatness exampled in "I have liv'd long enough." And though he may not have set the actual line to music, Verdi makes this flatness felt (EX. 9). His accompaniment, commonplace in its

Example 9

blandness, is powerful in the context of a swan song for a man who has supped with horrors. There is something both terrible and sympathetic in Verdi's choice of this tensionless rhythmic cliché. It illuminates that side of Macbeth which is not bear-like and which makes all the more awesome his final triumph of will in fighting out the course of his life. Macbeth's final aria is at first glance oddly out of character and something of a show-stopper, but Verdi as usual knew what Shakespeare was doing: there may be lyricism in the vocal line, but underneath all is powerlessness and despair. The musical rhythm here—as throughout the opera—follows the tragic rhythm of the play.

Lady Macbeth

More so than in Shakespeare, Lady Macbeth dominates the action of Verdi's opera. She has two brilliant scenes in Act I, commands the banquet with her drinking song (*brindisi*), and has the great sleep-walking scene. And for Paris Verdi restricted the role of Macbeth even further, replacing his *cabaletta* at the end of Act III with the present duet for both Macbeths and excising his death scene. It is not surprising that Lady Macbeth should loom so large, however, since the greater interest, suspense, and poetic splendor exist in the first half of the play, where she commands both her husband and the action. In the second half of Shakespeare's "Macbeth" a faceless destiny takes Lady Macbeth's place, and she is allowed to fade into the background. A second reason for her importance is quite simply that as a dramatic creation she is more impressive than her husband. Perhaps no woman in dramatic literature has been invested with such repellant yet fascinating grandeur as Lady Macbeth. No other could utter these words with such conviction:

> I have given suck, and know
> How tender 'tis to love the babe that milks me;
> I would, while it was smiling in my face,
> Have pluck'd my nipple from his boneless gums,
> And dash'd the brains out, had I so sworn as you
> Have done to this. [1.7.54-59]

A. C. Bradley has perhaps best argued the case for Lady Macbeth, calling her "one of the most commanding and perhaps most awe-inspiring figures that Shakespeare drew." The inflexibility of her will combines with complete immorality to make her uniquely overwhelming, and these qualities are realized in the opera. It will repay our interest to examine how Verdi developed this character through music.

The speech that epitomizes Lady Macbeth occurs just before the first interview with her husband. It displays those two qualities, extraordinary resolution and reckless immorality, which dominate in her:

> Come, you spirits
> That tend on mortal thoughts, unsex me here,
> And fill me from the crown to the toe topful
> Of direst cruelty! Make thick my blood,
> Stop up th'access and passage to remorse,
> That no compunctious visitings of nature
> Shake my fell purpose, nor keep peace between
> Th'effect and [it]! Come to my woman's breasts,
> And take my milk for gall, you murth-ring ministers,
> You wait on nature's mischief! [1.5.40-50]

This famous speech occurs in a scene structured in a manner very congenial to common bel canto organization. In the play Lady Macbeth enters reading the letter from her husband, she gives her initial reaction ("Glamis thou art, and Cawdor; and shalt be / What thou art promis'd"), a messenger announces Macbeth, and she is then left alone for the soliloquy just quoted. This fits almost perfectly the then-common scenic module consisting of an introduction, recitative, aria, bridge section, and *cabaletta* made popular by Rossini. This schema will clarify the parallelism:

PLAY (*Act I, scene v*)	OPERA (*Act I, scene 2, to Macbeth's entrance*)
"Enter Macbeth's Wife alone, with a letter"	—Introduction (allegro)
Lines 1-24 (letter read and Lady Macbeth's first reaction)	—Accompanied recitative
Lines 25-29 ("Hie thee hither")	—Aria (andantino) *Vieni! t'affretta!*
Lines 30-38 (messenger arives, tells of Duncan's arrival, exits)	—Bridge section (allegro)
Lines 39-54 (Lady Macbeth's soliloquy)	—*Cabaletta* (allegro maestoso) *Or tutti sorgete*

The challenge to Verdi's powers, then, was not in structuring but in reproducing the poetic enormity of this memorable entrance. And he indeed shows his control of Lady Macbeth's massive proportions in his brief introduction, which contains three central musical traits with which he will build her character (EX. 10). First are the stun-

Example 10

ning crescendos, crowded one upon another, which give the combined sense of pressure, urgency, and (evil) power bursting the (moral) bonds that contain it. Second are the half-tone progressions that will later be used to emphasize the evil indirection of her character—not to mention the slippery, involuted nature of evil itself. Finally, we have the up-shooting octave hammer blows, a perfect melodic means for describing the Lady's decisiveness and ambition. Before she utters a word, we know this woman is not to be trifled with.

Lady Macbeth's will is reasserted in yet another way in the brief recitative introducing her Act I aria—through coloratura. The age in which acrobatic vocalism commonly expressed passion or determination was not to end for decades, but in *Macbeth* Verdi kept this coloratura in firm theatrical control. It is used sparingly but effectively. For the line in the libretto, "Woe unto him who, fearful, after trying to climb . . . will then surrender!", Verdi provides a brief but potent display (EX. 11). The imperious roulades and the nastily emphasized inverted turn in the last bar provide just the right foretaste of this woman's evil "spirits" that Shakespeare intended. The recitative ends in prickly staccato figures as Lady Macbeth steps to the edge of the moral abyss and demonstrates her ambition in the leaping vocal line of *Vieni! t'affretta!*[9]

du-bi-to-so vi pone, e re-tro - ce - - - - - - - de!
af-ter try-ing to climb it, Will then sur - ren - - - - - - - der!

Example 11

A messenger announces the arrival of Duncan and Macbeth, and the following few bars make clear that the plot has been decided upon, alone, by Lady Macbeth. This second and more horrible resolution sets the stage for the full-blown *cabaletta, Or tutti sorgete, ministri infernali*—a vocal set-piece fully worthy of the poetic set-piece Shakespeare gave his Lady Macbeth.

In Lady Macbeth's next aria, *La luce langue,* Verdi deepens the sense of her reckless evil. The chromatic leading-notes in many phrases give an oblique "edge" to her role, while the incessant octave leaps (EX. 12) provide a countering forcefulness: Lady Macbeth can proceed in half-steps or great strides in pursuit of the crown. In the tiny andante section in the middle, Verdi provides a moment of almost unnerving and ironic false piety. The following explosion of heaven-storming evil looks forward to Iago's outburst at the end of

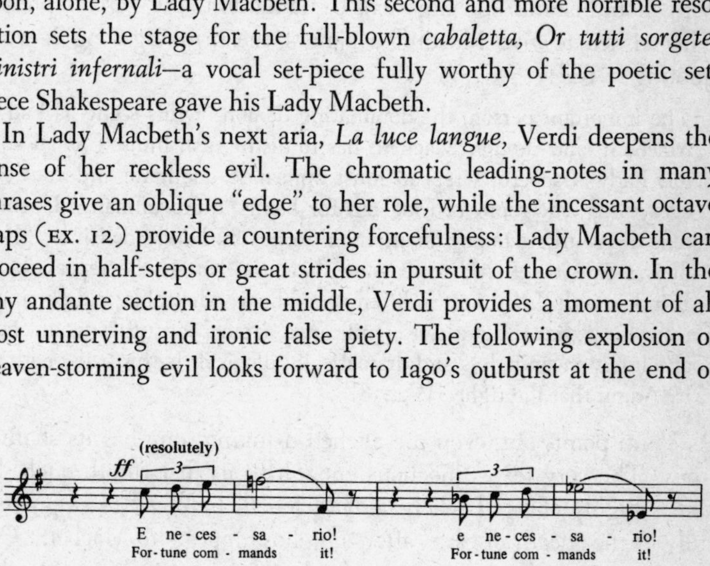
(resolutely)
ff
E ne - ces - sa - rio! e ne - ces - sa - rio!
For - tune com - mands it! For - tune com - mands it!

Example 12

the "Credo" in *Otello*. The transition here from a pianissimo andante to the forte allegretto after the line *Ai trapassati regnar non cale; a loro un requiem, l'eternità!* ("Those who've departed care not for glory; theirs be a requiem once and for all!") is a Verdian masterstroke. The *stretta* that comes next (*O voluttà del soglio!*) Verdi wanted sung "with a little tremor of pleasure and excitement in the voice," over an orchestra playing as softly as possible. If the dynamics and the directions for the singer are observed, this short climactic section will have an effect that justifies Verdi's interpolation of the text. In fact, this piece's fiery mixture of terror and joy is an instance of Verdi and his librettist Piave looking to Shakespeare's lines (in this case those of Macbeth to his wife: "There's comfort yet, they are assailable. / Then be thou jocund" 3.2.39-40) and finding between them room for appropriate musical expansion in a conventional way.

Verdi lavished subtle care upon what might at first seem the obligatory "festive" scene in the opera. The banquet scene is a great one for a singing actress, and the composer was adamant that Lady Macbeth should be in full charge. His explanation to the Paris impresario who wished to give Macduff a part of the drinking song is worth quoting in full:

> The important person, the dominating demon of this scene, is Lady Macbeth, and though Macbeth has to distinguish himself as an actor, Lady Macbeth, I repeat, must appear to dominate and control everything; she reproves Macbeth for being "quite unmanned," she tells the courtiers to pay no attention to her husband's delirium, "the fit is momentary," and to reassure them the better, she repeats her Brindisi with the utmost indifference. This is admirable and coming from her it has the greatest significance; from Macduff it would be absolutely meaningless and dramatically illogical. Is this true or isn't it? Admit that I'm right. [*W*, 238]

As Verdi points out, even the clichéd drinking song has its share of irony. The very text, innocuous enough in its first run-through, becomes highly charged when Lady Macbeth is forced to sing cheerfully of the "death of care" after the ghost appears to Macbeth. One might say the first entrance of the *brindisi* is pure bel canto, but that—though the notes are the same—the reprise relies far more on verismo dramatic power. That Verdi composed no "new" music at this point is perhaps an example of his belief, mentioned earlier, that the composer's art must sometimes be not to compose at all. As Macbeth deteriorates, his wife bravely attempts to chastise him back to normality in phrases constructed out of a nervous asymmetrical rhythm and the emphatic octave (EX. 13).

Example 13

The next time we see Lady Macbeth (except for an awkward appearance after Macbeth's second meeting with the witches) is in the sleepwalking scene. In terms of character development her insanity is abrupt, and one can excuse this only by noting that it is equally abrupt in Shakespeare's play. What we have is, in effect, a suddenly lobotomized heroine. Vaulting ambition is nowhere present. Her inflexible will is lost within a mind that cannot fix itself on a complete sentence, is capable only of rambling verbal associations. To Verdi's credit we do not for a moment think this sudden collapse silly. It is consistently terrifying. Even as a shell of her former self Lady Macbeth is a mesmerizing figure—largely due to the rhythmic construction of the scene already discussed. But there are other details of genius: the dark, lugubrious turns that remind us of her earlier coloratura, the tenuous reach of her last vacant octaves, and the gripping, momentary release from pain in a C-major modulation for Shakespeare's line "all the perfumes of Arabia will not sweeten this little hand."

Mary McCarthy has said of "Macbeth" that "the whole action takes place in a kind of hell and is pitched to the demons' shriek of hyperbole."[10] Lady Macbeth is a prime example of this exaggeration in character. Verdi, with his special gift for vitalizing hyperbolic figures and situations, seems to have been perfectly suited to the challenge posed by Lady Macbeth. If we find her and much in the opera coarsely drawn, it is because Verdi was faithful to the demons' shriek in the play.

The Paris Macbeth

After many years Verdi revised *Macbeth* for the Théâtre Lyrique in Paris. This revision is interesting because it forced Verdi to re-evaluate a work he had written nearly two decades before, prepare it for a new stage and different theatrical conditions, and simply improve upon it in accordance with Shakespeare and his own developing artistry. The task of revision was not a pleasant one for Verdi: "You can't imagine how tedious and difficult it is to work oneself up over a thing done at some other time, and to take up the thread broken so many years ago. It will be done—but I detest mosaic in music."[11] Verdi found five parts of the opera needed attention: Lady Macbeth's aria in Act II (*Trionfai!*), Macbeth's response to the ghost at the banquet, his aria concluding Act III, the opening scene of Act IV (including the chorus of refugees), and the death scene and finale. In addition, he was anxious about the Parisian requirement of a ballet. He felt one would be awkward in the second act (where the powerful Jockey Club preferred its dancing), but must have remembered the scandal of Wagner's Paris *Tannhäuser* of 1861, the failure of which hinged on this very matter.[12] Taken as a whole, however, Verdi changed relatively little for Paris. Tone and basic shape are substantially the same, and while many find the result a disconcerting mosaic, I do not experience differences in style grating enough to spoil pleasure in either the old or new parts of the score. Each of the changes must be judged separately and on its own merits.

The finest Paris addition is surely the aria *La luce langue*. In keeping with Verdi's later style, this aria has the basic function of a *cabaletta,* but its actual form is unique, comprising an allegretto exhortation, a brief andante, and a highly compact, emotionally dense *stretta.* The original *cabaletta* (*Trionfai! securi alfine,* EX. 14) is cut to the pattern of most of Verdi's early essays in this form. What doubtless must have troubled Verdi about the old number is the almost complete lack of dark undertones and the bouncy quality of

Example 14

the melodic line. And it is quite clear from *La luce langue* that Verdi felt he could improve upon the rather simple oompah accompaniment. All in all, a formulaic set-piece was lost and a more carefully tailored and complexly scored masterpiece of characterization gained.

The manner in which Verdi changed the details of the banquet scene is discussed by Budden. The next major change is the replacement of a rousing *cabaletta* (*Vada in fiamme*) for Macbeth at the end of his consultation with the witches in Act III. I find myself wishing Verdi had had second thoughts about disturbing this aria, for it parallels in its invocational quality the impressive speech Shakespeare gives Macbeth at this point:

> From this moment,
> The very firstlings of my heart shall be
> The firstlings of my hand. And even now,
> To crown my thoughts with acts, be it thought and done:
> The castle of Macduff I will surprise,
> Seize upon Fife, give to th' edge o' th' sword
> His wife, his babes, and all unfortunate souls
> That trace him in his line. No boasting like a fool;
> This deed I'll do before this purpose cool. [4.1.146-54]

This crude display of vindictiveness, it seems to me, Piave captured in his text and Verdi captured in his music. I have already noted that the dramatic interest of Macbeth in the last half of the play is his oscillation between desperate courage and profound fatalism. *Vada in fiamme* was the only focus of the former (as the last aria, *Pietà, rispetto, amore,* is of the latter), and it upsets rather too much this crucial balance to give up the old aria. Verdi may have been forced to write something new for physiological reasons. The old aria lies very high for a baritone and may simply have proved too taxing for the average run of Macbeths.

One might be happier with the disappearance of *Vada in fiamme* if Verdi's new music were more apt dramatically. Having Lady Macbeth suddenly appear at the dark cave is awkward (though Verdi thought it natural for her to have discovered Macbeth's whereabouts). In the play Lady Macbeth disappears from the action after the banquet scene, not to reappear until she is at her nadir. If anything, we may reasonably believe that the very stress of the banquet crisis is the beginning of her collapse. Whether this is so or not, Verdi was ill-advised to have her appear in her usual high dudgeon for the clichéd "revenge" duet that closes the new Act III. Her complete enervation in the sleepwalking scene simply follows too closely for comfort.

The final important change is the excision of Macbeth's death scene and the elaboration of the triumphal finale. In the play Macbeth has no final words of contrition. To many Englishmen of the eighteenth and nineteenth centuries this subdued conclusion to so momentous and shameful a career was unsatisfying. The great tragedian David Garrick went so far as to compose a dying speech for Macbeth:

> 'Tis done—The scene of life will quickly close,
> Ambition's vain delusive dreams are fled,
> And now I wake to darkness, guilt, and horror—
> I cannot bear it— Let me shake it off—
> It wo'not be— My soul is clog'd with blood,
> And cannot rise— I dare not ask for mercy!
> It is too late— Hell drags me down— I sink—
> I sink—Oh! my soul's lost for ever. (*Dies.*)

Garrick's speech, which was preserved by actors well into the nineteenth century, should make clear that opera did not have a monopoly on protracted death rattles.[13] Even if one agrees that Garrick's speech is trivial and anti-climactic, we can perhaps sympathize with the desire to see Macbeth die on stage (as do all of Shakespeare's other tragic heroes). It is the culminating event of the play, and we reluctantly relinquish it to the wings. How much pressure Verdi must have felt to include a death scene we can easily imagine by recalling all the elaborate operatic deaths of the time. Even with the short, two-page scene from the 1847 version (its text is not markedly different from Garrick, just shorter), Verdi felt he was doing something quite extraordinary, and he urged the baritone Varesi to attack it in an innovative frame of mind.

A death scene, however short, is the logical climax of the play, but for Shakespeare, and eventually Verdi, the triumph of the powers of good was the final focus of attention. Unfortunately for Verdi, the final fifty lines of the play are *pro forma.* They are decorative, undramatic—in short a letdown. Verdi was unable to rise above them: his final pages have an equally bombastic and anti-climactic effect. What is to be done in the circumstances? Perhaps the best solution, developed in recent decades, is to permit Macduff to defeat Macbeth on stage, insert the 1847 death scene, and then follow with the Scottish celebration (*Vittoria! Vittoria!*). This is not a purist's solution, but it seems the most satisfactory way of avoiding the opera's weak final moments.

The "Failure" of Macbeth: *One Critic's View*

After *Macbeth* suffered a marginal failure in Paris, Verdi wrote to Escudier: "Operas [in Paris] are only a pretext for the stage machinery." Sour grapes perhaps, but also the grapes of justifiable wrath. Although Verdi was not entirely comfortable with his revision, he admitted surprise that it had not fared better. To criticism that he misunderstood Shakespeare, however, he reacted more violently:

> I may not have rendered "Macbeth" well, but that I do not know, do not understand and feel Shakespeare, no, by heavens, no! He is one of my very special poets, and I have had him in my hands from my earliest youth, and I read and re-read him continually. [*W*, 243]

As the foregoing pages must suggest, Verdi's anger was understandable. This was not, though, the only point upon which Verdi must have been infuriated by the critical reception of *Macbeth*—particularly in Paris, whose musical criticism Verdi had always despised. He warned Parisians, in a letter to Escudier, "If you terrify the man of genius with your wretched measured criticism, he will never let himself go, and you will rob him of his naturalness and enthusiasm" (*W*, 252). The warning had autobiographical bite: Verdi (and most notably Berlioz) suffered often from wretched, measured criticism.

One example of such criticism is a review of the Paris premiere that appeared in the *Journal des Débats* on 29 April 1865. The remarks made there by the dean of Parisian musical reporters, Joseph d'Ortigues, are worth examining here not only for their historical interest, but because most of the common reservations expressed about *Macbeth* are retailed by d'Ortigues. Some deserve a defense.

D'Ortigues's first complaint is that Shakespeare's "beautiful and terrifying play has been disfigured, lacerated, knocked to pieces by the Italian librettist, Piave." The result is an "unfortunate" and "vulgar" melodrama. D'Ortigues doubtless uses the term melodrama pejoratively, as we now are also inclined to do. However, Shakespeareans have for a long time felt their author strong enough to suffer a more reasoned application of the term to his plays. Bradley asked challengingly: "Is not 'Hamlet,' if you choose to so regard it, the best melodrama in the world?" And the New Arden editor of "Macbeth" further softens the blow by observing that all of Shakespeare's mature tragedies "may be regarded as 'melodrama humanized.' " These critics were no doubt attempting to counter the connotation of unreality that melodrama seems to carry (and that is one burden of much criticism of opera). The defense for Shakespeare, as for opera, is that the plot and the characters, viewed superficially, may seem melodramatic and not as in real life, but that in fact the humane truth thus invented transcends the mere structure of the dramatic vehicle. Almost everything in the play—if one stops to think—is outlandish, arcane, exaggerated. Nevertheless, it illuminates the human condition. The same must be said of the opera; d'Ortigues was simply displaying an immunity beyond persuasion when he saw nothing but the surface "vulgarity" of the opera.

The question of vulgarity arises most commonly with reference to the witches. Toward them d'Ortigues is especially harsh: "The marvelous has given way to grotesquerie, the fantastic becomes a shadow-game of chinoiserie. And what is the legion of witches (we ought rather to say charladies) substituted for the three Shakespearean witches?" In Verdi's defense a few points may be made. First, even in the play the witches' scenes are extremely difficult to stage with the proper effect of horror. There is some feeling that, like the storm scenes in "King Lear," they can be most effective only in the reader's imagination, not in the theater. Second, while Shakespeare was catering to King James's published views on witchcraft, there is no reason to believe Shakespeare took the witches seriously as dramatic creations (though they are certainly the instruments of evil). They were for Shakespeare more likely scenic marvels that would help popularize his play. Their presence may finally be tangential, merely freakish (a plausible reason for Verdi to instruct Piave to treat the witches "as trivial but in an extravagant and original way"). This last possibility—there is no certainty in this obscure matter—is strengthened if we remember that the operative evil is not in the witches but in the central characters. The witches prove fatal to the Macbeths only because something in the couple's souls assumes control of their actions at the sound of the prophecies. In the play the witches are catalytic agents—to be taken far less seriously than the two sinners. Verdi, it seems to me, has done them no great injustice with their admittedly vulgar, clichéd music—though Budden is surely too dismissive in calling them "straight from St. Trinian's."[14]

D'Ortigues observes that the first part of the opera regretfully contains "the most remarkable and numerous beauties"—a complaint, we have seen, for which Shakespeare is largely responsible. He also expresses annoyance that the ballet that so worried Verdi should be slipped in late in the evening: "It perhaps would have been satisfactory at eight in the evening, but at eleven-thirty it is intolerable." He notes that it was inserted in the fourth act, which would make his timing approximately correct. To judge from the length and quality of the ballet, one can only agree with the critic. Its effect late in the evening would be ruinous indeed. This ballet, needless to say, is rarely performed in modern productions.[15] One should add, too, that Verdi would probably never have written his ballets had the task not been forced upon him by contemporary tastes. Other of the critic's remarks seem designed to madden Verdi. The cutthroats' commonplace chorus is singled out as "one of the best numbers in the work," and Verdi is even criticized for passing the drinking song to Macduff —precisely what Verdi had fought against.

Only when d'Ortigues turns to the music does he make comments that have the ring of truth. Though he shies somewhat from the "fantastic color" and "coarseness" of the score, he feels obliged to praise its "profound and energetic accents." He admires the "complete agitation and anxiety of the orchestra, somber and terrible at Macbeth's words spoken after the assassination," and to the sleepwalking scene he gives all that is due: "It is very beautiful. During it the oboes sound a plaint—a plaint of an expression so raw that it becomes unbearable, giving birth to a visceral sensation of sadness. Should one demand to know what realism in music is, it is here."

A Final Observation

In professional matters Shakespeare was one of the least opinionated of the world's great artists. He left no treatises, no memoirs or letters, and there are few "theorems" in the plays one can confidently call Shakespearean. He was of no particular school, seemingly had no axes to grind. His bias was neither academic, courtly, nor plebeian (unusual, if not unique in his time). His own resources were immense, but he nevertheless borrowed poetic ideas, plots, scenic material, and special effects constantly and unabashedly. No artist of Shakespeare's stature has been as eclectic as he. It appears, in short, that he thought his job was to write good, popular plays. If he is a mysteriously impalpable genius, it is because (as has been often observed) his true nature was "subdu'd / To what it works in, like the dyer's hand" (Sonnet 111).

Verdi, too, was unusually reticent when it came to theorizing or pontificating. He set rules for himself, and he set rules for the production of his operas, but he trembled to lay down rules for others. He refused to become a *magister musicus,* balked at the request to judge other men's music, and was annoyed by the convoluted musicological debates of his time. To a young composer who wished Verdi's opinion of his works, the old man replied: "I am quite capable, in private, of giving an informal opinion of a musical work—

but no more than that. Judgments are of no value, even when they are sincere" (*W*, 428). Music of the past, music of the future—these phrases Verdi heard but could not fathom. He merely knew his job was to write good, popular operas.

To do this Verdi became, like Shakespeare, a great eclectic; he shrank from nothing if it would lead to a more effective musical drama. Nor was he afraid of innovation if the means were not to hand. Again like Shakespeare, Verdi was a pragmatist: what worked he used, what did not he abandoned. He was, like Shakespeare, a latitudinarian in matters of art, as is eloquently expressed in a letter he wrote in 1882:

> In the matter of musical opinions we must be broadminded, and for my part I am very tolerant indeed. I am willing to admit the melodists, the harmonists, the bores—those who want to be boring at all costs, as it is smart—I appreciate the past, the present, and I would appreciate the future too, if I knew anything about it and liked it. In a word, melody, harmony, coloratura, declamation, instrumentation, local color (a word so frequently used, which in most cases serves no purpose but to hide the absence of thought): all these are only means. Make good music with these means, and I will accept everything, and every genre. [*W*, 362][16]

If one may venture a reason why Verdi felt so close in spirit to Shakespeare, it is because he sensed in the English playwright not only a "great master of the human heart" (*C*, 276), but also a fellow artist who rarely confused artistic means with the ultimate goal of engaging human drama. Verdi, who hated artistic refinements, naturally allied himself with the great poet of "Art without Art" (as Digges said of Shakespeare in 1640).

I am tempted to add another, biographical similarity between Verdi and Shakespeare—if Ben Jonson's description of the latter is trustworthy: "Hee was (indeed) honest, and of an open, and free nature: had an excellent Phantsie [i.e., imagination]; brave notions, and gentle expressions." Such is the man we come to know in Verdi's letters. *Macbeth* stands as the first hint of Verdi's devotion to his compatriot of genius, just as *Otello* and *Falstaff* represent the fulfillment of its promise of greater works to come.

seven

EUGENE ONEGIN

For the Russian-speaking people Alexander Pushkin (1799-1837) is, like Shakespeare for the English, the literary figure who has provided the richest mine of sources for transformation into other art-forms, particularly opera. Glinka, Mussorgsky, Cui, Rachmaninov, Rimsky-Korsakov, and Stravinsky all turned to Pushkin for inspiration. With the exception of the greatest of Russian operas, *Boris Godunov,* however, the most popular and endearing Pushkin setting remains Tchaikovsky's *Eugene Onegin,* which received its premiere on 16 December 1878.* As a transformation of literature for the lyric stage, this openhearted, passionate score is nevertheless highly problematic—and all the more intriguing therefor. Of the many circumstances and influences that may affect the musical translation of a literary work none is more crucial than the meshing or clashing of the creative intellects involved in the process, and *Onegin* sets out vividly the dangers lying near at hand when a composer finds himself attracted to a work with which he is spiritually and artistically incompatible.

In February 1824 Pushkin wrote disgruntledly about a critic's reaction to his poem-in-progress, "Eugene Onegin" (1823-31): "He expected romanticism from me and found satire and cynicism and failed to get the feel of much of it." Those who know Pushkin's masterpiece through the opera rather than from reading the poem (in non-Russian speaking countries this is probably a great majority) may also be shocked. In the annals of opera there is scarcely a more radical difference in tone and dramatic effect than exists between "Onegin" and its operatic counterpart. Between the intentions of Pushkin and Tchaikovsky lies a strange aesthetic warp that seems to divide—and make mutually exclusive—the essential qualities of poem and opera. We find in the music just what Pushkin's critic had expected: a lush, dreamily sentimental romanticism. In the poem this romanticism is specked and seared by the acid of irony and ridicule.

* To avoid confusion, the opera will be designated by italics and the Pushkin poem by quotation marks. Quotations from "Eugene Onegin" will be from Vladimir Nabokov's alternately forbidding, ruthless, charming, gratuitous, but literal translation published by Bollingen/Princeton Univ. Press (rev. ed., 1975, 4 vols.). The numbers in parentheses refer to chapter number and stanza. Citations from Modeste Tchaikovsky, *The Life and Letters of Peter Ilyich Tchaikovsky,* tr. Rosa Newmarch, will be made in the text (*L*).

Attempting to describe Pushkin's "novel in verse," one contemporary writer sought a musical analogy: "In music there is a special type of work called the *capriccio*—and [it] exists in poetry. 'Onegin' is one."[1] In Tchaikovsky's score, on the contrary, there is hardly a hint of the liveliness, brilliance, and wit we associate with musical *capriccios*. To him the story was a very serious matter and not, as among other things for Pushkin, a springboard for clever rodomontade. To understand why the two works differ so remarkably we must step back and consider the nature of Pushkin's "romanticism," the central traits of his poem, and the conflicting personalities and aesthetics of these two men.

The Romantic Impasse

Among literary scholars the definition of Romanticism is a notoriously vexed problem. The range of suggested formulations and the extent to which they contradict each other are both breathtaking and oppressive. The matter is raised here briefly and gingerly because Pushkin was the most prominent poet active during the Romantic period in Russian literary history and because, through a slow, relentless though not altogether justifiable process, he came to be seen as the quintessential Russian Romantic. It was a literary fate not unlike Byron's. We must look at Pushkin's Romanticism because in the musical domain Tchaikovsky is also considered an important exponent of late nineteenth-century musical Romanticism. If in fact both men—so utterly unlike each other—deserve to be called Romantics, we may have considerable right to throw away the term completely. Finally, we must note the various strains of Romanticism (and Pushkin's variable attitudes toward them) to appreciate the poem's complexity. For it is just these Romantic "complications" and ambiguities which do not survive in Tchaikovsky's opera.

The desire to understand what Romanticism implied was keen even in Pushkin's day. Nor was this, as now, a mere scholarly pastime but a much-debated, vital topic among artists of the 1820s. Even so, the true nature of Romanticism seemed to sink in the morass of words, definitions, and counter-definitions.[2] Pushkin attempted to describe what it was *not* ("French critics have their own concept of

Romanticism. They attribute to it all works which bear the stamp of dejection and dreaminess") and in most general terms what it might be ("Wouldn't it be better to follow the Romantic school—which is an absence of all rules, but not of all art?"). Still, these were merely tentative gropings. The muddle was too much. "I have noticed," he wrote to Prince Vyazemsky, "that everybody here (even you) has the most hazy notion of what Romanticism is." And, throwing up his hands, he said to another friend: "All I have read about Romanticism is just wrong."

Was Pushkin, then, a Romantic? This hulking question might be avoided best by saying that Pushkin was enough of a Romantic to be, along with Byron in "Don Juan" and Stendhal in *The Red and the Black,* one of its great satirists. He may have been steeped in Romanticism, quite capable of Romanticism, but he did not finally bear allegiance to the movement. A genuine Romantic might have said, as did Pushkin, "A writer should be master of his subject in spite of the hindrance of rules," but he would hardly have been responsible for observing:

> True taste consists not in an unreasoning rejection of a certain word, a certain locution, but in a sense of proportion and conformity.

—or—

> I confess that in literature I am a skeptic (not to say worse) and that all sects are equal for me, each presenting its positive and negative sides.

Pushkin's confession of skepticism may be closest to the point of "Eugene Onegin," for in this poem many of the stylistic symptoms of Romanticism (melancholy, revery, grotesquerie, *cris de coeur,* primitivism, fantasy) and many of its scenic features (emotive landscaping, mortuary architecture, apparitions, the moon in all its splendor) are treated with considerable skepticism—sometimes piquant, sometimes merciless. Pushkin was aware, perhaps too aware, of the vulnerabilities of the Romantic movement, and "Onegin" is a sparkling demonstration of this awareness. Here is an anti-Romantic manifesto written by the most dangerous kind of critic—one who has lived within the castle walls and who knows all the crotchets of design, the architectural and spiritual weaknesses of the movement from the inside. Intertwined with "Onegin's" criticism of the period's society and fashions is devastating criticism of the Romantic aesthetic. One should perhaps add that, because Pushkin does seem on occasion to be capable of unabashed, unashamed lyric and elegiac gestures, it is more to the point to say he is not merely an enemy-from-within but a double or triple agent vis-à-vis the Romantic aesthetic.

"Eugene Onegin" runs to 5500 lines—largely fourteen-line stanzas—organized into eight chapters. These chapters were published intermittently, beginning in 1825 and culminating in the first complete edition in 1833. The action opens in about 1819 in Saint Petersburg and closes there six years later. The model and inspiration for Pushkin was Byron's "Don Juan," a much longer, truly epic satire. "Don Juan" appeared in English between 1819 and 1824, but when Pushkin started his poem he had read only the first five of its sixteen cantos—and these in a wretched French prose translation. Miraculously, however, "Onegin" still approaches closely the ambience of Byron's free-wheeling mock epic.[3] In both style and content "Don Juan" and "Onegin" share many characteristics: poetic posturing, "literary" digressions, a consistent repulsion at moralizing cant and hypocrisy, the frequent imposition of the author's mischievous will [Byron: "my Muse is a capricious elf" (4.74); Pushkin: "my wayward Muse" (7.5)], and above all sophisticated manipulations of language for comic or ironic effect.

Numerous important themes in "Onegin" and Tchaikovsky's opera are prefigured in "Don Juan." In Byron's poetic persona we find Onegin's extravagant aloofness:

> Oh! never more on me
> The freshness of the heart can fall like dew,
> Which out of all the lovely things we see
> Extracts emotions beautiful and new,
> Hived in our bosoms like the bag o' the bee. [I.214]

And:

> My days of love are over; me no more
> The charms of maid, wife, and still less of widow,

Can make the fool of which they made before,—
  In short, I must not lead the life I did do;
The credulous hope of mutual minds is o'er. [I.216]

In Byron's poem is the frequent stepping to the brink of emotion and sudden withdrawal that Pushkin loved to indulge:

So Juan wept, as wept the captive Jews
  By Babel's waters, still remembering Sion:
I'd weep,—but mine is not a weeping Muse,
  And such light griefs are not a thing to die on. [II.16]

And: "But I grow sad—and let a tale grow cold, / Which must not be pathetically told" (5.4). Byron's hackles are easily raised at second-rate poetizing (for which Pushkin skewers Lensky):

When amatory poets sing their loves
  In liquid lines mellifluously bland,
And pair their rhymes as Venus yokes her doves,
  They little think what mischief is in hand. [V.1]

And the archly satirized, ethereal love-passion between Byron's Juan and Haidée is paralleled in the fun Pushkin's narrator has with the passions of Tatiana and Lensky (4.26-29). Byron, Pushkin, and Onegin stand aloof from such transports. For them, not women but marriage was the danger most greatly to be feared:

'T is melancholy, and a fearful sign
  Of human frailty, folly, also crime,
That Love and Marriage rarely can combine,
  Although they both are born in the same clime;
Marriage from Love, like vinegar from wine—
  A sad, sour, sober beverage—by Time
Is sharpened from its high celestial flavour
Down to a very homely household savour. ["Juan" III.5]

we, enemies of Hymen,
perceive in home life nothing but
a series of wearisome images. ["Onegin" 4.50]

Tchaikovsky, though he had some reason to fear marriage (his own being brief and catastrophic), was not of this party, as Gremin's warm-hearted Act III aria in praise of the institution might suggest.

The ambience of "Don Juan" and "Eugene Onegin" is practically the same: sprawling, digressive, mercurial, susceptible to flippant turns of event and wit, flooded with fine observations, nice judgments, and cruel deprecations. Both poems are immensely encompassing and seem able to hold virtually anything the poet takes it in his mind to say. Pushkin's description of his poem in a prefatory stanza could well serve for "Don Juan" as well:

> this collection of variegated chapters:
> half droll, half sad,
> plain folk, ideal,
> the careless fruit of my amusements,
> insomnias, light inspiration,
> unripe and withered years,
> the intellect's cold observations,
> and the heart's sorrowful remarks.

But for both poets "the intellect's cold observations" held ultimate sway. If a single phrase can be suggested for the method they use, it is satirical realism. They shared a rather chilly Muse who preferred disengagement and disillusioning judgment. It is indeed as representatives of the cynical, ironic strain of Romanticism that Byron and Pushkin will probably be best remembered.

In Tchaikovsky's *Eugene Onegin,* however, most emphatically the heart and not the intellect has captured the composer's imagination and governs his expression. The need to deflate, ridicule, and debunk that is present in Pushkin's verse is replaced by Tchaikovsky's need to sympathize with, draw near to, and grasp the innermost passions he is setting to music. His life and work, one might even venture, were based upon a deep-seated and ultimately unfulfilled longing for compassionate and satisfying human relationships—that Tchaikovsky was homosexual must largely account for this. To Nadejda von Meck he wrote:

> And, do you know—it seems to me you only care so much for my music because I am as full of the ideal longing as yourself. Our sufferings are the same. Your doubts are as strong as mine. We are both adrift in that limitless sea of skepticism, seeking a haven and finding none. [*L,* 236]

In the year this letter was written, 1877, he was composing *Onegin,* and it should not surprise us to find his imagination most inspired by the situations in Pushkin's poem descriptive of the idealist's yearning malaise.

Blind to Pushkin's caricatures of emotional idealism, Tchaikovsky gave himself up to just the excess of longing that is the tragedy of Tatiana, Lensky, and finally Onegin. Clues in his correspondence suggest that the power of this longing—and the consequent urge to express it in a sublimated, musical form—could not be denied. To von Meck's question whether he had ever known love that was other than platonic, Tchaikovsky replied: "Yes and no. If the question had been differently put, if you had asked me whether I had ever found complete happiness in love, I should have replied no, and again, no. Besides I think the answer to this question is to be heard in my music. If, however, you ask me whether I have felt the whole power and inexpressible stress of love, I must reply yes, yes, yes; for often and often I have striven to render in music all the anguish and the bliss of love" (*L,* 270). A better explanation of the musical values of *Onegin* could hardly be wished. In the opera's finest pages the "stress of love" is strongest—Tatiana's letter scene, Lensky's final aria, and the last interview between Tatiana and Onegin. Tchaikovsky ignored much of Pushkin's finely honed realism ("Realism argues a certain limited outlook," he wrote to von Meck, "a thirst for truth which is too quickly and easily satisfied," *L,* 236) and social satire in his eagerness to give imaginative life to those situations with which he identified. No matter that Pushkin's purposes in these situations were to show what fools mortals can be. The composer felt obliged to turn Pushkin's characters—"charming dunces"—into real people. In a long letter about his opera, Tchaikovsky warned, "I want to handle human beings, not puppets" (*L,* 255). All of the figures in the poem, major and minor, are caricatures or at best two-dimensional. Pushkin treats them precisely as puppets through the means of his omniscient first-person narrator. This narrator is part of the reason for the ironic distance in the poem, and it should not surprise us to find him nowhere in the opera. For the impact and communicative power of music are direct; music cannot, alone, say other than what it "means"—cannot itself create ironic distance. And so the operatic form is uncongenial to literary conventions, like the omniscient narrator, which distance the reader from the apparent meaning of a text. A fully "narrated" opera is difficult to imagine without flashbacks or the kind of narrative "frame" we have, for instance, in the Prologue and Epilogue of Offenbach's *Tales of Hoffmann*. Not only because Tchaikovsky was preoccupied with the direct impact of strong emotions but also because opera finds uncomfortable the complexities of an ironic perspective, it was perhaps inevitable that the composer should banish Pushkin's narrator from his opera.[4]

Tchaikovsky took Pushkin's characters seriously. It was the only way he knew how to write opera: "I would gladly compose an opera which was completely lacking in startling effects, but which offered characters resembling my own, whose feelings and experience I shared and understood" (*L*, 255). The composer was a man of sentiment rather than intellect, and nothing less than a direct, personal sympathy with his characters would suffice. It is not surprising that his most successful opera was also the one he thought closest to the nexus of his own personality.[5] Later in life he confided to von Meck: "If my music to *Eugene Onegin* has the qualities of warmth and poetic feeling, it is because my own emotions were quickened by the beauty of the subject" (*L*, 445).

The Central Characters

The nature of Tchaikovsky's aesthetic bias and its effects upon the original poem are best seen in the treatment of the three main characters. An examination of the two males makes especially clear the anomaly of the poem and the opera, for their creators identified themselves with different heroes. With Pushkin shadowing himself in the person of Onegin and Tchaikovsky drawn to Lensky, their divergent perspectives upon the bare-bones plot was inevitable.

The figure of Onegin particularly illuminates Tchaikovsky as a man and a composer. In the poem, Onegin and the narrator dominate the action: events are filtered through their skeptical eyes; Tatiana's letter, Lensky's poem, and Onegin's own letter are presented with the narrator's smirking comments; their exquisite social and literary judgments push to the foreground at will. Though Pushkin now and then obfuscates, mainly to disconcert or titillate the reader, we do not doubt that he is the figure behind the literary and social snob introduced in his first chapter:

> Now my Onegin is at large:
> hair cut after the latest fashion,
> dressed like a London Dandy–
> and finally he saw the World.
> In French impeccably
> he could express himself and write,
> danced the mazurka lightly,
> and bowed unconstrainedly–
> what would you more? The World decided
> he was clever and very nice. [1.4]

As Pushkin develops Onegin in his first brilliant chapter (ignored almost completely by Tchaikovsky), two facts become clear: Onegin possesses most of the characteristics for which Pushkin was well known, and Tchaikovsky lacked these traits almost completely. The poet's Onegin is witty, anecdotal, learned in that learning which is most easily displayed, and extroverted. Unlike Tchaikovsky, who hated society and the pressures of the salon, Pushkin's dandy is the picture of ease and control:

> How early he was able to dissemble,
> conceal a hope, show jealousy,
> shake one's belief, make one believe,
> seem gloomy, pine away,
> appear proud and obedient!
> How languorously he was silent,
> how flamingly eloquent,
> in letters of the heart, how casual!
> With one thing breathing, one thing loving,
> how self-oblivious he could be!
> How quick and tender was his gaze,
> bashful and daring, while at times
> it shone with an obedient tear! [1.10]

Again so unlike the composer, Onegin is a complete master of women:

How he was able to seem new,
to amaze innocence in sport,
alarm with ready desperation,
amuse with pleasant flattery,
capture the minute of softheartedness;
the prejudices of innocent years
conquer by means of wits and passion,
wait for involuntary favors,
beg or demand avowals,
eavesdrop upon a heart's first sound,
pursue a love—and suddenly
obtain a secret assignation,
and afterwards, alone with her,
amid the stillness give her lessons! [1.11]

This Onegin is an amalgam of arrogance and superiority.[6]

I indulge in this excursion upon the Onegin who is not in the opera because we must know him to realize Pushkin's original intentions and to see exactly how Tchaikovsky managed to subvert them. For Pushkin, Onegin represents the powers and pridefulness of intellect, and "Eugene Onegin" ends with the crashing irony of his final capitulation to passion. Pushkin foreshadows this irony at the end of his fourth chapter:

pitiful is he who foresees all,
who's never dizzy,
who all movements, all words
in their translation hates,
whose heart experience has chilled
and has forbidden to be lost in dreams! [4.51]

To such a figure Tchaikovsky was manifestly unresponsive. His score shows an inability or disinclination to develop the side of Onegin's character that is volatile, ingratiating, and humorous. There is in fact astonishingly little musical characterization for the title role in the opera.

Understandably, the composer had difficulty vitalizing the "sharp, chilled mind" (1.45) of Pushkin's anti-hero. It is almost as difficult to give musical stage life to a character who is touched by nothing as to obey Shakespeare's direction for Ariel to "enter invisible." Nevertheless, it is a crucial "fault" in translation, at least, that Tchaikovsky's music does not give a sharp undercutting bite to the pensive indolence Onegin affects. He is a master of Byronic gloom, a poseur whose pose is eventually crushed by one of life's massive ironies. But the composer sees no humor in this turn of events. While "Onegin" ends with a rollicking envoi, the opera ends with Onegin's last tragic words—there are none in the poem—and the fortississimo rush of chords that announce so many operatic catastrophes. Predictably, the only inspired pages Tchaikovsky wrote for Onegin come at the end, where the hero is no longer "harking to the stern reprovals of the mind" (8.30). Only Onegin abandoned to a yearning passion seems to have excited Tchaikovsky's interest.

Pushkin's Onegin verges dangerously on caricature. Tatiana glimpses this when she rummages in Onegin's abandoned library, a scene naturally avoided by the composer:

> Can it be—an imitation,
> an insignificant phantasm, or else
> a Muscovite in Harold's mantle,
> a glossary of other people's megrims,
> a complete lexicon of words in vogue?
> Might he not be, in fact, a parody? [7.24]

Tchaikovsky rejected this possibility out of hand, for parodic heroes cannot be receptacles of deep emotion or suffer a fate tinged with profound loss and tragedy. Consequently, he appears to have divested the figure of its frivolous airs and its ludicrous comic aura. Gone, in short, is the best part of Pushkin's hero. Tchaikovsky was unable to make a sufficiently dominant and developed hero with what was left.

If we are to take Tchaikovsky at his word when he asserts that he was moved by characters whose experience was most like his own, then we must turn to Lensky for a blossoming of musical empathy. The truth of his assertion is borne out by the limpidly beautiful Act I *arioso,* the first passionate bars of the Act I, Scene 1 finale, and the last aria before the duel. The attraction to Lensky was natural. Whether he was consciously aware or not, there is much of the composer's own life in the naïveté and virginal eagerness of Pushkin's young poetaster:

In matters of the heart he was a winsome dunce.
Hope nursed him,
and the globe's new glitter and noise
still captivated his young mind.
He would amuse with a sweet dream
his heart's incertitudes.
The purpose of our life to him
was an alluring riddle;
he racked his brains over it
and suspected marvels. [2.7]

All his creative life Tchaikovsky suffered the "heart's incertitudes." Unlike Pushkin, he lacked social finesse, self-control, and confidence. He was a ganglion of extraordinary shyness, sexual fears and inadequacies, and vacillating judgment. Even his favorite opera was subject to this last quality of oscillation: He wrote to his brother in 1878, "Yesterday I played the whole of *Eugene Onegin,* from beginning to end. The author was the sole listener. I am half ashamed of what I am going to confide to you in secret: the listener was moved to tears, and paid the composer a thousand compliments" (*L,* 304). But two years later he berated his overzealous publisher, "Good Lord, what a stupid idea to go and print that score!!! It is not profitable, is no use to anyone, not satisfactory in any respect—simply absurd" (*L,* 370).

In the anguished uncertainty of Lensky there is also a reflection of Tchaikovsky's own pathetic self-criticism. In 1886 he entered in his diary, "Played Massenet at home. How stale he has grown! The worst of it is, that in this staleness I trace a certain affinity to myself" (*L,* 515). A few years later he was to observe:

> I have suffered all my life from my incapacity to grasp form in general. I have fought against this innate weakness, not—I am proud to say—without good results; yet I shall go to my grave without having produced anything really perfect in form. There is frequently *padding* in my works; to an experienced eye the stitches show in my seams, but I cannot help it. [*L,* 569]

The crux of Lensky's character as Pushkin develops it is the "poetic" or artificial depth of his feelings; he is eager to show how these incapacitate Lensky and blind him to harsh realities. Inertia and naïveté are at Lensky's core, and these same qualities were noted in Tchaikovsky by his brother, Modeste. "He was incapable of clearing a direct way for himself to some definite goal; he could only desire intensely and await with patience the course of events, until the obstacles gave way of themselves" (*L*, 320-21). Modeste marveled at the "inconceivable degree of naïveté" in his brother; like Pushkin's maladroit but passionate poet, Tchaikovsky coped none too effectively with the riddle of life.

But perhaps most engaging to Tchaikovsky was Lensky's aesthetic bias: "His pen breathes love—/ it does not glitter frigidly with wit" (4.31). These lines could serve as the composer's artistic epitaph, containing as they do a capsule summary of his musical personality. They also explain much about the differences between poem and opera. Those emotions that moved Lensky also moved the composer, and to focus upon them he ignored the surrounding ironies Pushkin used to ridicule the poet's bathetic and cliché-ridden thoughts. Consider this stanza describing Lensky's artistic subject matter. It contains—once the phrases of satire and denigration I have italicized are filtered out—the essence of *Eugene Onegin*'s lyric richness and simplicity:

> He sang love, to love submissive,
> and his song was as clear
> *as a naïve maid's thoughts,*
> *as the sleep of an infant,* as the moon
> in the untroubled wildernesses of the sky,
> goddess of mysteries *and tender sighs.*
> He sang parting and sadness,
> *and something,* and the misty distances,
> remoteness, *and the romantic roses.*
> He sang those distant lands
> where long into the bosom of the stillness
> flowed his live tears.
> He sang life's faded bloom
> *at not quite eighteen years of age.* [2.10]

The opera is the result of such scrupulous separation of ironic and lyric content.

Like Lensky's, the composer's aesthetic was based on direct, spontaneous feeling; the sophisticated effects of judgment and ratiocination he did not seek. Toward the end of his life he wrote,

> The question: How should opera be written? is one I always answer, have answered, and shall always answer, in the simplest way. Operas, like everything else, should be written just as they come to us. I always try to express in the music as truthfully and sincerely as possible all there is in the text. But truth and sincerity are not the result of a process of reasoning, but the inevitable outcome of our inmost feelings. [*L*, 621]

Of course the result, for both Tchaikovsky and Lensky, was not necessarily simplicity but a confusion of the "heart's sorrowful remarks," an inability to cut through the crowding of stressed emotions, and a perhaps too easy reliance on clichés and formulas. Still, the taste for simplicity was marked in Tchaikovsky; in music he was especially taken by works whose impact was immediate, if not profound. He thought Bizet's *Carmen* the most perfect opera of his day, loved Delibes's ballet *Sylvia* and Lalo's "Symphonie Espagnole." He little cared for the three composers whose music is the most thickly textured and theoretically complex: to him Bach was "wearisome, but still a genius"; Wagner he felt had "killed his colossal creative genius with theories"; and Brahms he found inert in his lofty academicism.[7]

Lensky's yearning to feel as deeply as possible clearly appealed to Tchaikovsky. His famous scene in Act II shows this best, and its construction is typical of the changes Tchaikovsky made in Pushkin. The text for the aria is taken almost verbatim (plus fifteen added bars of "operatic" exordium) from Pushkin, but the circumstances are quite dissimilar. In the original, Lensky writes a love poem to Olga in the early hours of the morning of the duel. These verses "chanced to be preserved" by the narrator, who lays them before the reader. Before we come to the letter/poem itself we are warned that it is "full of love's nonsense" and that when the poetaster read them aloud to himself, he did so with "lyric fever." After the two-stanza poem is entered in evidence, the special pleading recommences:

> Thus did he write, "obscurely" and "limply"
> (what we call romanticism—

though no romanticism here in the least
do I see; but what's that to us?),
and, before dawn, at last
sinking his weary head,
at the fashionable word "ideal",
Lenski dozed off gently. [6.23]

Notwithstanding the delicate, slightly decadent beauty of Tchaikovsky's setting (certainly "limp" with all its drooping musical phrases), we must in the cold light of day observe that Lensky's poem is a conglomeration of clichés.[8] What Pushkin had offered with gentle but firm condescension the composer took at face value and transformed into the epitome of sweet regret.[9] The ironic subtext is ignored; Lensky's tender emotions are husbanded rather than punctured. Victimized himself by the stresses of unfulfilled love, perhaps Tchaikovsky had no other choice.

Tatiana is the most important character in "Eugene Onegin"; Dostoevsky thought Pushkin should have given the title of the poem to her, since "she is undeniably its protagonist." And we know from his letters that it was Tatiana who initially engaged Tchaikovsky's sympathies. The letter scene was the first part of the opera he completed. "I am in love with the image of Tatiana," he wrote to Modeste. "I am under the spell of Pushkin's verse, and I am drawn to compose the music as it were by some irresistible attraction" (*L*, 203). Pushkin's narrator makes a similar avowal of love, but it contains the certain air of mockery:

Involuntarily, my dears,
pity constrains me;
forgive me: I do love so much
my dear Tatiana! [4.24]

Pushkin's treatment of Tatiana's love passion is consistently ironic. We are given the text of her effusive letter, along with this devastating preamble:

Who taught her all that touching tosh,
mad conversation of the heart
both fascinating and injurious?
I cannot understand. But here's

an incomplete, feeble translation,
the pallid copy of a vivid picture,
or *Freischütz* executed
by timid female learners' fingers. [3.31]

In mock-defense of her abject capitulation to emotion, Pushkin asks a series of rhetorical questions whose answers, in the hands of this ironist, are clear enough:

Why is Tatiana, then, more guilty?
Is it because in dear simplicity
she does not know deceit
and in her chosen dreams believes?
Is it because she loves without art, being
obedient to the bent of feeling?
Because she is so trustful,
because by heaven endowed
with a restless imagination,
intelligence, and a live will,
and headstrongness,
and a flaming and tender heart? [3.24]

Because Tchaikovsky was inclined in his life and music to follow Tatiana's "bent of feeling," he chose to answer these questions differently. He took her plight with the utmost seriousness: "Tatiana is not merely a provincial 'Miss,' who falls in love with a dandy from the capital. She is a young and virginal being, untouched as yet by the realities of life, a creature of pure feminine beauty, a dreamy nature, ever seeking some vague ideal, and striving passionately to grasp it" (*L*, 445). Here is a heroine not of Pushkin's but Tchaikovsky's own invention. Here is the most serious misreading of the original, for Pushkin's Tatiana *is* a provincial maid; she is by no means beautiful (she is "*sauvage*, sad, silent" in the poem—it is Olga who is beautiful); and she is "merely" chased by the ache of love. The *merely* is vital to a reading of "Onegin," for Pushkin consistently soft-pedals her passion.

Tchaikovsky instead gave the love of this "innocent maid" the fullest lyric amplification. The letter scene is the great demonstration of his identification with Tatiana's "ache of love." This identification is, so to speak, musically verbatim; the text of the letter is taken nearly as it stands in the original. The result is surely the pièce de résistance of the composer's vocal writing.[10] His portrayal of the varying moods of the letter (there are eight distinct changes of emotion in the music), the breathless quality, the agitated atmosphere evoked by the rhythms—all amount to an operatic show of strength. If as with Lensky's aria the sentiments seem jejune and a bit timeworn—worthy of Richardson's impossibly sentimental Clarissa (Pushkin thought *that* heroine an "unbearably boring fool")—we are again obliged to add that Tchaikovsky has breathed passionate conviction into the scene.

His infatuation with Tatiana led him to play down or ignore important aspects of her role in "Onegin." He did not set the remarkable dream of Tatiana in which Lensky's death is foreshadowed, probably because of its heavily fantastic, ironic, and highly "literary" undertones. He spared himself the pain of mortification to which Pushkin subjects his heroine; nor does he delineate her collapse subsequent to Onegin's rejection. And in order to spare her injury added to insult (and perhaps to soften Onegin's cavalier behavior in the original), he tellingly changes a crucial passage prior to the Lensky-Onegin confrontation. In the original Onegin is maddened at the Larin ball by Tatiana's embarrassment at meeting him again so soon after his rejection:

> Tragiconervous scenes,
> the fainting fits of maidens, tears,
> long since Eugene could not abide:
> enough of them he had endured.
> The odd chap, on finding himself at a huge feast,
> was cross already. But the dolent girl's
> quivering impulse having noticed,
> out of vexation lowering his gaze,
> he went into a huff and, fuming,
> swore he would enrage Lenski,
> and thoroughly, in fact, avenge himself. [5.31]

Tatiana's pain being too great and Onegin's brutality too appalling, Tchaikovsky contrived instead to have Onegin overhear gossip about himself (culled from Pushkin's second chapter) as the basis for his irascible decision to revenge himself upon Lensky.

Finally, the composer chose not to incorporate any of Pushkin's narration of Tatiana's entry into the *grand monde* of Saint Petersburg society and her assumption of the dignities and reticence that go along with high social status. Tchaikovsky, after all, had fallen in love with an image of rustic, untutored passion, not a finely veneered *grande dame*. It is further quite doubtful that Tchaikovsky's muse would have been equal to the sarcasm and poignant details of social criticism in this Pushkin passage. What attracted him was Tatiana's struggle with emotions she could not control, and he clearly had his eyes on her final scene, in which that emotion threatens to break loose again, as of old. She is taken up again at just the moment when, to use the composer's own words, she is struggling with "the whole power and inexpressible stress of love." For a man who chose, or was forced to choose, a life of respectability and reserve rather than indulge his passionate inclinations, Tchaikovsky must have felt deeply the pain of Tatiana's final rejection of Onegin's advances. The final pages of *Onegin* show this.

Not all of the changes wrought in the original were constitutional. As it stood, the careening and multifocal poem was not fit for the stage. As the poet admits in his envoi, "Onegin" contains something for nearly everyone:

> Whatever you in my wake
> sought in these careless strophes—
> tumultuous recollections,
> relief from labors,
> live pictures or bons mots,
> or faults of grammar—
> God grant that you, in this book,
> for recreation, for the daydream,
> for the heart, for jousts in journals,
> may find at least a crumb.
> Upon which, let us part, farewell! [8.49]

To give his libretto unity and to narrow his focus to manageable proportions, Tchaikovsky selected themes "for the heart." And, though he pretended to have no vein for dramatic effects and ignored the necessity for them, he did make some major changes in order to heighten the drama of his libretto. In the poem there is no confrontation at the Larin festivities; Lensky leaves in a rage and sends Zaretsky with a challenge. In *Onegin* the action is brought on stage—where it belongs—with considerable fidelity to the feelings of the various Pushkin characters. Another instance of major surgery both well intentioned and successful is the last scene. Pushkin's ending is for theatrical purposes a disaster. Onegin is given his own impassioned letter, introduced as usual by the narrator, and during Tatiana's long lecture of rejection he says not a word. To overcome this static situation—drama, after all, was not the supreme value for the poet—Tchaikovsky blended the pleas in the letter and Tatiana's actual rejection into a highly charged dialogue. The achievement of a flowing conversational quality that still closely follows the Pushkin text required great dexterity.

Operatic composers are always on the lookout for "musical" moments in their sources, and Pushkin's poem offers a number of them which became memorable moments in the opera. As a part of his description of the stolid rural life Pushkin inserts a song for peasant girls. This the composer uses poignantly to "frame" Onegin's deflating interview with Tatiana in Act I. Pushkin mentions the title of the song Triquet presents to Tatiana at the Larin ball, and this is enlarged into a full-fledged near-parody that anticipates the Tenor's aria in *Der Rosenkavalier*.[11] The two festive scenes provided other openings for the master of the ballet style. If the choreographer can catch the flavor of Pushkin's reference to the waltz—

> Monotonous and mad
> like young life's whirl,
> the waltz's noisy whirl revolves
> pair after pair flicks by. [5.41]

—and to the mazurka—

> But in small towns, in country places,
> still the mazurka has retained
> its pristine charms:
> *saltos,* heel-play, mustachios
> remain the same. [5.42]

—in the Larin ball, he will capture one of the opera's subtle but important scenic effects. The stately polonaise and the divertissement-like gopak in Act III fit nicely into the grander scale of the Saint Petersburg scenes.

We should forgo with regret Tchaikovsky's other additions: The initial chorus of reapers, with its fleeting but atmospheric taste of *a capella* Russian choral sonorities, is an addition to Pushkin.[12] Also added by the composer is the ingratiating romance for bass assigned to Prince Gremin.[13] Though it stops the action in its tracks (much like *Di provenz'il mar* in *La Traviata*), the romance does make the anguish of Tatiana's dilemma all the more poignant. It is also well defended in *Stanislavsky on Opera* by Rumyantsev: "In consonance with the laws of the stage Tchaikovsky acted with great sensibility in giving Gremin such a warmhearted aria because it is a reflection of Tatiana, her pure, moral outlook, her spiritual beauty. What Onegin overlooked in Tatiana is now brought home to him by Gremin." One might add that a Russian opera without a bass aria is virtually inconceivable.

The Virtues of Passion and Judgment

Describing Onegin and Lensky, Pushkin wrote:

> They got together; wave and stone,
> verse and prose, ice and flame,
> were not so different from one another. [2.13]

We might add in conclusion that "Eugene Onegin" and *Eugene Onegin* are as dissimilar as Onegin and Lensky. Pushkin's poem is at center a work of icy intellect. C. S. Lewis once observed that "there is nothing so cold, so disinterested, as the heart of a stylist," and one cannot help feeling that the poem is the work of a supreme stylist. Extravagant and fussy wordplay abounds; the lines are full of opinions, indictments, and final verdicts; self-consciousness and self-indulgence exude from every page. What is most apparent to the reader is the *distance* of the writer from his characters, and this distancing is achieved through the abundant use of irony, burlesque, caricature, drollery, and assumed poetic identities. On the other end of the continuum is Tchaikovsky's opera, a work preoccupied with human *closeness* or (to use Byron's phrase) the "credulous hope of mutual minds." It is concerned with the urge that makes people draw closer to the objects of their affection—and the obstruction of this urge. Gremin's aria announces the wished-for goal, happy marriage, but the opera's three main characters never achieve it. The opera is a work of softness and warmth; its dominant sonorities are lush, plaintive, reclining, sweetly yearning, gently rounded.

The essential dichotomy of comedy and tragedy is also manifest in these two works. Horace Walpole noted that life is a comedy for those who think and a tragedy for those who feel. This is borne out by *Eugene Onegin*. The action of the poem is founded upon a sense of the "world's cold depravity," but the workings of Pushkin's skeptical mind almost always reach toward the comic. There is no tragedy in his poem. Even the final climax takes a puckish turn:

> She has gone. Eugene stands
> as if by thunder struck.
> In what a tempest of sensations
> his heart is now immersed!
> But a sudden clink of spurs has sounded,
> and Tatiana's husband has appeared,
> and here my hero,
> at this unkind minute for him,
> reader, we now shall leave. [8.48]

Yet as a musician, Tchaikovsky wore his feelings on his sleeve. Deep passions, not deep cerebration, are the core of his work. True to Walpole's aphorism, he reached in his score toward the tragic. If he does not finally achieve genuine tragedy in *Eugene Onegin,* it is because there is little support for it in the original, or because it was not within the compass of his peculiarly vulnerable genius to raise mere malaise and emotional deprivation to a truly tragic pitch.

"Eugene Onegin" is a masterpiece of diminution. Pushkin looked upon his world much as Onegin observed the Larin party:

> Triumphing beforehand,
> he inwardly began to sketch
> caricatures of all the guests. [5.31]

Nothing is too gentle, sincere, or virtuous for cynical sniping. The rural scenes so sympathetically treated by Tchaikovsky are by and large sprees for Pushkin ("What silly country!"). Humanity seems smaller through Pushkin's eyes, while the opera works in quite the opposite direction—enlarging, magnifying, idealizing human emotions. In this respect Tchaikovsky is very much like Lensky:

> the exalted Muses of the [poetic] art
> he, happy one, did not disgrace:
> he proudly in his songs retained
> always exalted sentiments. [2.9]

Yet again, we find a musical epitaph for Tchaikovsky in the lines for Lensky. His music, in common with all great opera, was founded upon exalted sentiments.

In the original, vice and self-love seem to triumph—with the notable exception of Tatiana. In Pushkin's world, virtue often seems tainted and love finally proves vulnerable, silly, or not even to be love at all. But in the opera virtue and love have the upper hand. Pushkin has occasion to observe with his usual snide detachment that "all poets / are friends of fancifying love" (1.57), and Tchaikovsky was such a friend. The theme of love in the poem is harassed unmercifully (see especially 4.24-34), but it emerges "fancified" in the extreme from the composer's pen. The scoring virtually glows around the passionate and the virtuous in *Onegin*—not only in Lensky and Tatiana, but in Madame Larin, the nurse, Olga, and Gremin.

I have refrained as much as possible from passing judgment upon the relative merits of the two works here under view—a sure invitation to injustice. Each work has its excellences, though it is clear they are almost entirely unrelated. Nevertheless, it is easy to condescend toward Tchaikovsky. In many ways he is neither the Pushkin nor the Byron of nineteenth-century opera, but its Tennyson. He was not a profound composer, and though his writing is ingratiating and often compelling, it is not intellectually challenging. As Tchaikovsky himself sensed, it often stales rather too quickly, and uninspired patches are no rarity. Perhaps we would be more impatient with the opera if we knew Pushkin's poem better and held it dearer.[14]

There would, however, be something hollow in this condescension, for the blunt fact is that *Onegin* succeeds very well within its limitations and in its Tchaikovskian way. As a faithful translation of literature it is a catastrophe, but it is nevertheless an *operatic* success. We should pause over the nature of its appeal. First, the composer was true to his own aesthetic. Operas in which sympathy for the characters was wanting, operas in which there was no immediate and direct impact, infuriated Tchaikovsky. Hence his dislike of *Tristan und Isolde:* "It is an endless void, without movement, without life, which cannot hold the spectator, or awaken in him any true sympathy for the characters on the stage" (*L,* 432). He followed no elaborate theories, indulged in no compositional pretences. What he said about his favorite contemporary opera *Carmen* could also be said of *Onegin:* "The music is not profound, but it is so fascinating in its simplicity, so full of vitality, so sincere" (*L,* 253). By the force of his simplicity and sincerity Tchaikovsky was able to insinuate genuine vitality into the puppets of Pushkin's invention. Real blood flows in their veins, and—what is most important for any opera—they are engaging characters.

Finally, the opera succeeds for the same reasons Tchaikovsky's music as a whole succeeds. It is imbued with brilliant Russian color. "I am passionately fond of the national element in all its varied expressions," he wrote, and this fondness is manifest throughout the opera—in the reapers' chorus, the maidens' chorus, and the droll charm of the nurse's scenes, to name the most obvious. As with Beethoven's *Fidelio* and Dvořák's *Rusalka,* we find often in *Onegin* the well-known personality of the composer as symphonist. The andante theme in the middle of the letter scene is quintessential Tchaikovsky in its glowing simplicity and dying fall (EX. 1). Nor is there anything in the opera as impassioned or typical of the composer's style as the

Example 1

Example 2

andantino con moto that ends the second scene (EX. 2). And, among so many possible choices, one might point to the exalted passion of a motive in the last pages of the would-be love duet between Tatiana and Onegin (EX. 3). The composer of *Swan Lake* and *Sleeping Beauty* is equally in evidence in this opera, and not only in the obvious dance passages.

Example 3

If this does not convince as a kind of apologia for *Eugene Onegin,* little more can be said. Perhaps those like myself who are attracted to it must take the position Tchaikovsky himself eventually assumed concerning the opera:

> If my enthusiasm for *Eugene Onegin* is evidence of my limitations, my stupidity and ignorance of the requirements of the stage, I am

> very sorry; but I can at least affirm that the music *proceeds in the most literal sense from my inmost being*. It is not manufactured and forced. [*L*, 257. Tchaikovsky's emphasis]

In an art-form where so much is indeed manufactured or forced, Tchaikovsky's achievement in *Eugene Onegin* is enviable.

A Note on Performance

Eugene Onegin is a difficult opera to stage successfully. Tchaikovsky himself was burdened by this realization even as he wrote it.[15] It takes considerable finesse to project strong passions without sliding into the ooze of sentimentality or bathos, to feel genuinely rather than merely exude strong emotions. In addition to these critical threshold matters, producers of the opera should cast a cold eye upon some aspects of the source and upon the score itself before succumbing to a number of dubious traditions that have arisen over the years.

The most important, perhaps, concerns the "size" of the opera—a matter that will remain problematic as long as major companies insist on doing *Onegin* on the largest stages. It was not merely the desire to avoid the "fatal invalids of both sexes" who reigned at the opera house that led Tchaikovsky to favor the Conservatoire's much smaller stage for the *Onegin* premiere: "The performances at the Conservatoire are private, *en petit comité*. This is more suitable to my modest work, which I shall not describe as an opera, if it is published. I should like to call it 'lyrical scenes,' or something of that kind" (*L*, 257). The Stanislavsky production took place likewise in the very intimate surroundings of the Bolshoi Studio Theater. We should not lose sight of the fact that the composer conceived the opera essentially as an "intimate and thrilling" story, and efforts to enlarge its enlargeable parts (the festive scenes, elaborate choreography, and choruses) for big houses will inevitably swamp the effect of the delicate main plot lines of the opera. In this respect *Onegin* is very much like Britten's *A Midsummer Night's Dream*. Both pieces blossom in a medium-sized house, but they assume quite another personality (and not a happier one) when performed in cavernous surroundings.

If opera directors are willing to revive *Onegin* in more intimate surroundings, they might also be more inclined to consider my next advice, namely, to attend to the ages specified by Pushkin for his Tatiana, Lensky, and Onegin—seventeen, eighteen, and twenty-four respectively. Though of course they need not—could not—be this young, the younger the principals for *Onegin,* the more potent are its dramatic possibilities—not to say its visual impact. Tchaikovsky keenly worried that the effect of his opera might be ruined because of the system (still in existence, one sometimes feels) "of retaining invalided artists and giving no chance to younger ones" (*L,* 257). Onegin in particular suffers from superannuated impersonators. As we have seen, Tchaikovsky makes no particular effort to point out the ludicrousness of one so young being so world-weary and bored. A young, still quite virile Onegin would serve to make this crucial point silently, while also making more moving Tatiana's passion for him. We should be made to feel that—but for his affected ennui—Onegin and Tatiana would make a perfect pair of lovers. Needless to add, younger voices could cope better with the demands of the score in a smaller house.

The casting for Lensky should, I think, also be approached anew. There is a tradition of casting a Don Ottavio tenor, very light and bordering on the effeminate, in this role. This is perhaps because Pushkin's introduction for Lensky encourages such a choice:

> He out of misty Germany
> had brought the fruits of learning:
> liberty-loving dreams
> a spirit impetuous and rather strange,
> an always enthusiastic speech
> and shoulder-length black curls. [2.6]

Opera directors typically cast Lensky as a vocal and physical "weak sister" who must face off a ruggedly masculine Onegin. But there is already such a tenor role in the opera, Monsieur Triquet, and Lensky's vocal personality ought to be distanced as far as possible from this French salon silverfish. Tchaikovsky has given Lensky supremely delicate music to sing, but it need not be sickeningly sweet. There is room in the role for virility which, if exploited, would again silently help to bring back a crucial aspect of the Pushkin original.

Stanislavsky was adamant on this point. His advice to Lensky: "Above all be manly. There is nothing more repulsive on the stage than a droopy, saccharine, effeminate tenor."

Both to follow Pushkin more faithfully and to heighten the drama of the opera, a director should pay careful attention to the characterization of Olga and Tatiana. In the original they have distinctly different personalities. Olga is the more strikingly beautiful:

> as winsome as love's kiss;
> eyes, azure as the sky,
> smile, flaxen locks,
> movements, voice, light waist—
> everything in Olga . . . but any novel,
> take, and you'll surely find
> her portrait. [2.23]

On the other hand, Tatiana almost takes on the cast of an ugly duckling:

> *Sauvage,* sad, silent,
> as timid as the sylvan doe,
> in her own family
> she seemed a strangeling. [2.25]

The virtues of "pointing" the contrast as much as possible are at least three: First, the pathos of Tatiana's first passion will be heightened and perhaps make more natural and affecting Onegin's avuncular rejection. Second, it will be an ironic touch true to Pushkin to have the conventionally passionate poet of love, Lensky, fall in love with Olga, the conventionally beautiful love object. Third, it will heighten the drama of Onegin's reacquaintance with the "new" Tatiana in Act III. In Pushkin's poem the transformation is meant to be striking in the extreme, and a director of the opera should also work for this effect. There should be something of Galatea or Eliza Doolittle in the transformation; it should strike us as a social miracle.

In scenic terms, the director should not forget that Acts I and II represent the *petit monde* and Act III the *grand monde*—and scale his designs accordingly. In both Pushkin and Tchaikovsky the Larin household is by no means lavish: a dilapidated fence and an ill-kept flower-garden surround the house. "Old-fashioned ball costumes" and a mazurka (out of fashion then in high society) figure in the Larin celebration. A director would be wise to "point" the rustic stolidity of Acts I and II. Again, Stanislavsky's direction is apt: "A soft smile should accompany the whole of the Larin Ball. What we need is a simple kindly, country atmosphere provided by rather eccentric but good-natured people. Remember you are playing Pushkin, not Gogol."[16] The director may properly venture upon grander proportions and gestures in Act III.

eight

SALOME

All art is at once surface and symbol. Those who go beneath the surface do so at their peril.

The Picture of Dorian Gray

If there was ever an artwork to which the epigraph applies, it is Wilde's own play "Salomé." Its surface is brilliant, exquisitely polished, mesmerizingly simple. One can scarcely avoid the imagery of precious stones—which Wilde so often indulged—when describing the play: its metaphorical facets sparkle in rich succession; its colorism has the luxuriance of ruby, emerald, pearl, onyx; and the characters themselves are like the hard-edged, frigid, soulless gems they wear. On its surface—in the words, sounds, and images Wilde savors to sybaritic excess—"Salomé" is a gorgeous creation.

Pristine and fascinating as the surface is, however, a turmoil of activity seethes underneath. This primarily psychosexual activity is coarse, violent, and ugly. With good reason Wilde bids us tread carefully below the surface of his art, for there we are liable to stumble on rather grisly implications. Behind the handsome, sophisticated Dorian Gray is a fetid sink of ethical corruption. In the feminine principal of "The Sphinx"—this Wilde poem should be read as a companion piece to the play—is a pulse that "makes poisonous melodies" and a power to "wake foul dreams of sensual life." Just as the poet-narrator is maniacally fixed upon the Sphinx, so are the secondary figures in "Salomé" bound with hypnotic tautness to the Princess of Judaea. She is in turn obsessed by the prophet Jokanaan. The result is an access of "poisonous melodies" reverberating inaudibly in the play's subterranean passages.

There are two potential levels of musicality in Wilde's play. The first is the superficial music of sound and expression—the poetic harmonies inherent in the sensual French of the original version. This level was clearly uppermost in Wilde's mind when he called "Salomé" a "beautiful coloured musical thing," or when he wrote to Edmund Gosse of this, his "first venture to use for art that subtle instrument of music, the French tongue."* Two very early responses to the play likewise draw attention to its surface harmonies. Lord Alfred Douglas, Wilde's paramour and translator of "Salomé," wrote in *The Spirit Lamp* of May 1893: "One thing strikes one very forcibly in the treatment, the musical form of it. Again and again it seems to one that in reading one is *listening;* listening, not to the author, not to the direct unfolding of a plot, but to the tones of different instruments, suggesting, suggesting, always indirectly, till one feels that by shutting one's eyes one can best catch the suggestion." Nearly the lone prominent drama critic who defended the play from censors, William Archer, also observed, "There is at least as much musical as pictorial quality in 'Salomé.' It is by methods borrowed from music that Mr. Wilde, without sacrificing its suppleness, imparts to his prose the firm texture, so to speak, of verse." (These judgments were based upon a reading of the play. It was not performed in England until 1905, and then in a private, unlicensed production.)

The critical reaction to Richard Strauss's operatic version of the play makes clear that he was little interested in the superficial beauties of Wilde's sonorous, bejeweled text. "Premeditated nastiness," "flagrant," "malevolent," "voluptuous"—these were the epithets heaped upon the score after its American premiere. The *New York Sun* critic typified the virulence and also, we must admit, accurately described the tone of the opera: "The whole story wallows in lust, lewdness, bestial appetites, and abnormal carnality."[1] As might be expected, French critics were even more sensitive to the havoc wreaked upon the original by Strauss's Teutonic libretto and abrasive orchestration. Louis Laloy wrote in *La Revue de Paris* after the 1907 premiere in that city: "Mr. Strauss has allowed all of the imperceptible irony, the skillful mosaics, and the secret and sophisticated sensuality to fall away from [Wilde's] subtle poem." For the most part the reaction to Strauss's heroine was very like the narrator's revulsion at the Sphinx:

* *Letters,* ed. Rupert Hart-Davis (1962), p. 331. Hereafter, quotations from the letters will be designated by (*L*). Citations from Wilde's writings, unless otherwise noted, are from the Viking *Portable Oscar Wilde* (1946) and will be cited in the text in parentheses.

For the sake of clarity, the title of the play will be enclosed in quotation marks, the opera italicized.

> Get hence, you loathsome mystery! Hideous animal, get hence!
> You wake in me each bestial sense, you make me what I would not be. [585]

All this suggests that the opera departed radically from the tone of Wilde's original. This assumption, however, is hasty and unjust, for Strauss did take into account the play's second, submerged level of potential musicality—the level upon which exist the poisonous melodies of sexual fixation and frustration, nervous exhaustion, and neurosis. Strauss, in short, responded to the psychological implications rather than the textual sonorities of "Salomé."

From Wilde's own standpoint (expressed often in his writings), Strauss's response may have been appropriate. Wilde felt the critic must be able to focus on "works that possess the subtle quality of suggestion, and seem to tell one that even from them there is an escape into a wider world" (89), and this task Strauss brilliantly fulfilled in his opera. From Salome's subtle allures he re-created the "wider world" of psychological malady that lies below the play's surface. Strauss's eventual collaborator Hugo von Hofmannsthal was to use a similar phrase in describing the composer's gifts:

> That mastery over the darker, wilder world, which I have purposely refused to provide for, is nevertheless a real force in you. Many a time when we have been discussing some new plot, I have been conscious of your desire for an opportunity to exploit this energy, for a further working of those mines which yielded so well in the case of *Salome* and *Elektra,* for something, in short, in the *furioso* vein.[2]

There was a furioso vein in the aesthetic that produced "Salomé"—but Strauss had to mine for it.

Wilde wrote in a letter to Frank Harris that "it is only when you give the poet a mask that he can tell you the truth" (*L,* 759).[3] The superficial music of "Salomé" is the poetic equivalent of Wilde's mask and, in a way, renders inaudible the harsh truths sounding at the core of the play. The *effect* of Wilde's play is beautiful and entrancing, but its *implications* are hideous. To understand the literary sources and intellectual milieu of "Salomé" as well as the consequences of Strauss's particular approach as its musical translator, we must explore the influences behind what Wilde called his "curious and sensual" play.

The Sources of Decadence: A Genealogy

Wilde's "Salomé" is in many ways representative of the pan-European artistic movement that thrived in the last decade of the nineteenth century. The characteristic outlines of this Decadent (or Aesthetic, or Art nouveau, or Jugendstil) movement are by no means sharply drawn. Nor is there complete agreement upon its historical sources, which are variously thought to be found in Romanticism, pre-Raphaelitism, and French Symbolism.[4] Because so many artistic traditions seem to lie behind "Salomé," the play makes a uniquely illuminating "abstract and brief chronicle" of its era, which Hamlet says a good play will be (though no one would claim it is great literature). An anonymous writer for the *Pall Mall Gazette* (27 February 1893), discussing the first printed edition, sensed that "Salomé" was an epitomal work: "Mr. Wilde has given, as it were, the quintessence of a school of writing. In this regard it is a library shelf, or perhaps it would be better to say a handbook to a library, a Primer." What is the library for which "Salomé" is an introduction? To find out—and to discern which qualities of literary Decadence Strauss eventually ignored and which he magnified—we must trace the literary genealogy that wends its way confusingly through the last half of the nineteenth century down to 1891, when Wilde wrote the play. Salomé has an ancestry alternately bizarre, fascinating, misty—as might be expected of a woman one early critic called "the daughter of too many fathers."

The literary ancestor whose style most illuminates the Wilde play and the Strauss opera is neither English, French, nor German. Wilde himself venerated Edgar Allan Poe, but it is largely through Poe's influence upon French writers that he figures in a discussion of "Salomé."[5] The American's macabre, highly charged stories and poems charismatically influenced the advance-guard for what was to become the French Symbolist movement. They deeply affected Baudelaire when he read them in 1847, and he eventually translated the stories. Mallarmé, the patriarch of the Symbolists, translated

Poe's poems; one of his most famous sonnets is "Le Tombeau d'Edgar Poe." In his *chef d'œuvre* "Hérodiade"—a clear influence upon Wilde—the mark of Poe's aesthetic is unmistakable.

Though the most immediate influences upon "Salomé" derive from French literature, much in Poe's writing is particularly relevant to the Strauss opera. Nothing in English so closely approximates the forbidding pall that Wilde cast over his play as do the tales of Poe. Baudelaire wrote of Poe that "no man has better described the exceptions of human life and of nature, the feverish curiosities that arise in convalescent states, the dying seasons, heavy with enervating splendours."[6] He could have had in mind the opening of "The Fall of the House of Usher": "There was an iciness, a sinking, a sickening of the heart—unredeemed dreariness of thought which no goading the imagination could torture into aught of the sublime." Poe was a master of gloom and the dim glow of moribund existences and civilizations, and this same expertise is apparent in Wilde's play. "It *is* wonderful," says the narrator of Poe's "Berenice," "what stagnation there fell upon the springs of my life." In Salome's world, too, the springs of life are still and contaminated.

Underneath this existential stasis, however, Poe was able to infuse a kind of nervous psychic energy. This Baudelaire sensed when he called Poe a "writer of nervous tension," or Walt Whitman when he found a "demonic undertone behind every page." Strauss was to evoke this primal restlessness in his opera: the same nervousness hanging in the dead air of the House of Usher hangs also in Herod's palace.

This nervous tension builds until it must be released in the stabs of terror that unsettle us in a Poe tale, just as in *Salome*. What causes this tension Baudelaire, among others, was quick to realize. Poe had rediscovered a great forgotten truth—the primal perversity of man:

> There is in man, he [Poe] says, a mysterious force which modern philosophy does not wish to take into consideration; nevertheless, without this nameless force, without this primordial bent, a host of human actions will remain unexplained, inexplicable. These actions are attractive only *because* they are bad or dangerous; they possess the fascination of the abyss. This primitive, irresistible force is nat-

> ural Perversity, which makes man constantly and simultaneously a murderer and a suicide, an assassin and a hangman.[7]

Such are the dramatis personae who surround Salome, herself a kind of apotheosis of the perverse. Wilde's play is virtually a pathology of perversity—one, incidentally, that can be remarkably complemented by two of Poe's own brief explorations of this irrational malady, "The Black Cat" and "The Imp of the Perverse."[8]

Wilde's play has much in common with the themes and preoccupations of Poe's tales. There is something of Salome in the narrator of "Ligeia" when he cries, "My memory flew back, oh, with what intensity of regret! O to Ligeia, the beloved, the august, the beautiful, the entombed . . ." There is even more of her in the last macabre pages of "Berenice," where the narrator, insanely fixated upon the teeth of his recently deceased cousin, breaks into the coffin and tears them from her skull. W. H. Auden finds a large group of Poe stories concerned with "states of willful being, the destructive passion of the lonely ego to merge with the ego of another," and this strikes close to the essence of the Salomé-Jokanaan relationship. And the "full, setting, and blood-red moon" hanging over the House of Usher bears kinship to the moon in the last pages of *Dorian Gray* and to the moon that becomes crimson during the Dance of the Seven Veils. The Decadent movement was nocturnal and avoided the harsh sunlight of conscience. Its unspeakable acts and intoxicating dreams required the cover of dark. What light the Decadents needed the moon could supply.[9]

Poe was among the first writers to explore so penetratingly the dark recesses of the psyche—that domain Freud was to lay open scientifically. In America and England Poe's explorations were unappreciated, but in France his aesthetic caught hold among a small but influential group of writers. In particular, Baudelaire was imbued with the qualities we find in Poe, and in him was already discerned a "decadent" literary trend. The very title of his life-work—*Les Fleurs du mal* ("The Flowers of Evil")—betrays a Poe-esque amalgam of threat, beauty, and horror. In one of the first attempts to capture the essence of French Decadence, Théophile Gautier wrote of Baudelaire's style:

> It expresses novel ideas in novel forms and uses words hitherto unheard. Contrasted to the classic style, it admits of the introduction of shadow, in which move confusedly the larvae of superstition, the haggard phantasms of insomnia, the terrors of night, the monstrous dreams that impotence alone stays in their realization, the gloomy fancies at which day would stand aghast.*

Poe initiated Baudelaire in this delectation of evil. He too became skilled in the mixture of fantastically strange and venemous ingredients. Especially in his femmes fatales do we have some of the first glimmers of the nature of Salome: "They are coldly, cleverly, perversely corrupt [and] transpose vice from the body to the soul. They are haughty, icy-proud, bitter, and find pleasure only in satisfied wickedness, insatiable as sterility itself, filled with hysterical, mad fancies, and lacking, like the Fiend himself, the power to love."

Like Poe, Baudelaire was expert in observing and expressing the subtle shading of neurosis, the twilight zone between mere lust and depravity, between hallucination and mania. He illuminated a sickened world of entropy and putrefaction, and over such a realm Herod rules. A stage designer for the Strauss opera would do well to follow the color chart of Decadence as Gautier described it in the works of Baudelaire:

> In order to paint the corruption which he abhors, he managed to find the morbidly rich hues of more or less advanced decomposition, pearly, shelly tones such as shimmer on stagnant waters, the bloom of consumption, the ghastly whiteness of anaemia, the gall yellow of overflowing bile, the leaden grays of plague mists, poisonous, metallic greens that stink of arseniate copper, sooty blacks washed by the rain down plastered walls, bitumens baked and browned in the frying-pans of hell and so admirably adapted to form a background to livid, spectral heads, in a word, a whole scale of exacerbated colors carried out to the most intense pitch, that corresponds to autumn, to sunset, to the extreme maturity of fruits, to the dying hour of civilizations. [58]

Baudelaire's credo might be taken from his poem "L'Irrémédiable": "Our sole glory and our solace— / Consciousness in doing evil!" This

* *Collected Works,* ed. F. C. de Sumichrast (1905), Vol. 23, p. 40. All Gautier quotations in this chapter are from this volume.

idea, Baudelaire's enthronement of Poe's perverse imp, lies behind the climactic last scene of "Salomé."

Passing from Baudelaire, we come to works that influenced "Salomé" in more obvious ways. First, the prose fiction of Gustave Flaubert—especially his more exotic pieces like *La Tentation de Saint Antoine* (of which Wilde began a translation), *Salammbô* with its Turandot-like heroine, and the long story "Hérodias." This last must have given Wilde the basic outline for his play—though it is rather removed from the aspects of the play Strauss was eventually to focus upon.[10]

A more important influence upon Wilde was Stéphane Mallarmé, particularly one of his two most important works, the 250-line poem "Hérodiade" (the other is "L'Après-midi d'un faune").

The composition of the poem became a lifelong occupation. Mallarmé appears to have commenced it in 1864; a version was published in 1871, but the poet continued to work on it until his death in 1898. An unfinished manuscript of the poem lay open on his desk when he died. It is a catalogue of Decadent poetic methods: highly contorted, disquieting language; fluid, ambiguous, attenuated tone; and macabre, vibrant imagery. Its texture is far closer to the Wilde play than Flaubert's story, especially in its underlying sexual energies. Mallarmé's poem is rich in epithets of decay ("last splendors," "sad dusk," "the grace of faded things," "languishing voice") and grotesquerie ("peculiar times," "fatal splendor," "dazzling abyss"). But most important is Mallarmé's central femme fatale. She is called a "glacier / Farouche"—fierce glacier. Her inner life is a mystery:

> You wander, solitary shadow and new furor
> Looking into yourself precociously with terror:
> But always adorable as an immortal,
> O my child, and terribly beautiful.

Beneath Hérodiade a sensualism threatens to erupt—and finally does in the third section of the poem at her union with the disembodied head. Here we begin to learn more of the side of Salome's character that survives in the opera. Hérodiade's speech to her nurse very nearly captures the charismatic awfulness of Wilde's heroine:

> The horror of my virginity
> Delights me, and I would envelope me
> In the terror of my tresses, that, by night,
> Inviolate reptile, I might feel the white
> And glimmery radiance of thy frozen fire,
> Thou that art chaste and diest of desire,
> White night of ice and of the cruel snow! . . .
> So rare a crystal is my dreaming heart,
> I live in a monotonous land alone,
> And all about me lives but in mine own
> Image, the idolatrous mirror of my pride,
> Mirroring this Hérodiade diamond-eyed.
> I am indeed alone, O charm and curse![11]

The mainsprings of Wilde's drama are contained in these lines: the central character who is chaste but racked with desire, who is abstracted from all around her, and whose pride and willfulness are dangerous, volatile, frigid, and yet incandescent.

England's poet laureate from 1850 to 1892, Tennyson, blamed the rise of Decadent literature on his side of the Channel upon the "poisonous honey stol'n from France." Perhaps it is now impossible to know just what combination of poisonous blossoms helped to produce this disagreeable honey and led to the creation of a work like "Salomé." Other names than those already mentioned might be added to our genealogy: Villiers D'Lisle-Adam for his Poe-like *Contes cruels,* Verlaine for the disturbing word-melodies of his poetry, or Maeterlinck for his chiming, hypnotically repetitious phrasing. Fortunately, however, a novel of the period re-creates much of the ancestry set forth above, and it is a novel whose testimony upon the nature of Decadence should be highly regarded: *A rebours* by Joris-Karl Huysmans.

This novel, which has been translated as *Against the Grain* and *Against Nature,* appeared in 1884 and immediately became (as one writer put it) the breviary of the Decadent movement. In his article "The Decadent Movement in Literature" (1893) Arthur Symons wrote that it "concentrates all that is delicately depraved, all that is beautifully, curiously poisonous, in modern art." Max Nordau in his great jeremiad against European Decadence, *Degeneration* (1893), called Huysmans's hero, the Duc des Esseintes, the ideal Decadent. *A rebours* is doubtless the strange yellow book that has such a deleterious effect upon Dorian Gray. The style of the novel is faithfully described by Wilde:

> The style in which it was written was that curious jewelled style, vivid and obscure at once, full of argot and of archaisms, of technical expressions and of elaborate paraphrases, that characterizes the work of some of the finest artists of the French school of *Symbolistes* . . . It was a poisonous book. The heavy odor of incense seemed to cling about its pages and to trouble the brain. The mere cadence of the sentences, the subtle monotony of their music, so full as it was of complex refrains and movements elaborately repeated, produced in the mind of the lad, as he passed from chapter to chapter, a form of reverie, a malady of dreaming. [281]

Wilde might have been describing his own style in "Salomé."

The peculiar tastes displayed by Des Esseintes are a catalogue of the interests, fixations, and crotchets of the Decadents. He inhabits a decomposing world we have already met in Poe and Baudelaire. He is also a nocturnal creature, "holding that night afforded greater intimacy and isolation and that the mind was truly roused and stimulated only by awareness of the dark."* He is ravished by visions of Oriental opulence. And it comes as no small surprise that his literary interests follow the path we have just explored. His tastes are uniquely satisfied by Poe's ability to explore the sphere of morbid psychology and the progress of mental disturbance from anxiety, to anguish, to stupefying terror. "With awful fascination," Des Esseintes observes, "Poe dwelt on the effects of terror, on the failures of will-power, and discussed them with clinical objectivity, making the reader's flesh creep, his throat contract, his mouth go dry at the recital of these mechanically devised nightmares of a fevered brain." Des Esseintes finds much the same attraction in Baudelaire, who possessed for him "the power to define in curiously healthy terms the most fugitive and ephemeral of the unhealthy conditions of weary spirits and melancholy souls." And he is drawn to just the works of

* All Huysmans quotations are from the Penguin paperback translation by Robert Baldick (1959).

Flaubert that were to attract Wilde—*La Tentation de Saint Antoine* and *Salammbô*.

The Duke's sweetest joys, however, are saved for the poet whose aesthetic is the key to Wilde's play—Mallarmé. "Hérodiade" has special power over him. He sits for hours in front of Gustave Moreau's paintings of Salomé, simultaneously reading the poem: "These precious, interwoven ideas he [Mallarmé] knotted together with an adhesive style, a unique, hermetic language, full of contracted phrases, elliptical constructions, audacious tropes." After a long appreciation, Des Esseintes concludes: "The truth of the matter was that the Decadents of French literature . . . had been embodied in Mallarmé in the most consummate and exquisite fashion. Here, carried to the further limits of expression, was the quintessence of Baudelaire and Poe; here their refined and potent substances had been distilled yet again to give off new savors, new intoxications." "Salomé" was yet a further savor and intoxication of the Symbolist aesthetic. The dyspeptic, morbid Des Esseintes would surely have applauded it; indeed, Wilde's play is a kind of theatrical *A rebours*.

"Salomé" and English Decadence

By the time Wilde wrote "Salomé"—probably in the few weeks before Christmas 1891 in Paris—the influence of the French school had been percolating into English letters for decades. Swinburne was probably the first to saturate himself in French Symbolist literature, and he was succeeded in the 1880s by Walter Pater, George Whistler, and Oscar Wilde. Still, in that decade the combined pressures exerted by the pre-Raphaelites and Art-for-Art's-Sake movements had not yet made sufficient inroads upon Victorian orthodoxies to permit a real blossoming. The great bastions were still occupied, as Symons phrased it, by the "elderly minded"—Tennyson and Browning in poetry, Ruskin and Arnold in aesthetics, Newman in theology. Only in the late 1880s did England seem ready for the aesthetic shock administered by Wilde and the illustrator Aubrey Beardsley in letters and art, just as Ibsen and Nietzsche were soon to shock in their respective fields. The blossoming of English Decadence was brief and almost exactly simultaneous with the literary rise and fall of Oscar Wilde. The movement's typical novel *Dorian Gray* appeared in 1891; its most characteristic poem "The Sphinx" appeared in 1894; and its most typical theatrical manifestation, "Salomé," was first published in France in 1893. But by 1895 Max Beerbohm announced with his usual trenchant whimsy that, as a member of the Decadent coterie, he found himself a bit outmoded. By 1895-97 Decadence was on the wane in England.

Few artistic movements have been so consciously "led" by one man as Oscar Wilde led the English Decadents. In every genre, but particularly in drama, he left the mark of his aggressive aesthetic: "I took the drama, the most objective form known to art, and made it as personal a mode of expression as the lyric or sonnet; at the same time I widened its range and enriched its characterization" (515). Tucked in one of Wilde's early reviews is perhaps the essence of the highly personal ideas that led him to create "Salomé": "Directness of utterance is good, but so is the subtle recasting of thought into a new and delightful form. Simplicity is good, but complexity, mystery, strangeness, symbolism, obscurity even, these have their value."[12] Biased in favor of the ornate and artificial, Wilde set out to explore strange worlds unheard of in England. And so he turned to the *haute cuisine* of French literature with its exotic, delicate themes. These central themes of the Decadent movement are worth glancing over briefly.

The charismatic power of the homme fatal gradually translated into the femme fatale as Romanticism changed by fine shades into, among other things, Decadence. Thus Des Esseintes's fascination with the power of a Salome: "The character of Salome, a figure with a haunting fascination for artists and poets, had been an obsession with him for years . . . She had always remained a dim and distant figure, lost in a mysterious ecstasy far off in the mists of time, beyond the reach of punctillious, pedestrian minds, and accessible only to brains shaken and sharpened and rendered almost clairvoyant by neurosis." Given Wilde's aesthetic, his creation of a Salome was natural, one might even venture to say inevitable. Here was the invitation to explore an exotic Byzantine ambience and the obscure psychic wellspring of fatal attractions. Here could be explored the confrontation of pagan, feminine naturalism and masculine intellectual idealism which consistently fascinated Wilde.[13] Here, too, was a creation worthy of Sarah Bernhardt, the great femme fatale of the era to whom Wilde first offered the part of Salome. Opera goers who are restive in the presence of superannuated Salomes should note that Bernhardt was nearly fifty when she first read Wilde's play and agreed to perform it (censors thwarted this plan). As late as 1900 Wilde could still write in the present tense, "What has age to do with acting? The only person in the world who could act Salome is Sarah Bernhardt" (*L*, 834).

Many commentators upon Decadence find the thirst for new experiences a central characteristic. This desire for novel sensations, imperceptibly nuanced and attenuated, fans throughout Decadent literature and is classically expressed in *A rebours* and *Dorian Gray*. This craving for experiential intensity arises from the sense that certain areas of being are simply not satisfied by everyday life. These areas the Decadents explored with a vigor sometimes whimsical, sometimes malign, sometimes obsessive, and sometimes simply shocking to the middle class.

What might be called the esoteric principle of the Decadents was early established in England by Pater's influential "Conclusion" to *The Renaissance* (1873). There Pater made it the task of philosophy, religion, and culture to startle the human spirit into a "sharp and eager observation." He asserts that experience, rather than the fruit of experience, is the proper end. The effect of this idea was scandalous in an era of the "high normalities" (Holbrook Jackson's phrase) of Tennyson and Ruskin, and he was forced to remove the "Conclusion" from the second edition for fear it would "possibly mislead some of those young men into whose hands it might fall." But the damage had already been done. Wilde and most of his followers idolized Pater, and much of what they were to write vindicates or indicts the "Conclusion," depending on one's view of Decadence. The "new Hedonism" prophesied by Lord Henry in *Dorian Gray* is a conscious paraphrase of Pater, and, though it might have horrified Pater to think so, the intense sensualism of "Salomé" is a logical extension of his ideas. What Salome says and does when given the silver charger is one of the last and, now, most famous gusts of pleasure in unusual experience the Decadent movement produced.

The search for new experience opened up strange realms of troubled sexuality, neurosis, and perversity. "Tired of being on the heights," Wilde relates in his autobiographical *De Profundis,* "I deliberately went to the depths in search for new sensation. What the paradox was to me in the sphere of thought, perversity became to me in the sphere of passion. Desire, at the end, was a malady, or a madness, or both" (515-16). There is something of Wilde in all of the characters in "Salomé," but in the heroine herself, with her lust for the touch of Jokanaan's body, hair, and mouth, is perhaps the strongest indication of the passionate perversity Wilde said he was searching for. In his play Wilde explores the misshapen joys, the vivid life which lurks in grotesques, and that sin which is "the only real color element left in modern life" (all phrases from *Dorian Gray*). The beauty of Salomé—and the play as a whole—is one of monstrous evil. Salome is both bejeweled and fatal, a combination irresistible to a true Decadent.

Those who were at least not ill-disposed to the Wilde-Beardsley party appreciated the strangely dual responses that any intentional artistic balance of beauty and monstrosity must invite. Max Beerbohm wrote in a letter, "I have just been reading 'Salomé' again—terribly corrupt but there is much that is beautiful in it, much lovely writing." Symons found it "filled with strange fascination, not easy to define." For the most part, however, the play's first critics were unable to see beyond the horror. The tone of the London *Times* makes this point sufficiently: "It is an arrangement in blood and ferocity, morbid, bizarre, and very offensive in its adaptation of scriptural phraseology to situations the reverse of sacred" (23 February 1893).

The relationship between Beardsley's drawings and the Wilde play requires a final observation. It is generally conceded that Beardsley's illustrations for "Salomé" are a more enduring and historically important artistic event than the play itself—and that they overwhelm the text. Wilde himself was not pleased with them. However, that the two men should have collaborated upon the Salome story, so important a thread in the history of the Decadents, is a fortunate coincidence. Both possessed the power to evoke the superficial, emotional, and subconscious mainsprings of the Decadent ethos. Wilde described Beardsley's work in a way that makes it clear why this artist was chosen for the project. The comparison to that favorite elixir of the movement is telling:

> Absinthe is to all other drinks what Aubrey's drawings are to other pictures; it stands alone, it is like nothing else; it shimmers like southern twilight in opalescent coloring; it has about it the seduction of strange sins. It is stronger than any other spirit, and brings out the subconscious self in man. It is just like your drawings, Aubrey: it gets on one's nerves and is cruel.[14]

Perhaps because the drawings work too much upon the nervous subterranean level of the play and not so much upon its genuinely alluring surface, Wilde was uncomfortable with them. Nevertheless, we can grant that the artist's special gift for the creation of distended, androgynous bodies and cruel, pleasure-sated mouths does complement aspects of the play. Beardsley's juxtapositions of youth and age, effeminacy and brutality, ugliness and beauty are part of "Salomé's" grotesquerie. His aura of ambiguity, mystery—even his rococo flourishes—reflect in Wilde's poetic prose. Because both Wilde and Beardsley could express cruel and insatiable craving, because both possessed theatrical imaginations of a shocking and atrocious bent, and because an eroticism at once languid and galvanic pervades their sensibilities—for these reasons the John Lane edition of "Salomé" (1894) containing Beardsley's drawings is the epitome of English Decadence.

Strauss and the Decadent Movement

In May 1907 the eminent French writer Romain Rolland wrote to his friend Richard Strauss about the Paris premiere of *Salome*. "I fear (forgive me if I am wrong) that you have been caught by the mirage of German decadent literature . . . There is in Europe today an unbridled force of decadence, of suicide . . . beware of joining forces with it. Let that which must die, die—and live yourself."[15] Rolland, no friend of the Decadents, raises the question of how Strauss was connected with the movement. Though we must finally dissociate Strauss from Decadent fashions, it is important to notice some aspects of their German-Austrian efflorescence. That the movement was as Rolland suggests dying, if not already dead, in 1907 is certain. The mere choice of "Salomé" for an opera may be the most "decadent" aspect of the entire transaction. The opera, when all is said, finally looks forward to the world of Schiele, Kokoschka, Munch, and the Expressionist painters and to the musical horizons shortly to be explored by Schoenberg and Stravinsky. While its subject matter is in the Decadent tradition, *Salome* is not of it. To see why, we should synchronize it with the rise and decline of the German Decadent movement.

Two aspects of Decadence are particularly remarkable, its pan-European influence and its brief and simultaneous vogue in the various countries it reached. Decadence manifested itself in German-speaking areas as what was called Jugendstil (named after the periodical *Jugend*—just as the "yellow nineties" in England were epitomized by *The Yellow Book*). Jugendstil flourished at almost exactly the same time Wilde reached the apex of his career. In 1891 Hermann Bahr could observe that "once more Art, which had been the market-hall of reality for a while, has become the 'temple of dreams,' as Maurice Maeterlinck has called it."[16] A few years later he could describe a new poetry that had all the qualities of Decadent poems like "The Sphinx" or the same bizarre interests as "Salomé." From the "entire group of lyric poets" of the day, Bahr cites as typical a poem called "Neurotika" by Felix Dörmann (*pseud.* Felix Biedermann, 1870-1928). A few stanzas are worth translating:

I love the hectic, slender
Narcissus with blood-red mouth;
I love tormenting thoughts
Which pierce and scar the heart.

I love the sallow and pale ones,
Women with wan demeanor,
Out of which the consuming glow of sin
Speaks in fiery hints.

I love the iridescent vipers,
So supple and yielding and cool;
I love the lamenting and anxious
Songs of the feeling of death.

I love what no one loves,
What no one could ever love—
My own deepest being
And all that is strange and diseased.[17]

Everything about Dörmann's poem—especially the title's conflation of *neurosis* and *erotica*—marks it as Decadent; Salome, Herod, and Herodias inhabit the same kind of world. Indeed, one could lodge against this poem the same criticisms that were made against the English "aesthetic" poets of the 1890s: it remains curiously decorative; the form and texture seem to overwhelm the poet; it speaks to us not from life but from bits and pieces of alien literature; and its intention is to shock and repel.

Dörmann's poem is a lurid and self-conscious example of German Decadence. A more general indication of the chronology of the movement is in the active years of the Viennese Secession, a group of artists that broke away from the high normalities of late nineteenth-century conventions. This group was led by the redoubtable Gustav Klimt, just as the early French Decadents were led by Gustave Moreau. The Secession was formed in 1897, climaxed in influence about 1902, and gradually evanesced around 1905—the year of *Salome*.

The chronology of Decadent/Symbolist/Aesthetic influence upon German-speaking artists, however, is perhaps most clear in relation to the early career of the poet Stefan George (1868-1933). Though George was not exactly in the forefront of Austrian Decadence, and though he was a strangely isolated writer, he was nevertheless an important conduit of such influences into German. At one time or another he translated Baudelaire, Verlaine, Mallarmé, and Swinburne into German. But by far his most important achievement was the establishment in 1892 of a periodical called *Die Blätter für die Kunst*. This publication was intended to present works of the new wave of poets and writers from all Europe, and as such it is an indication of how international the movement was: in the first five issues appeared the works of Mallarmé, Verlaine, Swinburne, D'Annunzio, Jens Peter Jacobsen (whose poetry is the basis for Schoenberg's *Gurrelieder*), in addition to works by George and Hofmannsthal.[18] George's reputation as the focus of the Austrian circle of the movement became similar to that enjoyed by Mallarmé in France (George and his disciples considered the French poet "le maître"). George was the only German poet asked to work on a book to raise funds for a statue of Baudelaire.

Die Blätter für die Kunst appeared regularly from its inception in 1892 until 1919, but—as with the Secession—it did not thrive much beyond 1907. It is interesting to note that Hofmannsthal contributed to the magazine until 1904, when his relations with George became strained. Within a few years Hofmannsthal was working with Strauss on *Elektra*. Whatever the reasons for the breakup, it is at least suggestive that by around 1905 the movement George had been leading was beginning to lose vitality. In art, the Beardsley movement in England and the Jugendstil movement on the Continent proved to be dead ends. Little in either was suitable for further development, simply because they were themselves artistic movements *in extremis*. Rolland was right: the logical end of decadence is death, and the death rattle of the movement was audible by the time Strauss set Wilde's play to music.

It is difficult to imagine Strauss really caught by the "mirage of German decadence" as Rolland feared. Everything we know about Strauss as a man and, during these years, an extremely busy conductor militates against the notion. He possessed a peasant streak, a hard bourgeois core of shrewdness and tightness, and an earthy pride and humor. He was a domesticated person, very much at home in the *Familienkreis*. His sensibility could scarcely have been further removed from the humid, artificial, languorous world of Wilde. It is more likely that Strauss, far from imagining himself one of Wilde's party, simply saw in the play the possibilities for a highly effective, absorbing and—not a small matter for the composer—profitable new opera. He was right: within two years some fifty German houses had staged *Salome*.

This leaves the question, Is the music of Strauss "decadent"? The answer lies in the fact that decadence is in the ear of the beholder. If history is an indication, musical decadence is largely a function of time, place, and personality. The epithet is usually trundled out whenever musical conventions are forced to change strikingly.

Strauss's early career supports this conclusion in an amusing way. Consider this thumbnail sketch of *fin-de-siècle* music:

> A dissonant interval must appear where a consonant interval was expected; if the hearer is hoping that a phrase in what is an obvious final cadence will be spun out to its natural end, it must be sharply interrupted in the middle of a bar. Keys and pitch must change suddenly. In the orchestra a vigorous polyphony must summon the attention in several directions at once; particular instruments, or groups of instruments, must address the listener simultaneously without heeding each other, till he gets as nervously excited as the man who vainly endeavors to understand what is being said in the jangle of a dozen voices.[19]

Pejorative tone apart, this is not an inaccurate description of the music for *Salome*. However, Nordau was thinking not of Strauss but Wagner. He could not see beyond Beethoven and so called Wagner decadent. Inevitably, those who could not see beyond Wagner were bound to call Strauss decadent. The great German music critic Eduard Hanslick—whose sensibility was akin to Nordau's, especially in his hostility to Wagner—took one of Strauss's least likely works, "Don Juan" (1888), as the occasion for assailing the "decadence" of his music. He accuses "these youngsters" of an aesthetic where "color is everything, musical thought nothing," of "false licentiousness," and of creating "musical narcotics"—all remarkably typical of abuse hurled at literary Decadents. Hanslick adds that some "have found it ["Don Juan"] repulsive, and this sensation seems to me more likely to be the right one. This is no 'tone painting' but rather a tumult of brilliant daubs, a faltering tonal orgy, half bacchanal, half witches' Sabbath."[20] It is impossible for us, today, to find in "Don Juan" those qualities Hanslick called decadent. One wonders what Hanslick, who died one year before the *Salome* premiere, would have said of *its* music.

This all serves to suggest that, although Decadence has been shown to be a useful if not entirely enlightening critical term in literature, the term rarely serves as other than an abusive shorthand for radical change on the musical horizon. The word has a way of flurrying about innovative composers—Gluck, Berlioz, Liszt, Wagner, Strauss, Schoenberg, Stravinsky, Webern, Cage, and so on.

One thing is certain: Strauss's music went far beyond the musical métier associated with literary Decadents. Our Decadent hero Des Esseintes could not, it seems, bear anything more daring than Schubert:

> Certain settings for the violoncello by Schumann had left him positively panting with emotion, choking with hysteria; but it was chiefly Schubert's *Lieder* that had excited him, carried him away, then prostrated him as if he had been squandering his nervous energy, indulging in a mystical debauch.

Though a Des Esseintes would have found Wilde's play appealing, the Strauss opera might well have been fatal to one of such delicate taste. Lord Henry Wotton and Dorian Gray sit in "rapt pleasure" listening to *Tannhäuser;* in Wilde's *The Critic as Artist,* Gilbert expresses the desire to play "some mad scarlet thing by Dvořák" for Ernest. The musical tastes of the Decadents were, to say the least, old-fashioned—practically the only old-fashioned taste they seem to have affected. Perhaps in this is a partial explanation why there was virtually no innovation or progress in music in the 1890s. As Constant Lambert observed, "The nineties themselves had no music, properly speaking."[21]

It is especially telling to find Arthur Symons, the foremost contemporary appreciator of Decadence, attacking Strauss in a long article entitled "The Problem of Richard Strauss" (1905): "Strauss is the only decadent in music, and he has tried to debauch music . . . for the satisfaction of a craving which is not 'simple, sensuous, and passionate' but elaborate, intellectual, and frigid." Again, it is vital to note that Symons could only be referring to the early tone poems; he had not yet heard the opera *Salome.* Doubtless, if he had, his criticism would have been the stronger. His displeasure with Strauss, at any rate, is indication enough that by the time Strauss composed *Salome* he had moved outside of the musical world in which the literary Decadents had luxuriated—the musical world of lush beauty, caressing harmonies, and pleasing cadences.

The genius of the Decadents was in *concealment:* behind highly artificial, outwardly brilliant forms, under the laminations of allusion, mystery, and obscurity, within such creatures as Hérodiade and Salome they concealed their intentions and their fears. Strauss's genius, on the other hand, was that for which music is peculiarly apt: the *revelation* of underlying qualities. "In music," he wrote to Rolland, "one can say anything." And Strauss certainly felt no reticence in *Salome*. In this he was allied to Freud, then just beginning to find recognition in Vienna. The revelations of Freud disturb the beautiful surface of "Salomé" in precisely the way Strauss's music virtually explodes underneath the action. Upon the psychology of "Salomé" Strauss performed a kind of musical pathology. If concealment, suppression, sublimation are at the heart of Decadent art and are left over from the Victorian era, and if (self)recognition is a sign of modernity, then the almost ghoulish psychological dissection of the Strauss score clearly sets it ahead in intellectual history. Wilde's play is essentially of the nineteenth century; Strauss's opera decidedly belongs to the twentieth.

Decadent Play and Expressionist Opera: Only the Shudder Counts

In the late nineteenth century there was much talk of the musical nature of nonmusical arts. In his famous "Art poétique" Verlaine wrote,

> You must have music first of all,
> and for that a rhythm uneven is best,
> vague in the air and soluble,
> with nothing heavy and nothing at rest . . .
> Never the Color, always the Shade,
> always the nuance is supreme.

As Verlaine suggests, the air of indefiniteness was an important effect for the Symbolists. The metaphor of music, the one impalpable art, proved very useful to them, and in this they were, as so often, looking back to Poe, who found in "true musical expression . . . a suggestive indefiniteness of vague and therefore spiritual effect." Music looms large, if only metaphorically in the period. Hence, poetic titles like Gautier's "Symphonie en blanc majeur" (pronounced "immortal" by Wilde), J. A. Symonds's "In the Key of Blue," and Wilde's own "Symphony in Yellow." Hence also Baudelaire, writing of "peintres symphonistes," and the paintings Whistler called Harmonies, Nocturnes, and Symphonies. Upon these last Beerbohm turned his bemused eye and announced: "Mr. Whistler's top-hat is a true nocturne and his linen a symphony in white major."

This was, of course, verbal game-playing—a way of explaining and justifying the purposeful ambiguity of poetic effects and sheer pleasure in the caressing sound of strange words embedded in strange syntax and metrics. To this level of musicality, as we have noticed, Strauss turned a deaf ear. Though his translation of the play into opera is in many ways a loyal one, it is by no means complete. Certain qualities of the original are absent:

(1) Strauss cut about 40 per cent of the play, and it is not surprising that much of Wilde's repetition of phrasing was removed. One example will suggest what happens throughout:

1st Soldier:	The Tetrarch has a sombre aspect.
2nd Soldier:	Yes; he has a sombre aspect.
1st:	He is looking at something.
2nd:	He is looking at someone.
1st:	At whom is he looking?

Strauss cut the third and fourth lines. Wilde filled his play with such repetitions, and these were the object of much scorn. One critic associated the French version with the then equivalent of a beginning French textbook; Mario Praz found little except "childish prattle" in the play.

The repetitiousness, however, can be defended. Wilde was no doubt working toward the same effect for which Maeterlinck, the Flemish dramatist who created the Symbolist theater, was just becoming notorious. Arthur Symons wrote of him: "As a dramatist he has but one note—fear; has but one method, that of repetition." The quality of stasis, of a kind of existential indolence, is best personified in the heroine of "Pelléas et Mélisande" (1892; English translation 1894; Debussy opera 1902). The result in this play was to make a figure like Mallarmé's Hérodiade viable on the stage, to make inertia stageworthy. Beckett was later to achieve the same effect in his repetitious dialogues. Strauss left Debussy to make the one valiant and, for most audiences, indigestible attempt to translate the ennui of French Symbolism into operatic form. The draw of spiritual indolence could not have been very great for the brisk, industrious Strauss. Other possibilities attracted him.

(2) There is a quality shared by much of the poetry and prose of the Decadent movement, by Beardsley's drawings, by Tiffany glass—indeed by most of the art and architecture of art nouveau: a curvilinear or fluid quality. Flowering, vegetal shapes pervade the artistic creations and imagery of the movement. The long, sinuous line—as in any Beardsley piece—is the essence of the erotic, too, and this is why that artist loomed so importantly in a movement that exulted in Eros and the willing capitulation to the pleasures of sensuality.

Strauss, however, was concerned with force and subjugation. That quality of more purely decorative and superficial eroticism in Beardsley's "Salomé" illustrations is not prominent in the opera. This was immediately apparent to Louis Laloy: "The music of Mr. Strauss is far from resembling the compositions of Beardsly [*sic*] . . . it recalls rather the crude and fiery colors of Böcklin."[22] It is interesting that Böcklin should have been called to mind. That painter (1827-1901) was one of the forerunners of German Expressionism, and there are elements of musical Expressionism in the score of *Salome*.

Another Parisian critic, writing for the *Revue des Deux Mondes* (June 1907), perceived a parallel between the opera and Impressionist methods as well: "Reduced to the formal minimum, both in space and time, they [*Salome*'s themes] no longer appear as lines, but as points. And if pointillism, as the aesthetic jargon has it, is disagreeable enough in painting where the work is presented and embraced all at once, the effect is all the more tedious and distressing in music, which by its nature is one of successive perception" (p. 693). Pointillism describes certain aspects of Strauss's compositional methods in *Salome*. While the story unwinds the music presents a conflation of musical "points." These points of sound which explode from various parts of the orchestra may seem at first haphazard, but they finally serve to create the single most overwhelming effect of the opera—that of nervous tension constantly frustrated or erupting.

Nervous tension is mercurial, unpredictable, and threatening. Such is the music of *Salome*. Like Beardsley's drawings, its music "gets on one's nerves and is cruel." To achieve this the composer forsook the pleasures of Eros in favor of the brutal realities of force in human relations. That Strauss's predilections ran this way his friend Rolland concluded after seeing *Salome* for the first time: "Above all, you love force."

(3) Inevitably, *Salome* lacks the tone imparted to Wilde's original by the French language. As we have seen, Wilde was referring to the harmonies of French when he called "Salomé" a "beautiful colored musical thing." To the English, French was the language of exoticism and nuance. It was also the language of the Decadent movement—an exhilarating métier for such a poseur and artist in outrage as Oscar Wilde.[23] The French reacted mildly to Wilde's use of their language; the text had after all been corrected by his friend Pierre Louÿs (to whom the play was dedicated). Seen as a work connected with the Symbolist tradition, its extravagances and crotchets raised hardly an eyebrow. The French critic Philippe Jullian comments simply that the play was written in the Symbolist idiom, and that it seemed to use slightly childish language and rather flowery diction. He does add in a boggling aside that, "In order that certain words should stand out as the author intended, 'Salomé' has to be acted with an English accent."[24]

What concerns us here is the transition from French to German—what happens when "C'est de ta bouche que je suis amoreuse" becomes "Deinen Mund begehre ich," or when "J'ai baisé ta bouche" becomes "Ich habe deinen Mund geküsst." One need not be a linguist to sense that the German is a less supply inflected, more strictly modular, more guttural language—one, in short, which can be more stark and harsh.[25] Strauss learned this lesson from Rolland during 1905 when he asked for advice on a French version of *Salome* he was personally preparing. After many complaints from the composer about seemingly capricious French inflections, Rolland finally lost his patience:

> I can see very well that you have no feeling for our literary French language at all. You imagine that it's like yours. Our language has

> no connection with yours. You have very marked stresses, very strong and continual contrasts between (´) and (˘), between the strong and the weak syllable. With you, it's either all one thing or all the other. And it's precisely in the interval which separates the (´) from the (˘), the *forte* from the *piano*, that our poetry lies. It has an infinite number of shades in the half-tone—accents much less stressed than yours are, but much more varied, more supple, more flexible. [*Correspondence* p. 37]

Rolland leaves little more to be said of the differences one senses in reading the play in French and hearing the opera in German. Strauss's score has just the powerful stresses, the immense contrasts Rolland describes. Even its nuances seem highly pointed. It would be facile to say the operatic styles of Debussy and Strauss developed as they did because one was working with French, and the other with German; one can only say that the differences between *Pelléas* and *Salome* do manifest essential parallels with the differences between the two languages In his review of the opera, Laloy tempered his disparagement with the observation, "While *Salome* is quite far from our [Parisian] experience, it is indeed almost as astonishing and, here and there, as shocking to our ears as *Pelléas et Mélisande* must be for a German listener. Few works carry such a marked nationalistic character as these."

To this generalization about the relative delicacy of French and German an obvious caveat should be added: had a great and resourceful German poet such as Hofmannsthal set Wilde's play, perhaps a far closer approximation of "Salomé's" feline grace and buoyancy might have been achieved. The German language is by no means exclusive of such effects, as Hofmannsthal was indeed to prove, almost too well, in his libretto for *Der Rosenkavalier*.

Rolland relates in his diary an amusing story of attending *Pelléas* with Strauss:

> Marnold tries to take part in our conversation, and says to him [Strauss] with his usual ponderousness: "There are musical phrases; but they are not stressed, underlined, so that the general public notices them." Strauss, rather hurt, but very calm, replies: "Yes, but

> I'm a musician, and I can't hear anything." We resume our conversation in an undertone. I try to make Strauss understand the restraint of this form of art, which is all in shades and half-tones, of its impressionism, delicate and poetic, using of little touches of color in juxtaposition, unobtrusive and vibrant. [*Correspondence,* p. 151]

Rolland is here defending the prime qualities of Symbolist and Decadent poetry. Strauss was clearly impervious to them, and the scene leaves little doubt that Strauss was intellectually alien to this aesthetic. In *Salome* he was not reacting to the French language of the play, nor to the French artistic movement from which it sprang. He was an Expressionist at heart, not an Impressionist. He was interested in the theater of action, situation, and conflict, not in the theater of attenuated mood, indirection, and inertia. Strauss made this bias apparent when he complained of *Pelléas,* "But it's just *Parsifal.*"[26]

It should by now be clear that Strauss was not artistically inclined or able to compose music for "Salomé" that was, as Verlaine desired of poetry, "vague in the air and soluble." Strauss chose to set the inner "Salomé," and this task required, not the fluid indirection of Impressionism, but the violent utterance and harsh "line" we associate with Expressionism in art. And so the opera lacks the play's dark allure; rather it is transparently terrific and ugly. There is reason to believe the author would not have objected to the result: to a friend who said he shuddered when he saw the play, Wilde replied, "It is only the shudder that counts."[27] In Strauss's opera the shudder counts. Indeed, it is supreme.

As we have noted, there are two levels to Wilde's play: the superficial, which is lubricious, fecund, sensual, and the concealed, which is brutal and ugly. The music of Strauss is addressed to the latter, as one early reviewer realized: "How odd it is that the decadence of two nations: [*sic*] France and Germany, should be incarnated in two men who represent it, the one with his effeminate refinement, and the other with his brutality!"[28] Wilde left the nuclear core of terror and repulsiveness in his play unspoken. Strauss was not so squeamish; his furioso vein (as Hofmannsthal called it) drove him to describe in music what lies at the center of "Salomé." It remains for us to pinpoint the means the composer used to delineate this part of the play. In the following pages I have avoided analysis of the leitmotifs of the opera. This has already been performed, for instance, by William Mann in *The Operas of Richard Strauss* and Norman Del Mar in *Richard Strauss*.

PERVERSITY AND IDÉE FIXE

Two common modes of expression in the music of *Salome* are those suggesting (1) the aimless, erratic, perverse release of energy and (2) the fixation or mania which may or may not derive from such energy. Strauss often captures the former through extended slithering motifs usually sounded by a single instrument or instrumental desk; the latter is most frequently expressed through the tremolo or trill and the short, repeated phrase. Throughout the opera these two methods are connected—sometimes in a linear form where the nervous energy issues from (EX. 1A and 1B) or vanishes into (EX. 2A and 2B) a tremolo of suspension. Often, as in the first bars of the

Example 1

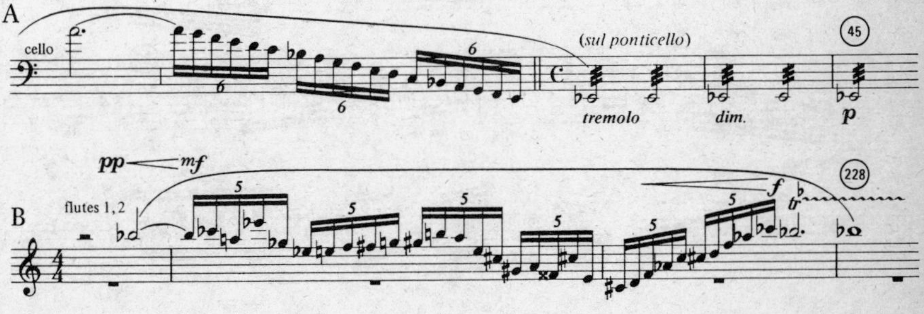

Example 2

opera, the two effects overlap each other (there the clarinet theme sprawls over a violin tremolo).

Particularly through instruments with low registers—bass violins, bass tuba, bass clarinet, bassoon, and contrabassoon—Strauss gives voice to the imp of the perverse that impels the characters to the edge of the abyss and then downward. Activated by sexual energies, the imp which leads Salome to destruction is best captured in the eerie descending line of the contrabassoon we hear as she awaits the sounds of decapitation (EX. 3), or by the insistent, grating bass tuba phrase

Example 3

introducing Salome's desire to kiss Jochanaan. A similarly erratic but propulsive theme, this time for solo flute, carries Salome to the height of ecstasy as she hears the prophet for the first time. This twelve-bar passage (EX. 4)—like so many events in the score virtually inaudible as such—is archetypal for the music of *Salome*. It lunges fitfully, diz-

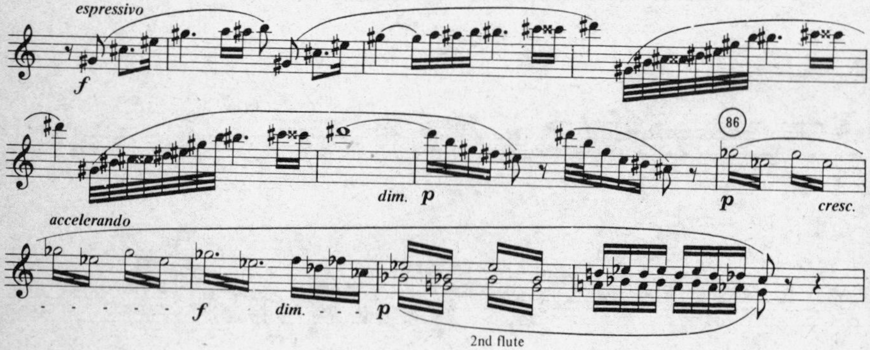

Example 4

zily to D-sharp, and in a few arpeggios decomposes into a tremolo with a dynamic crescendo bulge, and then evanesces in a few frenetic semiquavers. Such momentary ascents and descents (enjambed against, shuffled with, or simultaneous with similar events in other parts of the orchestra) give *Salome* that "coarse and jumbled declamation, all developing in starts and flashes" that Laloy experienced at the first Paris performance.

The terrifying combination of aimlessness and fixation, however, is most brilliantly captured by Strauss when we are permitted to see in music what Salome sees in the abysmal cistern where Jochanaan is imprisoned. He surrounds the passage of EX. 5 with numerous effects expressive of Salome's idée fixe. A trill on the bass drum and in two of the four bass violin desks sounds the depths, while the remaining two desks enter with an explosive row of B-flats. Above this hovers the entire brass section, all muted. Only two French horns, doubled by the kettle drum, display a hint of nervous excitement in a briskly attacked, repetitious interval of a third. With the entry of the strings in a coarse tremolo upon the bridge of the instrument, the contrabassoon commences its languorous descent. This combination of the fixating tremolo with a surrounding nimbus of nervous energy is frequent in *Salome*—and is most simply exampled in the two motifs associated with Salome's demand for the head of the prophet (EX. 5): as she asks for the silver charger, the clarinets play the increasingly ominous, literally nerve-racking trill, while the flute and even more astringent piccolo sound the cruel, galvanic flicker of Salome's theme.

Example 5

The psychic abyss is metaphorically present everywhere in *Salome*—in the cave of decadence which is Herod's palace, in the mouth of Jochanaan, in the moon, where each character sees the reflection of a personal abyss. Salome even sees the abyss in Jochanaan's horrible eyes: "They are like the black caverns of Egypt where dragons make their lairs." Strauss's orchestration for this line is again typical of his power to evoke a sense of evil horror: the meandering bass clarinet gives way to the Salome theme (compare EX. 5) in the clarinet; the string basses spread themselves into a three-note chord at the bottom of the orchestral chasm; against muted fluttering in the first violins, the harps and violas administer pizzicato pinpricks; and these are accented by bristling pizzicato stabs by a solo flute that are rendered even more coarse by full-octave grace notes. The overall effect, as Strauss intended, is grisly.

Lest there be any doubt that the sex drive is behind all of this, it is worth observing that the whooping, orgasmic figure in the horns just after Herod finally grants Salome's demand (EX. 6) may be com-

Example 6

pared with the sexual climax Strauss was later to portray in the more genteel context of the prelude to *Der Rosenkavalier*.

There is a comic aspect to perversity—one that is black and sick. The imp of the perverse (the very word *imp* relieves the story of the odium of systematic evil) controls the action of the play, just as it controls the texture of Strauss's music. The imp is behind what one critic called all the "recondite pranks" in the score. The imp of the perverse makes the opera, to use Strauss's own words, a scherzo with a fatal conclusion.

NERVOUS DISORDER

When Strauss played through *Salome* on the piano for his aging father, the latter said, "Oh God, what nervous music. It is exactly as if one had one's trousers full of May bugs."[29] Nervous the music of *Salome* certainly is: bustling, electric, violent. What makes the music sound this way is its lack of evenness, continuity and what might be called developmental thought. Most of the opera's music must be judged against those relaxing passages of "flow," normalcy, and symmetry that accompany the optimistic prophecies of Jochanaan (EX. 7). Overwhelming these moments of repose is the nervous orchestral

Example 7

maelstrom. The wealth of coarsening effects in *Salome* had not been so notably experienced since the Witches' Sabbath of Berlioz's "Symphonie Fantastique." Only a few of innumerable examples can be singled out here: the almost painful violin tremolo that wafts up to the second E above high C as Salome admires the moon (Sec. 30 of the score); the "spitzig" (barbed) oboe thrusts accompanying Salome's discomforting gaze upon Jochanaan (Sec. 81); the sinister muted brass when she calls his body hideous (Sec. 98); the prickling harp pizzicato when she finds his hair like a crown of thorns (Sec. 111); and the two glorious plucked chords at the moment Salome discloses her demand for the head (Sec. 254). The score is thick with phrases that give the sense of a sudden rush of energy, often followed by a temporary and uneasy suspension (EX. 8). Also common are the vertiginous rollercoaster phrases such as the clarinet line accompanying Salome's description of Jochanaan's hair (EX. 9).

The brutal tension of the score is also partially created through

Example 8

Example 9

bulging or distending dynamic markings. These accompany the harmonic distortions and contrasts for which the score is famous. The smallest phrases (of which three instances are given in EX. 10) may exhibit harsh dynamic change, and the sforzando (forced) marking is ubiquitous. The opera, as one Parisian critic well observed, is full of "accents explosifs."

The nervous character of the score is also derived in large part

Example 10

from the conflicting timbres, textures, and instrumental registers within the orchestra. In a way this is symbolized by the sectarian conflict between the five Jews, which lies at the center of the opera and which climaxes in complete musical pandemonium. In the score different motifs and instrumental "sects" continuously criss-cross, vanish suddenly in the musical underground, reappear just as suddenly.

Salome is a score of loose ends or, more specifically, exposed nerve-ends. Its orchestral underworld is thus like the mental underworld—full of false starts, shards of malicious desire, an ill-fitting mosaic of psychic bits whose conscious (i.e., audible) life represents but a brief foray out of the oblivion of the subconscious. This sense of shattered and truncated musical development is probably what led Bellaigue to the perceptive though ill-meant observation that *Salome* is "composed of nothings, nothings in the plural, innumerable nothings, but nothings nevertheless."

MALAISE

That a malaise pervades *Salome* is a commonplace and yet can hardly be underemphasized. Even its lighter moments, which are almost all in three-quarter time and verge on the Viennese waltz idiom, have a sickly, banal tinge. Strauss was at heart a Viennese, and so the distinctly Viennese banality was inevitable and no doubt intentional.[30] Still, it must be admitted that Strauss's deployment of waltz time (and its relatives 6/4 and 9/4)—in Herod's cajoling with the wine and grapes, in the ghastly heaving of the Dance of the Seven Veils, and in Herod's hysterical pleas after the Dance—all succeeds in capturing the malaise of the lumpish, gross-fleshed civilization of Judaea.

The last pages of the opera are surely the apotheosis in music of the Decadent malaise. They capture the crucial moment for that aesthetic, the moment when ecstatic experience of forbidden pleasure transforms into revulsion. The massive orchestral juggernaut, as it were, exhausts its energy as Salome observes, "the great mystery of love is greater than the mystery of death." Fully muted and pianissimo, the harmonies slowly twist until, as Salome pronounces the

word *Todes* (on a low B-flat!), the grim abysmal tremolo and the drum dirge indicate which of the mysteries Salome has indeed revealed. A deathly chill falls over the music.

Salome's impending moment of truth is briefly interrupted by an argument between Herod and Herodias. As Herod repeats a fear expressed earlier in the opera by the Page ("Something terrible is going to happen."), we are left to focus on the now-familiar tremolo and idée fixe theme (EX. 5). This is soon interrupted by a sickening pianissimo tonal cluster (EX. 11). This is given added depth by the

Example 11

organ as Salome kisses the severed head. Her next line ("I have kissed your mouth") must be uttered faintly (*matt*), and Strauss truncates and flattens the idée fixe into a ghastly three-note hint, in the violins and horns, of the enervation which follows upon the satisfaction of lust. The very flatness of Salome's vocal line adds an appalling effect. As the bitter taste of the blood works upon her, the theme of exultation staggers and reels. Exercising in the face of this unhinging, collapsing sensation a final heroic burst of erotic exultation, Salome brings the music back into the resplendent key of C-sharp major for a last gust of pleasure in the kiss. The two bars following her last words (EX. 12) are the quintessence of Decadence: here is ecstasy falling in upon itself, crumbling into the abyss at the sound of that most sickening chord in all opera in the second bar.

Plate 1. Gustave Moreau, "Salome Dancing Before Herod" (1876). *From the Collection of the Armand Hammer Foundation, Los Angeles.*

Example 12

Two paintings of the Salome story exist which are particularly helpful in summarizing the differences between the play and the opera. When Wilde complained about Beardsley's drawings, he explained: "My Herod is like the Herod of Gustave Moreau–wrapped in his jewels and sorrows. My Salomé is a mystic, the sister of Salammbô, a Sainte Thérèse who worships the moon; dear Aubrey's designs are like the naughty scribbles a precocious schoolboy makes."[31] Wilde was referring to Moreau's "Salome Dancing Before Herod" (1876–PLATE 1). And this work–made famous by Huysmans in a long appreciation in *A rebours*–certainly has much in common with the style of "Salomé." There is a profusion of lapidary detail, brilliant color, and sybaritic luxuriance. Also as in the play, however, there is a pervading coldness and unsettling ambiguity in the event Moreau has re-created. There are no natural human gestures in the painting; Moreau's Salome is, as Symons writes, "a rigid flower of evil, always in the midst of sumptuous glooms or barbaric splendors." The discomforting facets of this picture–its voyeurism, aura of sterility, and mystery–are all ingredients in the Wilde play. But most importantly, Moreau's elaborate symbolism in the picture and its great façade of detail-work serves to conceal the sexual implications of the event, and such artistic concealment, we have seen,

---

Plate 2. Gustav Klimt, "Judith II" ("Salome," 1909). *Galleria d'Arte Moderna di Cà Pesaro, Venice.*

is prominent in "Salomé." Moreau's picture, in short, is very close to Wilde's play in its interpretation of the story and its texture.

More akin to Strauss's achievement is a painting by Gustav Klimt dating from 1909 (PLATE 2).[32] Though both Klimt and Moreau shared a fascination with the feminine principle and femmes fatales, both practiced the art nouveau principle of decoration as content, and in the œuvre of both there is a constant sexual element—Klimt is nevertheless an artist of the twentieth century in his more direct expression of disturbing sexual implications. In his painting an alarmingly straight-forward sexuality—the sullen eyes, cruel hands, bare breast, and floating male head—can be seen literally breaking through an otherwise art nouveau style. Klimt's predatory and flesh-and-blood figure brings us much closer than does Moreau to the Strauss heroine. We know Strauss found Klimt's style congenial. "In the world of this painter of fantasy," Strauss remarked that he found "much of my own music, especially *Salome*."[33] Like Strauss, Klimt was intrigued to explore the psychic underworld; like Strauss also, he was, in his willingness to exploit, distort, and exaggerate form and color, a forerunner of Expressionism; and finally Klimt was also more given to the description of sexual energies in explicit terms. His gift was revelatory rather than—as with Moreau—concealing. The impact of Klimt's femme fatale is more direct, brutal, and modern. The same could be said of the Salome given us by Strauss.

nine

WOZZECK

A real phenomenon, this man Wozzeck.

Wozzeck

The career of Georg Büchner, whose *Woyzeck* is the basis for Alban Berg's first opera, is one of the most remarkable in theatrical history—the kind of career that encourages superlatives. Most astonishing perhaps was his death in 1837 at the age of twenty-three. No reputation for theatrical genius has ever rested upon so brief a career or a more slender body of works: *Danton's Death,* one of the most brilliant first plays ever written; *Leonce and Lena,* a short comedy with a tone of existential farce that looks forward to Brecht, Ionesco, and Beckett; and a garbled, unfinished conglomeration of approximately twenty-seven scenes called *Woyzeck,* which runs a mere thirty printed pages.* One might also venture that no writer for the stage has ever been more in advance of his own time than Büchner. His three plays were not performed until the turn of the century—*Danton* in 1902, *Leonce* in 1911, and a reconstructed *Woyzeck* in 1913. Nevertheless, Büchner's influence upon twentieth-century dramatic styles and schools was enormous. Brecht was reported to regard *Woyzeck* as the beginning of modern theater. From our modern perspective he appears the single most seminal and revolutionary dramatist of his century. Naturalist, Expressionist, Absurdist, Existentialist theater—it would be difficult to explore the sources of these dramatic traditions without reference to Büchner, and scholars of each of these movements have claimed Büchner's influence in one way or another.

* Berg based his libretto on an edition of *Woyzeck* that misspelled the title. This fortunate mistake will help keep references to play and opera in this chapter distinct.

Among many intricate questions this chapter will not discuss is the "proper" ordering of *Woyzeck*'s scenes. This issue is briefly treated in the edition of *Woyzeck* translated by Henry Schmidt (Avon paperback, 1969), which I have used in this chapter. Quotations from *Danton's Death* are also made from a Henry Schmidt translation (Avon paperback, 1971). References to *Leonce and Lena* and *Lenz* are from Michael Hamburger's translation (1972). An excellent recent book on Büchner is Maurice Benn's *The Drama of Revolt* (1976).

But in artistic matters influence need not be, rarely is, exclusive; so the warning should be quickly made that the Büchner of this chapter is not the complete Büchner. The context here is the so-called atonal or Expressionist epoch in music, and consequently it is in his Expressionist guise that the playwright will emerge.

Certain masterpieces seem to accord perfectly with the tastes and spirit of the time in which they first appear; their popularity is immediate and vast. As we have seen, Beaumarchais's comedy *Le Mariage de Figaro* was such a work. It appeared at just the moment when the expressive powers of music, moulded by a genius, were peculiarly complementary to the playwright's style. Within two years of its premiere the play had become a masterly opera. *Woyzeck,* on the other hand, was obliged to wait nearly a century for a similarly fruitful transformation. The case of *Woyzeck* (*circa* 1837) and *Wozzeck* (1925) is a strong one for arguing that contemporaneity may not necessarily affect the translation of literature into opera. Büchner was, as a thinker and writer for the stage, a thoroughly twentieth-century intellect, and his aesthetic and world view could not be appreciated until modernism came into existence after the turn of the century. His writing waited long to be understood and appreciated on its own dramatic and philosophical terms (as late as 1891 a German editor was jailed for reprinting *Danton's Death*). One can even say that only with the exhaustive German edition of Büchner's works by Werner Lehmann of 1967 did it become possible to see *Woyzeck* in its pristine state, unadulterated by the arbitrary editorial assumptions and emendations that flawed early versions of the play—including those Berg used.

The dramatist was also obliged to wait for nineteenth-century operatic conventions to be replaced by ones more congenial to his art. His dramaturgy required a musical embodiment not possible until Debussy, Strauss, Schoenberg, and Berg successively reacted to the Wagnerian and verismo aesthetics. Büchner's text remained effectively locked until a new generation of musical Expressionists appeared with the sensibilities and techniques to open it. In spite of the century-long postponement caused by that oddly warped time-frame that sometimes governs intellectual history, the combination Büchner's drama and Berg's music was a happy union. The equivalence of expressive modes and creative powers that ties the two men together helps explain the greatness of the opera *Wozzeck.*

Ode to Joy, Ode to Sorrow

Almost everything about *Woyzeck* is revolutionary, and to understand why it should have been ignored through the nineteenth century and why it would never have appealed to operatic composers of that time—even the most politicized like Verdi or Wagner—it is necessary to examine Büchner's revolutionary qualities. To see just how staggeringly estranged from the main currents of his time Büchner was, one need only observe his reaction to the dramaturgy of Friedrich Schiller—whose plays were still very popular in Büchner's time, notably among opera librettists. Schiller and Büchner were nearly polar opposites, and much that the latter wrote can be seen as a reaction to Schiller's Romantic idealism.[1] Leonce observes to Valerio: "Poor wretch, you seem to be in labor with ideals" (*Leonce and Lena,* I.i), and most of Schiller's ideals are mentioned by Büchner for the sake of parody or bitter sarcasm. Take, for example, the idea of freedom. "Liberty," wrote Schiller, "is everywhere vastly more attractive to a noble soul than good social order without it . . . liberty makes him a citizen of a better world." It was a sign of Büchner's modernity that he had little patience with "noble souls" and found the ideal of freedom to be a rather transparent mask for harsh, impenetrable determinism. "We are nothing but puppets," Danton says, "our strings are pulled by unknown forces, we ourselves are nothing, nothing!" (II.v.).

It is a thinly disguised counterblast to Schiller and to German idealistic philosophy that the Doctor in *Woyzeck* raises the subject of human freedom in connection with urination: "Haven't I proved that the *musculus constrictor vesicae* is subject to the will? Nature! Woyzeck, man is free. In man alone is individuality exalted to freedom. Couldn't hold it in!" (scene viii). Schiller's works are in aggregate an heroic assertion of human dignity and individual worth. Büchner's works searingly proclaim human indignity.[2] Schiller's aesthetic is essentially optimistic and vigorous; Büchner's is cynical and recessive.

Schiller's central characters, we saw in Chapter Four, embody an exhilarating upward thrust and are expert at taking noble stances. These larger-than-life figures—William Tell, Mary Stuart, and Joan of Arc, for instance—struggle heroically against palpable enemies. Lionel Trilling has described the hero as "one who looks like a hero; a hero is an actor—he acts out his own high sense of himself." Such are Schiller's central characters. Büchner's heroes are another matter. His French revolutionary leader, Danton, though he may seem to occupy the intense dramatic space of a hero, is in fact notable as the first truly passive hero in theatrical history. As one observer in the play says, "He would rather let himself be guillotined than make a speech" (II.i), conduct unbecoming a traditional heroic personage. A relentless examination of spiritual inertia, *Danton's Death* looks not backward to *Hamlet* but forward to *Waiting for Godot*. Danton and Vladimir and Estragon are alike in that they are waiting, not for someone or something, but for an end. They are waiting for nothing: God-knows-what = God-wot = Godot. Danton announces at the end of the play: "The world is chaos. Nothingness is the world-god yet to be born."

Büchner was the first to explore on the stage this demeaning heroism, and he was among the first to depict man suffering that peculiarly modern malaise induced by a sense of "negative" freedom. His other works make even more clear his hostility to the old Schillerian (and this is to say nineteenth-century operatic) heroics:

> *Valerio:* Then let's be heroes. (*He marches up and down, drumming and trumpeting.*) Bang-bang-bla-bla-bang.
>
> *Leonce:* But heroism frays horribly and starts getting hospital fever and can't be maintained without lieutenants and recruits. Spare me all the romantic driveling over Alexander and Napoleon! [I.iii]

Traditional heroics on which opera then thrived—based usually on high-flown ideals like patriotism, filial piety, or love—are even more devastatingly attacked in Büchner's short novel *Lenz:* "Ideal personages is what they ask for, but all I've seen is a lot of wooden puppets. This idealism is the most shameful contempt for human nature. If only artists would try to submerge themselves in the life of the very humblest person and to reproduce it with all its faint agitations, hints of experience, the subtle, hardly perceptible play of his features" (p. 46). Two aspects of this credo illuminate Büchner's art. First is its expression of concern for common humanity. This led the playwright to focus upon the actual events surrounding the execution in 1824 of a demented barber named Johann Christian Woyzeck. Second, it suggests what process was necessary to wear down the impressive but unwieldy conventions of traditional drama, namely, the process of *decomposition*. Before Büchner's aesthetic could come into its own, the elaborately plotted, idealistically arching Romantic theater typified by Schiller and then Hugo had to be broken down; a "smaller," more compact dramaturgy was necessary to capture existential realities on a proper human scale. For a poetic realist and pessimist like Büchner this meant a diminutive scale. The old style was too rich in rhetorical amplification to grasp the tinier aspects of life, the faint hints and barely perceptible sensations Lenz refers to in the passage just quoted. Büchner's aphoristic, disjointed, compressive style was perfect for this purpose, but not until this century did his methods and intentions become attractive.

Nor were Büchner's works suited to the operatic fashions of the mid-century. It was necessary that the genre be scaled down to a more instantaneously affective musical idiom; nothing Wagner or even Verdi might have written would suit the dramatist's terse style. Opera tied to the set-piece or the large-scale scene had to be "decomposed." The direction was "pointillist." (Fauvism might be more to the point, with its powerful experimentation in pure colors.) It was thus possible to avoid the expansive distortions that would have subverted Büchner's anti-heroic intentions. With that last stupendous achievement of German Romantic idealism, *Der Ring des Nibelungen,* a process of musical decomposition became almost inevitable. This process made a great Büchner opera possible.

I have spoken of stylistic aspects of the Büchner revolution. It is in their world view, however, that Schiller and Büchner present the greatest contrast. The disparity is worth describing because their works proved agreeable to such widely differing operatic epochs—Schiller to the mid-nineteenth century generally, Büchner to the Expressionist period dominated by Schoenberg. The contrast is also between a nineteenth-century strain of idealism and twentieth-century cynicism, humanist exhilaration, and existentialist mortification. Romantic art, according to Heine, attempted to represent or typify the infinite and the spiritual. That is the thrust of Schiller's drama. Büchner could bear none of this: he perceived the state of human affairs more darkly. He found his age utterly materialistic; he saw that "nothing in the world costs one so dearly as humanity." Schiller's gift was for capturing the ascendant and commanding sensation; Büchner's for the evocation of flatness and vacuity.

Many of the great notions of German idealism are found in Schiller's "Ode to Joy," made immortal by Beethoven. Büchner negates each of them. Schiller's ecstasy in the presence of a purposeful universe ("Brothers, surely a loving Father / Dwells above the canopy of stars") is balanced by the icy ennui of Danton ("Creation has spread itself out so far that nothing is empty, it's all a jumble. Nothingness has killed itself, Creation is its wound, we are its drops of blood, the world is the grave in which it rots" IV.vii). Schiller's cosmopolitanism and sense of human connectedness ("All men will become brothers") are countered not only by Büchner's grim view of society—

> Why should a society such as this walk around between heaven and earth? Its whole life consists only of attempts to dissipate its most terrifying boredom. Let it die out: that is the only new thing which it can still experience. [letter, 1836]

—but also by his near-obsession with the solitariness of man. His *Lenz* is one of the most moving tales of human isolation ever written. Nor is *Leonce and Lena* saved by its thin comic veneer from provoking a deep sense of loneliness. *Danton's Death* is quite simply structured upon what one critic called *Aneinandersprechen*—talking past one another. The theme of isolation is set forth in the opening interview between husband and wife:

> *Julie:* Do you believe in me?
> *Danton:* How do I know? We know little about each other. We're all thick-skinned. We stretch out our hands toward each other, but it's all in vain, we just rub the rough leather off . . . we are very lonely.

Julie: You know me, Danton.
Danton: Yes, whatever "knowing" means. You have dark eyes and curly hair and a nice complexion and you always say to me: dear Georges. But (*He points to her forehead and eyes.*) there—there: what's behind that? No, our senses are coarse. Know each other? We'd have to break open our skulls and pull each other's thoughts out of the brain fibers. [I.i]

Woyzeck and Marie do not possess the sophistication of Danton and his wife; they could never have this conversation. Nevertheless, they suffer from the same brutal fact of isolation and the impossibility of real communication. With Schiller all men are brothers. With Büchner man is hermetically self-contained.

Schiller's ode celebrates a sense of discovery, of finding what is valuable—be it a true friend, a noble wife, or simply a lust for life. He celebrates the act of finding that which sustains: "All the world's creatures / Draw joy from nature's breast." Büchner, to the contrary, was almost solely interested in describing a sense of loss and deprivation. "Something is missing in men," Danton says, and that is a good commentary upon the playwright's view of the human situation. Of the many passages one might choose, the Grandmother's fairy tale in *Woyzeck* (partially used by Berg in his Act III, scene 1) provides the most stark contrast to the "Ode to Joy." It is worth quoting in full:

> Once upon a time, there was a poor little child with no father and no mother. Everything was dead, and no one was left in the whole world. Everything was dead, and the child went and cried day and night. And since nobody was left on earth, he wanted to go up to the heavens, 'cause the moon was looking at him so friendly, and when he finally got to the moon, the moon was a piece of rotten wood, and then he went to the sun, and when he got there, the sun was a wilted sunflower, and when he got to the stars, they were little golden flies stuck up there like the shrike sticks them on the blackthorn; and when he wanted to go back down to the earth, the earth was an upset pot, and the child was all alone, and he sat down and cried, and there he sits to this day, all alone. [xix]

As the last lines of the ode suggest, Schiller's thrust is upward: "World, do you sense your Creator? Seek him beyond the stars. He must dwell beyond the stars." Büchner moves his reader, as he moved Lenz, in the opposite direction: "Now he felt in himself a stirring and teeming toward an abyss into which a relentless power was dragging him" (p. 51). It is not far thence to Woyzeck's own observation that "Every man is an abyss. You get dizzy when you look down into it." Schiller bids us hasten joyfully and follow the sun through "the glorious order of Heaven." Büchner opens to us a world of darkness—the kind of darkness that swallows meaning, direction, and sense. His world, like Woyzeck's, "gets so dark you have to feel your way around it with your hands."

The differences between Schiller's roseate ethos and Büchner's parched modernism could easily be extended, for it was Schiller's intention to assert human dignity and Büchner's generally to attack the notion that life is intrinsically valuable and also sustained by values. Dignity, beauty, morality, love—all those traditional ideals of art—are ridiculed or parodied by Büchner. He wrote, as he often avowed, from actual life and laughed at those who criticized him in the name either of morality or aesthetic beauty. He despised Schiller and artists of his kind who sought to transform and improve upon reality. It was his purpose to bring attention back to earth, a dreary and grim earth unpleasant to look at. His credo was at heart a realist's and is expressed in a passage from *Lenz* that is as good an introduction to *Woyzeck* and its operatic counterpart as one can find in his writings:

> One must love human nature in order to penetrate into the peculiar character of any individual; nobody, however insignificant, however ugly, should be despised; only then can one understand humankind as a whole. The most undistinguished face can make a deeper impression than the mere perception of abstract beauty. [p. 46]

Only a writer who believed these words could have produced a character like Woyzeck—an insignificant figure who does indeed make us better "understand humankind as a whole."

Wozzeck *and Aspects of Expressionist Drama*

We know from a letter Berg wrote to his wife (7 August 1918) that there was some autobiographical impetus behind his choice of *Woy-*

zeck as a libretto: "There is a bit of me in his character, since I have been spending these war years just as dependent on people I hate, have been in chains, sick, captive, resigned, in fact humiliated." But his affinities with the play go far beyond mere identification. They reach in fact to the fundamental nature of Büchner's proto-Expressionist dramaturgy and that Expressionist music (controversially called "atonal") that flourished roughly from the end of the first decade to the middle of the third decade of this century, that is, between the last glimmers of post-*Tristan* Romanticism and the ascendancy of serial or twelve-tone techniques. *Wozzeck* represents another of those remarkable moments when historically far-flung artworks fall into a natural symbiosis.

An operatic *Woyzeck* is hard to conceive of prior to the appearance of the works of Strauss and Schoenberg (though Mussorgsky might have made an interesting version if he had tried). Their works were seminal in the development of the highly personal musical style of Berg's opera. The result, as Theodor Adorno describes it, was a kind of consummation where Berg "attempts to redress what a hundred years have done to Büchner's scenes: he transforms a realistic draft into one of concealed but crackling inner vitality in which every artistic means used guarantees something extra beyond the mere surface of the text. To make manifest this additional meaning, this extra quality—that is why the music of *Wozzeck* is there."[3] But before we turn to specific parallels (and some differences), something should be said of the more general aesthetic ties that bind *Woyzeck* and *Wozzeck*.

At the outset one must observe that Büchner was perhaps the first dramatist to make Keats's "negative capability" theatrically viable: "That is when man is capable of being in uncertainties, mysteries, doubts, without any irritable reaching after fact and reason." Büchner's world, especially in *Danton's Death* and *Woyzeck*, is one of doubtfulness and ambiguity. Its focus is not upon the known, but the unknown, the unspoken, the unconsciously felt. Hence its pervasive sense of unease, even hysteria. In this it bears comparison with the later Expressionist movement proper.[4]

The scenes in Büchner's plays do not seem to "go" anywhere. Nor does he permit leading motives, if indeed he may be said to have any, to lead us in a sustained way. Grand themes do not proclaim themselves. There is not the faintest trace of dogmatism to distract us from the uncertain world his characters inhabit. Like the child in the *Woyzeck* fairy tale, his characters are more likely to cry in despair than to analyze or attempt to improve their situation. Nor is it useful to speak of plot and structure in Büchner's works. There are none, particularly in *Woyzeck*. Its scenes can be performed in the most various orders. *Eins nach dem andern* ("one thing after another"), the motto that occurs three times in the play, is a hallmark of Büchner's art in its hint of random, meaningless, yet inexorable connections. Miraculously, however, he maintains momentum and interest in spite of this apparent aesthetic anarchy.

Büchner's drama, then, is not that of the sky-scraping sort that requires great architectural skill. It is not beholden to the tidy concept of the "well-made play" but deals rather in the rubble, shards, truncations, and exaggerations that were to become tools of Expressionist drama after the turn of the century (the literary Expressionists were naturally associated with the Cubist movement in art). Indeed, the essence of Expressionism is the intentional disintegration of reality and its "expressive" reworking. Büchner's style was of this kind, though he has many "realistic" moments.[5] His aesthetic was firmly founded upon a devastating concision that combined with—or rather grew out of—his sense of the fragmentary nature of human perception and human existence.

To bring such an aesthetic alive musically a similarly truncated style was necessary, and such was forthcoming from the composers of the Schoenberg school, who were (in their leader's words) able to free music from the Procrustean bed of tonality. Büchner's verbal eclecticism and dizzying succession of scenes required the most extreme compositional flexibility, and yet there was little room in the text for the rhetorical expansion we find in the major-minor or tonic-dominant methods of composition in "traditional" music. Berg gave *Woyzeck* an operatic style that met these demands, one that could operate in the cramped hollows behind Büchner's words.[6] That Berg was able to accommodate these demands is clear from the very first reviews of the opera, which speak of his score's extreme differentiation and delicacy, great command of aphoristic nuance, spider's-web-fine orchestration of momentary effects, and grasp of Büchner's nearly imperceptible undertones. Just as Büchner's language does, Berg's music for *Wozzeck* unwinds in tiny explosive bursts. Its texture is one of multifarious, simultaneous, and conflicting events. In this it is a descendant of *Salome* and *Elektra,* though its formalism of composition owes more to Schoenberg.

Büchner was the most important nineteenth-century link between Germany's Storm and Stress writers of the previous century and the Expressionist dramatists like Wedekind, Toller, Kaiser, and Brecht in the next. Indeed, one can learn much about Büchner from the Expressionist drama, which was partially responsible for his rediscovery. Consider, for example, characterization. Extended and seamless character development was never a strength of the Expressionists. They were more interested in telling bits and pieces of the subconscious, eloquent idiosyncrasy, extremes of psychological stress. Expressionists were not so much concerned to describe those outer, elaborately prepared, modular emotions like love or vengeance (and their consequent theatrical stance or "gestus") as to capture fleetingly and incisively what Walter Sokel has called the "inner feel" of a figure in a given situation. Berg's music was well fitted to depict the inner feel of Büchner's characters because they were limned, not in the broad heroic lines of a Schiller, but in the vivid jottings and sharp truncations of the later Expressionists. The exaggerations and distortions of sound Berg created with his huge and unusually constituted orchestra served to capture in music that "beautiful *aberratio*" affecting most of *Woyzeck*'s characters.

The method of exaggeration so important to the Expressionist aesthetic was also apt for operatic purposes. One important spokesman for the movement, Paul Kornfeld, even went so far as to praise operatic heightening as a useful model for the dramatist:

> The melody of a larger-than-life gesture says more than the most extreme perfection of that which one calls naturalness ever could. One thinks of the opera in which the singer, dying, is still able to burst forth one last high C and who expresses more about death with the sweetness of his melody than if he were to twist and writhe. For that death is a great shame is more important than that it is hideous.[7]

Though there is only a parodic high C for the Captain in *Wozzeck,* Berg nevertheless shows himself able to accompany in music Büchner's strong theatrical gestures. The score is rich in extreme exaggerations of sound, as well as in the powerful flux of style that is so vital in following the playwright's swift changes of tone from parody, ballad-like simplicity, vertiginous terror, almost mystical alienation, to anchoring ennui.

Büchner, in keeping with Expressionists generally, avoids sentiment or what we call the pathetic urge. He more often expresses feelinglessness than feeling. The figure of Lenz shows this most strongly: "The world which he had wished to put to some use had suffered an immense rift; he felt no hatred, no love, no hope—a terrible emptiness, and yet a torturing restlessness, an impatient impulse to fill this void" (p. 58). Woyzeck is closely related to the insane Lenz: he is a sufferer distinctly lacking the intellectual power to confront a strangely vacuous world. And—hard to appreciate sufficiently—neither figure is maudlin or sentimental.

Now, Büchner's art would be much less prized if he had tainted his deeply unaccommodated characters with condescension. The isolation of his characters is overwhelming simply because their creator alienated himself from them by artistic choice. This is the key to his greatness. Büchner was loathe to burden his writing with artistic "purpose" or avuncular moralizing. He never set the template of purpose upon nature or humanity because he could see none in the scheme of things: "Nature does not bother itself with ends; it does not devolve in an endless row of purposes where one necessitates the next; rather it is in all its manifestations self-sufficient in its own immediacy."[8] This passage might also serve as Büchner's artistic credo. Such is life, he says, and all teleological explanations are just so much folly and intellectual arabesque.

What *Woyzeck* asked for, then, was musical alienation, that is, a musical embodiment that could break away from the traditional operatic modes of identification, sympathy, and easily labeled emotions. Again, the ethos of the Schoenberg school prepared the way for Berg: "The actual revolutionary moment for him [Schoenberg] is the change in function of musical expression. Passions are no longer simulated, but rather genuine emotions of the unconscious—of shock, of trauma—are registered without disguise through the medium of music."[9] *Woyzeck* required a music that could seep through the pores and into the psychic underground, a music that could capture inner turmoil rather than rhetorically articulated feelings. Not Büchner's words but the existential void behind them is crucial. It is one mark of the opera's genius that Berg's music does not "parallel" the text, but develops apart from the vocal line and leads an expressive life of its own while never departing from the dramatic action. Berg's music inhabits and makes us constantly aware of the language within Büchner's language.

Berg achieved this feat through the synchronization of *Woyzeck*'s random, varied style with time-honored musical forms. He committed himself "to realize musically the intellectual content of Büchner's immortal drama," and he fortunately sensed that part of this content was its choatic structure and multiple tones. To preserve the integrity of the play, Berg chose to avoid Wagnerian through-composition and turned instead to structures of absolute music like the theme and variations, fugue, or dance suite. In this way, according to Berg, he followed "the demanding task of giving each scene and each entr'acte (either as preludes, postludes, transitions, or interludes) its own unmistakable musical countenance and unity." Those with highly trained ears may detect these musical countenances in his fifteen scenes, but it would be dubious to say they are the better for it in the sense of experiencing the drama: Berg certainly does not encourage them:

> No matter how much one might know about the musical forms within the framework of this opera, how everything is strictly and logically "worked out," what skill lurks in all details . . . from the moment when the curtain goes up to the moment when it goes down for the last time, no one in the audience should be aware of these diverse fugues and inventions, suite and sonata movements, variations and passacaglias—no one who is suffused with anything besides the central idea of this opera.*

It is important to emphasize here the symbolic parallel of Berg's traditional musical forms with the Büchner dramaturgy. How the world in which Woyzeck lives, suffers, and dies actually works—this the dramatist does not say. Woyzeck's fate unwinds in a relentless and yet unfathomable way, and Büchner uses images of abyss, darkness, and vacuum to assure this effect. Of morality and immorality, he once wrote to his family, "I have my own thoughts." This reticent motto applies to *Woyzeck.* Berg's methods capture this indirection; his forms, in other words, do not have the disconcerting effect of formality. Aside from giving clarity of tone to each scene, these forms are tailored to the drama. Pierre Jouve has perhaps best described the result: Berg's innovation "is that the connection between the lyric drama and absolute music is *cryptic.* The listener, as Berg himself has said, does not realize this; he feels himself conveyed by an imperious force, though one which is secret and internal."[10] Thus, Berg succeeded in re-creating musically the play's single most crucial and yet nameless quality—the sense of an impersonal and imperious force that destroys Woyzeck. It is not important that Berg's scenes are elaborately wrought as absolute musical entities, but rather that for dramatic purposes his methods are "secret and internal."

The miracle of the opera is that Berg was able to remain faithful to Büchner's terse, unexpansive play while providing a kind of interlinear version of the text based upon absolute musical forms (like the fugue) whose very essence is expansion of musical ideas. Perhaps one must finally conclude that it was not so much Berg's insistence upon the composer's art (and some have castigated the score as "arrogantly overloaded"), but the ultimate effect of restraint one senses in actually listening to the opera that makes it such a successful musical translation. For the paradoxically momentous exaggeration and curtness of *Woyzeck* Berg provided music that is implosive and obliquely effective.

Wozzeck's *Musical Precursors*

Before we look at the music of *Wozzeck,* it is worthwhile to pause over the opera's musical ancestry. One early reviewer called the opera the final song of farewell to the spirit of Tristan. Another offered this genealogy: "Grandfather, *Tristan;* French offshoot, Debussy's *Pelléas et Mélisande;* last descendent (via Debussy and Schoenberg),

Wozzeck." Joseph Kerman calls it "a very Straussian work." Theodor Adorno finds a more strictly Schoenbergian product:

> Berg's great opera *Wozzeck* . . . resembles *Erwartung* in detail as well as in conception—as the portrayal of anxiety; it resembles *Die glückliche Hand* in the insatiable successive strata of harmonic complexes, and the allegory of the multilateral character of its psychological subject.

In a short article, called by Berg himself "three pages of intelligent praise," Ernst Viebig ventured to set *Wozzeck* down in the "direct line from Franz Schreker's *Der ferne Klang*"—now a quite forgotten work. One can see strains of many styles in *Wozzeck*—a little bit of *Der Ring,* something of Bach, and hints of Webern. Clearly, hunting for sources in either literature or music can be risky. Still, one might mention briefly three scores without which an appreciation of *Wozzeck*'s music would be difficult: *Salome, Erwartung,* and *Pierrot Lunaire.* If there is a main line of ancestry for the opera, these works must have a prominent place on it.

What has been said of *Salome* in the preceding chapter should suffice to make clear how important that opera (and *Elektra,* too) was in the discovery of musical means for describing psychological abnormality, fragmentary experience, existential horror, and ennui. Strauss's busyness, blatant sound-coloring, frequent distortions of instrumental sound, and the extreme unpredictability of his huge orchestral juggernaut—all these qualities are present in the score of *Wozzeck.* Just as one might say the Expressionist dramaturgy was prefigured by Büchner, so was the disengagement from the Wagnerian system announced in *Salome* (and in other ways in *Pelléas*) a prefiguring of Expressionism in music. There were things not dreamed of in the Wagnerian aesthetic, and it took the double wave of Strauss and Schoenberg to bring these new powers of musical expression into plain view. The greatest results of this development in opera were *Wozzeck* and *Lulu.*

Even before the Dresden premiere of *Salome* this scene, as remembered by Egon Wellesz, took place in Schoenberg's Vienna home:

Arnold Schoenberg, cigarette in hand, his head inclined, pacing ceaselessly to and fro. On a chest, a parcel of unusually large music paper—the still incomplete score of the *Gurrelieder*. On the music desk of the piano, the recently published vocal score of Strauss's *Salome,* open at the first page. Schoenberg said: "Perhaps in twenty years' time someone will be able to explain these harmonic progressions theoretically."[11]

It was symbolic that the *Gurrelieder* (the last gargantuan monument of nineteenth-century Romanticism) should have been placed to the side and *Salome* on the piano. As Schoenberg's comment indicates, in Strauss's opera something radically new had appeared, and it is impossible in view of Schoenberg's developing musical style to think it was not an important influence on him. One thing is certain, though: it took Schoenberg scarcely twenty years to outstrip *Salome*'s innovative qualities. Proof that he did just that appeared within a few years, in the form of the short monodrama *Erwartung* (written 1909, premiere 1924). This work may be seen as the midpoint or bridge between *Salome* (1905) and *Wozzeck* (written 1917-21, premiere 1925). *Salome*'s influence on *Erwartung* both in content and form is obvious—even its apocalyptic blood-red moon reappears in the monodrama (as it will again in *Wozzeck*).

Like *Salome, Erwartung* has as its subject a disturbed proto-psychotic heroine. There is no plot to speak of. The subject is simply the mental suffering of a woman who has lost, perhaps even murdered, her lover. Schoenberg himself called the piece an *Angsttraum* or nightmare—a favorite mode for Expressionist painters and writers. His score is structured like *Salome* upon an extraordinarily short rhythmic attention-span: there are over a hundred metronome changes in the four hundred bars of the piece. The overall sense is of something unstructured, fragmentary, compulsive (in literary terms not unlike Molly Bloom's stream-of-consciousness monologue at the end of *Ulysses*). The degeneration of the woman's logical faculty is mirrored in a fractured and unpredictable vocal line, if line is the proper word for the contortions Schoenberg requires. What especially marks *Erwartung* as a sign that musical Expressionism had reached a quick maturity is its brilliant evocation of the "inner feel" of the heroine. The piece depends not so much on articulation of the text, which in any case has few complete, grammatical sentences, but upon evocation of the sheer nervous tension and disorder engulfing the solitary figure.

As in *Salome,* the composer of *Erwartung* has succeeded in performing a kind of musical pathology on the heroine. The score is probing and dissective, and this may explain why Robert Craft describes it as the first Freudian music drama, or why Adorno observes that the heroine is consigned to music in the same way a patient is to analysis.[12] *Erwartung* shows an advance in the power to express a complex psychic state. To achieve this power Schoenberg went beyond Strauss's radical departure from traditional operatic structure; he fashioned an even more complex musical texture, forsook entirely the areas of tonality already under siege in *Salome,* and increased the alienation in the dialogue between voice and orchestra.

The leading trends of Schoenberg's "new music" after the appearance of *Salome* and *Erwartung* were, first, in the concentration and contraction of musical utterance and, second, the increasing alienation of the singing voice from the musical accompaniment. Schoenberg's song cycle based on poems from Albert Giraud's *Pierrot Lunnaire* is an important landmark for both trends. Here is a tour de force of the tiniest musical gestures, the most exquisite nuancing. The critic who said with malicious intent that *Pierrot* (1912) represented "the decomposition of art" was on the right track. These adroit, witty Expressionist miniatures anticipate *Wozzeck*'s needle-sharp clarity of effect.

Even more significant was Schoenberg's attempt to complete the alienation of vocal and musical material through the *Sprechstimme* and rhythmic declamation. This opened the full range between speaking and singing voice. Short of recitation, this technique made the strongest possible break between voice and orchestra, and Schoenberg was not afraid to claim all expressive burden for the music. In the foreword to the *Pierrot* score he wrote:

> In this work, the performers at no time have the task of shaping the mood and character of the individual pieces according to the meaning of the words, but rather according to the music. To whatever ex-

tent the composer felt a tone-pictorial representation of the actions and feelings indicated in the text to be important, it is simply to be found in the music.

Pierrot is an important introduction to the music of *Wozzeck* for many reasons, not the least being Berg's own admission of its influence upon him. In fact, the foreword to the opera's score refers the reader to Schoenberg's explanation of the *Sprechstimme* in the *Pierrot* score. The passages of chamber-music delicacy in *Wozzeck,* and there are many, owe much to *Pierrot.* The work is also a small-scale demonstration of the potential in contrapuntal absolute music for capturing the spirit of a verbal text. Stravinsky pointedly called *Pierrot* a "brilliant instrumental masterpiece," but it sets the texts effectively and rises fully to the various challenges of the Giraud poems. Schoenberg may not in a technical sense have "set" the words, but he did succeed in grasping the subjective moods—the "inner feel"—of the poems themselves. Schoenberg was able to set the music free from verbal, syntactic bonds while remaining faithful to their spirit.

It would be difficult to underestimate the importance of *Pierrot Lunaire,* especially for the history of twentieth-century opera. Walter Schrenk, assessing its place in that history in 1924, put the work in august operatic company:

> This melodrama is one of those unique, unrepeatable creative works which, both positively and negatively, point the way for, and mark the destiny of, the art of music. Seen in this lofty historical perspective, it takes its place in the line of works such as Mozart's *Don Giovanni,* Beethoven's *Missa Solemnis* or late quartets, Wagner's *Tristan,* Mahler's *Song of the Earth,* and Richard Strauss's *Elektra.* This is not a matter of drawing comparisons: *Pierrot Lunaire* is placed alongside these works only to point out that, like them, it was in a sense created at a crucial moment for music.[13]

It was certainly a fortunate moment for Schoenberg's student Alban Berg, whose *Wozzeck* is easily the most important opera in the standard repertory to venture toward the new horizons made possible by *Pierrot Lunaire.*[14] At least one reviewer recognized at the premiere of the opera that the potential of Schoenberg's early innovations had finally been fulfilled.

Woyzeck and Berg's Compositional Principles

The paradox of *Wozzeck* is that Berg succeeded in creating an intensely theatrical version of Büchner's systemless fictional world through extraordinarily systematic techniques. The problem posed by *Woyzeck*'s chaotic state forced Berg into this radical solution:

> In order to provide variety for my grouping of fifteen scenes, whereby their musical clarity and memorableness would be guaranteed, I was prevented from simply "through-composing" them according to their literary content, as is so often done.

Berg's sense of the need for individual scenic "clarity and memorableness" was crucial, for Büchner's dramatic art is ultimately one of piercing local effect rather than large-scale movement. Through-composition, Berg rightly feared, would not only have rendered the many short scenes monotonous, but would have subverted its random *Eins-nach-dem-andern* quality.

Büchner was a great despiser of theory. In a letter to a friend he wrote: "With all my energy I am throwing myself into philosophy. Its artificial language is abominable; I mean, for human affairs one ought to find human expressions." No wonder he was so hostile to intellectual giants like Kant, Fichte, and especially Hegel. It is therefor ironic that *Woyzeck* should eventually be turned into music by one of the most rigorously systematic of composers. Unlike Büchner, Berg was friendly to analysis, a lover of symmetry and orderly architecture. Also unlike Büchner, he was a friend of traditional art, and his *Wozzeck* is a masterpiece of traditional art in some respects. *Woyzeck* is a work of exaggerated, self-conscious carelessness; *Wozzeck* is a work of exaggerated care. Composition cost Berg so much time that, realizing his eventual output as a composer would be small, he ceased assigning opus numbers with the number seven of *Wozzeck*.

In spite of the startling variance of methods, Berg makes a musical reality of *Woyzeck* with surprisingly little distortion on the level of individual scenes. The listener hears the music in its dramatic dimension and rarely as a structural "format." This was Berg's overriding desire:

> I simply wanted to compose good music; to develop musically the contents of Georg Büchner's immortal drama; to translate his poetic

> language into music. Other than that, when I decided to write an opera, my only intention, as related to the technique of composition, was to give the theater what belongs to the theater. The music was to be so formed that at each moment it would fulfill its duty of serving the action.

In this Berg succeeded, and so it seems gratuitous to call his score arrogantly overloaded. It would be arrogant indeed if he had desired to call our attention to his compositional legerdemain in the actual process of listening. But he does not. The structure is for most ears inaudible.

The trend toward the use of absolute musical forms for ulterior dramatic purposes, as in Mozart's operas, began in this century with Schoenberg. Berg himself described this trend in 1930 as being essentially a return to contrapuntal methods: "At the moment, we are passing slowly but irresistibly from the harmonic period, which in fact dominated the entire Viennese classical period, into an epoch of predominantly polyphonic character." Succeeding upon the high harmonic adventures of the nineteenth century, then, was a turn toward more complex textures and multivoiced patterns—largely the heritage of Bach.[15] Not surprisingly, those methods Schoenberg professed to have learned from Bach are also the methods at work on almost every page of *Wozzeck:*

> 1. To think contrapuntally, i.e. the art of inventing figures that can be used to accompany themselves.
> 2. The art of producing everything from one thing, and of relating figures by transformation.
> 3. Disregard for the "strong" beat of a bar.[16]

An almost cabalistic awareness of the niceties of craftsmanship was characteristic of the Schoenberg school, but to the lay listener these niceties were not intended to be a matter of concern.

For our present purposes, however, we cannot entirely ignore the impact of Berg's abstract musical methods. The artist Paul Klee gives one reason why: "The more horrifying this world becomes (as it is these days) the more art becomes abstract; while a world at peace produces realistic art." Büchner's was a horrifying world, and Klee's comment may be a hint why Berg's abstract accompaniment is able to plumb the depths of this horror so effectively. One need only think of the complacent Dutch realists and the frenzied German Expressionists to sense the plausibility of Klee's observation. One might even see in Klee's precise use of geometrical forms a parallel to the precise use of abstract musical forms in the music of Schoenberg and Berg.

Another remarkable paradox of the *Wozzeck* score is Berg's almost complete unrestraint in the choice of techniques and sonorities and yet the music's ultimate air of restraint. Jouve has remarked upon the "stupefying scaffolding of means" Berg used: most obviously the fifteen musical forms for the fifteen scenes, but also the three separate orchestras, the extreme range of orchestral sound and sound-combinations, the complicated marshaling of tiny soloistic events, the greatest variation from a refined chamber-music mode to monumental tutti gestures, and of course the full range from spoken text to coloratura vocalism. So it is that *richness* is a common epithet in descriptions of Berg's *Wozzeck* music. And yet, richness is not really apt as a description of the mood or effect of Berg's music. Rather the mood is one of reserve—what Adorno called "the restrained sympathy of sound." Büchner's peculiar potency as a dramatist derived partly from his willingness to leave effects understated and momentous implications barely hinted at. He was the first to practice exhaustively on the stage the Bauhaus axiom that "less is more," and Berg's music is finally also faithful to this procedure. Seldom (in the murder scene and in the magnificent cathartic interlude that follows Wozzeck's death, for instance) does Berg permit great surges above the eerily flat emotional landscape of *Woyzeck*. Berg well said of his version of the play that it is "a *piano*-opera with outbursts."

Herbert Lindenberger speaks of a dispersion technique in Büchner's *Woyzeck,* "whereby the central themes are dispersed spatially within the speeches and songs of a large number of characters, many of whom have little or no connection with the temporal sequence."[17] Dispersion may be an accurate way of describing *Wozzeck*'s music, for dispersion is the essence of the polyphonic style, that is, the breakdown, transformation, and repetition of given melodic elements. This metaphor of dispersion is not very far from that of atomization which Adorno has used in speaking of *Wozzeck* ("The impulses of the composition—alive in its musical atoms"), nor is it far from the concept of the "basic cells" from which some musicologists find the entire musical structure of Berg's *Lulu* derives.

Büchner's play is filled with tense, momentary, and haphazard encounters, behind which lies the artistic belief that fragmentary statements are sometimes more powerful in an appropriate context than full statements. Berg's score is a testimony in music to this principle, namely, that shards of melody, tantalizing obeisances to tonality, mere hints of banality can be more effective than fully worked out musical ideas. Brevity and truncation are part of Büchner's world view: "Life becomes an epigram," he wrote in *Danton,* "who ever has enough breath and spirit for an epic?" (II.i). Fortunately, Berg's gift as a composer lay in the epigrammatic direction. The epic was for the bygone Wagnerian aesthetic.

The world of *Woyzeck* is edged with hysteria. It portrays a kind of hallucinatory nightmare for a tortured and doomed Everyman. What we have called the process of decomposition was useful to Expressionists who were seeking to capture this ambience of psychic distress. Busoni accurately summarized the methods of Expressionism in music:

> "Hysteria" is maintained by using short disconnected forms of sighs and of runs, in the obstinate repetition of one or more sounds, in fading away and using the highest of the high and the deepest of the deep sounds, in the pauses and in the accumulation of different rhythms within one bar. All available means of expression are used as far as they can have a place appointed for them within the structure of a composition.[18]

Surprisingly, Busoni had not heard *Wozzeck* before writing these words (the premiere took place three years later), for he touches upon many of the notable qualities of the score: the will-o-the-wisp utterances of the violins, scurrying runs and glissandi, the use of ostinato forms (in no less than six scenes), the gamut from the most ear-piercing upper register of the violins to the abysmal low notes of bass tuba and contrabassoon, and the keenest differentiation and opposition of various rhythms. All this serves to give the opera what a critic in 1925 called an unheard-of multivocal quality (*Vielstimmig-*

keit). One need only peruse the piano-vocal score—surely the most splendid reduction of an opera ever made, and beautifully printed—to sense the complexity of the work.[19] It becomes obvious that *Wozzeck* simply cannot be reduced to a mere two hands; extra staves are often necessary to compass the multilayered musical events. For this reason the tinier nuances and smallest musical events are always in danger of perishing virtually unheard as we listen.

To the general effect of decomposition and the sensations it best evokes—malaise, confusion, terror—one must add numerous other specific effects that Berg re-creates musically from Büchner's text. The harsh and cruel distortions Berg requires from his orchestra mirror the monstrous and torturing psychic events in the play: be it a sickening, whining glissando, a stinging pizzicato (as when the Doctor berates Wozzeck), a cutting, metallic xylophone tremolo, or ominously muted brass or string passages that hint obliquely at the misery of Wozzeck's life. The scene between Wozzeck and Andres on the open field is a miracle of bizarre, unnerving orchestration as well as a moving description of Wozzeck's mental instability. The second scene of Act II between Wozzeck, the Doctor, and the Captain proves beyond cavil that parodic humor is not beyond the reach of the Schoenberg school.

It would be overzealous, however, to argue that *Woyzeck* was left utterly unmodified in its musical transformation. Significant changes, mainly in overall structure, did take place and deserve mention. First, *Woyzeck* comes to us in the form of various manuscript drafts left unordered at Büchner's death. The exact order in which its scenes should be played is therefor impossible to discern. What we do know about Büchner is that he was a revolutionary dramatist, and we can be reasonably certain that *Woyzeck* was not intended to be a play of ordinary structure. The obvious warning, then, is offered by Lindenberger: "*Woyzeck* is no conventional drama, and there is no reason that its scenes should be arranged to fit conventional notions about drama." Berg, however, did have some conventional notions about drama, or at least about opera. He chose to order *Woyzeck* quite arbitrarily and with characteristic symmetry in three acts, each with five scenes. Further, Berg superimposed a kind of Aristotelian format by designating Act I the Exposition, Act II the Denouement, and

Act III the Catastrophe. If there is one thing Büchner was not, it is an Aristotelian. His forte was not plotting action, but evoking mood and inner psychic states, most notably ennui. This encompassing inertia Berg managed to a considerable degree to subvert, perhaps mainly because he wrote—with the exception of the moving "commentary" in D-minor on Wozzeck's death—connective music for the scenic changes. This inevitably gave the entire opera what one critic called an unrelaxing "forward thrust" (*Vorwärtsdrängen*). And so the frightening randomness of the play is somewhat vitiated by Berg. That his score is often praised as "cinematographic"—highly anachronistic of course for the play—is another hint of the change from Büchner's original intentions.

We cannot blame Berg entirely for these radical changes, for he was after all using an imperfect edition (Franzos, 1879, or Landau, 1909—it is not clear), made when the idea of the well-made play was still strong. Early editors all made changes in the Büchner manuscript in order to rationalize it and give it a more traditional contour. Franzos, for instance, put the seemingly expository shaving scene first, and also made the decision—we now see it as quite arbitrary—that Woyzeck must drown at the end of the pond scene. Berg seems to have taken up such changes without questioning them.[20] To wish that he had done otherwise, in view of the skimpy knowledge of Büchner at the time, is to press beyond the limits of reasonable expectation.

The other major question of change concerns the alleged sentimentality of Berg's opera. As we have noticed, Büchner was utterly unsentimental, one might even say merciless in the treatment of his characters. Whether Berg escaped completely, or even sufficiently, from the temptations to sentimentalize Wozzeck's plight is an open question. Critics have answered the question both ways. We know, of course, that Berg identified with his hero in some ways, and this very sympathy may explain why he focused more single-mindedly upon Wozzeck's suffering than does the original—and why his famous outbursts are so memorably set to music. Of course, it may have been Berg's keen desire to clarify and unify the action of his opera that dictated a more unblinking focus upon Wozzeck himself. And it may be that the closer observation of the tormented creature naturally made the risks of sentimentalism, apparent or real, all the greater. How the listener reacts must finally be a personal judgment.

We should at this point recall Büchner's observation in *Lenz* (page 296 above) that love of human nature is an artistic necessity if one is truly to penetrate the human situation. Behind Büchner's impassive cynicism and laconic style are sufficient indications that he did care profoundly for humanity. He was no misanthrope. Berg, too, was deeply responsive to the human predicament in a way that goes beyond mere sentimentality, as the D-minor interlude alone might amply suggest. *Wozzeck*'s music is *lebensnahe* or close to life as Büchner portrays it. As an undeniably sympathetic response to human suffering, *Wozzeck* is not only a masterpiece of translation but also a great opera.

A Postscript on Lulu

Though the plays of Frank Wedekind (1864-1918) upon which Berg based *Lulu* are by no means great dramatic works (they do not possess the profundity or artistic economy of Büchner's plays), there are many reasons for discussing them briefly in a postscript. First, an extraordinary number of aesthetic similarities bind the Büchner and Wedekind dramaturgies; what recommended *Woyzeck* so strongly to Berg's musical idiom also served to recommend the Lulu plays *The Earth Spirit* and *Pandora's Box*. Second, *Lulu* is important in Berg's career, not only because of its long period of gestation (He first saw the plays in 1905, started work on the libretto in 1928, and began composing the next year, leaving the opera virtually complete at his death in 1935), but because it represents—along with the also unfinished *Moses und Aron* of Schoenberg—a culmination in opera of the use of the tone-row system.[21] Finally, *Lulu* is a great work (more so, certainly, than its sources) and—when its mysteriously undivulged third act is finally restored—may well be seen as Berg's masterwork. Critics most familiar with the full *Lulu* score are inclined to think so.*

* A form of censorship practiced by Berg's widow (who died on 30 August 1976) and/or the publishers controlling Berg's music appears to be the cause of the suppression. For a discussion of this situation, see Karl Neumann,

Wedekind's place in theatrical history is intimately related to Büchner's—a point made most obvious to us today by the fact that Berg chose these writers for his two operas. Wedekind, though it may be wrong to call him a genuine Expressionist, was nevertheless a seminal figure for that movement. Walter Sokel has identified his play, *Spring's Awakening* (1891), as the first drama to reveal Expressionist tendencies, and he has been singled out as the writer who influenced the Expressionists more than any of the older generation of German dramatists.[22] One might add that the Expressionist movement was largely responsible for the change in theatrical tastes that made possible Büchner's rediscovery. German Expressionist drama culminated in the second decade of the century, and that is when Büchner enjoyed great prestige.

Wedekind's personality and nature as a thinker are astonishingly like Büchner's. At least during his early career (when the Lulu plays were written) he was an isolated artist and very controversial—which Büchner would also have been if his plays had reached the stage in his lifetime. Also like his predecessor, Wedekind was a revolutionary. Paul Kornfeld, in an obituary that appeared in *Das Junge Deutschland* in 1918, wrote: "We know that he was a strong-willed, possessed, belligerent man—fighting against the great masses, against the public and the critics." In the same issue Rudolf Kayser made a more direct connection, saying that since Büchner, "Wedekind is the first German who has stalked the warpath, not in order to trace 'a new path in drama,' but to attack spiritual poverty and unfreedom (*Ungeist und Unfreiheit*)." Both men spoke in bloody earnest and were ardent despisers of bourgeois morality. Büchner's attacks were largely social and political; whereas, Wedekind set himself the task of fomenting a sexual revolution, an overthrow of Victorian morality. Just as Büchner prophetically saw the grinding effects of an oligarchic society upon the common man and the eventual revolt this would produce, Wedekind foresaw the eventual revolt of natural sexual ener-

---

"Wedekind and Berg's *Lulu*," *Music Review*, Vol. 35 (1974), pp. 47-57. George Perle was able to examine the withheld materials and describes them in great detail in "*Lulu*: The Formal Design," *Journal of the American Musicological Society*, Vol. 17 (1964), pp. 179-92.

gies against the hypocritical pseudo-morality of a decaying middle class.

Wedekind shares with Büchner a decided pessimism. He is also intrigued by the dark inner malaise. Woyzeck's remark about the abyss in every man might well apply to Wedekind's characters. Both dramatists saw human society as a jungle and men merely as animals. Wedekind, especially, focused upon the animalistic sensuality of man—the reasonless instinctual forces that motivate human beings. This willingness to observe man naked and unaccommodated by idealism, continuity, purpose, or even self-knowledge—is a characteristic we have already seen in Büchner. If one must choose just one passage that hints at the interest in the "dark side" Wedekind shared with Büchner, it is from a speech by the Countess Geschwitz just before her death (compare this with the passage from *Danton's Death* quoted on page 294 above):

> People don't know each other—they have no idea what they're like. The only ones who know them are those who aren't human themselves. Every word they utter is untrue, a lie. But they don't know that, because today they're this and tomorrow that, and it all depends on whether or not they've eaten, drunk, loved . . . Men and women are like animals; not one of them knows what he's doing. [*Pandora's Box,* Act III]

Büchner and Wedekind are both interested in the alienating egoism that produces the situation Geschwitz describes. Büchner focused upon the egoism of society itself, which crushes helpless nonentities like Woyzeck with consummate indifference. Wedekind focused upon the egoism of sexuality which, in its crudest essence (and that is in the form of Lulu herself), is a highly destructive force for those who come in contact with it and who make themselves vulnerable to its attractions.

Wedekind's dramatic style also bears important similarities to that of *Woyzeck*. Büchner influenced Wedekind's style considerably, particularly in the loose connection between scenes, in a highly disjunctive dialogue, and in that *Aneinandersprechen* where characters seem to exist in isolation and talk in simultaneous monologues. This quality is part of Wedekind's message that, as Lulu puts it, "No one knows anything about anyone else. Everyone thinks himself the unhappy victim." True dialogue would subvert this notion.

The main themes of the Lulu plays parallel *Woyzeck* too. Overriding all is a sense of deterioration: Lulu's demise is just as inevitable as Woyzeck's. The theatrical world is in both cases one of entropy. Both are full of characters with bad cases of "nerves"; Woyzeck's "beautiful *aberratio mentalis partialis*" is re-echoed frequently in the Lulu plays, where all the surrounding figures are in one way or another obsessed with Lulu as a sexual object. Most important, though, is the sense of rootlessness in the central figures. Both are profoundly distant—Woyzeck made so by his utter innocence of the "reason" in his tormenting world, Lulu made so by her innocence of the devastating sexual energy she releases in the lives around her. Both suffer with a terrifying indifference. Both are almost skeletal versions of humanity. Woyzeck possesses only a piece of paper indicating his identity:

> *Woyzeck.* (*Pulling out a piece of paper*) Friedrich Johann Franz Woyzeck, soldier, rifleman in the second regiment, second battalion, fourth company, born on the Feast of the Annunciation. Today I'm thirty years, seven months, and twelve days old. [xvii]

Lulu hasn't even this—no real name, no parents, no desires, and no self-knowledge, as we learn from her interview with the painter.

The sense of rootlessness is also created by a surreal estrangement from reality, as well as by use of highly eccentric language. There is, in short, a dearth of "normal" theatrical style in the Lulu plays. One scene does not make another, there is no natural or rational evolution, the spectator does not really become involved. These are, in other words, not the kind of plays for which traditional operatic methods would have been apt. What was needed, in fact, was a style like Berg's—which in *Wozzeck* had already proved its ability to deal with these revolutionary aspects of Expressionist drama. Berg's style is, from the listener's standpoint, one of rootlessness and flexibility, extreme distortion and nervous tension. This suited Wedekind's dramaturgy.

Wedekind's plays offer another opportunity to note that Expressionism was peculiarly appropriate to the exigencies of the operatic stage. Opera is an unavoidably unrealistic art-form, and in this respect it has much in common with Expressionism, which rejects realistically prepared motivation and depends upon modes of stylization. The operatic medium is one of selective heightening, and Expressionists cherished this method too. They deplored psychological realism and preferred instead to exaggerate or distort their artistic visions. In a credo for Expressionist theater Paul Kornfeld wrote: "Psychology says just as little about the nature of men as does anatomy . . . the art that remains in the bonds of reality will never rise to the truth."[23] We have already seen that Kornfeld was drawn to opera in the pursuit of these views. Wedekind employs a general method of heightening that is close to opera's essence—that is, a broadening and deepening of the portrayed figure through the added dimension of music. The way Wedekind goes about creating his characters parallels the methods of the operatic composer: "He distills these forces [of sex and lust for power] from actual society in which they are hidden in layers of hypocritical convention and, with provocative glee, exhibits their 'pure essence' embodied in empirically impossible specimens."[24] The process of "musicalizing" a character requires the same reduction to a kind of pure essence, and the result is the singing actor—indeed an empirically impossible specimen. One might add that the exaggerations of the operatic stage do little harm to Wedekind, since he himself introduced a radically unrealistic method of acting in his own plays.[25]

One might say of Wedekind's style that it generally cries for sound rather than sense. Friedrich Gundolf made this point in the 1920s when he observed that Wedekind's words were meant to express life rather than thought, "sound, ringing, the scream—not sense and syntax."[26] Indeed, in the following summary of Wedekind's typical modes of expression one can already see parallels with the music invented for *Lulu:*

> Wedekind [is] at his most aggressive in inventing a language so completely rootless, a mode of communication which Walter Sokel describes as "never heard in actual life, and yet remarkably expressive of the alienation, confusion, and hysteria characteristic of modern life." The dialogue is an explosive mixture of epigram, lyricism,

and banality, delivered by people in asides, simultaneous speech, past one another, so that language is finally reduced to a kind of surrealistic stream-of-consciousness.[27]

Berg's musical language has much in common with this. It is, in relation to the old landmarks of tonality and melodic development, a rootless musical language. It is an explosive mixture of differing expressive modes—of chromatic, twelve-tone, and diatonic elements. And the end result is the same: a musical score surrealistically estranged from the actuality on stage and expressing the hysteria and alienation pervading the Lulu plays.

Over the characters in the Lulu plays rules an elemental power—blind, accidental, violent, and irrational. The effect of Berg's music for *Lulu* might be described in the same terms, though as *Wozzeck* would lead us to expect, this does not mean the music is not very carefully constructed.[28] *Lulu*'s sound-world matches the dynamic psychological tensions, the brutal collision of passion and passionlessness, the ominous anxiety and idée fixe which make Wedekind's plays such an unsettling experience. Berg's score matches the frenzy of sexual energy underneath their thin surface. There is a tone of urgency in the Lulu plays; Wedekind, like Büchner before him, was always on the attack. So it is fitting that Berg, as a symbolic comment upon his music, put the direction *attacca* above the very first bar of the *Lulu* score.

Near the end of the unreleased Act III Berg specifies that Lulu emit a *Todesschrei* or death cry (it is heard in the "Lulu Suite," which is used in most current productions). It ought to remind us of the shrieked "Hilfe" at Marie's moment of death—both Marie and Lulu, incidentally, are stabbed in the neck—and the scream of utter horror portrayed by Edvard Munch in his quintessential Expressionist painting "The Cry." The Expressionists, and Berg among them as a composer, desired to show us the darker side of man and society that induces this terrified response. Hermann Bahr, a prominent writer of the period, even singled out the scream as a chief characteristic of Expressionist art:

> Never yet has any period been so shaken by horror, by such fear of death. Never has the world been so silent, silent as the grave. Never

> has man been more insignificant. Never has he felt so nervous. Never was happiness so unattainable and freedom so dead. Distress cries out aloud; man cries out for his soul; this whole pregnant time is one great cry of anguish. Art too joins in, into the great darkness she too calls for help, she cries to the spirit: this is Expressionism.[29]

In 1924 Webern published his "Six Bagatelles." For this Schoenberg wrote a preface which might be called musical Expressionism's equivalent of Bahr's summary. He alludes again to the cry:

> Art is the cry of distress uttered by those who experience at firsthand the fate of mankind. Who are not reconciled to it, but come to grips with it. Who do not apathetically wait upon the motor called "hidden forces," but hurl themselves in among the moving wheels, to understand how it all works. Who do not turn their eyes away, to shield themselves from emotions, but open them wide, so as to tackle what must be tackled.[30]

The unsettling plays of Büchner and Wedekind, as well as Berg's two operas, are artistic versions of the cry of distress induced when fearless and deeply sympathetic minds observe the enormities men commit upon each other and themselves. Berg's music may indeed absorb some of the shock value of the Expressionist scream; the full horror of the Büchner and Wedekind world view may appear somewhat muted and even mitigated from the stark originals. But within Berg's operas there is still potential for the scream of anguish. The horror of human degradation is still vivid enough to induce such a response.

Philippeau observes in *Danton's Death* that "there is an ear for which our deafening screaming into each other and vociferation [*Ineinanderschreien und Zeter*] are a stream of harmonies." The Expressionists had such an ear, and they turned this primal screaming into an aesthetic of appropriately strange harmonies—harmonies for which, to this writer at least, Berg was able to provide appropriate music in *Wozzeck* and *Lulu*.

ten

DEATH IN VENICE

Into me, with fury hot,
Like a dart himself he shot,
And my cold heart melts; my shield,
Useless, no defence can yield;
For what boots an outward screen
When, alas, the fight's within.

"The Combat between Cupid
and Anacreon" (6th century B.C.)

Throughout his career Benjamin Britten sought out the challenge of literature in difficult and—at least at first glance—operatically infertile works. A genius of foresight, not to say musical invention, was necessary to see in Crabbe's *The Borough* the potential for *Peter Grimes,* in Melville's *Billy Budd* the viable musical "space" for operatic treatment, or in Henry James's two stories "The Turn of the Screw" and "Owen Wingrave" the possibilities for musical amplification. Britten's history of choosing daring librettos, however, could scarcely prepare us for his last opera based on Thomas Mann's novella *Der Tod in Venedig.** With its nondramatic plot (the story is cast almost entirely in interior monologue) and dense prose style, *Der Tod in Venedig* made peculiarly heavy demands not only upon the composer's expressive and evocative skills but also upon what might be called the power of reticence. Mann's intricately quilted and yet seamless masterpiece demands understatement and withdrawal from comment quite as much as it requires Britten's genius for orchestral coloring in its brilliant but finally peripheral exoticism. The story balances upon hairline distinctions, carefully articulated ambiguities, the most delicate and numerous verbal leitmotifs. The success of Britten's score is largely dependent upon the composer's ability to match these qualities of the story with a commentary that

* In this chapter the German title will refer to the novella, the English title to the opera. All quotations from *Der Tod in Venedig* appear in parentheses in the text and are taken from the translation by Kenneth Burke (1965). Citations from *Stories of Three Decades,* tr. H. T. Lowe-Porter (1936) are indicated thus: (*S*).

likewise avoids crude, hasty, or simply overwhelming musical assumptions. It depends also upon a willingness to follow with tightrope care our (and Mann's) paradoxically detached and passionate observation of Gustav von Aschenbach's ironic tragedy. Mann's story challenged Britten and his librettist Myfanwy Piper to proceed with a very light but firm touch, and this—with a few exceptions—they were able to do.

Anyone familiar with the scholarship lavished upon *Der Tod in Venedig* will know how perfect a trap the story is for generalizations—even those not made in haste—and how unavailable its full value is to those with a specialist's focus. It is all too easy to write about such a work in impertinent clinical or scholarly jargon. Merely uncovering beyond a certain point its bare outlines is in a way shameful. Literary anatomists can nevertheless be shameless, and so over the years the story has been burdened with just such jargon ("manic replacive object," "disintegration of artistic sublimation"), far-fetched psychoanalysis ("Tadzio is an ecstasy-provoking embodiment of the maternal breast"), silly moralizing ("Why does Aschenbach never envisage fruitful love between himself and Tadzio, or any healing or beneficial outcome of his love? He could have introduced himself to the family with propriety, and sought appropriate expressions of love."), mercilessly reductive simplification (a "story . . . of latent and unrecognized homosexuality leading to self-destruction"), or mere revulsion (D. H. Lawrence calling the story "absolutely, almost intentionally unwholesome").[1] It is easy for critics to say too much and, it would seem, nearly impossible to say too little about *Der Tod in Venedig,* where silence rather than assertiveness would often be more telling. As yet another commentator upon the action of the story, Britten, we shall see, exercised more discretion than many of his scholarly counterparts—though he too was for "operatic" as well as interpretative reasons unable to avoid simplifying the original. Still, *Death in Venice* ennobles Mann's story; it increases the fictional amplitude and heightens the dramatic impact of the original through the added dimension of music.

Der Tod in Venedig is an excellent example of the limitations that affect the transformation of a literary work into another medium or, as in opera, into other media. Frost said that poetry is what is lost in translation, but that is perhaps the aspect of the novella most strongly translated in *Death in Venice.* What is lost, however, is the sense of a multileveled creation—a fictional machine with many moving parts that presses forward inexorably. *Der Tod in Venedig* is an extraordinary mixture of allusive elements. In it the forces of myth (Apollonian devotion to reason versus Dionysian devotion to passion), religion (Protestant ethic versus paganism), the psyche (id in conflict with ego and superego), society (the self in conflict with sexual mores), and of perception itself (objectivity versus hallucination)—all of these exist in an oscillating world of attraction and repulsion. The story's setting—a diseased but mesmerizingly beautiful city—is perfect for Mann's purposes. The great challenge of *Der Tod in Venedig,* then, is to match one's experience of the story with Mann's subtle combination of these conflicting values. This challenge is all the sharper because Mann's story is so pellucid—even if its texture at first strikes us as thick. If we are surprised by the story or its effects upon us, it is because we have surprised ourselves rather after the fashion of Aschenbach himself. If we suddenly find ourselves bound to the psychological, the mythic, or the realistic level of the story's meaning, it is not the author's fault but our own.

This task of keeping all avenues of the imagination open is easiest for the armchair reader, far more problematic for those, like the movie director Visconti or Britten, who seek to render the story visually. Visconti, chained to the realistic level, was able to focus only the clinical eye of the camera upon Aschenbach's Venetian excursion. He captured brilliantly the outer life the author leads in Venice; his observation of life in a pre-World War I Grand Hotel and the decadent-beautiful city insensibly stole our attention. But the film scarcely touched upon the keenly cerebrated terror Aschenbach experiences in his own mind. It simply could not explore the great interior monologues of the novella.[2] The level upon which Visconti approached *Der Tod in Venedig* was, in short, its least important.

Britten, on the other hand, found himself limited in quite the reverse direction. As a composer he could not hope to compete with the cinematic version in its panoramic visual opulence; at best, he could render Mann's Venice and Hotel des Bains in the merest outlines of musical suggestion and with minimal scenery. Though, it should be noted that the structure of the opera—rapid changes of venue, seventeen brief scenes, and extremely short, through-composed musical intervals—is still essentially cinematic. Rather, Britten was obliged to re-create *Der Tod in Venedig* from the inside out, focusing as in the original upon the inner tragedy of Aschenbach. The nature of Britten's artistry and sensibility, as well as the nature of opera itself, led *Death in Venice* to be centered on its most important level—that of the hero's increasing inner psychic distress. To appreciate fully how Britten and Piper achieved this focus and to judge the faithfulness of their translation, however, we are obliged to make an excursion into the literary and philosophical underpinnings of Mann's story. Before approaching the music itself, we must inquire into the circumstances surrounding the composition of the story, Mann's thoughts upon art and the sources of creative power, as well as the story's themes and their Platonic and Nietzschean background. Without such consideration the Aschenbach of both Mann and Britten cannot be appreciated.

Aschenbach, Mann, and His Early Works

The early works of Thomas Mann—largely stories except for *Buddenbrooks*—frequently betray themes and details of clearly autobiographical significance. *Der Tod in Venedig* is a case in point. In mid-May 1911 Mann traveled with his wife to Brioni, an island off Istria; from there they proceeded to Venice, where they stayed at the Hotel des Bains near the Lido from 26 May until 2 June. Here he experienced a "series of curious circumstances and impressions" or what he called elsewhere a "personal and lyrical experience while traveling." Years later, Mann reminisced about the novella and its gestation:

> The "pilgrim" at the North Cemetery, the dreary Pola boat, the gray-haired rake, the sinister gondolier, Tadzio and his family, the journey interrupted by a mistake about the luggage, the cholera, the upright clerk in the travel bureau, the rascally ballad-singer, all that, and *anything else you like,* they were all there.[3]

Whether phrasing himself euphemistically or, as above, challenging us more aggressively to assume what we suspect, Mann apparently never divulged, at least publicly, the true nature of his Venetian experience. Lately, more light has been thrown on the event by Karl Pringsheim, who enjoyed unusually close ties by marriage to Mann: each of them married the other's sister. As Pringsheim relates:

> In 1911, in May or perhaps the end of April, Thomas Mann and his wife went to Venice. There, on the first or second day, Mann saw that fabulous young Tadzio and the entire story, as it developed, was Thomas Mann's own personal experience. It did not go so far as in the novella. It did, however, go *rather* far. He was absolutely captivated. It was a great experience, and in a direction in fact alien to him. He was still young—I mean it would have been something else again for a man of 50 or 60, but Mann was 35 years old. It was entirely his own experience.[4]

Pringsheim is being disingenuous when he says this homoerotic event was "alien" to Mann; the prima facie evidence strongly hints at the novelist's vulnerability. The main point, at any rate, is that the superficial events of the story may be accounted for through Mann's own experience. To this experience he began in July 1911 to add fictional dimensions. On 18 July he wrote of a story in progress that was "serious and pure in tone, concerning a case of love for a boy in an aging artist." This same progression from real experience to fiction is mirrored in the linear progress of *Der Tod in Venedig:* the staid, prosaic, finely observed opening parts (the second of the story's five sections, largely cut in the opera, is an autobiographical description of Aschenbach's professional career) slowly give way to the mythic hallucination and richly lyric imagery of the last pages. Mann's triumph over the deepening implications of his story was not effortless: writing the seventy-five-page story took a full year.

If the facts of Mann's Venetian adventure were novel and startling, the themes that finally emerged in *Der Tod in Venedig* were not. Indeed their very frequency in Mann's early stories argues a continuing interest in and struggle with existential problems besetting Mann himself. If we accept Mann's assertion that "every piece of work is a realization, fragmentary but complete in itself, of our individuality,"[5] then these themes provide even more important autobiographical data than the registry of the Hotel des Bains for 1911 or the Venetian public health records. Fragments of Aschenbach's individuality and varying perspectives on his artistic agony are scattered in Mann's earlier writings.

Aschenbach's debilitating struggle between egotistic complacency and a sudden, forbidden passion is mirrored in one of Mann's first stories, "Little Herr Friedemann" (1897). We see a Venetian glimmer when a little hunchback falls in love with the beautiful but unattainable Frau von Rinnlingen: "He was gazing horror-struck within himself, beholding the havoc which had been wrought with his tenderly cherished, scrupulously managed feelings" (*S*, 12). In the denouement of this grotesque precursor to *Der Tod in Venedig*, Friedemann is crushed by the "dead weight of impotent, involuntary adoration" and commits suicide, precisely Aschenbach's fate.

The central characters of "Disillusionment" (1896), "Tonio Kröger" (1903), and "Felix Krull" (1911) all display an egotistic malaise and a self-satisfaction somehow baffled by passion. All feel an "indefinite ache" and yearn for a fulfillment that eludes them in their otherwise comfortable lives. When we first meet Aschenbach he is becoming aware that, in the words of Mann's "Dilettante," "besides my satisfaction and confidence something else stirred in me, a faint sense of anxiety and unrest, a faint consciousness of being on the defensive" (*S*, 38). Such is Aschenbach's pose from the very first pages set in Munich.

A second theme important in *Der Tod in Venedig* is the sophisticated artist's isolation from what Aschenbach calls "the varied amusements of the great world" (8). Mann's dilettante expresses this sense of splendid isolation at its height, and his final "fall" is all the more melodramatic. In Mann the wages of ironic aloofness are usually paid with a vengeance. The fate of Tonio Kröger, who provides us with a picture of Aschenbach in his childhood, exemplifies this. Devoted to the powers and pleasures of the intellect, he develops a "queer, aloof relationship" to his own humanity and that of others. Kröger's self-analysis, like Aschenbach's, is incisive and decidedly not self-serving:

> [The artist's calling] begins by your feeling yourself set apart, in a curious sort of opposition to the nice, regular people; there is a gulf of ironic sensibility, of knowledge, scepticism, disagreement between you and the others; it grows deeper and deeper, you realize that you are alone; and from then on any *rapprochement* is simply hopeless! What a fate! That is, if you still have enough heart, enough warmth of affections, to feel how frightful it is! [S, 104]

Like feelings and circumstances are experienced by Siegmund in "The Blood of the Walsungs" (1905), by Adrian Leverkühn in *Dr. Faustus,* Hanno Buddenbrooks, and—perhaps most parallel to Aschenbach—by Felix Krull. Still, if one story must prepare us for *Der Tod in Venedig,* it is "Tonio Kröger"—whose plot and central thesis are intimately parallel to Mann's great story.

As *Der Tod in Venedig* would amply suggest, Mann profoundly questioned, even suspected, the creative act and the creative life. When Aschenbach finishes an essay written in Tadzio's presence, he remarks darkly: "Certainly it is better for people to know only the beautiful product as finished, and not in its conception, its conditions of origin. For knowledge of the sources from which the artist derives his inspiration would often confuse and alienate" (69). Mann had touched upon this very same problem in the earlier story: "[People] assume that beautiful and uplifting results must have beautiful and uplifting causes, never dream that the 'gift' in question is a very dubious affair and rests upon extremely sinister foundations" ("Tonio Kröger" *S,* 105). Kröger's painter friend tries to talk him out of his cynicism by reminding him of

> the purifying and healing influence of letters, the subduing of the passions by knowledge and eloquence; literature as the guide to understanding, forgiveness, and love, the redeeming power of the word, literary art as the noblest manifestation of the human mind. [S, 106]

This recalls Aschenbach's own elaborate attempts, based largely upon Plato's *Phaedrus,* to drive the chilling wedge of intellect between himself and Tadzio. For Aschenbach as for Tonio, however, the idealized eloquence of the written word is savaged by the reality of passion. Both characters find themselves sorely torn by the problem of how to relate their artistic and human aspects. As Mann's earlier story closes, the hero looks at himself: "Eaten up with intellect and introspection, ravaged and paralysed by insight, half worn out by the fevers and frosts of creation, helpless and in anguish of conscience between two extremes, flung to and fro between austerity and lust; *raffiné*, impoverished, exhausted by frigid and artificially heightened ecstasies; erring, forsaken, martyred, and ill" (*S*, 131). Aschenbach, too, dies of rather more than Asian cholera.

Aside from these central themes, more modest aspects of *Der Tod in Venedig* are prefigured in "Tonio Kröger." Aschenbach's late adventure of the feelings takes place in the spring, and there are hints in the earlier story that this is not propitious: "Spring makes me nervous," Kröger admits, "I get dazed with the triflingness and sacredness of the memories and feelings it evokes . . . for the truth is it makes me ashamed; I quail before its sheer naturalness and triumphant youth" (*S*, 102). In his story, too, Italy is associated with "ardent wine, the sweets of sensuality." Aschenbach's startling dream is likewise foreshadowed in the "confused and ardent" dreams Kröger experiences on his emotional hegira, and Aschenbach's characteristic pose is well formulated by Kröger: "Happiness is in loving, and perhaps in snatching fugitive little approaches to the beloved object" (*S*, 97). The effeminate fop on the steamer is related to Kröger's dancing master Knaak (*S*, 93; *S*, 333). Finally, as background to the vague feelings "so long dormant and neglected" (7) and elicited by Tadzio, the juvenile homoerotic events in "Kröger" and "The Fight between Jappe and Do Escobar" (1911) are relevant.

Few novelists have questioned so self-consciously, so devastatingly, the writer's task, and I have referred to Mann's earlier works in order to emphasize this level of the novella's meaning which is so easily lost sight of (and non-existent in the Visconti film). The crux of the story is not sublimation of homosexual instincts, but more generally the sublimation of vital instincts—the instincts of life—which is a danger courted by the superior intellect—an intellect like Mann's own. To understand how Aschenbach responds to his Venetian crisis, we must turn to the Socratic "illusion" he falls back upon while under duress.

Aschenbach and the Fine Socratic Line

Britten and Piper focused upon the literary and philosophical level of Mann's theme of disintegration. This intentional preoccupation with the most difficult, crucial, and in a sense anti-operatic aspect of *Der Tod in Venedig* was daring, for the oppressive mood of entropy and decay might have been captured in more obvious, more theatrically attractive ways. Daring, too, because this led inevitably to *Death in Venice*'s rather low musical profile. Nietzsche called music the Dionysian art, and the forces of Dionysus do ultimately triumph in the story. But the object of interest is an Apollonian artist, that is, an artist dedicated to the word and its power to liberate man from the bondage of his emotions. Mann's first interest was not to praise Dionysus and the "sweets of sensuality," but to undermine and question the Apollonian intellect, with its complacent reliance upon logic, judgment, syllogism, and the precisions of a finely chiseled prose. Perhaps because Britten—no modern composer has responded so masterfully to the written word—and Mann are at heart Apollonian artists, the word (i.e., the libretto) is rarely overwhelmed by the music in *Death in Venice*. Only once, and then appropriately in Aschenbach's traumatic dream, is the full Dionysian power of music unleashed.

The psychic entropy captured by Britten, then, is not to be discovered in the progress of the Asian cholera, in the sense of a movement from "intellectual and youthful masculinity" (16) toward homoerotic debauchery, nor even in the carefully modulated development of Aschenbach's relation to Tadzio from artist, to father, to worshipper, to lover. Rather, we must look to the philosophical decay that takes place—and to the aesthetic ideals which slowly crumble in the face of his confrontations with Tadzio. We must look in short to Plato—quotations from whom give the operatic Aschenbach his most affecting lyrical moments. The plot of the story is simply the slow ruin of Aschenbach's self-esteem, and this esteem is based upon a Socratic assumption that existential and artistic truth can be grasped through the exercise of reason. The *Phaedo* contains a *locus classicus* for this view:

> The clearest knowledge will surely be attained by one who approaches the object so far as possible by thought, and thought alone, not permitting sight or any other sense to intrude upon his thinking, not dragging in any sense as accompaniment to reason: one who sets himself to track down each constituent of reality purely and simply as it is by means of thought pure and simple: one who gets rid, so far as possible, of eyes and ears and, broadly speaking, of the body altogether, knowing that when the body is the soul's partner it confuses the soul and prevents it from coming to possess truth and intelligence. [65E-66A]

Such is Aschenbach's belief when we first meet him. We hear of discipline, inward barriers, tenacity, endurance in the face of normal social impulses, aloofness, and a coldly passionate service to art. We learn that he has as a true Platonist "restrained and chilled his emotions, since he was aware that they incline to content themselves with a happy approximate, a state of semicompletion" (10). This distrust of the senses is the ground-bass of *Der Tod in Venedig*.

However, for Socrates as for Aschenbach this rigidly intellectual bias is threatened by physical beauty. How the Greek philosopher escaped from this agonizing dilemma is set forth in the *Phaedrus*. Socrates, inspired by the ravishing young Phaedrus, discourses upon beauty and the kind of love it ought to inspire. According to the famous parable of the charioteer and his two horses, the beloved evokes two responses in the lover—one intellectual and one physical. The former results in an aspiration after truth leading ultimately to temperance. The physical response is simply a desire for pleasure and leads finally to excess. Love or *eros,* then, is a concept motivated by the belief that the beloved is good, embodies the truth, contains the "form" of beauty, and that physical beauty must merely provide a bridge to the appreciation of this intrinsic "form" of beauty.

Socrates' oration in the *Phaedrus* demonstrates this dualism of divine, philosophical and profane, sensual love. Socrates loves Phaedrus, but this love is sublimated, transformed, and then offered in the form of an oratorical love-gift. Indeed, Socrates expresses the true lover's self-abnegation by assigning Phaedrus—with typical Socratic irony—as the real creator of the rhetorical tour de force ("that speech of yours which found utterance through my lips"). Precisely in this spirit does Aschenbach fashion in Tadzio's presence that "page and a half of choice prose which was soon to excite the admiration of many through its clarity, its poise, and the vigorous curve of its emotion":

> He even went so far as to prefer working in Tadzio's presence, taking the scope of the boy as a standard for his writing, making his style follow the lines of this body which seemed godlike to him . . . Never had his joy in words been more sweet. He had never been so aware that Eros is in the word. [69][6]

Aschenbach's brave attempt to live the Socratic ideal, however, is disconcertingly effusive. An air of desperation surrounds it. In the harsh light of the next dawn Aschenbach wonders again if his Platonic pretensions have not already been hopelessly dismantled: "Too late! Too late!" Mann then makes one of his few authorial intrusions: "But the fact was that Aschenbach did not want soberness: his intoxication was too precious." As the story progresses, Aschenbach is drawn irresistibly to Tadzio. He begins to experience the psychomachia Plato allegorized in the charioteer of the *Phaedrus:*

> Now when the charioteer sees the vision of the loved one, so that a sensation of warmth spreads from him over the whole soul and he begins to feel an itching and the stings of desire, the obedient horse [reason], constrained now as always by a sense of shame, holds himself back from springing upon the beloved; but the other [appetite], utterly heedless now of the driver's whip and goad, rushes forward prancing, and to the great discomfiture of his yoke-fellow and the charioteer drives them to approach the lad and make mention of the sweetness of physical love. [253-54]

In *Der Tod in Venedig* Socrates' "good" horse straining for detachment is insensibly overmastered by the "bad" horse straining for union. His mind wearied and spent, Aschenbach at this moment in his life does not have the psychic energy to withstand the onslaught.[7]

Socrates, describing the aging lover who feels the carnal sting, sets Aschenbach's essential pose in the novella: "He is old but his companion is young, yet he is driven on by an irresistible itch to the pleasures which are constantly to be found in seeing, hearing, and touching his beloved, in fact in every sensation which makes him conscious of his presence; no wonder then that he takes delight in close attendance on him." And the climax of the Socratic description reflects, with clinical exactness, the hastening final pages of Mann's story:

> In this state of mingled pleasure and pain the sufferer is perplexed by the strangeness of his experience and struggles helplessly; in his frenzy he cannot sleep at night or remain still by day, but his longing drives him wherever he thinks that he may see the possessor of beauty. When he sees him and his soul is refreshed by the flood of emanations the closed passages are unstopped; he obtains a respite from his pains and pangs, and there is nothing to equal the sweetness of the pleasure which he enjoys for the moment. From this state he never willingly emerges . . . the conventions of civilized behavior, on whose observance he used to pride himself, he now scorns; he is ready to be a slave and make his bed as near as he is allowed to the object of his passion; for besides the reverence which he feels for the possessor of beauty he has found in him the only physician for sickness of the most grievous kind. [251-52]

Mann crushes Aschenbach with ironies: the last and greatest is that, true to the prediction of the *Phaedrus* he so dearly believes in, the ailing artist accepts Tadzio as his only physician and consequently dies of the cholera.

The Nietzschean Overview

The time-honored Platonic theory of love is of no avail to Aschenbach, and Nietzsche—a thinker who strongly influenced Mann—can tell us much about the character's fate. "To make the individual *uncomfortable,*" Nietzsche proclaimed, "that is my task" (*N*, 50).* This he performed relentlessly, and his targets were invariably men like the dour, steadfast, abstinent Gustav von Aschenbach.

Nietzsche was the first modern philosopher to make a direct frontal attack upon Platonism and the hypertrophy of the powers of ratiocination which he said it encouraged. Because Aschenbach fancies himself a Socratic, many of Nietzsche's excoriatory remarks upon

* Quotations, with Nietzsche's own emphasis, are either from the Viking Portable edition, ed. Walter Kaufmann, designated by (*N*) or *The Basic Writings of Nietzsche,* also ed. Kaufmann (1968), designated by (*B*).

"that most brilliant of all self-outwitters" reflect back on Mann's hero. Nietzsche found the Platonic theory transparently and dangerously biased. He realized that it could mask over but not fill the psychic abyss:

> When one finds it necessary to turn *reason* into a tyrant, as Socrates did, the danger cannot be slight that something else will play the tyrant. Rationality was then hit upon as the savior; neither Socrates nor his "patients" had any choice about being rational: it was *de rigeur,* it was their last resort. The fanaticism with which all Greek reflection throws itself upon rationality betrays a desperate situation; there was danger, there was but one choice: either to perish—or to be *absurdly rational* . . . one must imitate Socrates and counter the dark appetites with a permanent daylight—the daylight of reason. One must be clever, clear, bright at any price: any concession to the instincts, to the unconscious, leads *downward.* [*N,* 478]

The fictional Aschenbach might have read these words fearfully, for when the story opens instinctual feelings long ago outgrown and forgotten—Nietzsche's dark appetites—are beginning to cause anxiety. They will give him the unsettling dreams during his sleep of reason in Venice. They will culminate in the final orgiastic vision that becomes Scene 13 of the opera.

Concerning the theory of love expounded in the *Phaedrus* that so entices Aschenbach, Nietzsche was brutally sarcastic:

> [Plato] says with an innocence possible only for a Greek . . . that there would be no Platonic philosophy at all if there were not such beautiful youths in Athens: it is only their sight that transposes the philosopher's soul into an erotic trance, leaving it no peace until it lowers the seed of all exalted things into such beautiful soil . . . Philosophy after the fashion of Plato might rather be defined as an erotic contest, as a further development and turning inward of the ancient agonistic gymnastics and of its [homoerotic] *presuppositions.* [*N*, 528]

Nietzsche questioned what he called the "cheerfulness" of Greek art, that is, its complacent optimism and delusive intellectual serenity. He was the first to criticize the prevailing view of the Greeks epitomized by Winckelmann, Goethe, and the famous neo-Classical motto *edle Einfalt, stille Grösse* (noble simplicity, calm grandeur).[8] Common sense warned Nietzsche against this aesthetic idealism: "To smell out 'beautiful souls,' 'golden means,' and other perfections in the Greeks, or to admire their calm in greatness, their ideal cast of mind, their noble simplicity—the psychologist in me protected me against such 'noble simplicity,' a *niaiserie allemande* [German folly] anyway" (*N*, 559). Aschenbach's elaborate rationality does appear a piece of transalpine folly under the glare of the Mediterranean sun and in that city described by Balzac in "Massimilla Doni": "Here in Venice love and its thousand vagaries, the luscious business of genuine happiness, engrosses each moment of time." Aschenbach's erotic contest takes place in this venue.

In a letter Thomas Mann described the general character of *Der Tod in Venedig* as "rather Protestant than Classical."[9] This précis draws us again to Nietzsche, for he saw a close connection between the evils of Socratism and the evils of the Protestant/Prussian ethic—he even called the Greek philosophers "pre-existently Christian" in their rejection of the natural human passions lying at the root of the individual personality. Nietzsche found monstrous all morality that gratuitously inhibited the experience of one's own sexuality: "It was Christianity, with its *ressentiment* against life at the bottom of its heart, which first made something unclean of sexuality" (*N*, 562). In his *Attempts at a Self-Criticism* (1886) prefacing *The Birth of Tragedy*, Nietzsche describes the effects of Christian moralism in terms that give us yet another glimpse of the ruinous presuppositions Mann's respected novelist makes. Nietzsche sees in Christian teaching "a *hostility to life*—a furious, vengeful antipathy to life itself," "condemnation of the passions," and "fear of beauty and sensuality" (*B*, 23). Aschenbach struggles with all of these feelings.

Nietzsche, then, attacked with equal vehemence the philosophical mode (Socratic) and the religious/social mode (Christian/Prussian) upon which Aschenbach has gained the world's esteem and his own. Unsurprisingly, the qualities of the hero's agony are also expressed by Nietzsche:

> There are two kinds of sufferers: first, those who suffer from the *overfullness* of life and want a Dionysian art as well as a tragic in-

sight and outlook on life—and then those who suffer from the *impoverishment* of life, and demand of art and philosophy, calm, stillness, smooth seas, or, on the other hand, frenzy, convulsion, and anesthesia. Revenge against life itself—the most voluptuous kind of frenzy for those so impoverished! [*N*, 669-70]

Aschenbach's suffering is of the latter variety. There is even a Nietzschean hint of the psyche's revenge for repression in the first pages of *Der Tod in Venedig*: "Were these enslaved emotions now taking their vengeance on him, by leaving him in the lurch, by refusing to forward and lubricate his art . . ." (10). And the frenzy Nietzsche refers to is an important aspect of the last third of Mann's story, as much a study in self-hatred as in love for Tadzio. The prideful artist is engulfed in a flood of self-accusation that exhausts the lexicon: *transgression, folly, hysteria, mania, dissolution, abject, degenerate, ignoble, unseemly*. The mixture of violence and exhilaration in Aschenbach's self-criticism gives the last pages their fascinating power. As so often for the novella, Nietzsche's gloss is apt: "Man is the cruelest animal against himself; and whenever he calls himself 'sinner' and 'cross-bearer' and 'penitent,' do not fail to hear the voluptuous delight that is in all such lamentation and accusation" (*N*, 330).

What is the Nietzschean ideal? How, finally, does it relate to Aschenbach? Walter Kaufmann has perhaps best expressed the central Nietzschean theorems that "wisdom consists in seeing the limitations of one's own knowledge," and that the ideal man is "a passionate man who can control his passions."[10] Aschenbach's psyche, like his physique, has grown too weak to bear the sudden pressures of emotion with such Nietzschean equanimity. Nietzsche wanted man to discipline himself to wholeness, to the full measure of his will, but Aschenbach discovers in Venice—when he is physically and spiritually beyond hope—that he has in his past life disciplined himself to emptiness. He has shown the ignoble caution Nietzsche criticized in Plato: "Plato is a coward before reality, consequently he flees into the ideal; Thucydides has control of *himself*, consequently he has control of things" (*N*, 558-59). Aschenbach, though he may fancy himself a Thucydides when he arrives in Venice, loses control of himself. His world begins to display a "faint but irresistible tendency to distort itself" (29); he becomes "no longer even sure of his directions" (106). With unwonted indolence he gives himself over to destiny after he has lost any ability to control it—yet another irony of the story.

Nietzsche preached that man must not flee from the reality of his passions, for they may vanish and leave him permanently impoverished or break forth unpredictably. This latter event Aschenbach experiences with initial pleasure: "Past emotions, precious early afflictions and yearnings which had been stifled by his rigorous program of living, were now returning in such strange new forms. With an embarrassed, astonished smile, he recognized them" (73). But wonderment succeeds to uncontrollable desire, desperation, and an eventual symbolic suicide. The Nietzschean lesson Aschenbach learns in Venice is one of general import: "The degree and kind of a person's sexuality reach up into the ultimate pinnacle of his spirit" (*N*, 444). It is a mark of the faithfulness and value of Britten's *Death in Venice* that its focus remains on this universal level and does not merely communicate a moral tale for pederasts.

Apollo and Dionysus

It is a critical commonplace that *Der Tod in Venedig* allegorizes the struggle between the Apollonian will to judgment and the Dionysian will to pleasure; the story is, after all, full of mythological and classical allusions. Mann inherited this particular dualism from Nietzsche's *The Birth of Tragedy,* which was dedicated to Richard Wagner. Britten and Piper give voice to the two gods in *Death in Venice:* the musical climax of the opera is a dream in which Apollo and Dionysus vie for ascendancy over Aschenbach. This mythical opposition bears closer scrutiny.

The Birth of Tragedy (1872) was Nietzsche's first published book. Its purpose was to describe the beginnings of tragedy in the Dionysian or bacchic festivals of the early Hellenes, the infusion of Socratic or Apollonian dialectic into theater (for which Euripides is castigated), and the final emergence of the dual nature of Attic drama. His bias was unmistakable: "I was the first to take seriously, for the understanding of the older, the still rich and even overflowing Hellenic instinct, that wonderful phenomenon which bears the name of Dionysus" (*N,* 560). Because the Apollonian Aschenbach preoccupies us in *Death in Venice,* we ought to begin with a summary of that side of the dualism.

The Apollonian instinct is to isolate; it triumphs in a complete self-sufficiency achieved through the exercise of reason. It gives man the strength to deliver himself from the flood of Dionysian passion. "Apollonian power erupts to restore the almost shattered individual with the healing balm of blissful illusion" (*B,* 127). At the heart of this ethos was Socrates' "sublime metaphysical illusion" that "thought, using the thread of causality, can penetrate the deepest abysses of being, and that thought is capable not only of knowing being but even of *correcting* it" (*B,* 95). Hence, Nietzsche finds the Apollonian influence in tragedy to be the same that Aschenbach esteems in his own prose: "Everything that comes to the surface in the Apollonian part of Greek tragedy, in the dialogue, looks simple, transparent, and beautiful . . . Thus the language of Sophocles' heroes amazes us by its Apollonian precision and lucidity" (*B,* 67). To Nietzsche's mind the Apollonian demand for measure, restraint, harmony, and proportion drove Dionysian vigor out of Greek tragedy.

As a visual suggestion of the Apollonian ethos, we have the sculpture of Bertel Thorvaldsen (PLATE 3). Thorvaldsen, like Aschenbach, was obsessed with juvenile masculine beauty. He made five studies of Ganymede, as well as numerous other archetypes of Classical masculine beauty like Mercury and Cupid. His quintessentially neo-Classical sculpture of repose, idealized form, harmony of line, and almost luminous beauty serves as a key to the Apollonian admiration Aschenbach tries to sustain for Tadzio. Indeed, his attempts to describe the boy remind us of Thorvaldsen's works:

> His face, pale and reserved, framed with honey-colored hair, the straight sloping nose, the lovely mouth, the expression of sweet and godlike seriousness, recalled Greek sculpture of the noblest period. [37]

> The flowering head was poised with an incomparable seductiveness—the head of an Eros, in blended yellows of Parian marble. [43]

Plate 3. (left) Bertel Thorvaldsen, "The Shepherd Boy" (1822-25). *Photograph by Ole Woldbye København, Copenhagen. By courtesy of the Thorvaldsen Museum, Copenhagen.*

(below) Bertel Thorvaldsen, "Cupid Received by Anacreon—Winter" (1823). *Photograph by Jonals Co., Copenhagen. By courtesy of the Thorvaldsen Museum, Copenhagen.*

> His armpits were still as smooth as those of a statue; the hollows of his knees glistened, and their bluish veins made his body seem built of some clearer stuff . . . Yet the pure and strenuous will which, darkly at work, could bring such godlike sculpture to the light—was not he, the artist, familiar with this? [66]

And the very qualities Aschenbach describes in his own prose—"a discriminating purity, simplicity, and evenness of attack which gave his productions such an obvious, even such a deliberate stamp of mastery and classicism"—are not these the qualities of Thorvaldsen's sculpture? (Incidentally, Mann has Tonio Kröger stand "long before Thorvaldsen's noble and beautiful statuary" (*S*, 122) when he visits Copenhagen.) And are they not the qualities Nietzsche identified as Apollonian?

Dionysian forces upset Aschenbach's self-sufficiency. This opens, as Nietzsche puts it, the way to "the innermost heart of things." When Nietzsche speaks of the eternal phenomenon of Dionysian art, the omnipotent expression of individual will, and the "eternal life beyond all phenomena," we may well think all this more relevant to *Tristan und Isolde* than to *Death in Venice*. But the fact is that the Dionysian climax in the Britten opera is very closely related to the *Liebestod* in Wagner's opera. The dream—like the last moments of *Tristan*—permits the music to achieve its fullest Dionysian expression, and this moment symbolizes the tragedy of Aschenbach: "This is the most immediate effect of the Dionysian tragedy, that the state and society and, quite generally, the gulfs between man and man give way to an overwhelming feeling of unity leading back to the very heart of nature" (*B*, 59). There is little real difference between Isolde dying over the lifeless form of Tristan, and Aschenbach giving himself over simultaneously to Tadzio as Eros, a summoner to love, and as Hermes, a summoner to death. Each is a love-death—an ultimate symbol of spiritual union.

A visual equivalent of the Dionysian ethos may help to capture the stupendous axis on which *Der Tod in Venedig* and the opera rest. Indeed, Mann attempts at the outset to give a palpable sense of the brimming, subversive forces at work within Aschenbach:

> His yearnings crystallized; his imagination, still in ferment from his hours of work, actually pictured all the marvels and terrors of a

> manifold world which it was suddenly struggling to conceive. He saw a landscape, a tropical swampland under a heavy, murky sky, damp, luxuriant and enormous, a kind of prehistoric wilderness of islands, bogs, and arms of water, sluggish with mud; he saw, near him and in the distance, the hairy shafts of palms rising out of a rank lecherous thicket, out of places where the plant life was fat, swollen, and blossoming exorbitantly; he saw strangely misshapen trees lowering their roots into the ground, into stagnant pools with greenish reflections; and here, between floating flowers which were milk-white and large as dishes, birds of a strange nature, high-shouldered, with crooked bills, were standing in the muck, and looking motionlessly to one side; between dense, knotted stalks of bamboo he saw the glint from the eyes of a crouching tiger—and he felt his heart knocking with fear and with puzzling desires. Then the image disappeared. [7-8]

This hallucination is the first hint of and early counterpart to the dream which is the climax of the story and the opera. What is pictured here is aptly illustrated by one of Henri Rousseau's last jungle pictures, "The Dream" (PLATE 4).[11] Rousseau captures many of the effects of Mann's psychic or subconscious jungle—its air of unreality (the perspective, like Aschenbach's, is ajar), its hallucinated fecundity, its Dionysian sense of natural excess. The Apollonian-Dionysian extremes of *Der Tod in Venedig* are paralleled in Thorvaldsen's "The Shepherd Boy" and Rousseau's "The Dream": the former is reposed, idealized, harmonious, colorless, flawless; the latter is luxuriant, richly colored, subtly disturbing, erotic.

In *Death in Venice* Dionysus vanquishes Apollo and the "sweet and wild orgy" of Scene 13 proceeds. It is the opera's climax. What follows, though splendid, is merely the tragic addendum. Again, we may ask, what is the Nietzschean ideal underlying the dualism set forth above? It is something symbiotic; it lies in a fraternal union of the two deities, Dionysus speaking the language of Apollo and Apollo the language of Dionysus. Nietzsche was not predisposed to

---

Plate 4. Henri Rousseau, "The Dream" (1910). Oil on canvas, 6′ 8½″ × 9′ 9½″. *Collection, The Museum of Modern Art, New York. Gift of Nelson A. Rockefeller.*

Socrates' "good" horse or the "bad"; he knew that both horses require rein and freedom. For Aschenbach, unsure of his control, the attempt to manage the two is catastrophic. Nietzsche thought the Dionysian state "most apt to seduce us to life," but for Aschenbach—the victim of yet another grotesque irony—Dionysus proves fatal.

The Britten Transformation

The first audiences for *Death in Venice* (and many critics) were disappointed by its spare musical economy. Whether this was justified or not, it was natural: something richer, more lush—in short more Wagnerian—might have seemed in order. Mann, after all, is perhaps the one modern novelist most consciously indebted to Wagner, and *Der Tod in Venedig* has even been called "the most Wagnerian of all short stories."[12] Nor is it inapt to observe that the love music for *Tristan und Isolde*—a companion work to Britten's opera in its expression of the Eros-Thanatos theme—was composed in Venice, where Wagner was eventually to die. Mann's story rises out of a complex of leitmotifs; themes of encounter, unfulfillment, beauty, evasion, and death crowd in upon the simple action of the story, giving it a rich Wagnerian texture. And the sheer mythic understructure of the novella owes something to Wagner's musical drama.

Failing the presence of Wagner, we might have expected something along Mahlerian lines. We know Mann was greatly taken with that composer's music and personality, that Mahler died while Mann was sojourning in Venice, and that the story of Aschenbach became an artistic salute to the dead composer. Wrong though Visconti may have been to turn Aschenbach into a composer, his choice of Mahler's lush adagietto for the film soundtrack did provide a perfect accompaniment for the artist's decline into Venetian indolence. There is something profoundly akin to Aschenbach's experience in the psychologically overwrought, nearly schizophrenic moodiness, and plush contours of Mahler's music.

Finally, a first-night audience might have hoped for a recurrence of the full-blown orchestral scale of Britten's early masterpiece *Peter Grimes*. The very similarity of themes—the mesmerizing presence of the sea, the focus upon a social outsider, the hero's fatal destiny—might well have encouraged a return to the grand operatic style.[13] But for plausible, even predictable reasons there is in *Death in Venice* no Mahler, little Wagner (short of an unprepossessing cluster of motifs gingerly but frequently used), and only brief hints of the younger Britten. The reasons for this are numerous, and we shall explore some of them here as we attempt to account for the culminating place this opera occupies in Britten's body of vocal writing.

The most obvious and important reason for the un-Wagnerian and un-Mahlerian cast of *Death in Venice* is, quite simply, Britten's respect for and invariably gifted response to the written word. Wagner and Mahler are at their best when describing *how* staggering emotional experiences are felt rather than *why*. The confusion of thought in the text of *Tristan* is great (and explains, and is explained by, its convoluted, alliterative syntax), and yet it is finally of little matter, since Wagner's concern was to explore emotion. Similarly, with Mahler we may be uplifted and moved, but we rarely experience in his music a sense of rational resolution, of thought imposing restrictions upon or illuminating emotion. Wagner and Mahler remain the two great protagonists of the inundating power of music.

In *Der Tod in Venedig,* however, Mann was preoccupied with a description of *why* Aschenbach feels as he does, and to just this analytical, essentially philosophical level of the story Britten and Piper responded. It is also the level for which Britten's gifts as a composer are most apt. No twentieth-century composer responded more feelingly, successfully, and self-effacingly to verbal expressions of human experience. Britten's settings of Donne's Holy Sonnets, Shakespeare's *A Midsummer Night's Dream,* the poems of Blake, Hölderlin, and Michelangelo, the "Serenade" and the "Nocturne" have all displayed this talent. In all these works (and, though one might not sense it at first, as early as *Peter Grimes*) Britten's intention was to keep the music subordinate to the text, to make the music a form of accompaniment and comment upon the words. This intention, moreover, became stronger as Britten's career developed: *Death in Venice* might well be seen as a supreme example of the bias, *prima le parole, doppo la musica.* For him the word is supreme, and this perhaps explains why the most distinctive orchestral writing in his operas often occurs when voices are silent and music can be allowed its fullest expressive power. If Britten's operas err, it is almost always on the side of understatement and simple paucity of impact; where they succeed is, as one might expect, in the subtle, finespun evocation of mood.

Britten's powers of musical understatement, however, were never tried as greatly as in *Death in Venice,* especially since the vastly fascinating atmosphere and setting of the story could so easily have been expanded upon musically at the expense of the novella's long, static, interior monologue. Britten must have realized that to make his opera a musical fashionplate—as Visconti made his film a visual one—would ultimately trivialize the story. He must likewise have sensed that the central role of his opera was (and he must have trembled a little at the thought) not a "musical" one properly so called. Throughout most of the story Aschenbach is a reasoner, an observer, an abstainer from emotion. His cold voice of judgment virtually enjoins traditional operatic heightening (one should note, though that the opera is weighted toward the "emotional" end of the story: Act I covers the first two-thirds of the story, Act II the last third). Britten's solution for this problem was to develop a freely declamatory vocal line, with pitch notations but no rhythmic indications (EX. 1). Aschenbach's isolation is emphasized by scoring his introspective moments with piano punctuation; the result is the most stark, the driest of recitative. On stage these soliloquies are set off by having

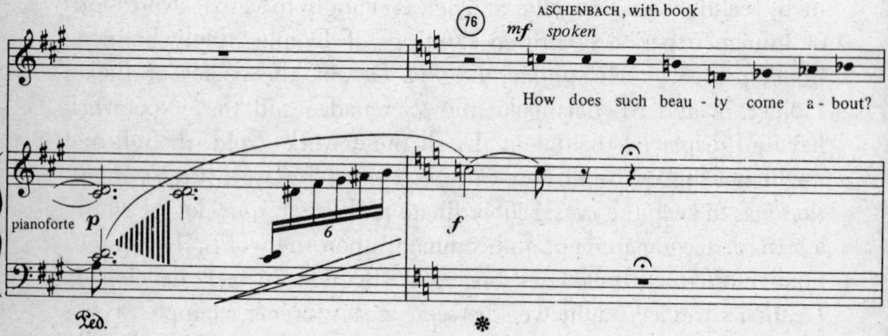

Example 1

Aschenbach produce "a small book the symbol of his novelist's trade." It is not a coincidence that for the characterization of the almost monkish novelist Britten turned to pre-Classical traditions with a vocal line that hints at ancient Greek hymn, the melisma of Schütz's *Passions,* and the chaste qualities of plainsong. If Aschenbach's role is criticized as largely recitative, one can only reply that the stiff, cerebrating protagonist fairly demanded such a compositional strategy.

Another reason for the recessiveness of the score is to be sought in the original's pervasive ambiguity. Ambivalence, whether referring to sexuality, to the sources of artistic inspiration, or to the sources of any emotion, is central to our experience of *Der Tod in Venedig.* This blurring pervades everything. Venice itself is "flatteringly and suspiciously beautiful" and "half legend, half snare for strangers" (84).[14] The nationality of the demonic figures is undiscernible. The influences ("psychic or physical?") that send Aschenbach south are vague. Softness, luxury, and death seem everywhere in league, as in the gondola. There is a "perilous sweetness" in the air related to the sweet and terrible joy of Aschenbach's love for Tadzio. Even the clues we are given about Tadzio's visual aspect are strangely ambiguous.

The miracle of Mann's story is that by the most economical and glancing references he was able to load his story with the full freight of ambiguity without stretching credibility, or indeed without drawing us too startlingly to the realization that nothing Aschenbach sees or feels can be taken as a dependable datum of experience. As with the Asian cholera, much of the Venetian adventure is inscrutable to Aschenbach: "Certainty was impossible" (86). He loses his bearings precisely because the graspable certainties of his life and his present surroundings gradually blur. Mann achieves this dismantling of Aschenbach's "reality" through the subtlest minutiae of observation and altered tone, and Britten matches this low-profile artistry (its equivalent in plastic art is intarsia) through similarly understated local musical effects. Britten proceeds, too, by means of intimation and adumbration. The scoring for Tadzio's entrances is an example of the hovering ambiguity Britten cultivates. The vibraphone motif associated with him is entrancingly simple, yet it has at the same time an ominous quality of suspended animation.[15] A fluttering, breathy flute (familiar from Britten's *Curlew River*) and a harp provide surrounding arabesques, and as the opera progresses the "other" world of sensuality represented by Tadzio is given richer exotic character through the use of the xylophone, marimba, glockenspiel, harp, and assorted percussion instruments.

On the other side, Britten's music obliquely evokes the heart's disease in Aschenbach and its slow progress. As Mann wrote in "Tonio Kröger," artistic careers are built on "extremely sinister foundations," and so might one describe the reticent score of *Death in Venice:* its delicate lyricism is underlaid by hollow woodwinds, mordant and deep-throated brass emerging from the psychic and orchestral underground, and the bass drum, double bass, and gong virulently echoing *de profundis.* All of this often takes place under a darkly textured and oppressively formless string tutti. Throughout the score the measured rhythms of Venice's bells, the motion of the Adriatic, and an ever-present dirge are hauntingly intertwined. Especially in the gut-wrenching dirge does Britten capture the tragic undertow of Mann's story. It reappears in virtually all of the opera's important moments: during Aschenbach's ride in the gondola, when he first watches Tadzio on the beach, when he first tries to leave Venice. It is deployed even more powerfully in the prelude to Act II, in the Saint Mark scene, and in the opera's last moments. In its "mortifying" sound-world Britten's opera is comparable to *Wozzeck.* With distressing eloquence these operas describe dying, entropic worlds—one primarily psychological, the other social.

Faithfulness to his own developing style also helps explain Britten's approach to *Der Tod in Venedig,* and this recent development in his vocal writing (with the exception of *Owen Wingrave*) may not be familiar to Britten's operatic audience. *Death in Venice* was the composer's first opera composed for the stage since he made his two-act version of *Billy Budd* in 1961. In the intervening years his writing for the stage was represented primarily by the strange, little-known church parables, *Curlew River* (1964), *The Burning Fiery Furnace* (1966), and *The Prodigal Son* (1968). As the first example of this new direction in Britten's music, *Curlew River* is particularly interesting. This short piece was inspired by the tradition of Japanese Noh drama. It is stylized in text, plot, and characterization, and its music, intricately based upon a medieval plainsong, is of the sparest. Notation for the vocal line is rhythmically free, and in order to assure a very thinly textured, linear freedom in his score, Britten invented the "curlew" (⌒⌒) to give the singers room for extemporaneous pacing.[16] The curlew reappears frequently in *Death in Venice*. As well, the orchestral comment in *Curlew River* is highly simplified, and there is more strict alternation of vocal and instrumental parts. This alternation occurs often in *Death in Venice* and naturally tends to exalt the text. This linear simplicity is not unrelated to Winckelmann's neo-Classical principle that the thinnest line is most apt for limning a beautiful human form. Britten's vocal line in *Death in Venice* is thus in another way particularly congenial to Aschenbach's classicizing intellect.

Curlew River is also a breathtaking display of Britten's evocative powers. The small chamber ensemble, dominated by harp, flute, and horn, gives an exotic aura to this partly medieval, partly Oriental, partly primitive work (this was to help Britten evoke the Asiatic origins of the cholera in his Mann opera). The ambiguous beauties and harshnesses of *Curlew River* are further accented by the mercurial portando and glissando sliding of the strings (reminiscent of the "fairy" music in *A Midsummer Night's Dream*).[17] These methods reappear in *Death in Venice*. *Curlew River* portrays a theatrical world in which reality and unreality, mythic symbolism, and precisely observed details are subtly mixed. To achieve this Britten necessarily had to break away from the conventions of "normal" opera. This break ultimately made him better able to cope with the similarly dualistic world of *Der Tod in Venedig*, for normal operatic conventions would never have served Mann's story adequately. It is not Britten's more famous operas but the church parables that are the best introduction to *Death in Venice*.

Finally, one cannot explain the composition of the opera without reference to Peter Pears, for whom the role of Aschenbach was written. Nearly all of the composer's vocal writing focused upon Pears, who created the central roles of his operas, parables, and song cycles. *Death in Venice* must surely be seen as the crowning event of their long companionship and their unparalleled thirty-five-year artistic collaboration. Many of Britten's finest works have showcased Pears's tenor voice, but none of these is as strongly wedded to this singer's chaste-toned, silvery voice as *Death in Venice*. The role of Aschenbach, as one might expect, does not require a Heldentenor (Pears was sixty-one the week of the Aldeburgh premiere), though because Aschenbach is rarely offstage it does require Wagnerian stamina. If not heroic voice, the role does require heroic intellect. Extraordinary humanity and emotional energy suffuse the vocal line, and the singer must be constantly wary of slipping into mere recitative in the role's numerous soliloquies. Pears's perspicacity as an interpreter of songs, as well as his long schooling in the expressive, declamatory Britten style, needless to say, made him superbly able to cope with the limited lyric and melodic values of the role. Pears's voice has always made up in finesse, purity of tone, and restraint for what it lacks in warm timbre and force. No other tenor's instrument is so much one of reason, and this is apt both for the Mann story and the opera. The role of Aschenbach is a tour de force of what might be called intellectual coloratura and highly suited Pears's art.

The most problematic crux of any visual rendering of *Der Tod in Venedig* is Aschenbach's relationship to the Polish family and to Tadzio. The difficulty lies in the fact that, as we read the story, our sense of what the boy looks like is filtered through Aschenbach's own increasingly rhapsodic vision. We are of course aware of his real existence, but what actually absorbs us is the separate, fantasized existence he takes on in Aschenbach's mind. When, in the cinema or the opera house, we are allowed to view Tadzio (and to begin creating our own fantasies), the effect may be to jolt us suddenly outside the privileged inner sanctum of Mann's interior monologue. Once this happens we find ourselves in the position of Visconti's camera, that is, on the outside looking at the implacable Aschenbach exterior, catching a glimpse of physical decline now and then but finally not sharing the inner turmoil.

Rejecting mime in favor of the more symbolic potential of ballet, Britten and Piper turned Tadzio into a young dancer, his mother into a ballerina, and the children on the beach into a kind of balletic pre-school. Perhaps their initial inspiration was the Dionysian dance in Aschenbach's last dream, a fine moment for operatic ballet. Even Nietzsche—who felt dance revealed the Dionysian spirit because "the greatest strength remains only potential but betrays itself in the suppleness and wealth of movement" (*B*, 67)—might have approved of this radical change. That Aschenbach should be seduced from his repressive life-style through ballet, with its exalting release of physical energy and its self-conscious display of beauty, is an immediately attractive idea.

The *Death in Venice* ballet, however appealing in theory, does not work so well in practice: as a means of expressing the mythic implications of the story, the ballet is quite appropriate (the dream sequence can have a brilliant impact), but in the earlier scenes where we should prefer naturalness and realism, the ballet seems peculiarly out of synchronization with the action. Piper was led by the corps de ballet at her disposal to the one large-scale addition and vulgarity in the text, the "Games of Apollo" in Act I. This pseudo-pentathlon not only has the invidious effect of burlesquing Aschenbach's theme of formal Greek beauty, but is very difficult for a group of children to perform without ludicrousness. As well, the choral observation of the five events contains the least inspired lines in an otherwise splendid libretto. Thus inserted in the action, the ballet gives an unavoidable and unpleasant sense of divertissement—a jejune moment in an otherwise deadly serious work. One should add that Tadzio, as the *premier danseur jeune*, is allowed to win all the contests, something that Mann's Tadzio could never have done.[18]

The decision to cast Tadzio as a dancer was ingenious but unfortunately also carried some aesthetic and practical traps. Specifically, the ballet requires that Tadzio have the musculature of a dancer (i.e., of a man), that he be the self-conscious poseur classical balletic style requires, that he be notoriously athletic, and—the last straw—that he have a brief but pointedly erotic pas de deux with his mother (cut in subsequent productions). All this blithely disregards numerous hints in *Der Tod in Venedig* that Tadzio is not a young balletic god, but one of a rather different, Platonic sort:

> The person we shall see him [the carnal lover] running after will be soft rather than tough, the product of a breeding in chequered shade rather than clear sunshine, a stranger to manly toil and honest sweat, accustomed to luxurious and effeminate living. [*Phaedrus*, 239]

Mann takes great pains to show Tadzio is such a figure. This is obvious from his first appearance: "It was clear that in his existence the first factors were gentleness and tenderness . . . The English sailor suit, with its braids, stitchings, and embroideries, its puffy sleeves narrowing at the ends and fitting snugly about the fine wrists of his still childish but slender hands" (38).[19] We are reminded again and again of his delicate figure, and further details are added to suggest Tadzio is less than a perfect specimen: a weak voice, imperfect teeth, jaundiced complexion, a thin envelope of flesh on his torso. "He is very frail," Aschenbach muses, "he is sickly. In all probability he will not grow old." Finally, Tadzio is "about fourteen" years old—a rather important fact if we as an audience are to give some credibility to the pure and virginal adoration Aschenbach at first pretends for Tadzio. To have a fully developed dancer as Tadzio severely undermines what Mann calls the aura of "chaste delight" which must breathe around him. If it does not—and a balletic Tadzio causes problems—it becomes all the more difficult for the audience to rise to the more ennobling levels of Mann's story.

One must draw back, finally, and observe that the casting for a Tadzio—whether the androgynous boy in the film or the vigorous athlete in the opera—is extremely difficult. Perhaps this is because Mann has so carefully typecast him as a figure from the impossibly idealized, unspeakably beautiful figures of Thorvaldsen. Perhaps the problems presented by a visible Tadzio will serve to make *Death in Venice* an opera far more effective for the armchair listener, who alone can imagine for himself the ravishing, fatal summoner.

The other major alteration made by Piper and Britten is the gathering of three demonic characters (The Traveler, The Old Gondolier, and The Leader of the Players) and three peripheral but important figures (The Elderly Fop, The Hotel Manager, and The Hotel Barber) into one role for a baritone—who is also assigned the Voice of Dionysus. Aschenbach has an appointment with death, and it is plausible to make all these figures part of the final summoning process.[20] Mann carefully emphasizes the similarities of the former three—grotesque, threatening physiognomy, red hair, odd teeth, uncertain nationality, mysterious appearance and disappearance. These three—and the other characters too—disconcert Aschenbach, and the composite role enforces an awareness that these troubling momentary encounters are part of a single, gradual awakening to his inner life forces. Each of the figures plays an important part in the story (Britten gives them a roughly similar five-note motif—EX. 2). The

Example 2

Traveler evokes the initial consciousness of "widening inward barriers" that leads to the first exotic vision and subsequent travel plans. In the opera The Traveler himself is given lines describing Aschenbach's jungle vision. A musical figure recurrent in Britten's music that combines a major third and a minor third is introduced at the phrase "Marvels unfold" (EX. 3). This becomes, in later orchestral

Example 3

transformations, symbolic of the epidemic: the marvel unfolding for Aschenbach is life—and death. The Elderly Fop (with his gaudy falsetto vocal leaps of the ninth and eleventh interval) is a hint of the novelist's own later transformation. He also foreshadows Aschenbach's growing self-disgust. Mann's purposes are perhaps most obvious on the gondola trip:

> The strange craft, an entirely unaltered survival from the times of balladry, with that peculiar blackness which is found elsewhere only in coffins—it suggests silent, criminal adventures in the rippling night, it suggests even more strongly death itself, the bier and the mournful funeral, and the last silent journey. [30-31]

The dirge underlining this scene in the opera and the Gondolier's words, "Nobody shall bid me," make clear that behind the impassive mask is another face of death. The Hotel Manager and Barber serve, for their own venal purposes, to keep Aschenbach at his ease. Like them, the Leader of the Players lies about the cholera. This last figure —the most carefully worked out in the story with his equivocal appearance, vicious and aggressive carriage, mocking laughter—in effect nearly unmasks Mann's thematic purposes. The vulgar subject-matter that Britten and Piper give to the strolling singers, incidentally, is "pointed" at Aschenbach's dilemma. When next we hear the baritone voice, it is etherealized: Aschenbach's final traumatic breakdown comes in his dream, so it is appropriate that the voice that has followed him should appear now—as the voice of Dionysus.

The amalgamation of these figures was a particularly happy inspiration. Aside from the elegance of the economy, it emphasizes the story's haunting unity and fatal momentum. *Der Tod in Venedig* mixes ironic-demonic playfulness (a Nietzschean effect achieved largely by means of the surrounding characters) with a tragic recognition of personal failure (focused in Aschenbach). That these two aspects of the story are balanced in two continuously interacting vocal roles is perhaps most responsible for the opera's finely weighed balance of irony and tragedy—the very balance Thomas Mann said he had striven for in his story.

Britten's opera will doubtless please those most who esteem Mann's novella. It not only captures the essentials but also fills the gaps that prose, however fine, cannot fill: the glorious lyric opening-out as Aschenbach first looks across the sea from his hotel room, the climactic moment of repose and death at the end, and, in general, the sheer "magical" atmosphere of Aschenbach's entire "belated adventure of the emotions." It will please Mann's readers most—and those who prefer their opera full of orchestral panoply, unsubtle vigor, and melodic richness least—because it is a thinking man's opera. Its methods are spare, transparent, and articulate. Britten's works have always been notable for their artistic economy: among them *Death in Venice* is perhaps the supreme example of this. Theodor Adorno has written derisively of the "triumphant meagerness of Benjamin Britten." If we soften meagerness to simplicity, masterfully controlled understatement, then the opera is indeed a triumph. Nietzsche observed that "the greatest events—those are not our loudest but our stillest hours." This certainly applies to *Der Tod in Venedig*. It is a mark of Britten's loyalty to the Mann story that its greatest moments—Tadzio's first entrance, Aschenbach's apostrophe at the end of Act I, the Phaedrus monologue in Scene 16, and the death scene (marked "always *pianissimo*")—are not its loudest but its stillest.

AFTERWORD: THE CRISIS OF MODERN OPERA

In 1962 Samuel Beckett wrote a short radio play entitled *Words and Music*. It has three characters: Music (played by a small orchestra), Words, and a controlling figure called Croak. The tone of the play is acrimonious, for it turns out that Words and Music have considerable trouble "getting together." The imbroglio of Beckett's play reflects the crisis of modern opera itself. Music is confronted, for instance, with utterly unmusical and pedestrian subject matter, next with a running-at-the-mouth, then with philosophical bombast, and finally with an inert, cryptic text. Croak finally disappears in anguish, and the play ends as Words utters a "deep sigh"—one imagines it is a sigh of disgust and unfulfillment. Beckett's pessimistic vision of the delicate relationship between words and music aptly opens the question, how is opera faring in the realms of modern music and literature? Or, as composer Ned Rorem has phrased it: is there room for just plain opera?

To find an answer necessarily brings us back to the question: What is operatic? The eighteenth-century musician Pierre-Jean Joubert may have hit upon the simple answer when he observed that the lyre is a winged instrument and must transport. The same can be said of opera, which requires from its literary sources the quality of transport or "wing"—be it a poetic surge in the language itself, eloquent characters, lyrical human predicaments, or overarching symbolic forces. It is the quality of wing that makes the translation from word into music not merely plausible but artistically profitable.

Unhappily, modern composers have not found modern literature congenial for their purposes. One looks in vain for operas that combine modern masterpieces and genuinely avant-garde compositional techniques. W. H. Auden called opera librettos the last refuge of the high style, and it does seem as if those qualities of grandeur that lend themselves naturally to operatic emphasis have atrophied in this century. We are living in a "leveling period," and this leveling down to the common reality and "prose" of life, along with a consequent fear of the altitudes of high tragedy and fear of the heroic (all staples of opera in its nineteenth-century heyday), has resulted in literary weather inclement for opera.

In the forties Wallace Stevens looked about him and complained that "the idea of nobility exists in art today only in degenerate forms or in a diminished state, if, in fact, it exists at all."[1] This situation resulted from the immense negative vitality this century has manifested in the arts—a zest for dismantlement and devaluation, denial and detachment. In Joyce's *Ulysses* the noble style became the object of parody, and in its place Joyce relied upon informal, popular, substandard speech. His *Finnegans Wake* will always stand as the monumental reduction of language to its sub-syntactical, subliminal state. Beckett has likewise almost single-handedly whittled the theatrical event down to its barest essentials with such plays as *Act without Words* (calling solely for mime), *Not I* (focusing only on a mouth that disgorges a rapid-fire monologue), and *Breath* (lasting exactly thirty-five seconds and dispensing altogether with actors and words). In painting Bracque, Picasso, and eventually Pollock—among others—abandoned perspective and the niceties of spatial composition, just as the composers of the second Viennese school—Schoenberg, Berg, Webern—unhinged music from traditional harmonic and melodic traditions in the name of formal purity. The atmosphere of this century, to speak generally, has seemed to favor the smaller over the larger than life, realism over romanticism, non-heroes over anti-heroes and heroes. The overwhelming urge has been deflationary. This trend is not salutary for opera. Opera is essentially an inflationary and elevating art form and requires a certain altitude in order to take wing. Unfortunately for composers of opera, many of the most important modern authors are distinctly afraid of heights.

The musical avant-garde also presents a bleak picture. Between the Scylla of random composition and the Charybdis of "*musique concrète*" and computer-generated sound, the operatic art-form has had a perilous voyage. Or one might look at it as no voyage at all, for it tests the imagination to think of successful opera by a Webern, Varèse, Partch, Messiaen, Cage, Babbitt, Boulez, Crumb, or Stockhausen. Composers preoccupied with the deployment of sound-materials rather than notes, with exhaustive taxation of our capacity to listen, with exploration of a sound-world rather than a human world—such composers are unlikely to find opera congenial. Stravinsky observed of that crucial avant-garde figure Webern, "if you are seeking strange gods you might do worse than continue to revere St. Anton."[2] It often sounds to the listener as though modern composers do indeed worship strange gods. Unfortunately, such men do not produce viable opera, a genre ruled by more traditional deities—in particular those two concepts anathematized by the avant-garde, rhythm and melody.

Drama has historically been the genre upon which operatic composers have most depended, and a survey of the postwar dramatic terrain makes clear just how infertile it is for operatic purposes. And —what is perhaps not so surprising when one thinks about it—the non- or anti-operatic qualities of the modern theatrical mainstream are often paralleled by adverse characteristics of the musical avant-garde. What has been called the "de-theatricalization" of the theater has been to some degree mirrored in the reluctance of major modern composers to create the gestures and intelligible plotlines that are necessary for sustained theatrical interest. Ernst Krenek has seen in this trend a "depersonalization of the act of composing." Pierre Boulez approvingly calls it a "search for anonymity."

Just as the concept of the well-made play now seems passé, so traditional musical forms apparently are out of favor. Boulez has declared: "I want the musical work not to be that series of compartments which one must inevitably visit one after another; I try to think of it as a domain in which, in some manner, one can choose one's own directions."[3] This central axiom of the "new" music expresses a bias in favor of the aleatory and opposed to the plotted and composed. This bias has made opera, necessarily tied to plot, a derelict genre for the most significant modern composers. The hauteur of Boulez speaks for all of them: "I stay outside the theater . . . operatic gestures excuse nothing." Those recent composers who have achieved a measure of success with opera tend in fact to be ones who are outsiders in the eyes of the avant-garde: Orff, Thomson, Britten, von Einem, Floyd, Henze, Menotti.

The effect of much postwar drama can be summarized in the process—one quickly senses its adverse implications for opera—of *de*composition. The process arose partially out of the effects of existentialist philosophy, with its presumption that human experience is fundamentally disconnected, and the absurdist theater, with its rejection of cause-and-effect logic and linguistic normality. Playwrights began to develop a taste for ellipsis and a preference for anonymity. Concepts of plot, character development, and realistic dialogue lost hold, along with the proscenium arch, "settings," curtains, or act-scene divisions. The dramatist's quest became a highly negating effort. Critics could thus begin writing of the "logic of denial," the "disavowal of identity," the "aesthetics of silence," and the "poetics of stasis." The famous line from *Waiting for Godot*—"Nothing happens, nobody comes, nobody goes, it's awful."—could stand as a motto for some of the most important modern drama.

In many of the important plays of our time the themes of attrition, stalemate, waiting, retreat, and stasis are central: O'Neill's *The Iceman Cometh,* Stoppard's *Rosencrantz and Guildenstern are Dead,* Pirandello's *Six Characters in Search of an Author,* Albee's *All Over,* Ionesco's *The Chairs,* and Beckett's *Happy Days,* to name just a few. Maeterlinck was of course the first to explore immobility dramatically in *Pélleas et Mélisande,* and Debussy made perhaps the sole effective translation of the power of inertia into operatic form. But it is difficult to imagine a theatrically engaging opera that would issue from drama focusing on the tedium and purposelessness of existence.

Such drama must avoid the eloquence of character and situation that is almost always the igniting spark of successful opera. "All life long," says Clov in Beckett's *Endgame,* "the same inanities": such is a major theme, even obsession of modern dramatists. This is not material on which the expansive art-form of opera is nourished. Modern dramatists tend to look through the wrong end of the telescope: they see man smaller than he is. Operatic composers and their librettists, on the other hand, have always tended to look through the end of the telescope which enlarges.

If one characterizes Beckett as representing a number of those stylistic traits that one instinctively feels are subversive of opera, then his musical counterpart is Anton Webern. Webern's aesthetic could not be less operatic. His music is extraordinarily lean and condensed. Indeed, his entire life's work barely fills three long-playing records, and only one piece lasts more than ten minutes. Stravinsky found his art "essentially static" and "wholly unrhetorical." There is in his music no gesture for his audience; it is strictly speaking neither expressive nor communicative, for Webern found alien the exaggerated gesture required by opera. His postwar disciples have carried music even further in this anti-operatic direction. The avoidance of musical effects that can produce a dramatic "shock of recognition" in the listening audience is a tendency shared by many prominent exponents of modern music. One might say that, instead of establishing or regaining that common ground between composer and listener/viewer upon which theatrical, operatic life is supportable, modern composers have displayed a more scientific, a colder exploratory bent. For them sound *is* something; it cannot *be* and also *express* at the same time. And so John Cage is compelled to warn the composer to "let sounds be themselves rather than vehicles for man-made theories or expressions of human sentiments." The composer who follows this advice will, one fervently hopes, never attempt to write opera.

The acoustic unknown beckons the avant-garde. Their concern is for what Boulez has called "the unexploited worlds in one's ear." Ear, not mind. One cannot help feeling—when Boulez goes on to say that "We are at the edge of an unheard-of sound-world rich in possibilities and still practically unexplored."—that the human arena, the operatic arena, has been left behind. Explorations into "pure" *vocalise,* verbal collages, fragmented syllables, onomatopoeia, and electronic distortions of the voice are simply not enough for opera. It is a truism among the musical avant-garde that the purpose of hearing music is to enlarge the capacity to listen, and works like Cage's *Aria* (1958) and Luciano Berio's *Visage* (1961) are the result. Operatic music, however, cannot merely explore sonic landscapes, cannot merely sharpen our auditory sophistication. It must also provide a means for exploring the human situation. The musical avant-garde on the whole has been unable to produce music that can effectively accompany such exploration, at least in an operatic context.

A literary source, if it is to serve as a libretto, must provide living-space for music "between the lines," and one abundant quality in modern theater is open space—silence—that might plausibly be filled by music. Beckett's dialogue is shot through with the "pause" stage direction, and it is now a critical cliché that the tension and richness of Harold Pinter's plays derive from the balloons of silence that keep his desiccated dialogue airborne. Dramatic silence of this kind, however, provides no breathing-room for opera; it creates an atmosphere too heavy with metaphysical implications, too elliptical and oblique to produce flesh-and-blood characters—characters who might conceivably sing. The dramatic orchestration of silence is paralleled in the methods of Webern, as Boulez describes them: "Webern accords great importance not only to the register in which a given sound is located, but also to its temporal position in the unfolding of the work, a sound enclosed by silences acquiring by that isolation a much stronger significance than a sound in the matrix of an immediate context . . . He aerates his positionings in time and space."[4] Without change, this could describe the dramaturgy of Beckett or Pinter. Webern's music, like their dialogue, seems "to float in isolation between frightening airpockets of total silence."[5]

This pursuit of silence has been carried to extraordinary lengths in the theater and in music: Beckett's *Act without Words* and Cage's *4′ 33″* (his notorious "Silent Sonata" in which the pianist appears, sits at the instrument for the specified time, then departs without having played a note). The point of these not-so-idle jokes is a serious one: silence is just as important an entity as sound.[6] Nevertheless, when it is too abstractly conceived it is not of much use in the operatic idiom. Silence is the logical conclusion of many prominent modern literary themes—impotence, inarticulateness, boredom, and depression. For many modern writers, as for T. S. Eliot, "Words, after speech, reach / Into the silence." Much they have produced reaches into silence, not into music.

Another general feature of postwar drama that discourages operatic translation is a climate of indirection and metaphysical complexity. We find plays filled not so much with characters, plot, and meaningful dialogue as with philosophical, linguistic, and symbolic contrivances. Martin Esslin, speaking of *Endgame* and *Waiting for Godot* in his *Theater of the Absurd,* makes this point: "They lack both characters and plot in the conventional sense because they tackle their subject-matter at a level where neither characters nor plot exist." Behind the studied inarticulateness of much modern drama is metaphysical stalemate, intentional ambiguity or merely confused thought; it is often exceedingly difficult simply deciding what a given work is about. Such are the plays—some of them like Chinese puzzle boxes—of Pinter, Arden, Albee, and Stoppard. One consequence of such equivocation is bound to be a weakening of sheer dramatic force and narrative tautness.

Highly cerebral drama poorly suits the necessities of the operatic stage. As René Char has observed: "No bird has the heart to sing in a thicket of questions." Nor has the typical operatic character. Music cannot express ideas or conceptual states; it can cope but poorly with the intricate paradox of a Pirandello, the metaphysical mystification of a *Tiny Alice,* or the profound ambiguity of a typical Pinter piece. Opera is strongly tied to human character and human action, which must somehow issue in the motivation to "break into" vocal utterance. But dramatists of abstraction, discussion, and philosophical excursion care more about developing ideas than vital stage figures. For them an element of stasis is salutary: "What a curse, mobility!" says Winnie in Beckett's *Happy Days*. Eric Salzman has described the music of Messiaen as "built, like that of Varèse, in densities and in static volumes of revolving (not evolving) sound,"[7] and this might be applied to many of today's play-conundrums. The result is a theater of non-events, non-persons, and non-plots—not a very likely atmosphere in which to find that human wilfullness and variety of which opera is a celebration.

The cerebral and abstract have also appeared ascendant in recent music—partially the result of serialism and computer techniques and partially because, as Rorem has observed, there are now many "verbal musicians who think music more than they feel it." Just as modern dramatists have rejected the normalities of plot and character development, modern composers have rejected traditional compositional strategies, notational systems, designated pitches, rhythmic devices, and musical instruments. And just as dramatists, following Brecht, have rejected through various alienating methods the bond between characters and audience, so any number of modernist composers have rejected the kind of rhetoric and gesture that is necessary for the operatic event.

Such composers are unwilling to address themselves to a central practical problem: namely, how to hold the interest of an audience over an evening. Virgil Thomson summarizes the difficulty of modern music as a theatrical vehicle with his usual directness in a discussion of the music of Cage:

> What his kaleidoscopes and arabesques lack is urgency. They can hold the attention but they do not do it consistently. The most dependable device for holding attention is a "theme" or story, the clear attachment of art patterns to such common human bonds as sex and sentiment. How far an artist goes in this direction, or in the opposite, is up to him. "Abstraction" in art is nothing more than the avoidance of a clear and necessary attachment to subject matter. It is ever a salutary element in art, because it clears the mind of sex and sentiment. Only briefly, however, because the human mind can always find ways of getting these back into the picture.[8]

Opera demands a "clear and necessary attachment" between the musical, verbal, and human levels of the work. Carl Orff, whose vocal works have proved among the most attractive and engaging theatrical events, has gone further and expressed what will always be the single most important credo for the successful opera composer: "Melody and speech belong together; I reject the idea of pure music."

Postwar dramatists have largely failed the operatic composer in another important respect, that of characterization. Most estimable operas draw their strength from strong as well as strongly developed characters—figures like Dido, Don Giovanni, Lady Macbeth, Isolde, Salome, or Peter Grimes. But there are relatively few such roles among the prominent plays of recent decades. Bred from a cynical view of human nature and a low estimate of man's ability to communicate, many modern protagonists display mediocre, low-grade mentalities. Those heightening reverberations that give a character, however ignoble his circumstances (one thinks of Wozzeck), plausible operatic dimension seldom vitalize modern plays. Where operatic characters tend to be writ large, many contemporary dramatic characters are writ small. The hero of John Osborne's *Inadmissible Evidence* calls himself "irredeemably mediocre," and this phrase might apply to Willie Loman, Rosencrantz and Guildenstern, all of Beckett's down-at-the-heel solipsists, as well as many of the personae of Albee, Pinter, Arden, Storey, and Miller.

When stage characters become too obviously part of a cerebral puppet show, they will somehow lack the spiritual exaltation or lyric core for which a composer must find a musical equivalent. These characters may be decked out in lavish philosophical costume, they may be charged with symbolic tensions, but if they do not have a compelling flesh-and-blood dimension, they will very likely remain operatically inert. That is why it is not easy to find protagonists in the historically important plays of recent years whose utterances might sound plausible on the operatic stage. The mind's ear cannot hear them sing.

One further characteristic of modern drama that discourages operatic transformation needs mention: the tendency for language to lose its transparency as a communicative medium and become itself an object of scrutiny. Playwrights often seem preoccupied, in Eliot's words, by "the intolerable wrestle/With words and meanings"—to the exclusion of real human beings and significant human actions. They eagerly denigrate the romantic, flourishing language of the last century, as well as the language of everyday speech. The result is a word-conscious, word-weaving, and word-assailing drama. Characters caught in verbal labyrinths (as often in Stoppard), spouting ready-made, lifeless words (as in Ionesco), or saddled by a language that decomposes practically as it is spoken (Beckett and Feiffer)—such characters are unlikely to produce the theatrical momentum we associate with memorable operatic roles.

Opera is likewise uncomfortable in the presence of literature where stylistic technique and linguistic manipulation are observable. Here the author's eloquence overwhelms that of his characters. Language subsumes character, plot, and psychology; language itself becomes the protagonist. The operatic composer, who must finally work from human rather than conceptual or syntactic materials, is at a disadvantage in such drama where linguistic devices, strategies, and games carry the action.

To sum up, those qualities on which, in varying combinations, opera thrives are not found in abundance on the modern stage, or indeed in modern literature generally: lyric expansiveness, extensive narrative vigor, implicit or explicit largeness of scale, impressive individuality of character, passionate force, psychological focus, and directness of impact. Instead we have what Eric Bentley has called the "little, twitching plays of today"—serious yet unexalted, steeped in ambiguity, lacking emotional breadth or depth, populated by faceless and bloodless personages, cynical, anchorite, reductive. In short, plays that are operatically inanimate.

In view of all this one cannot help feeling that opera is an endangered species if it must depend upon alliances between modern composers and dramatists in order to survive. Though, of course, it may survive through recourse to reactionary or "neo-Classical" compositional methods and to time-honored literary masterpieces. The careers of two composers—one an operatic elder statesman, the other young and prolific—tend to bear out one's fears.

No one in this century has proved as perspicacious and successful a musical translator of literature as Benjamin Britten. His name, among modern composers, stands perhaps the best chance of maintaining a hold in the standard repertory. But, just as Britten in his personal life rejected the essentially urban culture of his time and secluded himself on the Suffolk coast, so did he ignore modern literary culture in his search for operatic inspiration. He turned instead to Shakespeare, Crabbe, de Maupaussant, Melville, Henry James. His most nearly contemporary source, Mann's *Der Tod in Venedig*, was published in 1912.

The case of Thomas Pasatieri (b. 1945) is intriguing because he is, among composers of his generation, almost uniquely committed to writing for the lyric stage and also successful in gaining good artistic conditions for his premieres. Yet he too has shown a clearly antiquarian instinct in his choice of librettos: *Black Widow* (Unamuno), *Signor Deluso* (Molière), *Ines de Castro* (fourteenth-century Portuguese story), *The Seagull* (Chekhov), and *Washington Square* (James). Is it coincidence or, as I fear, conscious artistic choice that has led Pasatieri to avoid a modern source?

What passes now for opera that is truly modernist in musical style and libretto? Very little, to judge from the world premieres of the last decade or so.[9] Represented among these new works are all the great world dramatists: Euripides, Aristophanes, Shakespeare, Jonson, Racine, Ibsen, Wilde, Synge. But modern dramatists turn up rarely. There is Ward's opera based on Miller's *Crucible,* Lee Hoiby's setting of *Summer and Smoke,* Argento's *Krapp's Last Tape.* Weisgall's *Six Characters in Search of an Author,* and Villa-Lobos's version of Lorca's *Yerma* are at best borderline "modernist" collaborations. I doubt that any of these will escape oblivion.

To make matters worse, American opera has always shown a strong nostalgic bent. Witness such titles as *The Mighty Casey* (Schuman), *Lizzie Borden* (Beeson), *The Ballad of Baby Doe* (Moore), *The Jumping Frog of Calaveras County* (Lukas Foss), and *The Mother of Us All* (Thomson). The epidemic of Bicentennialitis in 1976 served only to heighten the reactionary preoccupations of native composers. But there are glimmers for those who hope for successful modernist opera: Conrad Susa's setting of Anne Sexton in his *Transformations;* the premiere of Andrew Imbrie's new opera based on Wallace Stegner's *Angle of Repose;* Leon Kirchner struggling for ten years with Bellow's *Henderson the Rain King*. It is still not enough.

Elsewhere in the world the situation is likewise disturbing. Again the sources of inspiration read like a roll-call in the Pantheon: Chaucer, Shakespeare, Racine, Milton, Defoe, Dostoevsky, Flaubert, Ibsen, and so on. Particularly disconcerting are current projects of certain composers whose idioms would seem apt for much modern literature. Alan Hovhaness preparing a *Pericles* opera on an NEA grant; Krzysztof Penderecki commissioned by the Chicago Opera to do a *Paradise Lost;* György Ligeti writing yet another *Oedipus* for the Stockholm Opera. Though one awaits these works with interest, they are indicative of current opera's reactionary bent. Of settings for living authors of some reputation, well, there are virtually none to speak of. For operatic composers and librettists, contemporary literature lies down the path not taken.

This is not to imply that genuinely modernist operas would necessarily be better than operas in which contemporary composers set old masters. In this there is no good and bad; as Rossini long ago pointed out, the only crucial distinction is between interesting and boring opera. Still, I believe contemporary opera is failing us when it ignores the literary creations of our own time. I am concerned to find out—and only time will tell—whether this current impasse between music and literature is a fact of modern artistic life to which we must become accustomed or a phenomenon that will pass and lead to a brighter future. Perhaps it will require a major change in literary fashion—away from the status quo—to make a "contemporary" nexus between literature and music possible.

The epithet *operatic* is not a complimentary one to modern writers. One of the most operatic of modern playwrights, Tennessee Williams, was crushed when his literary agent rejected *The Rose Tattoo* because "it was material for an opera, not a play." Whether this negative connotation will last is impossible to say. One can at least venture that the atmosphere for opera will not improve so long as we continue to live in fear of what Nietzsche called "the *lie* of the great style." Opera as a genre depends unavoidably on the grand style, the elevated gesture, and resounding utterance. So long as dramatists and composers mistrust these effects—and this mistrust is general today—opera will remain a troubled art-form.

LITERATURE AS OPERA: A SYMPOSIUM

It is not possible to transform any sort of play into opera without modifying it, disturbing it, corrupting it more or less. I know this. But there are many intelligent ways to prosecute this task of profanation [*ce travail profanateur*] that is imposed by musical exigencies.

> Hector Berlioz, Review of *I Capuleti e i Montecchi* by Bellini, in *A travers Chants* (1862; reprint 1970), p. 317.

In Spiritual Harangues, the Disposition of the Words according to the Art of Grammar, hath not the least Use, but the Skill and Influence wholly lye in the Choice and Cadence of the Syllables; Even as a discreet *Composer,* who in setting a Song, changes the Words and Order so often, that he is forced to make it *Nonsense,* before he can make it *Musick.*

> Jonathan Swift, *A Discourse Concerning the Mechanical Operation of the Spirit* (1710), *Prose Works* (1939; reprint 1965), Vol. 1, p. 182.

What the librettist needs is a command, not of great poetry, but of operatic dramaturgy . . . Great poetry set to music is not an ideal recipe for opera, in fact there is no great dramatic poetry written that operatic music would not ruin.

> Eric Bentley, *The Dramatic Event* (1954), pp. 235-36.

Instead of the mere opera-making musician, tied to his poem as to a stake, and breaking loose whenever it gives him an excuse for a soldiers' chorus, or a waltz, or a crashing finale, we have [in Gluck] the poet-musician who has no lower use for music than the expression of poetry.

> George Bernard Shaw, *The World,* 12 November 1890, in *Shaw on Music* (1955), p. 65.

What then is the Composer, who would aim at true musical Expression, to perform? I answer, he is to blend such an happy Mixture of Air and Harmony, as will affect us most strongly with the Passions or Affections which the Poet intends to raise: and that, on this Account, he is not principally to dwell on particular Words in the Way of Imitation, but to comprehend the Poet's general Drift or Intention, and on this to form his Airs and Harmony, either by Imitation (so far as Imitation may be proper to this End) or by any other Means. But this I must still add, that if he attempts to raise the Passions by Imitation, it must be such a temperate and chastised Imitation, as rather brings the Object before the Hearer, than such a one as induces him to form a Comparison between the Object and the Sound. For, in this last Case, his Attention will be turned entirely on the Composer's Art, which must effectually check the Passion. The Power of Music is, in this Respect, parallel to the Power of Eloquence: if it works at all, it must work in a secret and unsuspected Manner.

Charles Avison, *An Essay on Musical Expression* (1753), p. 69.

I consider the subject too slight, too thin for a spoken play—it is predestined for a libretto.

Richard Strauss, Letter to Hugo von Hofmannsthal, 6 July 1908, *Correspondence Between Richard Strauss and Hugo von Hofmannsthal 1908-1917*, tr. Paul England (1927), p. 17.

[The composer's] success lies less in comprehending the words he is setting than in feeling them musically, and in being able to convince us of the necessity of his feeling.

Ned Rorem, *Pure Contraption* (1974), p. 7.

He [Beethoven] tried to think in music, almost to reason in music; whereas perhaps we should be contented with *feeling* in it. It can never speak very definitely. There is that famous "Holy, Holy, Lord God Almighty, etc.," in Handel: nothing can sound more simple and devotional: but it is only lately adapted to these words, being originally (I believe) a love song in *Rodelinda*. Well, lovers adore their mistresses more than their God. Then the famous music of "He layeth the beams of his chambers in the waters, etc.," was originally fitted to an Italian pastoral song—"Nasce al bosco in rozza cuna, un felice pastorello, etc." That part which seems so well to describe "and walketh on the wings of the wind" falls happily in with "e con l'aura di fortuna" with which this pastorello sailed along. The character of the music is ease and largeness: as the shepherd lived, so God Almighty walked on the wind. The music breathes ease: but words must tell us who takes it easy.

Edward FitzGerald, Letter to F. Tennyson,
31 March 1842, *Works* (1902; reprint 1966),
Vol. 1, p. 133.

Late-romantic opera liquefies words, drowning them in the passionate inarticulacy of music.

Peter Conrad, *Times Literary Supplement*
23 July 1976, p. 920.

The duration prescribed for a stage performance by general usage, and the given number of roles to which one is confined by the same, as well as several other considerations of prudence, of costume, of place, and public, constituted the reasons why I have not made a translation of that excellent comedy [*Le Mariage de Figaro*], but rather an imitation, or let us say an extract.

Lorenzo Da Ponte, Preface to the
original libretto, *Le Nozze di Figaro*.

The Numbers of Poetry and Vocal Musick are sometimes so contrary, that in many places I have been obliged to cramp my Verses, and make them rugged to the Reader, that they may be harmonious to the Hearer: Of which I have no Reason to repent me, because these sorts of Entertainment are principally design'd for the Ear and Eye; and therefore in Reason my Art, on this occasion, ought to be subservient to his [Purcell's].

John Dryden, Letter of dedication for Henry Purcell's *King Arthur* (1691).

Only—that independence claimed by the literary conception, how to maintain it in alliance with that of musical form, which is nothing but *convention?*—you yourself used the word! For if one must obey the sense of complete logic, it goes without saying that when speaking, one does not sing; an angry man, a conspirator, a jealous man does not sing! An exception, perhaps for lovers, whom, in a strict sense, one can have *coo* . . . But even more forceful: does one go to one's death singing? *Convention* in opera, then, from beginning to end.

Gioacchino Rossini, conversing with Richard Wagner, *Rossini's Visit With Wagner,* Edmond Michotte, tr. Herbert Weinstock (1968), p. 60.

What is bad literature (or poetry) may be good libretto language.

Donald Grout, *A Short History of Opera* (1965), p. 5.

The very title of this work suggests that it is not based on the principal theme of Goethe's *Faust,* since Faust is saved in that illustrious poem. The author of *La Damnation de Faust* has merely borrowed from Goethe a certain number of scenes whose attraction upon his mind proved irresistible, and which suited the plan he had devised. But granted he had been faithful to Goethe's idea, he would still have incurred the reproach of having disfigured a monument which already has been leveled at him (and partly with bitterness) by several individuals.

Actually it is common knowledge that it is impracticable to set to music a poem of some length, not written for the express purpose of being sung, without subjecting it to numerous changes. And of all the dramatic poems in existence *Faust* is certainly the least suited to be sung integrally from beginning to end. But if, in preserving the theme of Goethe's *Faust,* one must change that masterpiece in a hundred different ways in order to render it suitable for composition, the capital crime against genius is just as apparent in this as in the other and, accordingly, merits equal reprobation.

It follows, then, that composers should be forbidden to choose famous poems as subjects for composition. We would thus be deprived of Mozart's *Don Giovanni,* whose libretto is Da Ponte's adaptation of Molière's *Don Juan*. Nor would we possess *Le Nozze di Figaro,* whose librettist has hardly respected Beaumarchais's comedy, *Il Barbiere di Siviglia* (for the same reason), or Gluck's *Alceste,* which is a somewhat crude paraphrase of Euripides' tragedy. The same applies to Gluck's *Iphigénie en Aulide,* in making which one has uselessly marred certain of Racine's verses which, with their spotless beauty, would have perfectly suited the recitatives. The numerous operas based on Shakespeare's plays would have remained unwritten.

Hector Berlioz, Preface to *La Damnation de Faust* (1846), in Weisstein, pp. 210-11.

To me, the all-important condition is the choice of a libretto. While for drama there are boundless possibilities of material, it seems that for opera the only suitable subjects are such as could not exist or reach complete expression without music—which demand music and only become complete through it.

Ferruccio Busoni, "The Essence and Oneness of Music" (1921), in *The Essence of Music and Other Writings* (1957), p. 7.

Operatic conventions are not necessarily anti-dramatic, but they are anti-literary.

> Paul Henry Lang, "The Composer," in
> *Man Versus Society in 18th-Century Britain*,
> ed. James Clifford (1968), p. 92.

Musick, Architecture, and Painting, as well as Poetry and Oratory, are to deduce their Laws and Rules from the general Sense and Taste of Mankind, and not from the Principles of those Arts themselves; or in other Words, the Taste is not to conform to the Art, but the Art to the Taste. Musick is not design'd to please only Chromatick Ears, but all that are capable of distinguishing harsh from agreeable Notes. A Man of an ordinary Ear is a Judge whether a Passion is expressed in proper Sounds, and whether the Melody of those Sounds be more or less pleasing.

> Joseph Addison, *Spectator* No. 29 (3 April
> 1711), ed. Donald Bond (1965), Vol. 1, p. 123.

Ludwig: Why did you refuse, at the time when we shared the same artistic ideals, to write the libretto I so ardently desired?

Ferdinand: Because I consider it to be the least rewarding of all tasks. You must admit that nobody is more stubborn in his demands than you composers. And if you claim that one cannot impose upon the musician to acquire the mechanical skill required for versification, I maintain that the poet is greatly handicapped by having to consider your needs, the structure of your trios, quartets, finales, etc., in order not to sin every moment—as is frequently the case—against the forms cherished by you with goodness knows what justification. When we have striven ever so hard to give the proper poetic expression to every portion of our work, and paint each situation in glowing words and charming, smoothly running verses, it is frightful to see how mercilessly you obliterate our finest lines and mangle our best verses by twisting, inverting, or drowning them in music. This much about the vain attempt to work out details carefully. And how many admirable subjects which we have conceived in a state of poetic frenzy and offered to you in the hope that they will satisfy your demands, you reject as being unsuited to and unworthy of musical treatment. Often this is sheer obstinacy on your part. For frequently you settle on texts that are of the poorest caliber.

E. T. A. Hoffmann, *The Poet and the Composer* (1816), in Weisstein, p. 169.

It is very gratifying to know that you have so high an opinion of my poetic diction, but we must not expect too much from poetic diction alone. "There is nothing in the skin," says Goethe somewhere, "but what was bred in the bone." If the framework failed to satisfy your imagination, no poetic text would suffice, by itself, to attract and inspire you—this must always be borne in mind.

Hugo von Hofmannsthal, Letter to Richard Strauss, 25 May 1911, *Correspondence Between Richard Strauss and Hugo von Hofmannsthal 1907-1918,* tr. Paul England (1927), p. 111.

A compelling opera can be made to an "inanimate" libretto if the composer discovers the right tone, as Debussy with *Pélleas,* or Thomson with *Four Saints,* white on white. But white on white was not proper, say, for *Summer and Smoke,* and Lee Hoiby's music vanished beneath Tennessee Williams' words.

Ned Rorem, *Pure Contraption* (1974), p. 79.

Music will express any emotion, base or lofty. She is absolutely unmoral.

George Bernard Shaw, *The World* 2 May 1894, in *Shaw on Music* (1955), p. 50.

Dramatic composers of my "manner" . . . I would recommend never to think of adopting a text before they see in it a plot, and characters to carry out this plot, that inspire the musician with a lively interest on some account or other. Then let him take a good look at the one character, for instance, which appeals to him the most this very day: bears it a mask—away with it; wears it a garment of a stage-tailor's dummy—off with it! Let him set it in a twilight spot, where he can merely see the gleaming of its eye; if that speaks to him, the shape itself will now most likely fall a-moving, which perhaps will even terrify him—but he must put up with that; at last its lips will part, it opens its mouth, and a ghostly voice breathes something quite distinct, intensely seizable, but so unheard-of (such as the "Guest of stone," and surely the page Cherubino, once said to Mozart) that—he wakes from out his dream. All has vanished; but in the spiritual ear it still rings on: he has had an "idea."

Richard Wagner, *On Operatic Poetry and Composition, Prose Works* (1892-99), ed. W. A. Ellis, Vol. VI, p. 170.

A librettist is always at a disadvantage because operas are reviewed, not by literary or dramatic critics, but by music critics whose taste and understanding of poetry may be very limited. What is worse, a music critic who wishes to attack the music but is afraid to do so directly, can always attack it indirectly by condemning the libretto. A librettist is at a further disadvantage because music is an international language and poetry a local one. Wherever an opera is performed, audiences hear the same music but, outside the country of its origin, either they hear alien words which are meaningless to them or a translation which, however good—and most translations are very bad—are not what the librettist wrote.

W. H. Auden, Review of *The Correspondence Between Richard Strauss and Hugo von Hofmannsthal,* reprinted in *Forewords and Afterwords* (1973), p. 349.

My labors are rendered a thousand times more distasteful still, in consequence of all the divers impediments to which I am subjected. To begin with, all Greek or Roman subjects are ruled out of court, since our chaste nymphs will in no wise countenance such improper costumes! I am obliged to resort to Oriental history, in order that all the noble ladies playing male parts may be duly and decently swaddled from head to foot in Asiatic draperies. Anything so bold as a contrast between vice and virtue is of necessity excluded from these dramas, because none of the ladies is prepared to play the part of a villainess. I may employ but five characters, for the excellent reason once given by the Governor of a certain stronghold, that it is impolitic to allow one's superiors to get lost in the crowd. The length of the performance, the number of scene-changes, the arias, everything, is laid down by immutable decree. Tell me, is this not sufficient to drive the most tractable of men into the pit of distraction?

Metastasio, Letter to a friend, quoted by
Stendhal in *Haydn, Mozart, and Metastasio*
(1814; tr. Richard Coe 1972), p. 235.

The mind has to relax from time to time. After the strenuous hours of business everybody follows his inclination when amusing himself. Some hunt, some drink, some play cards, and some busy themselves with intrigues. And I, who do not care for any of these things, write a modest opera.

Beaumarchais, Preface to *Tarare* (1790),
in Weisstein, p. 141.

Hence, the *genuine* Charm of Music, and the *Wonders* which it works, thro' its great Professors. A Power, which consists not in Imitations, and the raising *Ideas;* but in the raising *Affections,* to which Ideas may correspond. There are few to be found so insensible, I may even say so inhumane, as when GOOD POETRY IS JUSTLY SET TO MUSIC, not in some degree to feel the Force of so *amiable a Union.* But to the Muses' Friends it is a Force *irresistible,* and penetrates into the deepest Recesses of the Soul. . . . And farther, it is by the help of this Reasoning, that the *Objection* is solved, which is raised against the *Singing of Poetry* (as in Operas, Oratorios, &c.) from the want of *Probability* and *Resemblance to Nature.* To one indeed, who has no musical Ear, this Objection may have Weight. It may even perplex a Lover of Music, if it happen to surprise him in his Hours of Indifference. But when he is feeling the Charm of Poetry *so accompanied,* let him be angry (if he can) with that which serves only to interest him *more feelingly* in the Subject, and support him in a *stronger* and *more earnest* Attention; which enforces by its Aid the several Ideas of the Poem, and gives them to his Imagination with unusual Strength and Grandeur. He cannot surely but confess, that he is a *Gainer in the Exchange,* when he *barters* the want of a single Probability, that of *Pronunciation* (a thing merely arbitrary and every where different) for a *noble Heightening of Affections* which are suitable to the Occasion, and enable him to enter into the Subject with double *Energy* and *Enjoyment.*

James Harris, *A Discourse on Music, Painting, and Poetry* (1744; 1783 ed.), pp. 99-101.

NOTES

Chapter One

1. Joseph Desaymard, *Emmanuel Chabrier d'après ses lettres* (1934), p. 119. The letter was probably written in 1886.

2. Michel de Chabanon, *De la musique considerée en elle-même et dans ses rapports avec la parole, les langues, la poésie, et le théâtre* (1785), p. 6.

3. One good reason to avoid a law-giving approach to the question of what is operatic is simply that the legislative record of writers on opera is not very encouraging, even those writers who speak from practical experience. Consider these pronouncements: Wieland: "Plays whose action requires a lot of political arguments, or in which the characters are forced to deliver lengthy speeches in order to convince one another by the strength of their reasons or the flow of their rhetoric, should, accordingly, be altogether excluded from the lyrical stage."

Tchaikovsky: "Operatic style should be broad, simple, and decorative."

R. Strauss: "Once there's music in a work, I want to be the master, I don't want it to be subordinate to anything else. That's too humble. I don't say that poetry is inferior to music. But the true poetic dramas—Schiller, Goethe, Shakespeare—are self-sufficient; they don't need music."

Adorno: "It has never been possible for the quality of music to be indifferent to the quality of the text with which it is associated; works such as Mozart's *Così fan tutte* and Weber's *Euryanthe* try to overcome the weaknesses of their libretti through music but nevertheless are not to be salvaged by any literary or theatrical means."

All these statements have at least two things in common. First, they have much truth in them. Second, they have all been ignored—sometimes with conspicuous success. One could easily point to well-known repertory works to prove as well as disprove each of the above attempts to legislate the mercurial process of connecting words with music for theatrical purposes. In this realm of translation, as in other artistic realms, an aesthetic code is impracticable and even undesirable. Shaw made this point in *The Sanity of Art:* "The severity of artistic discipline is produced by the fact that in creative art no ready-made rules can help you. There is nothing to guide your own sense of beauty and fitness; and, as you advance upon those who went before you, that sense of beauty and fitness is necessarily often in conflict, not with fixed rules, but with precedents."

Gluck expressed a similar idea in his dedication for *Alceste* (1769): "I have not cherished the invention of novel devices except when they were demanded by the situation and the expression. There was, finally, no rule which I did not gladly violate for the sake of the intended effect."

4. The aesthetic of opera is remarkably like that of the modern Expressionist movement. If this passage on operatic style were not written by Diderot (in *Rameau's Nephew*), it could easily be taken as an Expressionist credo: "It is the animal cry of passion which ought to determine our course. These expressions must press hard upon each other . . . The passions must be strong, and the tenderness of both poet and composer extreme. The aria is almost always the peroration of a scene. We need exclamations, interjections, suspensions, interruptions, affirmations, and negations; we call, invoke, shout, weep,

cry, and laugh copiously. No wit, no epigrams, no subtle phrases—these are far removed from simple nature."

Diderot is here echoing Rousseau, who specified this "Expressionist theorem" in his article on opera in the *Dictionary of Music* (1764): "The force of all the emotions and the violence of all the passions are, then, the principal object of the lyrical drama."

5. George Bernard Shaw wrote in a review: "There are two extremes. One is to assume full dignity for the creative musician, and compose an independent overture which, however sympathetic it may be with the impending drama, nevertheless takes the forms proper to pure music, and is balanced and finished as a beautiful and symmetrical fabric of sounds, performable as plain Opus 1000 apart from the drama, as satisfactorily as the drama is performable apart from it . . . The other extreme is to supply bare *mélodrame,* familiar samples of which may be found in the ethereal strains of muted violins which accompany the unfolding of transformation scenes in pantomimes, the animated measures which enliven the rallies of harlequinades, or the weird throbbings of the ghost melody in *The Corsican Brothers.*"

6. The desire to capture speech patterns in the vocal line is a typically Eastern European trait (Mussorgsky's operas and those of Janáček especially) and was of course important for the eighteenth-century *tragédie lyrique* in France (Rameau's operas in particular). And this was the stated goal of Italian musical humanists—Monteverdi, Peri, Caccini.

7. Busoni wrote: "Goethe had thought of his second *Faust* half 'operatically.' He wished (it would seem from his communications) that the choruses should be *sung* throughout, and he expressed the opinion that it would be very difficult to perform Helena's part because it required a tragic actress as well as a prima donna."

8. "Certain great musicians—Haydn and Beethoven for example—possess a sense of drama, but they do not have a theatrical sense: sentiments quite distinct and utterly different." Paul Dukas, *L'Art de la musique* (Paris, 1961), p. 403.

9. "Some Reflections on Music and Opera," *Partisan Review,* Vol. XIX (1952). This article is reprinted in Weisstein.

10. Two instances of theory not coinciding with practice, in the cases of Wagner and Verdi, are explored by Jack Stein in *Richard Wagner and the Synthesis of the Arts* (1960), and Philip Gossett in "Verdi, Ghislanzoni, and *Aida:* The Uses of Convention," *Critical Quarterly,* Vol. I (December 1974), pp. 291-334.

Chapter Two

1. The finest book on Handel is Winton Dean's *Handel's Dramatic Oratorios and Masques* (1959). Dean's *Handel and the Opera Seria* (1969), the result of a series of university lectures, is naturally more cursory. A major study of Handel's operas, on which Dean is now working, has not yet appeared.

2. By 1725 one could write confidently about the "formula" for Italian

opera in England: "In England people like very few recitatives, thirty airs, and one duet at least distributed over the three acts. The subject must be simple, tender, heroic—Roman, Greek, or possibly Persian, but never Gothic or Lombard. For this year, and for the next two there must be two equal parts for Cuzzoni and Faustina. Senesino takes the principal male character and his part must be heroic." Giuseppe Riva, Modenese Ambassador in London, quoted by R. A. Streatfeild, "Handel, Rolli, and Italian Opera," *Musical Quarterly*, Vol. III (1917), p. 433. Stendhal gives a more elaborate description of the *opera seria* formula in *Haydn, Mozart and Metastasio* (1814; 1972 tr. Richard Coe), pp. 234-35.

3. Except perhaps for Benjamin Britten, no composer has served so successfully so many English literary figures as Handel: John Gay set the words for the exquisite pastoral *Acis and Galatea* (one of Handel's most popular works in his lifetime); Dryden's poetry provided the text for *Alexander's Feast* and the *Ode for Saint Cecilia's-Day;* Pope and Arbuthnot collaborated upon the words for the early oratorio *Esther;* Congreve wrote the libretto upon which *Semele* was eventually based; and Milton inspired two of Handel's supreme masterpieces, *L'Allegro and Il Penseroso* and *Samson.*

4. *Essays on Poetry and Music, as They Affect the Mind* (3rd ed., 1779), p. 56. "Musical expression was the expression of the passions of *men,* not of man. Hence the 'objectivity' that eighteenth-century musical expression, vocal or instrumental, seems to have. The doctrine of music as imitation and expression reflected the generalizing and universalizing aim of neo-Classical thought and art. The particular and the individual were to receive emphasis later, but for the time being the typical in human passion or even sentiment held full sway." Herbert Schueller, "'Imitation' and 'Expression' in British Music Criticism in the Eighteenth Century," *Musical Quarterly,* Vol. XXXIV (1958), p. 564.

5. *Several Letters Written by a Noble Lord to a Young Man at the University* (1716), p. 8; on Shaftesbury's ideas, see Stanley Grean, *Shaftesbury's Philosophy of Religion and Ethics* (1967).

6. *Sermons Preached upon Several Occasions* (1737), Vol. I, p. 59. In this matter, see Donald Greene's "Augustinianism and Empiricism: A Note on Eighteenth-Century English Intellectual History," *Eighteenth Century Studies,* Vol. I (1967), pp. 33-68. The thesis of this article is "that the dominant ethic of the intellectual life of eighteenth-century England . . . was one of disinhibition, of the release of human potential, emotional and intellectual, for good, the freeing of the human spirit from the bondage of the self and its narrow lusts and fears, the growth of the human capacity for awareness and feeling, for love and understanding" (p. 67). Handel's art has much to do with this ethic.

7. "The critical standards that governed the painting of passions were roughly the same for each of the major arts, though of course special conventions varied with the medium employed . . . Though there was no one official name for the technique of painting the passions, it was perhaps most frequently known as the Pathetic style; and its province was the whole scale of human affections." Brewster Rogerson, "The Art of Painting the Passions," *Journal of the History of Ideas,* Vol. XIV (1953), p. 68.

8. *Das Neu-eröffnete Orchestre* (1713), pp. 160-61. Among other things, Mattheson was the German translator of Mainwaring's first biography of Handel, Richardson's *Pamela,* and Defoe's *Moll Flanders*. He also founded the first German musical journal in 1722.

9. *Handel* (1909), p. 275. So apt is the metaphor to Handel's works that Streatfeild uses it on three other occasions: *Israel in Egypt:* "It is like a vast series of frescoes painted by a giant on the walls of some primeval temple" (278); *L'Allegro:* "a series of exquisite genre pictures sketched with the lightest touch and elaborated with the most intimate detail" (282); *Solomon:* "It is like a series of gorgeously coloured frescoes in some wondrous palace of the East" (319).

10. Handel collected paintings, one of which was a Rembrandt. Another important Handelian of this century, Romain Rolland, wrote often of Handel's pictorial powers (*Essays on Music,* pp. 231-33): "I do not know any great German musician who has been as much a visual as Handel . . . This evocatory character of Handel's genius should never be forgotten. He who is satisfied with listening to this music without *seeing* what it expresses . . . will never understand it. It is a music which paints emotions, souls, and situations . . . In a word, his is an art essentially picturesque and dramatic."

11. "On Modern Gardening" (1785), p. 537; in Walpole's *Works* (1798 ed.), Vol. II, pp. 517-47.

12. See Addison's *Spectator* on the subject (1 July 1712, No. 419). The English-reading public must have thought otherwise: by the mid-eighteenth century over sixty editions of *Orlando Furioso* had appeared in England.

One great man of the Age of Reason lived to recant his early dislike of Ariosto. "Once upon a time," wrote Voltaire, "I did not dare put Ariosto among the epic poets; I considered him only the first of the grotesques: but on re-reading him I have found him as sublime as he is agreeable." In 1761, at age 67, he wrote: "Ariosto is my god! All poems bore me but his. I did not love him enough in my youth; I did not know enough Italian. The Pentateuch and Ariosto are nowadays the enchantment of my life" (*Correspondence,* No. 8772).

13. John Lahr, *Astonish Me* (1973), p. 15.

14. It is not within the scope of the present chapter to examine the details of the reworking of the Ariosto episodes by Handel's librettists (only one—Antonio Salvi for *Ariodante*—is known). The relevant passages and major alterations from the original may be briefly noted:

Ariodante: (Canto IV.50-72; V; VI.1-16—130 stanzas) The action of Acts I and II of the opera is, in the original, related after the fact by Dalinda to Rinaldo; the opera, of course, makes all this "direct" action. The crucial acts performed by Rinaldo in the Ariosto denouement are divided between Lurcanio and Ariodante in Act III of the opera.

Orlando: (VIII.73ff; XIX.17-39; XXIII.97-133; XXX.7-9; XXXIV.65-85; XXXIX.44-61—115 stanzas) The figure of Zoroastro—magician overseer of the action—is not in the original, though his functions are performed by other figures in the poem. In Ariosto, Orlando regains his sanity through Astolfo's trip to the moon. There was apparently a limit upon credulity even in opera seria: a less spectacular special effect replaces the moon trip in Act III. Dorinda's character is not in the original.

Alcina: (VI.16 through VIII.19—164 stanzas) The most striking innovation in the opera is the centrality and depth of Alcina's characterization.

15. *The Allegory of Love* (1936), p. 308. See also C. P. Brand, *Ariosto: A Preface to the Orlando Furioso* (1974).

16. William Hazlitt, *Lectures on the English Poets* (1818) *Complete Works* (1930), Vol. V, p. 35. Mario Praz makes a similar comment in *The Flaming Heart* (1958): "The same adventures take place [in Spenser], the same battles, or nearly the same, are fought; but those of Ariosto are on the earth, and those of Spenser in the sky, among rainbows, in mid-air, so to speak."

17. *Letters and Literary Works* (1906; reprint 1966), Vol. II, p. 169.

18. Jonathan Richardson, *Explanatory Notes and Remarks on Milton's Paradise Lost* (1734), p. cxliv.

19. Lahr, *Astonish me,* p. 13. That *Orlando Furioso* has a peculiarly "modern" ring to it is also suggested by Harold Clurman in *The Nation* (23 November 1970), p. 541.

20. "It was from Handel that I learned that style consists in force of assertion. If you can say a thing with one stroke unanswerably you have style; if not, you are at best a *marchand de plaisir;* a decorative *litterateur,* or a musical confectioner, or a painter of fans with cupids and *cocottes.* Handel had this power . . . You may despise what you like; but you cannot contradict Handel." *How To Become a Musical Critic,* ed. Dan Laurence (1961), p. 278.

21. Letter to F. Tennyson, 6 February 1842, *Works,* Vol. I, p. 123.

22. Streatfeild's sensible and sensitive approach, expressed in *Handel* (1909), remains a model: "Handel followed the fashion of his day in the construction of his librettos, in the introduction of the inevitable confidantes and the no less inevitable underplot, but within certain limits he permitted himself all the freedom that he desired. The conventions of one age always appear foolish to another, but we must not let them blind us to the value of the work with which they are associated. But apart from convention, Handel's view of opera differed widely from that of our day. He treated it lyrically rather than dramatically, and who shall say that he was wrong? In our time opera has tended more and more to approach the confines of drama. Disregarding the one immutable convention by which opera exists as an art-form—the substitution of song for speech—we aim at a bastard realism, striving to bring the song of opera as near as possible to the speech of drama. Nothing can make opera realistic; it is conventional in essence; the less lyrical and the more dramatic it is, the less has it a reason for separate existence" (223).

23. *Observations on the Florid Song* (1723; Eng. tr., 1743), p. 91. Tosi's translator adds this footnote to the quoted passage: "Suppose the first Part expressed Anger, and the second relented, and was to express Pity or Compassion, he must be angry again in the Da Capo. This often happens, and is very ridiculous if not done to a real Purpose, and that the Subject and Poetry require it."

24. For a modern argument against embellishment, see Paul Henry Lang's review of the unoramented Richter version of *Giulio Cesare* in *High Fidelity* (February 1971), pp. 65-67.

25. Rudolf Steglich makes a cogent defense of da capo repetitions in "Über das Lebendige in Händels Opern," *Händel Jahrbuch* (1958), pp. 29-31.

26. Dean's study of the oratorios (see note 1) contains an admirably lucid and fair-minded discussion of Handel's borrowings (pp. 50-57).

27. Again, Dean provides an illuminating discussion of the modern alternatives to the presentation of the castrato roles (substitution of female voices, octave transposition) in *Handel and the Opera Seria,* pp. 206-14.

Chapter Three

1. Women's Liberation may put *Così fan tutte* on the defensive again. We should note, however, that Mozart was a fair judge of human nature: as a study of feminine frailty in love, *Così* is a sequel to *Le Nozze,* in which the frailty and arrogance of men in love are the focus. Mozart and Da Ponte might well have taken a line from Beaumarchais's Comtesse—"Les hommes sont bien coupables" ("all men are guilty")—and called their *Figaro* opera *Così fan tutti.*

2. *Prose Works* (1892-99), tr. W. A. Ellis, Vol. VI, pp. 152-53.

3. George Bernard Shaw made a similar observation in *The Sanity of Art* (1st ed., 1908, p. 29): "The first modern dramatic composers accepted as binding on them the rules of good pattern-designing in sound; and this absurdity was made to appear practicable by the fact that Mozart had such an extraordinary command of his art that his operas contain numbers which, though they seem to follow the dramatic play of emotion and character without reference to any other consideration whatever, are seen, on examining them from the point of view of the absolute musician, to be perfectly symmetrical sound-patterns."

4. Quoted in Cynthia Cox, *The Real Figaro* (1962), p. 196. Rosen finds this same equipoise in the piano concerto K.271: "What shall we term this manner of creation, freedom or submission to rules? Eccentricity or classical restraint? License or decorum? With a sense of proportion and dramatic fitness unsurpassed by any other composer, Mozart bound himself only by the rules he reset and reformulated anew for each work" (p. 210).

5. Robert Niklaus, *A Literary History of France: The Eighteenth Century* (1970), p. 329.

6. *The Private Diaries,* ed. Robert Sage, p. 240. W. J. Turner expressed the same idea in slightly different terms when he observed that *Giovanni, Così,* and *Figaro* are "works in which the elements of darkness and light are both present" (*Mozart: The Man and His Works,* 1938, reprint 1966, p. 304).

7. Turner, *Mozart,* p. 305. A related perception ("The creative consciousness is bisexual; otherwise there can be no creation.") provides G. Wilson Knight with his essential approach to Shakespeare. See *The Mutual Flame* (1955), especially pages 33-57.

8. In order to comment upon certain literary-musical parallels, I thought it useful to associate Mozart with an epithet from literary criticism. I am aware of the problems and vaguenesses which attend the use of what one critic calls "this maddeningly opaque term," but one must add that the common alternative epithets for eighteenth-century literature—Age of Reason, neo-Classical, Classical, Age of Elegance, Age of Prose, Enlightenment—are, if anything more clumsy and problematic. I use the term Augustan as a convenient means of opening a general discussion; the choice simply follows common usage. According to James W. Johnson (in Chapter I "Some Terms and Their Uses," *The Foundations of Neo-Classical Thought,* 1967, p. 28), "In the present century, English critics almost unanimously have used Augustan rather than Neo-Classical as the epithet for English literature of the Restoration and eighteenth century."

The reader concerned with the pitfalls and follies involved in "defining" artistic epochs with specific catchwords will find interesting Donald Greene's "Augustinianism and Empiricism: A Note on Eighteenth-Century English Intellectual History," *Eighteenth Century Studies,* Vol. 1 (September 1967), p. 33-68. There is also an interesting exchange between Greene and Vivian de Sola Pinto in Vol. 2, No. 2 of the same periodical (pp. 286-300). Also useful as a general introduction is Ian Watt's anthology *The Augustan Age* (Fawcett paperback, 1968).

9. Samuel Johnson, *The Life of Dryden.* What Johnson says of Dryden's prose style should also remind us of the felicities of Mozart's music: "Every word seems to drop by chance, though it falls into its proper place. Nothing is cold or languid; the whole is airy, animated, and vigorous: what is little is gay; what is great is splendid . . . Every thing is excused by the play of images and the spriteliness of expression. Though all is easy, nothing is feeble; though all seems careless, there is nothing harsh."

10. "It appears to me that the nobility showed a want of tact and restraint in applauding it; in doing so they gave themselves a slap in the face. They laughed at their own expense, and, what is worse, they made others laugh too. They will repent this later. The witticisms that amused them were directed against themselves, and they do not see it. Their own caricature has been held up before them, and they reply: 'This is it; we are very much like this.' What strange blindness!" *Mémoires de la Baronne d'Oberkirch,* ed. Suzanne Burkard (1970), p. 304. The Baroness nevertheless lavished high praise on the play, calling it "sparkling, a veritable fireworks."

11. Richardson's *Pamela* was the basis for Piccinni's *La Buona Figliuola* (1760)—one of the most successful works of its kind and hailed a masterpiece throughout Europe.

12. Walter Rex, *"Figaro's* Games," *PMLA,* Vol. 89 (May 1974), p. 525.

13. Henri Lemaître, *La Littérature Française,* Vol. II, p. 454.

14. "Mozart's *Figaro:* The Plan of Act III," *Music and Letters* 46 (1965), 134-36.

15. W. D. Howarth comes to the same conclusion for the play in "The Recognition Scene in *Le Mariage de Figaro,*" *PMLA,* Vol. 64 (1969), pp. 301-11.

16. Ann Livermore believes *Le Nozze* was influenced by the writings of

Rousseau ("Rousseau and Cherubino," *Music and Letters,* Vol. 43 (1962), pp. 218-24). She finds a passage from *The Confessions* particularly reminiscent of *Deh vieni.* Though there can be no certainty of influence, the beauty of Rousseau's prose parallels Mozart's music:

> It had been a very hot day, the evening was delightful, the dew moistened the fading grass, no wind was stirring, the air was fresh without chillness, the setting sun had tinged the clouds with a beautiful crimson, which was again reflected by the water, and the trees that bordered the terrace were filled with nightingales who were continually answering each other's songs. I walked along in a kind of ecstasy, giving up my heart and senses to the enjoyment of so many delights, and sighing only from a regret of enjoying them alone . . . the trees formed a stately canopy, a nightingale sat directly over me, and with his soft notes lulled me to rest: how pleasing my repose. (Book IV, W. C. Mallory translation).

17. Both *Le Mariage* and *Le Nozze* have had full-length, exhaustive dissections performed upon them. These are intensely humorless, nearly unreadable books, though useful as references for specific passages: J. B. Ratermanis and W. R. Irwin, *The Comic Style of Beaumarchais* (1961); Siegmund Levarie, *Mozart's Le Nozze di Figaro: A Critical Analysis* (1952).

18. Much about the Count reminds one of Don Giovanni. *Crudel! perchè finora* (the courting duet between a lecherous Count and an affectedly naïve Susanna) has the same structure and dramatic intent as *La ci darem la mano.* Many passages, like the recitative *Hai già vinto la causa!*, remind us of the basically nasty relationship between Giovanni and Leporello, which is just a more venal and corrupt version of the Count-Figaro *entente désagréable.* Even the last *Allegro assai* that closes *Le Nozze* works in a way similar to the sextet epilogue of Giovanni, sealing the fate (in this case a comic one) of the opera's central "villain" with a resounding moral.

19. *A Literary History of France: The Eighteenth Century* (1970), p. 328.

Chapter Four

1. Arthur Symons, referring to Rossini in "The Ideas of Wagner" (1905) in *Studies in the Seven Arts* (1910), p. 245.

2. The note here praised is the high B-flat at the end of "M'appari" from Flotow's *Martha,* admittedly no bel canto opera. Simon Dedalus is singing this aria in the Ormond Bar in the "Sirens" chapter of *Ulysses.*

3. *Selected Works,* tr. Helen Mustard (1973), p. 168. In *The Death of Tragedy* (1961) George Steiner wrote of Schiller's Romanticism: "He was a romantic by virtue of his militant liberalism, of his love for the wild and picturesque in nature, of his keen sensitivity to local colour and the stress of history. In his dramas and heroic ballads, the romantic generation found its repertoire of emotion" (p. 173).

4. Discussions of Scott's popularity in Italy, France, and Germany may be found, respectively, in: Mary Ambrose, "'La Donna del Lago': The First

Italian Translation of Scott," *Modern Language Review,* Vol. 67 (January 1972), pp. 74-82; E. Preston Dargan, "Scott and the French Romantics," *PMLA* Vol. 49 (1934), pp. 599-609; Paul Ochojski, "Waverley Über Alles —Sir Walter Scott's German Reputation," *Scott Bicentenary Essays,* ed. Alan Bell (1973), pp. 260-70.

5. Herbert Cysarz, *Schiller* (1934; reprint 1967), p. 336. In *The Theatre of Goethe and Schiller* (1973) John Prudhoe calls *Mary Stuart* "Schiller's greatest play" (p. 139). Charles Passage, the editor of the version used in this chapter (Ungar Press, 1961), calls it "his technically finest work" (p. xv). It should be added that there is a strong opinion among specialists in German drama that Schiller wrote only one major work, the *Wallenstein* trilogy.

6. Lavinia Mazzucchetti, *Schiller in Italia* (1913), p. 135.

7. H. B. Garland, *Schiller the Dramatic Writer* (1969), p. 201.

8. During rehearsals for the Naples premiere the two sopranos, sworn personal enemies, came to blows at these lines. When Giuseppina Begnis (Maria) spat her *"vil bastarda"* at Anna Delserre (Elisabetta), the latter forgot her role, took the text personally, grabbed her rival by the hair, and pummeled her severely enough to send her to bed for two weeks. In this story is some insight into the nature of bel canto, in which the personalities of the singer and the character were very close—almost one and the same. Begnis and Delserre were in typical bel canto fashion very nearly playing themselves as arrogant, indomitable souls. The performances must have been spectacular.

9. It was customary for heroines to be given a rousing rondo or *cabaletta* at the end of a bel canto opera. Donizetti, however, chafed at this if the drama did not suggest it. Two years earlier he had refused to give Méric-Lalande the bravura number she demanded for the end of *Lucrezia Borgia,* feeling it was ridiculous for a mother to carry on in the presence of the body of her son. Donizetti, however, lost that particular battle and finally wrote *Era d'esso il figlio mio* for her. Theatrically speaking, Donizetti's heart, if not always his practice, was in the right place.

10. Cysarz, *Schiller,* pp. 338-39.

11. *Memoirs of the Life of Sir Walter Scott* (1837-38), Vol. IV, p. 274. Bulwer-Lytton, who carried on the cause of historical romance after Scott's death, called *The Bride* "the grandest tragic romance our language possesses." Emerson, hard though it may be to believe, admired the Aeschylean nature of its plot. Hardy found it a nearly perfect specimen of form. It was Poe's favorite Waverley novel. A more recent critic well describes it as "an almost archetypal example of historical romance" (Andrew Hook, "*The Bride of Lammermoor:* A Re-Examination," *Nineteenth Century Fiction,* Vol. XXII, 2 (1967), pp. 111-25.)

Other Waverley novels which compete with *The Bride* for highest praise are *The Heart of Mid-Lothian, Old Mortality,* and *Guy Mannering.*

12. Critical comments on Scott cited in this section can be conveniently found in *Scott: The Critical Heritage,* ed. John Hayden (1970). As early as 1852 Turgenev could write (in a review of *The Niece* by Evgeniia Tur): "The historical, Walter Scott novel—that broad solid edifice, with its sturdy foundation dug into the national soil, with its broad introductions like por-

ticos, with its front rooms and dark corridors for ease of communication—this novel is almost impossible in our era, it is anachronistic."

13. In Paris a bourgeois class was slowly growing in the 1820s and 1830s in its patronage of opera, and taste for politically adventurous libretti likewise grew. Italy—whose revolution was still to come—was not as yet opened to explicitly politicized opera. Witness the trouble Verdi had with his *Rigoletto* in 1851 and *Un Ballo in Maschera* as late as 1859. One must add, of course, that ensembles in certain operas—notably Rossini's *Mosé in Egitto* and Verdi's *Nabucco*—were tremendously popular for their political undertones.

14. Unsigned review, *Athenaeum* (11 March 1828).

15. The accusation of lack of depth in character was leveled often at Scott, as for instance by Carlyle: "We might say . . . that your Shakespeare fashions his characters from the heart outwards; your Scott fashions them from the skin inwards, never getting near the heart of them! The one set become living men and women; the other amount to little more than mechanical cases, deceptively painted automatons."

The same charge can fairly be leveled at much bel canto characterization.

16. A droll hint of the extent of Donizetti's apoliticism is found in a letter he wrote to Antonio Vasselli (5 October 1837) giving his reaction to the idea of setting Bulwer-Lytton's *Rienzi*: "As for Rienzi, it doesn't strike me as the right thing now . . . does it seem so to you? A man who tries to establish a free government?" All quotations from Donizetti letters are from Guido Zavadini, *Donizetti: Vita, Musiche, Epistolario* (1948).

17. There were four prior operatic attempts on *The Bride*, by Carafa (1829), Ricci, Mazzucato (1834), and Bredal (1832). The University of Alabama Press plans to publish Jerome Mitchell's *Operas of Sir Walter Scott* in 1977.

18. It was the French grand opera stage that overwhelmed the bel canto hero and heroine with crowds and armies—in such operas as *La Muette de Portici*, *Guillaume Tell*, *Benvenuto Cellini*, and *Les Huguenots*. Donizetti's bias against huge stage forces is made clear in a letter he wrote to Gaetano Melzi (28 June 1838). There he complains of a militaristic libretto sent to him by Scribe. It contained, Donizetti says, "only military things, and I want emotions on the stage and not battles."

19. Scott was an unsparing critic of his own heroes. In an anonymous review of his own works, published in the *Quarterly Review* in 1817, Scott wrote: "In addition to the loose and incoherent style of the narration, another leading fault in these novels is the total want of interest which the reader attaches to the character of the hero . . . very amiable and very insipid sort of young men."

Hazlitt wrote in his essay "Why the Heroes of Romances are Insipid" (1827): "I do not say that his [Scott's] heroes are absolutely insipid, but that they have in themselves no leading or master trait, and they are worked out of very listless and inert materials."

20. The role of Edgardo practically made Duprez (1806-96) the king of European tenors overnight. He went on to create Donizetti heroes in *Les Martyrs*, *La Favorite*, and *Dom Sebastian*. He went on to sing most of the great roles written for Adolph Nourrit—Arnold in *Guillaume Tell*, and Raoul

in *Les Huguenots* for instance. He also created the role of Cellini in Berlioz's opera (the subject of a subsequent chapter). Berlioz's opinion of Duprez was low.

21. *The Memoirs of Hector Berlioz,* tr. David Cairns (1969), p. 208.

22. Ibid., p. 326. Schröder-Devrient was famous for a wide variety of roles: Agathe in *Freischütz,* Leonora in *Fidelio* (she was highly praised by Beethoven), Donna Anna, Norma, Amina in *La Sonnambula,* and Desdemona in Rossini's *Otello.* She also created the Wagnerian roles Senta, Venus, and Adriano in *Rienzi.*

Chapter Five

1. Andrew Porter nearly echoes Delacroix, calling *Cellini* "a sorry muddle (though touched with genius)" *The New Yorker,* 16 December 1974. It would appear from Porter's subsequent review of the Boston Opera's production of *Benvenuto Cellini* (*The New Yorker,* 2 June 1975) that he softened his views on the opera considerably.

2. Quoted in *Berlioz and the Romantic Century* by Jacques Barzun, Vol. II, p. 53. In *Hector Berlioz sa vie et ses oeuvres* (Paris, 1888), Adolphe Jullien speaks of "the abundance of themes, the warmth of the melodic fancy, the vehement brilliance of the inspiration" of *Cellini.*

3. Letter to Prince Vyazemsky (November 1825), in *Pushkin on Literature,* tr. Tatiana Wolff (1971), p. 163.

4. "There I go, you see, on the point of failing in modesty again; and if I tell you of the packed hall, the prolonged applause, the recalls, the chamberlains coming up to congratulate the composer on behalf of Their Highnesses, the new friends waiting at the stage door to shake his hand and forcibly keep him up till three in the morning—if, in short, I chronicle a success, I shall be set down as a vulgarian, an indelicate person, a buffoon, a—enough" (*M,* 290). See also pp. 387, 410-11, and 423.

5. A letter to Lobe, quoted in *Romain Rolland's Essays on Music,* ed. David Ewen (1959), p. 310.

6. *The Civilization of the Renaissance in Italy* (1860; Mentor paperback, 1960), p. 244.

7. Gilbert Duprez was the malfeasant tenor. Unfortunately it was in 1838 too late for the great progenitor of French grand operatic tenors, Adolphe Nourrit, to assume the role. Nourrit, who made his Opéra debut in 1821, had left the Opéra in 1837 when his successor and rival Duprez was allowed to make his debut in a role (Arnold in *Guillaume Tell*) created by the older singer. In his review of the *Cellini* premiere Jules Janin observed: "What a pity for this score, what poor luck for Berlioz, that Nourrit was not present to perform, to sing the principal role! Surely he, that excellent artist, would not have appeared to retreat, in the very first measures, from a role which was entrusted to him."

8. Janin's review appeared on 15 September 1838. François Henri-Joseph Blaze (also known as Castil-Blaze), "De l'Ecole fantastique et de M. Berlioz," *Revue des Deux Mondes,* 4. trimestre 1838, pp. 97-121.

9. In *French Grand Opera* (1948) William Crosten described Scribe as a man whose "words are prosaic enough not to draw undue attention to themselves" (p. 100). Gautier was less oblique: "If he tried, no one could write lines as bad as those of Scribe" (Vol. V, p. 289).

10. Its shock effect was not unlike that of *Hernani* at its premiere, which was famously described by Gautier (Vol. VIII, p. 149): "It would be a difficult task to describe the effect produced upon the audience by the striking, virile, vigorous verse, that had so strange a ring, and a swing that recalled at once both Corneille and Shakespeare, for nowadays [Gautier was writing in 1872 of 1830] the very innovations that then were considered barbarisms are accounted classical. It must also be carefully borne in mind that in France, at that time, adhorrence of plain speaking and of the use of crude words was carried to a fairly unimaginable extent."

11. This won him Berlioz's undying hatred, which the composer trumpeted in the journals whenever occasion arose. Berlioz despised "improvers": "Mozart assassinated by Lachnith, Weber by Castil-Blaze; Gluck, Grétry, Mozart, Rossini, Beethoven, Vogel, mutilated by this same Castil-Blaze; Beethoven's symphonies corrected by Fétis (as I shall describe), by Kreutzer and by Habeneck; Molière and Corneille cut down to size by obscure hacks at the Théâtre-Français; Shakespeare still performed in England as 'arranged' by Cibber and his kind. . . . Such corrections, I would suggest, come not from above but from below—perpendicularly!" (*M,* 91).

12. This unjust accusation has been perpetrated by many, including Saint-Saëns, who wrote that "the past did not exist for him" (*Portraits et Souvenirs,* 1903, p. 7). One might note in Berlioz's defense that he passed *four* courses in fugue from the old lion Cherubini, though it appears he succeeded in following the advice of another great critic George Bernard Shaw, to learn how to write a fugue and then don't do it. Gautier points out admirably (Vol. VIII, pp. 211-12) that Berlioz and most Romantic innovators were "all deeply versed in the techniques of their respective arts. A man must know much before he can reform. Every one of the so-called wild-haired, uncurbed artists who, so it was alleged, wrote only under the influence of delirium, were on the contrary consummate contrapuntists, each one in his own sphere, and perfectly capable of ending a fugue in the most regular fashion." One might add that many modern musicians feel that Berlioz's musical Romanticism was firmly based on—imbued with—Classical precepts and style.

13. A letter Liszt wrote to Berlioz after the *Cellini* revival has a remarkably similar flavor. In Liszt's eyes, Berlioz had become a modern Perseus: "I esteem you, Berlioz, for you have thus struggled with invincible courage, and if you have not yet subdued the Gorgon, if the serpents are still hissing at your feet, menacing you with their hideous fangs, if envy, folly, malignity, and perfidiousness multiply around you, fear nothing, for the gods will aid you; they have given you like Perseus the helmet, the wings, the shield and sword, that is to say, the energy, the alertness, the wisdom and the power. Combat, suffering and glory are the destiny of genius" (*Letters of a Bachelor in Music, Gesammelte Schriften,* Vol. II).

14. Gautier described Berlioz's sacrifice for his music in more lurid, Ro-

mantic terms: "He felt that he was a Titan capable of scaling high heaven and of standing face to face with Jupiter; yet he was condemned to remain nailed with diamond nails, by Force and Power, to the cross on Caucasus, like the hero of Aeschylus, while vultures gnawed at his heart. Nor did he even have the consolation of seeing the two thousand Oceanids, borne on winged chariots, coming to weep at the foot of his mountain" (Vol. XVI, p. 219).

15. Berlioz finally lost this strength. He died later in life than a Romantic ought—the same judgment, incidentally, that Berlioz himself passed on Goethe (*M*, 288). One of the most melancholy developments in all musical biography is the slow, ruthless crushing of this most generous of men into the withering cynicism of his old age, which is observable in his writings. Those of his later life are filled with a Goyesque sense of degradation; a few random citations capture this:

> The unsolvable enigma of the world, the existence of evil and pain, the fierce madness of mankind, and the stupid cruelty that it inflicts hourly and everywhere on the most inoffensive beings and on itself—all this has reduced me to the state of unhappy and forlorn resignation of a scorpion surrounded by live coals. The most I can do is not wound myself with my own dart. [Quoted in *Romain Rolland*, p. 296]

The last paragraph of the *Memoirs:*

> When I see what certain people mean by love and what they look for in the creations of art, I am reminded involuntarily of pigs snuffling and rootling in the earth with their great coarse snouts at the foot of mighty oaks and among the loveliest flowers, in search of their favourite truffles . . . But let us try to think no more of art. [*M*, 515]

Berlioz's dismal envoi to *Les Grotesques de la musique* (1859) might be an epitaph for Romanticism:

> One may observe a singular contrast between the activity of musicians in Paris during the present epoch and the musicians who busied themselves twenty years ago. Almost all the latter had faith in themselves and in the results of their efforts; today, almost everyone has lost his conviction. They persevere nevertheless.

16. What the opera managers were obliged to do to keep a bovine public from falling asleep is catalogued by Berlioz:

> Drastic methods followed in hopes of shaking it into wakefulness: high C's from every type of chest, bass drums, snare drums, organs, military bands, antique trumpets, tubas as big as locomotive smokestacks, bells, cannon, horses, cardinals under a canopy, emperors covered with gold, queens wearing tiaras, funerals, fêtes, weddings, and again the canopy, always the canopy, the canopy beplumed and splendiferous, borne by four officers as in *Malbrouck*, jugglers, skaters, choirboys, censers, monstrances, crosses, banners, processions, orgies of priests and naked women, the bull Apis, and masses of oxen, screech-owls, bats, the five hundred fiends of hell, and what have you—the rocking of the heavens and the end of the world, interspersed with a few dull cavatinas here and there and a large claque thrown in. [*E*, 109]

It is worth quoting this passage from the *Memoirs* in which Berlioz has fun at the expense of Duponchel, the director of the Opéra at the time of the *Cellini* premiere:

> Then there are the infatuated directors, the directors obsessed with a particular kind of idea or object, a particular period of history, particular settings and costumes and stage effects, a particular singer or dancer, as the case may be. Whatever happens, a place must be found for their hobby-horse. The hobby-horse of M. Duponchel, director of the Opéra, was, is and ever shall be a cardinal in a red hat under a canopy. Operas without canopies, cardinals or red hats (and they exist in considerable numbers) have never appealed to him. If the good Lord himself had a part in a new work, as I once heard Méry remark, Duponchel would insist on his wearing the cherished headgear. It would be no use pointing out that, as the good Lord, it wouldn't look right if one were to come on like a cardinal. "Excuse me, Almighty," Duponchel would reply, "it's essential that Your Eternity should kindly agree to put on this handsome costume and appear beneath the canopy, otherwise *my opera* will not be a success." And the good Lord would have to give in. I pass over M. Duponchel's enthusiasm for horses, a serious passion too respectable to be mentioned in this context. [*M*, 395-96]

Berlioz was not ignoring the director's penchant for scenic spectacle and grand effects in *Cellini;* he gave Duponchel no less than a Pope for his dais. Whether he wore a red biretta is not recorded.

17. It is interesting to note how Shakespearean allusions surface in Berlioz's mind at poignant points in his career. Both the Author's Preface (1848) and the last pages of the *Memoirs* (1854) carry Macbeth's famous lines beginning "Life's but a walking shadow . . ." In *Evenings with the Orchestra* the authorial figure admits "that it is my yearly habit to make a *poetical* retreat. I shut myself in at home and read Shakespeare or Virgil, sometimes both" (*E,* 60). The first envoi to the *Memoirs* (dated 18 October 1854) ends: "For you, morons, maniacs, dogs, and you, my Guildensterns and Rosencrantzes, Iagos, Osrics, gadflies, crawling worms of every kind: farewell my . . . friends. I scorn you, and hope not to die before I have forgotten you" (*M,* 473).

18. *L'Art de la musique* (1961), p. 234. The *Evenings* remain his most wonderful excursion in satiric fiction. His delightful collection of essays and reviews, *Les Grotesques de la musique* (1859) has unfortunately not yet been translated. Saint-Saëns, incidentally, thought Berlioz "incontestably the finest critic of his time."

19. Quoted in Barzun, *Hector Berlioz and the Romantic Century,* Vol. I, p. 110.

20. Berlioz, too, once became an avenging fury. While in Rome he learned that his fiancée, Camille Moke, had married another man in Paris. Berlioz immediately set out to "kill two guilty women [Moke and her mother] and an innocent man" and then commit suicide. His rage did not last beyond Nice, and the *crime passionnel* was abandoned. This amusing story is related in the *Memoirs,* pp. 152-58.

21. Letter to Lewis Gruneisen, 8 February 1853, in *New Letters of Hector Berlioz,* ed. Jacques Barzun (1954), p. 101.

22. Letter to Liszt, 29 August 1851, quoted by Tom Wotton, *Hector Berlioz* (1935), p. 147.

Chapter Six

1. *Opera as Drama* (1956), p. 130. See also, Roy Aycock, "Shakespeare, Boito, and Verdi," *The Musical Quarterly,* Vol. 58 (October 1972), p. 590. In one important respect—that of the purely *poetic* relationship between play and opera libretto—Kerman's assertion is well taken. Shakespeare's poetic textures and the complex web of imagery were but poorly treated by Verdi's librettist, and that is why *Otello* and *Falstaff* are incomparably better Shakespearean translations. What Verdi did not have to help him with in his struggles with *Macbeth* was a librettist of genius like Boito. My remarks in this chapter upon the poetic aspects of the libretto will therefor be brief.

2. Had Verdi consummated his long-agonized plans to set "King Lear" it might have been the most innovative work of his career. To Cammarano he wrote: "You know, we need not turn 'Lear' into the usual sort of drama that has been customary up to now. We must treat it in a completely new way, on a grand scale, without any regard for convention" (*W,* 152).

3. *Shakespearean Tragedy* (1st ed., 1904; paperback rpt., 1965), p. 327. Bradley's two lectures on "Macbeth" are still the best introduction to the play.

4. Kenneth Muir, ed., New Arden "Macbeth" (1968), p. liii.

5. Giulia Cora Varesi, "L'interpretazione di *Macbeth* (con lettere inedite di Giuseppe Verdi)," *Nuova Antologia,* Vol. 67 (Nov.-Dec. 1932), 433-40. All my translations from Verdi's letters to Varesi are from this article. The same priority Verdi observed when he came to the task of cutting his extremely long initial version of *Don Carlos:* "I shall strip the Carlos/Posa duet of everything that is purely musical, and keep just what is necessary for the drama." Quoted by Andrew Porter in "Preamble to a new *Don Carlos,*" *Opera* (August 1974), p. 671.

6. I do not mean to suggest Verdi was the first composer ever to make such a demand. There is an amusing letter from Mozart to his father (*Briefe und Aufzeichnungen,* Vol. VI, pp. 72-73) concerning his difficulties with the tenor Raaff, who was to create the role of Idomeneo: "Raaff thought it [the quartet *Andrò ramingo e solo*] would not be effective. He told me so while we were alone, 'There isn't room for expanding the voice; it is too narrow [*non c'e da spianar la voce—es ist zu Eng*].' As if in such a quartet one ought not much rather speak than sing! [*viel mehr reden als singen sollte*]." However, Mozart goes on to make a concession to the tradition-bound Raaff: "I have put myself out to serve you in your two arias and will do likewise with the third one . . . but what concerns trios and quartets must be left to the composer's free will." It remained for Verdi to exert his will in all aspects of his operas.

7. "In its unity of action (in all senses of the latter word) 'Macbeth' is obviously at opposite poles from 'Hamlet' among Shakespeare's tragedies. Its action is simply the yielding of a great and good man to temptation and the

degeneration of his moral nature resulting from his first deed of sin." Virgil Whitaker, *The Mirror up to Nature* (1965), p. 260.

8. *Shakespeare: A Critical Study of His Mind and Art* (1897 ed.), p. 217.

9. Another noteworthy instance of dramatic vocal display is Lady Macbeth's imperious two-octave descent ending her brief but decisive first interview with her husband (at the line: *Lieto or lo vieni ad incontrar con me*).

10. "General Macbeth," *Harper's Magazine* (June 1962), p. 39.

11. Quotations in this section are from Verdi's letters to Léon Escudier, *Music and Letters,* Vol. IV (January 1923), pp. 62-70.

12. Interestingly, the world premieres (1847, 1845) and Paris premieres (1865, 1861) of *Macbeth* and *Tannhäuser* closely parallel each other. Both were revised, and both failed. Many opera houses have recently opted for the earlier and cruder version of the Wagner opera for reasons of musical purity and stylistic integrity. It is very doubtful that the earlier version of *Macbeth* will receive the same treatment, however.

13. Consider Jean Noverre's 1760 description of a Garrick performance: "His gestures, without losing their expression, revealed the approach of his last moment; his legs gave way under him, his face lengthened, his pale and livid features bore the signs of suffering and repentance. At last, he fell; at that moment his crimes peopled his thoughts with the most horrible forms; terrified at the hideous pictures which his past acts revealed to him, he struggled with death; nature seemed to make one supreme effort. His plight made the audience shudder, he clawed the ground and seemed to be digging his own grave, but the dread moment was nigh, one saw death in reality, everything expressed that instant which makes all equal. In the end he expired. The death rattle and the convulsive movements of the features, arms and breasts, gave the final touch to this terrible picture." *Letters on Dancing,* (1760; 1930 tr. Cyril Beaumont), pp. 84-85.

14. Concerned with the charge of vulgarity directed at the witches, Dowden responded: "Shakespeare is no more afraid than Michelangelo of being vulgar . . . the great ideal artists—Michelangelo, Dante, Blake, Beethoven—see things far more dreadful than the vague horrors of the romanticist; they are perfectly fearless in their use of the material, the definite, the gross, the so-called vulgar. And thus Shakespeare fearlessly showed us his weird sisters, 'the Goddesses of destinie,' brewing infernal charms in their wicked caldron."

While we are considering the charge of vulgarity, this may be the point to observe that many of what might at first seem the most obvious set-pieces in the opera have a clear basis in the original play. Verdi deftly turns the egregious, time-consuming platitudes of Duncan's initial scenes into the musical platitude of the royal march in Act I—a fair transaction, it seems to me. The drinking song derives from Macbeth's line: "anon, we'll drink a measure/ The table round" (3.4.11). The Act IV chorus *Patria oppressa* (aside from having important historical implications for Italy oppressed by the Austrians) is based faithfully upon the many passages in Act IV describing the "suffering country/ Under a hand accurs'd" (3.6.48; see also 4.3.4-8/4.3.39/4.3.103-5). The relatively low-relief romance for Macduff (*Ah, la paterna mano*) is, of course, based upon the great scene in Act IV where Macduff learns of the slaughter of his family.

15. The ballet—based upon the witches' invocation of Hecate—is really an interpolation based upon an interpolation. For the Hecate scenes in the play are considered highly suspect and probably not from Shakespeare's pen.

16. Pragmatism must be the word to describe the Verdi, writing as late as 1880 of the *cabaletta* so much despised by Wagner and "modernists" of Verdi's time:

> I have no such horror of *cabalettas,* and if a young man were born to-morrow who could write any as good as, for instance, *Meco tu vieni a misera,* or *Ah! perchè non posso odiarti,* I would go to hear him with all my heart, and let the harmonic fancies of our learned orchestration go. Ah, progress, science, realism! Alas, alack! Be a realist as much as you please, but Shakespeare was a realist, only he did not know it. He was a realist by inspiration; we are realists by design, by calculation. [*W,* 360-61]

The two *cabalettas* Verdi refers to are from Bellini's *La Straniera* (1829) and *La Sonnambula* (1831). Berlioz, too, admired the *Straniera* piece—and for reasons Verdi would probably have agreed with: "I come to a very short aria, scarcely fitted to its surroundings, lacking all development, without any orchestral plan, virgin of any ambitious vocalization—simple, in a word—but in my view offering the type of the young maestro's most touching elegies . . . Certainly here is inspiration or it never existed." Quoted in Herbert Weinstock, *Vincenzo Bellini: His Life and His Operas* (1971), pp. 355-56.

Chapter Seven

1. Quoted in *The Critical Prose of Alexander Pushkin,* ed. and tr. Carl Proffer (1969), p. 294.

2. John Mersereau Jr.'s "Pushkin's Concept of Romanticism," *Studies in Romanticism,* Vol. III (1963), pp. 24-41, comes to no real conclusion, most likely because none is to be won from the poet's scattered comments on the matter. In a long footnote for a reference to Romanticism in "Onegin" (6.23), Nabokov wryly offers a list of eleven extant forms of Romanticism invented by critics. These are introduced amusingly: "As happens in zoological nomenclature when a string of obsolete, synonymous, or misapplied names keeps following the correct designation of a creature throughout years, and not only cannot be shaken off, or ignored, or obliterated within brackets, but actually grows on with time, so in literary history the vague terms 'classicism,' 'sentimentalism,' 'romanticism,' and 'realism,' and the like straggle on and on, from textbook to textbook."

3. Pushkin's first description of his new poem mentions Byron: "Something like "Don Juan"—it is useless to think of publication; I am writing quite casually" (Letter to Prince Vyazemsky, 4 November 1823). He also wrote in late 1823, "I am now writing a poem in which I babble on to excess" (Letter

to Baron Delvig, 11 November 1823) and "I am now writing a new poem . . . in which I choke in gall" (Letter to A. Turgenev, 1 December 1823).

4. In his article on Pushkin in *Nineteenth-Century Russian Literature* (1973), J. Fennell describes the way the narrator "works": " 'Eugene Onegin' is the most 'intrusive' of all Pushkin's works: the narrator continually thrusts himself to the fore. From time to time he may retreat into the wings in order to describe an action or let his characters speak for themselves. But never for long. Back he comes, often with what looks like unquenchable garrulity, to chat, to comment, to explain, to reminisce, and to treat his readers to huge asides" (p. 37). Hugh McLean, in "The Tone(s) of 'Eugene Onegin'," *California Slavic Studies,* No. 6 (1971), p. 15, discusses the narrator and then describes the effect of his absence in the opera: "One of the functions of the author-narrator in the novel . . . is to force us to keep our distance from the characters and to judge them intellectually and rationally. In this the author himself is our model. His heart may be hot, but he keeps a cool head. And his irony, the jocular, mocking aspect of the novel's 'tone,' is the literary expression of that cool head. Irony is a kind of spiritual air conditioner. . . . Tchaikovsky's opera, incidentally, shows what happens to the story of Onegin and Tatiana, Olga and Lensky, if you turn off this machine. The atmosphere becomes sticky, the underpinnings of the wonderfully delicate, intricate, balanced structure rot, and it collapses. You are left with a banal, trite, and sentimental bore—which may nevertheless be a vehicle for some delightful music."

5. Tchaikovsky's dicta upon the business of writing opera are few and unpretentious ("Opera style should be broad, simple, and decorative," *L,* 355) and go little beyond this need for a personal emotional involvement: "I am looking for an intimate yet thrilling drama, based upon such a conflict of circumstances as I myself have experienced or witnessed, which is capable of touching me to the quick" (*L,* 256).

6. Such appears the measure of Pushkin himself. In the early 1820s the poet was described thus in Eugene Baratinsky's elegy *The Feasts* (1820):

> . . . the enchanting minstrel
> of love, and liberty, and pleasure—
> young P., volatile and wise,
> a confidant of fun and fame . . .

7. "In the music of this master [Brahms] (it is impossible to deny his mastery) there is something dry and cold which repulses me. He has very little melodic invention. He never speaks out his musical ideas to the end. Scarcely do we hear an enjoyable melody, than it is engulfed in a whirlpool of unimportant harmonic progressions and modulations, as though the special aim of the composer was to be unintelligible. He excites and irritates our musical senses without wishing to satisfy them, and seems ashamed to speak the language which goes straight to the heart" (*L,* 570).

8. As a footnote to the first line of the poem's translation ("Whither, ah! whither are ye fled?") Nabokov archly offers seven nineteenth-century appearances of this cliché from *English* literature!

As one might expect, Nabokov's opinion of the opera is low. He refers to it as "silly" and "slapdash," as would any writer so imbued with Pushkin's own aesthetic biases and powers of harsh judgment. He is particularly annoyed that Tchaikovsky makes "a whining weakling of Pushkin's virile Lensky." Also raising his ire is the famous painting of the duel by Repin, which makes Lensky look effeminate: "As in the opera, everything in the picture insults Pushkin's masterpiece." We should note that Nabokov has admitted elsewhere that music is to him an alien art-form.

Tchaikovsky's music tends to bring out the boorish in men of rigorous, debunking intellect. Thus H. L. Mencken: "What ails the music of all the Tchaikovskys, Mendelssohns—and Chopins? What ails it is that it is the music of shallow men. It is often, in its way, lovely. It bristles with charming musical ideas. It is infinitely ingenious and workmanlike. But it is hollow, at bottom, as a bull by an archbishop. It is music of second-rate men" (*Mencken on Music*, 1961, p. 36).

9. Tchaikovsky never alludes to Olga's eventual betrayal, as it would destroy the effect of the aria:

> My poor Lensky! Pining away,
> she did not weep for long.
> Alas! The young fiancée
> is to her woe untrue.
> Another fascinated her attention,
> another her suffering managed
> to lull with love's flattery. [7.10]

See 7.11 for Pushkin's harsh moral to this love story.

10. The importance of this scene for the staging of the opera is emphasized in *Stanislavsky on Opera* (1975), by Constantin Stanislavsky and Pavel Rumyantsev (p. 41): "For Tchaikovsky the essence of the Letter Scene is the revelation of Tatiana's soul, conveying all the shadings of her thoughts and feelings; it is this scene which defines the character of the whole opera. When Stanislavsky grasped the meaning of this scene and was able to convey its essential quality, he held the key to the entire production." The nearly hundred pages in this book devoted to Stanislavsky's famous 1922 production of *Eugene Onegin* contain many important insights into the nature of the opera.

11. In the matter of Triquet's song Nabokov betrays the itch of the true pedant: "It is typical of Tchaikovsky's slapdash opera *Eugene Onegin* that *his* Triquet sings a totally different tune [from the French original by Dufresny]".

12. Stanislavsky did not like this scene: "Does Pushkin make any slightest mention of such a rite? He could not possibly have produced such a cheap, pinchbeck scene. This is nothing but an incrustation due to time, a sop to saccharine sentimentality. I am not at all certain that even Tchaikovsky cared for having a folk dance in the first act, but he was under some compulsion to gratify the taste of the theatre in his day."

13. The identity of Tatiana's husband is never revealed by Pushkin. He is

referred to only as "Prince N." Though Nabokov chides the "bright minds who made the libretto" for lighting on Gremin—a name seems necessary given the figure's purpose in the opera.

14. We might then feel like Nabokov. Nabokov's disgust with the opera might seem more plausible if we English-speaking people were to imagine, for instance, Frederick Delius bending Lord Byron's "Don Juan" to *his* musical aesthetic.

15. "Where shall I find a Tatiana such as Pushkin dreamed of, and such as I have striven to realize in music? Where is the artist who can approach the ideal Onegin, that cold-hearted dandy, impregnated to the marrow of his bones with the fashionable notion of 'good tone'? Where is there a Lensky, that youth of eighteen, with the flowing locks and the gushing and would-be-original manners of a poetaster à la Schiller? How commonplace Pushkin's charming characters will appear on the stage, with all its routine, its drivelling traditions, its veterans—male and female—who undertake without a blush to play girl-heroines and beardless youths! Moral: it is much pleasanter to write purely instrumental music which involves fewer disappointments" (*L*, 246).

16. A director, incidentally, should be wary of stage directions in the printed score. There are frequent comments on the dramatic and musical inefficacy of these in the Stanislavsky volume (e.g., "The stage directions in the libretto were written without the slightest regard for the music," p. 87).

Chapter Eight

1. "*Salome*—The Storm-Center of the Musical World," *Current Literature* (March 1907), pp. 294-98. This article contains a synopsis of the critical reaction to the New York *Salome*. The circumstances of this premiere are interesting. Every year the Metropolitan's manager H. Conried acquired the services of his principal singers for a benefit performance. The *Salome* premiere was chosen for the occasion. As a result the opera was preceded by an operatic concert with eighteen participants, including Sembrich and Caruso! Olive Fremstad sang Salome and Alfred Hertz conducted. Puccini was in the audience. Puccini, incidentally, had expressed interest a year before in setting another Wilde one-act play, "A Florentine Tragedy." The governing board of the Metropolitan forced the withdrawal of *Salome* after this lone performance. Whether positive or negative, the reaction to *Salome* was enormous. The *Nation* (24 January 1907, p. 89) reported that it was "more talked and written about than any other opera since the first production of *Parsifal* in 1882, with the exception of *Cavalleria Rusticana* [1890]." Mahler was prevented from giving *Salome* its Austrian premiere by the Imperial censors.

2. *Correspondence between Richard Strauss and Hugo von Hofmannsthal 1907-1918*, tr. Paul England (1927), p. 166. This letter was dated 8 March 1912.

3. The idea was not new. Compare Steele's farewell *Spectator* No. 555: "It is much more difficult to converse with the world in a real than a personated character." And Nietzsche in *Beyond Good and Evil:* "Everything pro-

found loves the mask . . . Every profound spirit needs a mask." (tr. R. Hollingdale p. 51)

4. This is not the place to enter the lists of controversy. The full panoply of scholarly argument and numerous references to germane studies, however, may be found in a trio of articles in the *Journal of Aesthetics and Art Criticism:* (1) Clyde de L. Ryals, "Toward a Definition of *Decadent* as Applied to British Literature of the Nineteenth Century" (September 1958, pp. 85-92); (2) Robert L. Peters, "Towards an 'Un-Definition' of *Decadent* as Applied to British Literature of the Nineteenth Century" (December 1959, pp. 258-62); (3) Russell M. Goldfarb, "Late Victorian Decadence" (Summer 1962, pp. 369-73). At the close of his article, Goldfarb ventures a thumbnail sketch of Decadence; I include it here for the convenience of the unfamiliar reader:

> We understand that late Victorian decadence refers to poetry and prose which does not emphasize philosophical, historical or intellectual concerns, but which does emphasize the value to be gained both from experience of all sorts and from indulgence in a life of sensations. Because of this emphasis, decadent literature is animated by the exploration of immoral and evil experiences; never does it preach morality, nor does it strongly insist upon ethical responsibilities. Decadent literature is characterized by artistic concern for the morbid, the perverse, the sordid, the artificial, the beauty to be found in the unnatural, and the representation of the cleanliness in unclean things; it is characterized by self-conscious and weary contempt for social conventions such as truth and marriage, by an acceptance of Beauty as a basis for life.

The most incisive and readable study of English Decadence remains Holbrook Jackson's *The Eighteen Nineties* (1913; Capricorn paperback, 1966). Karl Beckson's *Aesthetes and Decadents of the 1890s* (Vintage paperback, 1966) is the best anthology of English Decadent literature.

5. It is worth adding that Hedwig Lachmann, whose translation of Wilde's play Strauss used as the basis for his opera, was also a translator of Poe. A more unusual coincidence lies in the fact that the world premiere of "Salomé" was produced in Paris in 1896 by Aurélien-François Lugné-Poe (1869-1940), who took the American poet's name when he entered the theatrical profession. Lugné-Poe, at the age of twenty-seven, was the first Herod.

6. *Selected Writing on Art and Artists* (1972), p. 185.

7. Baudelaire's essay on Poe is included in *The Recognition of Edgar Allan Poe,* ed. Eric Carlson (1966), pp. 43-60.

8. From "The Black Cat" (1843): "And then came, as if to my final and irrevocable overthrow, the spirit of PERVERSENESS. Of this spirit philosophy takes no account. Yet I am not more sure that my soul lives, than I am that perverseness is one of the primitive impulses of the human heart—one of the indivisible primary faculties, or sentiments, which give direction to the character of Man." From "The Imp of the Perverse" (1845): "Nor will this overwhelming tendency to do wrong for wrong's sake, admit of analysis, or resolution into ulterior elements. It is a radical, a primitive impulse—elementary."

9. Bernard Muddiman wrote in *The Men of the Nineties* (1920, p. 136): "*Buveurs de lune* after the manner of Paul Verlaine, they evoked something of the ethereal glamor of moonlight itself." The combination of evil, eroticism and a nocturnal setting is found in another important proto-Decadent poetic work—the "Hymns to the Night" (1800) by Novalis.

10. The reviewer for the *Mercure de France* (1 June 1907, p. 532) jocularly referred to the Strauss opera as an "énorme éléphantaisie biblique d'après St. Mathieu, St. Jean et St. Gustave Flaubert."

The differences between the Flaubert story and "Salomé" should be noted. Flaubert was much more preoccupied with Herod's political relations with the Romans and their representative Vitellius, as well as with the Jews (Pharisees and Sadducees). The story is on the whole more realistic and less sensational than the play; Flaubert does give the court of Herod the trappings of voluptuousness, but somehow there is no terror in the story. There is no real mania or neurasthenic horror. Also, in the story Herodias uses her daughter Salome to retaliate against the prophet; the daughter is virtually a marionette. In this regard, Massenet's opera *Hérodiade* (1881) follows Flaubert more closely. There Herodias is the dominant villainess and Salome a typical Massenet heroine—almost the exact opposite of a femme fatale.

11. From Arthur Symons's translation, which is included in Beckson (see note 4 above).

12. *Complete Works*, ed. Robert Ross (1908; reprint 1969), Vol. XIII, p. 355.

13. Richard Ellmann makes an interesting case for seeing in Wilde's Jokanaan-Salome conflict a partly symbolic, partly autobiographical representation of the conflict between the pagan naturalism of Pater and the Christian idealism of Ruskin. Ellmann suggests that Wilde felt himself to occupy the place of Herod, who is susceptible to the contrary impulses of both Jokanaan and Salome. He also notes that Beardsley may have sensed this autobiographical element in Herod, for one of the figures of Herod has Wilde's face. See "Overtures to Wilde's 'Salomé'" *Tri-Quarterly*, Vol. XV (Spring 1969), pp. 45-64.

14. Quoted in Philippe Jullian, *Oscar Wilde*, tr. Violet Wyndham (1968), p. 258.

15. *Richard Strauss and Romain Rolland Correspondence*, ed. Rollo Myers (1968), pp. 83, 85-86.

16. *Die Überwindung des Naturalismus*, p. 153.

17. *Studien zur Kritik der Moderne* (1894), pp. 88-90.

18. George and Hofmannsthal enjoyed a very close relationship beginning in 1891. I am indebted to *Stefan George* by Michael Metzger (1972) for material in this section. George was in many ways a German Wilde. See Eric Bentley's discussion of the poet's "homosexual mind" in *Partisan Review* IX (1942), 321-30. The influence of Wilde upon George is interestingly discussed by Victor Oswald Jr. in "Oscar Wilde, Stefan George, Heliogabalus," *Modern Language Quarterly*, Vol. X (1949), pp. 517-24.

19. Max Nordau, *Degeneration* (1893; Eng. tr., 1895), p. 13.

20. *Musical Criticisms 1846-1899*, tr. Henry Pleasants (rev. ed., 1963), pp. 291-92. Hanslick's "Don Juan" review appeared in 1892.

21. *Music Ho!* (1934), p. 34.

22. *La Revue de Paris* (15 June 1907), p. 760. Curiously, Debussy described Strauss's talents in much the same way: "He undoubtedly thinks in color-pictures and he seems to draw the line of his ideas by means of the orchestra . . . it is no longer the rigid and architectural method of Bach and Beethoven, but the working out of a scheme of rhythmic colors." See *Monsieur Croche the Dilettante Hater* in *Three Classics in the Aesthetics of Music* (Dover paperback, N.D.), pp. 44-45.

23. John Davidson burlesqued the English view of French in his *Earl Lavender* (1895). One character observes, "It's *fang-de-seeaycle* that does it, my dear, and education, and reading French" (p. 68). Another: "I knew a woman who read French, and she ran away from her husband, and died of consumption. For it's in the language. My husband says it's rotten and corrupt, and he ought to know, being a chemist by examination" (p. 73). Wilde's tongue-in-cheek test of true poetic insipidity was whether a work could be translated into French and still not be harmful.

24. Jullian, *Oscar Wilde*, p. 247.

25. The dissimilarities between French and German are perhaps best captured in the two operatic instances where their respective qualities are forced to the greatest extremes: in *Pelléas et Mélisande* the fluid, highly nuanced French serves Debussy's undelimited musical ethos and Maeterlinck's diffuse dramaturgy, and in *Der Ring des Nibelungen* the German is forced back to its monosyllabic, alliterative wellsprings by Wagner's *Stabreim*.

Rolland defended the *Pelléas* libretto to Strauss (*Correspondence*, p. 49): "You don't like Debussy's musical declamation, my friend? It's a bit flabby for my taste, too. But as refined, aristocratic, society French declamation, it is perfect. Of course, there's nothing popular about it (in any case Maeterlinck's "Pelléas" requires a certain monotony of diction); but it has opened up the way to true French musical declamation."

26. *Correspondence*, p. 152. Rolland democratically records Debussy's reaction to Strauss: "He has the sound disease" (p. 156). *Parsifal* is, incidentally, perhaps the strongest foretaste in opera of the Decadent aesthetic.

27. *Oscar Wilde: An Idler's Impression* (1917), p. 22.

28. Related in Rolland's diaries for 5 May 1907, a remark made by Edouard Colonne, *Correspondence*, p. 143.

29. Richard Strauss, *Recollections and Reflections* (1949), p. 152.

30. Paris critics were especially disconcerted by these passages. Bellaigue found that the music "unrolls, or rather disgorges in the style of a coffee concert, even a German coffee concert." Gauthier-Villars (in the *Mercure de France* of 15 June 1907) thought Salome's entrance sounded like "une mazurka bénigne."

31. Quoted by Charles Ricketts in *Oscar Wilde: Recollections* (1932), pp. 51-52. The best studies of Moreau are Jeffrey Meyers, "Huysmans and Gustave Moreau" *Apollo* (January 1974), pp. 39-44, and Julius Kaplan, *Gustave Moreau* (1974).

32. Klimt titled this painting after Judith (from the Biblical Judith-Holofernes story), but it was widely considered—and reprinted as—another of the countless Salome paintings of the time. See Alessandra Comini, *Gustav*

Klimt (1975). Incidentally, Alfred Roller, a good friend of Klimt, was the stage designer for the Viennese premiere of *Salome.*

33. Quoted in Peter Vergo's *Art in Vienna 1898-1918* (1975), p. 202.

Chapter Nine

1. In a letter to his family of 23 July 1835 Büchner wrote: "As far as the so-called idealistic poets are concerned, I find that they have produced hardly anything besides marionettes with sky-blue noses and affected pathos, not men of flesh and blood, with whose sorrow and happiness I sympathize and whose actions repel or attract me. In a word, I think much of Goethe or Shakespeare, but very little of Schiller."

2. One can perhaps best make this point by sampling passages from Büchner's other works:

> We are all buried alive and entombed like kings in triple or quadruple coffins—under the sky, in our houses, in our coats and shirts. For fifty years we scratch on the lid of the coffin. Oh, to believe in obliteration—that would help. There's no hope in death . . . it's only a simpler—and life a more complicated—form of decay. [*Danton's Death,* III. vii]

> A horrifying thought has occurred to me: I think there are people who're unhappy, incurably so, only because they *exist.* [*Leonce and Lena,* II. iii]

> I find in human nature a terrible likeness, in human relationships an ineluctable desire to give away everything and nothing. The solitary person is only foam on the wave, a celebrity is utterly accidental, the mastery of genius a puppet play, a ridiculous struggle against a brazen law—to understand it is the utmost, but to overmaster it is impossible. [letter, 1834]

Particularly notable are the eerily flat last lines we have of *Lenz:*

> [Lenz] did everything just as the others did; but there was a terrible emptiness inside him, he no longer felt any fear, any desire, his existence was a burden to him, a burden he must bear. So he lived on . . .

3. *Berg: Der Meister des kleinsten Übergangs* (1968), p. 92. This, perhaps the best study of Berg hitherto, has unfortunately not yet been translated.

Since this chapter is not intended as a detailed study of the actual process of translation from play to opera, reference should be made here to studies of a more specific nature. The best one is Jack Stein, "From *Woyzeck* to *Wozzeck:* Alban Berg's Adaptation of Büchner," *Germanic Review,* Vol. 47, 3 (1972), pp. 168-80. See also George Perle, "*Woyzeck* and *Wozzeck,*" *Musical Quarterly,* Vol. 53, 2 (1967), pp. 206-19. More subjective and a bit arrogant is John Klein's "*Wozzeck*—A Summing Up," *Music and Letters,* Vol. 44 (1963), pp. 132-39.

See also H. R. Redlich, *Alban Berg: The Man and His Music* (Eng. tr., 1957); Pierre Jouve, *Wozzeck, ou le novel opéra* (1953); Willi Reich, *Alban Berg* (1965). Joseph Kerman also discusses *Wozzeck* at length in *Opera as Drama* (1956).

Berg's own brief but important discussion of *Wozzeck* is reprinted in the Avon *Woyzeck* edition, as well as in Ulrich Weisstein's anthology *The Essence of Opera* (1964).

4. "Expressionism is the symbol of the unknown in us in which we confide, hoping that it will save us. It is the token of the imprisoned spirit that endeavours to break out of the dungeon—a tocsin of alarm given out by all panic-stricken souls." Hermann Bahr, *Expressionism* (1920; Eng. tr., 1925), p. 88. This was one of the first studies of the movement; it referred mainly to the plastic arts.

5. The discontinuous quality Lee Baxandall finds in *Danton's Death* is also present in *Woyzeck:*

> The epigrammatic form of speech, the lack of considered exposition, the beginning at the high point of scenic conversation, the discontinuity of conversation, the expressive rather than declarative character of speech, the eruptive explosion of words—all these speak for the substitution of expression in place of classicism's reflectivity and pondered finality. Büchner's characters do not know what they will say next, their words are scarcely ordered within a causal procession; they are spontaneous, of the moment, new in every word and every scene. ["George Büchner's *Danton's Death*," *Tulane Drama Review*, Vol. 6 (1962), p. 145].

Another commentator finds the same emphasis upon local effects and a highly constricted attention-span in Büchner's diction:

> Words, everywhere in Büchner's work are such strange, isolated objects: now like gaudy beads of poison, now like knives quivering in the target, now like scalpels dissecting limbs, now again like gory wounds. Büchner's style is 'dramatic' if by 'dramatic' we mean, not the coherence of sustained conflict recognizable to both parties and made meaningful by motivation, but annihilating tension and conflict compressed into momentary haphazard encounters. [J. P. Stern, *Re-Interpretations* (1964), p. 119]

6. As a student of Schoenberg, Berg was well-prepared in an aesthetic opposed to traditional "expansion." In *The Philosophy of Modern Music* (1948; Eng. tr., 1973), Adorno writes of the Schoenberg school: "No works could exhibit greater concentration and consistency of formal structure than Schoenberg's and Webern's shortest movements. Their brevity is a direct result of the demand for the greatest consistency. This demand precludes the superfluous. In so doing this consistency opposes expansion in time, which has been the basis for the conception of the musical work since the eighteenth century, certainly since Beethoven. The work, the age, and illusion are all struck by a single blow . . . Music compressed into a moment, is valid as an eruptive revelation of negative experience" (p. 37).

A remark from Anton Webern's lectures *The Path to Twelve-Note Composition* (Eng. tr., 1963) is also worth reproducing: "All the works created between the disappearance of tonality and the formulation of the new twelve-tone law were short, strikingly short. The longer works written at the time were linked with a text which "carried" them (Schoenberg's *Erwartung* and *Die Glückliche Hand,* Berg's *Wozzeck*), that's to say, with something extra-musical. With the abandoning of tonality the most important means of building up longer pieces was lost" (pp. 53-54).

7. "Der beseelte und der psychologische Mensch," *Blätter des Deutschen Theaters* (1918; reprint 1969), p. 12. This periodical was a principal outlet for Expressionist dramatic theory.

8. From Büchner's inaugural lecture on the cranial nerves at the University of Zurich. He became a permanent member of the anatomy faculty there four months before he died.

9. Adorno, *The Philosophy of Modern Music* (1948; Eng. tr., 1973) p. 39.

10. Jouve, *Wozzeck, ou le nouvel opéra* (1953), p. 39.

11. Quoted by Willi Reich, *Schoenberg: A Critical Biography* (1968; Eng. tr., 1971), p. 25.

12. Robert Craft, "Note," for the Columbia recording of *Erwartung;* Adorno, *Philosophy of Modern Music,* p. 42. Charles Rosen's *Arnold Schoenberg* (1975) contains an excellent discussion of *Erwartung,* pp. 39-49.

13. *Richard Strauss und die neue Musik* (1924), p. 190.

14. I cannot resist adding reference to two other works relevant to *Wozzeck.* Schoenberg's George songs (*Das Buch der Hängenden Gärten,* op. 15, 1908) stand at a crucial moment which ushered in the composer's atonal-Expressionist period. They hover just barely on the traditional side of the line from *Sprechstimme,* but they show the creeping alienation of vocal line and musical accompaniment that is pregnant for *Wozzeck.* Though the George poems are decidedly *fin de siècle,* the moods of despair, oppression, ennui slashed with passion, isolation, and tentativeness which they elicit forcibly remind me of moments in Berg's opera. Erwin Stein's description of a 1910 performance of the George songs suggests the powers of expression we know in *Wozzeck:* "In a strange light, the most delicate gradations of psychic excitement became clear. One heard new harmonies, with the luminous quality of the colorful garden flowers they portrayed. At one moment the sounds would float, released from any division into meter, as if time were trying to stand still; the next, sharply rhythmical figures, together with harsh chords, drew sound pictures whose dynamics approached the threshold of pain" (quoted in Reich, *Schoenberg,* p. 49).

Of more symbolic relevance are the "Six Bagatelles" for string quartet by Anton Webern, the third of the triumvirate of musical expressionists. These miniatures (the shortest lasts fifteen seconds, the longest just over a minute) were written in 1913 but not published until the time of *Wozzeck*'s premiere. They are epitomes of that brevity of utterance which is one aspect of the opera's style. Of Webern's prose style it was once observed: "His language is simple with the greatest intensity, often noticeably shy and suppressed: the most soul-shattering things are hinted at in a few words." This comment is borne out for Webern's musical style in the "Bagatelles," which provide yet another atmospheric introduction to the music for *Wozzeck.* Webern dedicated these pieces to Berg.

15. One of the best introductions to this period in musical history is An-

ton Webern's set of lectures, intended for laymen, published as *The Path to the New Music* (1963).

16. Reich, *Schoenberg*, p. 175.

17. *Georg Büchner* (1964), p. 91.

Berg's two related methods of breakdown and increased complexity of orchestral events remind one of the development of Joyce's literary style. From his early *Portrait of the Artist* to *Ulysses* and then to *Finnegans Wake,* Joyce subjected language to increasing disjunctions. As his style became more allusive and complex, the operative level of his prose contracted until, in *Finnegans Wake,* it dropped even below the normal threshold of single words and into a world of bizarre hybrid syllabic combinations. This parallels the changing mode of musical expression effected by the development from Wagner through Strauss and Schoenberg. In his Berg study Adorno was attempting to make a similar point by relating his music, "at once elaborately constructed and tangled full of thickets," to the prose of Marcel Proust.

J. P. Stern hints at the extensive influence of fragmented reality in Büchner: "Almost every line he wrote speaks to us of life experienced as a thing fragmentary, unsustained—but also undimmed—by the consolations of continuity. Abrupt openings, exclamatory and sudden endings predominate in his life, in his dramas, as well as in *Lenz*" (*Re-Interpretations,* (1964), p. 78).

18. *The Essence of Music and Other Papers* (Eng. tr., 1957), p. 25.

19. Viebig wrote of the score in 1923: "All in all the piano version is a masterpiece, and one cannot praise fully enough the care and love which were dedicated to it." Viebig was still astounded by the difficulty of the opera in purely pianistic terms and was quite naturally reluctant to criticize the opera without a full orchestral score at his disposal.

20. Indication of just how "modern" *Woyzeck* is was really made possible as late as 1967, with the definitive Lehmann edition. Lehmann's reconstruction of the play is the basis for the Schmidt translation used in this chapter. In his Büchner study Herbert Lindenberger discusses in more detail the changes Berg made in the tone and emphases of the original (pp. 127-28). See also the Stein article cited in note 3.

21. The opera is dedicated to Schoenberg.

This is no place to become involved in a discussion of the compositional technique of *Lulu.* Some critics find it the triumph of the tone-row system (see, for example, Willi Reich, "Alban Berg's *Lulu,*" *Musical Quarterly,* Vol. 22 (1963), pp. 383-401); others find Berg's use of the tone-row more a pyrrhic victory. Stravinsky wrote that a case could be made for *Lulu* "as the end of the twelve-tone system," and Adorno observed that in *Lulu* "the essential rigidity of twelve-tone construction has been softened to the point that it is unrecognizable." Perhaps the wisest, and most latitudinarian, view is expressed in George Perle's "The Music of *Lulu:* A New Analysis," *Music Review,* Vol. 12 (1959), pp. 185-200. Perle rejects the idea of a solely twelve-tone method and instead describes a musical métier of diatonic, chromatic, and dodecaphonic elements.

22. Sokel, *The Writer in Extremis: Expressionism in Twentieth-Century German Literature* (1959), p. 97; Claude Hill, "Wedekind in Retrospect," *Modern Drama,* Vol. 3 (1960), p. 92.

23. Kornfeld (see note 7), p. 2, p. 9. Walter Sokel gives an illuminating brief summary of Expressionist dramaturgy in *The Writer in Extremis* (p. 40): "The realist aims at the variety of accents and idioms which the social and geographical diversity of actual life suggests. The Expressionist reverses this principle, since speech for him is not a means of characterization, but a function of expression. A character changes his speech as he changes his mood. While emotional nuances are mirrored in the speech of characters in the realistic drama, too, Expressionism exaggerates such changes enormously. In moments of despair, joy, illumination, or bliss, the Expressionist character takes on wings, as it were, both physically and linguistically. He rises from his seat, abandons his ordinary dry bookish prose, and breaks out into hymnic, rhapsodic, or elegiac lyricisms. Most Expressionist plays exhibit such operatic arias." Needless to add, what Sokel describes is very like the methods of operatic librettists and composers.

24. Sokel, *The Writer in Extremis,* p. 61.

25. Sol Gittleman, *Frank Wedekind* (1969), p. 22.

26. Friedrich Gundolf, *Frank Wedekind* (1954), p. 45.

27. Gittleman, *Frank Wedekind,* p. 73. On the surreal quality of Berg's opera see Douglas Jarman, "Berg's Surrealist Opera," *Music Review,* Vol. 31 (1970), pp. 232-40.

28. The formalism of the *Lulu* score is even more extreme than in *Wozzeck,* and yet the same amalgamation of absolute music and the situational demands of the drama is achieved. In an excellent "Talk on Alban Berg's *Lulu*" for the Böhm recording, Adorno describes the process: "While Wagner demanded that musical drama should incorporate all the qualities of great absolute music . . . this was first fully achieved by Berg. He actually succeeded in making the musical texture as varied yet at the same time as logical as had previously been the case only in purely instrumental compositions. His music attains its individuality not by going its own way wilfully and superfluously, but by reflecting faithfully a sense of single-minded devotion to the drama and its heroine."

29. *Expressionism* (1920; Eng. tr., 1925), p. 84.

30. Quoted in Reich, *Schoenberg,* p. 57.

Chapter Ten

1. The four quotations are taken, respectively from: (1) Raymond Tarbox, "*Death in Venice:* The Aesthetic Object as Dream Guide," *American Imago,* 26 (1969), p. 135; (2) A. E. Dyson, "The Stranger God: *Death in Venice,*" *The Critical Quarterly,* Vol. XIII (Spring 1971), p. 19; (3) Albert J. Guerard, *André Gide* (1951), p. 113; (4) D. H. Lawrence, *Selected Literary Criticism,* ed. A. Beal (1966), p. 264.

2. Of many thoughtful reviews of the movie, two are especially incisive: David Grossvogel, "Visconti and the Too, Too Solid Flesh," *Diacritics,* Vol. I, 2 (1971), pp. 52-55, and B. M. Kane, "Thomas Mann and Visconti," *Modern Languages,* Vol. 53 (June 1972), pp. 74-79.

3. *A Sketch of My Life* (1930), p. 46 (emphasis added). For an excellent

discussion of *Der Tod in Venedig*'s autobiographical aspects, see Herbert Lehnert, "Thomas Mann's Interpretations of *Death in Venice* and Their Reliability," *Rice University Studies*, Vol. 50 (Fall 1964), pp. 41-60. See also Erich Heller, "Autobiographie und Literatur: Über Thomas Manns *Tod in Venedig*," in *Essays on European Literature in Honor of Liselotte Dieckmann*, ed. P. U. Hohendahl (1972), pp. 83-100. T. J. Reed hints strongly that scholars have been too constrained in their search for the truth about Mann's homosexuality ("The Measure of Mann," *Times Literary Supplement*, 10 October 1975, p. 1207).

4. The *Times* (London), 14 June 1973, p. 9 (original emphasis).

5. *A Sketch of My Life*, p. 44.

6. The Aschenbach-Tadzio relationship is interestingly paralleled in the real-life events surrounding the German poet Stefan George (1868-1933) and his relationship with a young boy, Maximilian Kronberger. The latter—nicknamed "Maximin" by George—died of meningitis at the age of sixteen in 1904. The events are briefly related in *Stefan George* by Michael Metzger (1972), pp. 35-39. A number of poems in George's *The Seventh Ring* are written to Maximin.

7. The decline of Aschenbach is subtly underlined by the novelist's deteriorating view of Platonic *form*. His first encounter with Tadzio leaves him contemplating "general problems of form and art" (41). The view of Tadzio in the surf conjures up a vision of a male Venus: "It was like some poet's recovery of time at its beginning, of the origin of forms and the birth of gods" (49). The grip of sensual attraction becomes stronger: "What rigor, what precision of thought were expressed in this erect, youthfully perfect body" (66). When in the last pages Aschenbach talks to his Phaedrus in his own shattered persona, the theory of forms is utterly renounced: "Knowledge, Phaedrus, has no dignity or strength. It is aware, it understands and pardons, but without reserve and form. It feels sympathy with the precipice, it *is* the precipice" (109).

8. Nietzsche called sculpture the archetypal Apollonian art (*B*, 33), and nineteenth-century neo-Classicism indeed found its most pristine expression in the sculpture of Canova (1757-1822) and Thorvaldsen (1768?–1844).

9. Thomas Mann, *Briefe an Paul Amman 1915-1952*, p. 32.

10. These are, of course, really Socratic ideas, and Kaufmann is concerned to emphasize in his *Nietzsche: Philosopher, Psychologist, Antichrist* (3rd ed., 1968), Chapter 13, that Nietzsche was, if anything a Socratic at heart—harshly though he criticized his mentor. As Nietzsche wrote: "Socrates, to confess it frankly, is so close to me that almost always I fight a fight against him" (quoted p. 398).

11. Coincidentally, Rousseau painted "The Dream" just one year before *Der Tod in Venedig* was written. Also coincidental is the fact that Rousseau was then sixty-three and vainly in love with a much younger widow. Daniel Cattan Rich speculates that "his awakened amorous spirit found sublimation, perhaps, in 'The Dream'" (*Henri Rousseau* (1964), p. 69).

12. William McClain, "Wagnerian Overtones in *Der Tod in Venedig*," *Modern Language Notes*, Vol. 79 (1964), pp. 481-95. It is well known that Mann was steeped in Wagner as a young artist. See, for example, his

story "The Blood of the Walsungs." The Heller article cited in note 3 above contains interesting sidelights on the Wagnerian aspects of the novella.

13. The homoerotic implications of the Tadzio-Aschenbach relationship are prefigured by Peter Grimes and his apprentices, Claggart and Billy Budd, and the spectral butler and the boy in *The Turn of the Screw*. Certain thematic parallels also connect Aschenbach with Captain Vere in *Billy Budd*.

14. The ambivalent effect of Venice is strikingly exampled in the letters of Tchaikovsky. On 29 April 1874 he wrote of Venice: "It is a place in which—had I to remain for long—I should hang myself on the fifth day from sheer despair . . . Venice is very gloomy, and like a dead city." Three years later, however, he reported: "Venice is a fascinating city. Every day I discover some fresh beauty . . . Venice has bewitched me" (28 November 1877).

15. The unusually extensive musical analysis included with the libretto of the London recording of *Death in Venice* contains a musical quotation for this and many other crucial passages from the opera. Musical quotations made there will support many of the comments made in this chapter.

16. The curlew is explained in the rehearsal score's introduction by Imogen Holst (p. ix):

> There are many occasions throughout *Curlew River,* where an ordinary pause sign is not adequate for conveying the flexible fitting-in of the different tempi. The sign ⌒⌒ ('curlew' sign) over a note or rest shows that the performer must listen and wait till the other performers have reached the next barline, or meeting-point.

Britten's advancement in this first of the parables is well summarized by Eric White:

> If the score of *Curlew River* is compared with that of *Billy Budd* or *A Midsummer Night's Dream,* it will be seen that the new linear supremacy has led to the abandonment of most of the old triadic [i.e., chordal] procedures with their polytonal implications . . . The result is invariably to exalt the musical line at the expense of independent harmony—heterophony in the place of polyphony. [*Benjamin Britten: His Life and Operas* (1970), pp. 211-12]

17. Another sign, introduced in *Curlew River,* to achieve this effect of modulation (··ıı||||) is described in the rehearsal score as indicating "tremolando with a gradual, unmeasured accelerando" (p. ix). This sign occurs often in the *Venice* score.

18. The original ballet was created by England's dean of choreographers, Sir Frederick Ashton. It was hence bound to be an essentially classical conception, danced by young students of the Royal Ballet School. Free-form, nonclassical dance may ultimately be found preferable in performance as a means of rendering less harsh the symbolic discontinuities of Tadzio's and Aschenbach's worlds. Indeed, projections invoking actual Greek vase representations of athletic events might replace the ballet entirely.

19. The figure of an androgynous boy is important in other Mann stories: see "Tonio Kröger," "Felix Krull," "The Fight Between Jappe and Do

Escobar," and "Blood of the Walsungs." Even the sailor suit appears under similar circumstances in the first three stories.

20. Herbert Lehnert feels all the surrounding figures are "Death in person." See "Thomas Mann's Early Interest in Myth and Erwin Rhode's *Psyche*," *PMLA*, Vol. 79 (1964), p. 298.

Afterword

1. *The Necessary Angel: Essays on Reality and the Imagination* (1942), p. 13.

2. Preface, *Anton von Webern Perspectives*, ed. Demar Irwin (1967), p. xxvii.

3. *Notes of an Apprenticeship* (1968), p. 26. The inevitable results of such an aesthetic are summarized by Leonard Meyer in *Music, the Arts, and Ideas* (1967): "The music, art, and literature of the avant-garde is characteristically unkinetic and unfocused" (p. 78).

4. *Notes of an Apprenticeship*, pp. 384-85.

5. Ernst Krenek, "A Profile," *Anton von Webern Perspectives*, p. 4.

6. Joseph Kerman, in *Listening* (2nd ed., 1976), p. 381, says of "4′ 33″": "What Cage is saying is that silence is an entity, too, as well as sounds." Joan Peyser writes in *The New Music* (1971), p. 178: "Cage's 'music' here is the collection of unintentional sounds that occur during this particular period. His point is that silence is never absolute."

7. *High Fidelity*, Vol. 16 (April 1966), p. 92.

8. "The Abstract Composers" (*Herald Tribune*, 3 February 1952), in *Music Reviewed 1940-54* (1967), p. 345.

9. The *Central Opera Service Bulletin* (Winter 1975) contains a fascinating compilation of American and foreign world premieres between 1967 and 1975.

INDEX